Georgetown at Two Hundred

GEORGETOWN AT TWO HUNDRED

Faculty Reflections on the University's Future

William C. McFadden, Editor

Georgetown University Press
WASHINGTON, D.C.

Printed in the United States of America

Library of Congress Cataloging-in-Publication Data

Georgetown at two hundred : faculty reflections on the university's future / William C. McFadden, editor.
p. cm.
ISBN 0-87840-502-X. — ISBN 0-87840-503-8 (pbk.)
1. Georgetown University—History. 2. Georgetown University—Planning. I. McFadden, William C., 1930- .
LD1961.G52G45 1990
378.753—dc20 90-32745
CIP

FOR THE GEORGETOWN FAMILY —

STUDENTS, FACULTY, ADMINISTRATORS,

STAFF, ALUMNI, AND BENEFACTORS,

LET US PRAY TO THE LORD.

Daily offertory prayer of
Brian A. McGrath, S.J.
(1913-88)

Contents

FOREWORD

A Bicentennial celebration provides a university with a distinctive opportunity to reflect on its past and present and to focus its vision and energy on the future. Georgetown University's Bicentennial maintained such reflection and focus as a primary objective. The chapters in this volume are a result of that effort.

In the fall of 1987, after broad consultation and discussion, a faculty seminar of seventeen members was convened under the leadership of Dorothy M. Brown and William C. McFadden, and with the enthusiastic support of then-president, Timothy S. Healy, S.J. Seminar members were challenged by the president to "take a good, hard look at ourselves," with confidence that "we have something helpful to say to ourselves and to others as we enter our third century." The seminar began with very candid and open-ended discussions prior to choosing topics for individual papers. To provide a context for these discussions, and to situate Georgetown within the universe of Catholic higher education in the United States, a John Carroll Lecture Series was organized on the topic of "American Catholic Higher Education: Challenges for the Third Century." Scholars from sister institutions around the country joined Georgetown faculty to explore a range of contextual questions prior to our own reflection.

Beginning in February 1988, seminar members met to discuss one another's papers before revising them for this publication. On September 23, 1989, during the closing weekend of the Bicentennial year, seminar members engaged in a series of campus-wide "Conversations on the Future of Georgetown University." Leo J. O'Donovan, S.J., Georgetown's new president, actively participated in these discussions, thus emphasizing their importance for the University.

The Bicentennial theme chosen by Georgetown, "Learning, Faith and Freedom," is an attempt to capture the synthesis which was originally intended by its founder, John Carroll, and to characterize the best of Georgetown for two hundred years: a community committed to a vigorous life of the mind within a climate of faith and a tradition of freedom.

These pages reveal how that theme is expressed today and raise important challenges for how it will be expressed in the future.

No one volume can embrace all of the important issues Georgetown faces on the threshold of its third century, but it is safe to say that every issue explored here is important for the present and the future of the nation's first institution of Catholic higher education. While many of the particulars will vary from institution to institution, it is also safe to say that much of what is contained here will be helpful to other colleges and universities.

I am most grateful to each seminar member and to the cochairs, Dorothy Brown and William McFadden, for their generous and wise contributions to this important component of the Bicentennial. Special thanks are also due to the Loyola Foundation for their support which helped make the seminar possible.

Charles L. Currie, S.J.
Director of the Bicentennial

INTRODUCTION

When Jesus preached about the kingdom of God, he described its nature through a series of arresting images. One of them, the image of the mustard seed, has been very much on my mind over the past few years. The kingdom of God is a mystery of hidden growth and utterly surprising results. To teach this, Jesus compared it to the mustard seed, which is "the smallest of all the seeds on earth" and yet "grows up and becomes the greatest of all shrubs" (Mark 4:30-32). I used to think that "shrub" was something of a letdown. Why not a majestic cedar of Lebanon? Now I think it provides an insight into Jesus' understanding of the kingdom. Let Pharaoh be compared to a cedar in Lebanon with its top among the clouds (Ezekiel 31:3). God's kingdom is more on a human scale but, nonetheless, its growth can result in some unexpected outcomes.

This parable has often come to mind recently because in 1989 we celebrated the two hundredth anniversary of Catholic higher education in the United States. From St. Joseph's College in Maine and Barry University in Florida, to St. Martin's College in Washington and the University of San Diego in California (and let us not forget Chaminade University in Hawaii), Catholic colleges and universities are spread across the nation. They run alphabetically from Albertus Magnus College in Connecticut to Xavier University (there is one in Louisiana and another in Ohio), the largest of which is St. John's University of New York (over 19,000 students). Catholic devotion to Mary is reflected in twenty-two different ways in the names of fifty-one schools, including the College of Notre Dame of Maryland, the first Catholic college for women in the United States to award the Bachelor of Arts degree (1899). There are well over two hundred of them, enrolling more than half a million students at last count. A shrub, to be sure, but a sizable one, and many an attractive bird comes to nest in the shade of its branches.

All of this two-hundred-year growth began in a two-story brick building which John Carroll had constructed in 1788 on the banks of the Potomac at George Town in Maryland. Carroll's "modest academy" celebrated its Bicentennial with a year-long series of lectures, symposia, and events of an artistic and celebratory nature. It was also a time to reflect on the past and to make plans for the future.

In the fall of 1986, then-president Timothy S. Healy, S.J., expressed his desire that there be a "reflective center" during the celebration of the upcoming Bicentennial. He asked the director of the Bicentennial, Charles L. Currie, S.J., to organize a faculty seminar to look critically at the present state of the University and identify problems which Georgetown should be addressing as it begins its third century. The seminar's task was not to engage in self-congratulation or to weave a rug under which Georgetown's failures could be swept out of sight. It was to strive for a completely honest description of the present state of the institution as a stimulus for internal debate.

They say, if you want to get something done, entrust it to someone who is busy. So, Currie turned to Dorothy M. Brown, of the History Department. Until I met Professor Brown, my image of "busy" was a fellow in an old vaudeville act. He would first set up a row of ten thin wands across the stage. Then, he would balance a plate on top of the first wand by spinning it, then a second, and a third, then, beyond belief, a fourth. As he added new ones, he had to keep going back to give each of the old wands a little jiggle to keep its plate spinning. By the time he got the tenth plate spinning on its wand, he defined for me the word "busy." On the Main Campus the closest act we have to that is Dorothy Brown, who, while serenely engaged in an astonishing variety of other activities, also managed to get this seminar spinning and keep it going till the end.

In December 1986, we thought a ten-member seminar would be the right size. Five meetings later, the number was up to twelve and the seminar was beginning to take shape. During the fall of 1987, there were seven planning sessions, in which topics were proposed and suggestions were made as to who might address them. By November, the membership had risen to sixteen, the topics had all been decided upon, and it was time to start writing the papers. Subsequently, one topic was divided in two and the seminar welcomed its seventeenth member.

During the 1987-88 academic year, the members of the seminar attended a series of lectures, organized by Dorothy Brown, on "American Catholic Higher Education," and afterward dined with each speaker to explore further some of the issues raised in the lecture. Thus, we all had the opportunity to hear and to dine with the president of Catholic University, William J. Byron, S.J., the past and present presidents of the

University of Notre Dame, Theodore M. Hesburgh, C.S.C., and Edward Malloy, C.S.C., and Notre Dame historian, Philip Gleason, David O'Brien (Holy Cross) and Carol Hurd Green (Boston College), Mother Constance Fitzgerald, O.C.D. (Carmelite Monastery, Baltimore), John Brademas (New York University), Sister Ann Ida Gannon, B.V.M. (Mundelein College), and David Tracy (University of Chicago Divinity School). We also met with James H. Billington, the Librarian of Congress, to discuss the address he delivered at the formal opening of the Bicentennial, October 1, 1988.

Finally, by a happy coincidence, some nine hundred representatives of the twenty-eight Jesuit colleges and universities came to our campus in June 1989 to attend "Assembly '89: Jesuit Ministry in Higher Education." Several of our seminar members were able to attend different sessions of the four-day meeting and engage our colleagues in informal discussion of the issues raised in our seminar. We also had the opportunity to hear Peter-Hans Kolvenbach, the superior general of the Society of Jesus, who came from Rome to address this assembly.[1] In the past three decades, he noted, the entire context of Jesuit education has changed "irrevocably." He urged his fellow Jesuits not to spend time lamenting this fact or trying to deny it. They should recognize that "this changed world of ours is the only one in which we are called to work out our mission. How best to exercise our apostolic influence in the present is the only question worthy of our attention."[2]

In the grand tradition of Ignatius Loyola, Kolvenbach did not presume to answer that question in detail since, as he remarked, "all answers must be concrete ones; every means to the end must be inculturated, taking into account the myriad circumstances of the local scene, recent history and personalities involved."[3] (I wanted to cheer when he pointed out that in working toward a goal we must take into account the "personalities involved"!) Even so, he was willing to give an answer to the question: what is Jesuit education? His reply was wonderfully concise: it is education which is inspired by the spirituality of Ignatius Loyola.[4]

He reminded me of an incident which I think is pertinent here. A few years ago, I asked the Theology faculty to comment on a statement about Jesuit education and Ignatian spirituality which contained the following passage:

> Liberal education in the Jesuit tradition is rooted in a world-affirming spirituality which reverences the worth of the natural and

> the human, and which seeks to find God in all things, and through action to collaborate with God in the redemption of the world.
>
> Current Jesuit concerns would affect higher education at Jesuit schools by stressing the link between religious faith and the promotion of individual and social justice in the world.

My colleague, Rabbi A. Nathan Abramowitz, marked these two paragraphs and wrote in the margin, "Judaism, too!" When I saw his comment, I had to laugh. He was right, of course. In so many ways, we share a common goal and a common spirituality.

Similarly, when Kolvenbach spoke of the Jesuit concern for the poor, I thought of the seminar presentations of Gwendolyn Mikell, Anne Sullivan, and Bruce Douglass, all of whom made specific recommendations in favor of the admission to Georgetown of economically disadvantaged students.

There has been much discussion in recent years about the "Jesuit identity" of this school. Kolvenbach's address has helped me to formulate my own conviction on this question as follows: Georgetown's future as a Jesuit university depends largely on our ability to attract faculty members, administrators, students, and staff personnel, whose spirituality so resonates with that of Ignatius Loyola that it moves them to view education in the same value-oriented way.

Now, a word about the format of this book. Each paper was distributed to the membership ahead of time so that the entire meeting could be devoted to discussion of it. Subsequent revisions were the responsibility of the individual author. No attempt has been made to arrive at common positions on disputed issues. The papers, then, in their final form are independent of one another and may be read in any order. Since some of them address related topics, they have been grouped together for the reader's convenience as follows:

Past as Prologue: R. Emmett Curran, History Department, who is currently completing a two-volume history of Georgetown University, gives the reader a sense of the school's early years and the achievements they were celebrating at the Centennial in 1889, providing a useful benchmark from which to measure the school's growth in the subsequent hundred years.

The Catholic Identity: Monika K. Hellwig, Theology Department, describes the changing patterns in the Catholic church's self-image and the implications of that for a Catholic university. R. Bruce Douglass,

Government Department, addresses the problem Georgetown must face in maintaining its Catholic identity in the face of the academic revolution in American higher education, resulting in an autonomous and pluralist professoriat. William V. O'Brien, Government Department, argues that Georgetown should serve as a scholarly resource for the church in providing the research, reflection, dialogue, and writing necessary to advance Catholic thought on international relations.

Georgetown's Curriculum: Dorothy M. Brown, History Department, shows all the twists and turns in the development of the curriculum from the very beginning, and offers suggestions for improving liberal arts and intercultural education at Georgetown. John B. Brough, Philosophy Department, charts the rise of Scholastic philosophy to a position of unrivaled dominance in the curriculum, its decline, and the new role that the Philosophy Department now plays on the Hilltop. William C. McFadden, Theology Department, traces religious education in John Carroll's academy from its humble beginnings as extracurricular catechetical instruction at four o'clock on Saturday afternoons to its present situation as one of the core requirements for all undergraduates.

Science, Study, and Story: John F. Haught, Theology Department, makes the proposal that science education, especially for nonscience students, might become more interesting and captivating if it were presented in a narrative framework. Joseph E. Earley, Chemistry Department, argues that scientists should provide their students with examples of rigorous scientific reasoning applied to particular questions, and that responsibility for initiation of students into the narratives that shape culture is shared by the whole academic community.

The Challenge of Cultures: Anne D. Sullivan, Assistant Dean, College of Arts and Sciences, presents the case that admission of minority students is only a small first step toward the goal of interracial education: preparation of all students for life in a multiracial society in a multiracial world. Gwendolyn Mikell, Sociology Department, noting that from its beginning Georgetown was committed to openness, describes today's challenge of welcoming even greater diversity in the faculty and student body in seeking to provide interracial and intercultural education.

New Worlds and Old: Women's Studies and Jesuit Education: Leona M. Fisher, Department of English, Coordinator of Women's Studies, shows that the field of Women's Studies has discovered not only new issues to study but also new methods of learning which ought to transform the whole curriculum. James P. M. Walsh, Theology Department, details how his approach to teaching and to learning has been shaped by his experience directing and making the Spiritual Exercises of Saint Ignatius, leading him to positions strikingly like those of Professor Fisher.

The University Challenge: Graduate and Professional Education: Richard B. Schwartz, Dean of the Graduate School, looks at the recent growth of Georgetown's Graduate School, and presents the options the school faces for future growth. Milton Corn, Medical Center, reviews the history of medical education at Georgetown since the founding of the school in 1849, and reflects on its present and future prospects. Mark Tushnet, Law Center, explains the process and implications of becoming a national law school, and what that entails for legal education at a Catholic university.

Architecture on the Hilltop: Elizabeth Prelinger, Fine Arts Department, shows how buildings create environment on the Main Campus, and explains current plans for developing our limited acreage.

The topics we discussed are important ones for the future of the school and were approached with the seriousness they merit. But, for all that, this is a most enjoyable group of people and they know how to salt with laughter a serious conversation. Meeting with them every few weeks over the last two years has been a great learning experience for me. I undertook the task of editing these papers with the conviction that many readers would enjoy meeting them too.

I would like to express my appreciation for the valued guidance of John B. Breslin, S.J., director of the Georgetown University Press, and the skilful editorial corrections and suggestions supplied by its senior editor, Eleanor E. Waters.

It is only fitting that the final word come from my cochair of the Bicentennial faculty seminar. It is one of Dorothy Brown's favorite expressions: "We live in hope."

November 1989 William C. McFadden

Notes

1. Kolvenbach's address is printed in *Origins* 19:6 (22 June 1989), 81-87.
2. Ibid., 83.
3. Ibid., 83.
4. Ibid., 83.

R. Emmett Curran, S.J.
History Department

Georgetown's Self-Image at Its Centenary

By the measure of time allotted—three days in late February 1889—Georgetown's celebration of its centenary was a modest one. What it lacked in length, however, it made up in elaborate ceremonies, involving the most distinguished representatives of church and state. From the firing of cannon to welcome James Cardinal Gibbons of Baltimore to the Main Campus on Tuesday evening, to the Friday afternoon convocation presided over by President Grover Cleveland, speeches and dinners, academic assemblies and reunions brought together alumni, faculty, students, and dignitaries to honor Georgetown on the completion of its first century. The Marine Band provided the music for the three days. The student corps of cadets acted as honor guard for visitors. Banners with Latin, Greek, and Russian inscriptions adorned buildings and archways throughout the campus. Sixteen hundred candles illuminated the windows facing Washington and the Potomac. On the final evening there was a massive fireworks display. As the official Jesuit diarist noted, "This was the greatest event in the history of Georgetown College."[1]

It also marked the first time in which the University had celebrated its own beginnings. In 1839 no one seemed aware that the year was in any way special. Three years later there was a grand celebration. It had nothing to do, however, with Georgetown's origin but rather with the beginnings of Catholic Maryland in 1634. Historically, there was little notable about 1789. Carroll's plan for the school had been drawn up in 1786. He had broken ground for the first building two years later. The building itself was not completed until 1791, shortly after the first student arrived in November. Classes began in January 1792. The only thing of significance that had occurred in 1789 was Carroll's obtaining of the deed to the property, hardly the normal basis for a founding date.

Why did the University choose this date to celebrate? It seems to have stemmed from a mistake over the date of the first building. During the Centennial festival a banner flew from the original building, which stated in Latin: "The house which here you see, tottering from weight of years, John Carroll, of the Society of Jesus, under happy auspices began, by laying the foundation stone, in the year 1789."[2] This provides an important clue to the decision, fifteen years later, to raze the building to make room for Ryan Hall, but the date for the laying of the cornerstone is a year too late. Carroll himself gives testimony about the construction of the building in 1788.[3] Nonetheless, for more than four decades the founding of Georgetown had been equated with the erection of the first building, supposedly in 1789.[4] In 1851, the first catalogue of the University stated that "in 1789 the first house was built." This information was repeated in every catalogue for the next twenty years until the 1873 catalogue declared on the inside cover "Founded as a college 1789," thereby implicitly connecting first house and founding. Fifteen years later, 1889 was the conventional date to commemorate the completion of the University's first century.

The person responsible for the idea of the Centennial was the Rector/President from 1882 to 1888, James Doonan, S.J. According to the official historian of the centenary, John Gilmary Shea, Doonan had been promoting the idea of a centenary for two or three years among the alumni (who had been organized by his predecessor, Patrick Healy, in 1881). Doonan, himself an alumnus of the College, had inherited a university with a small enrollment, no endowment, and a crushing debt of nearly $300,000, mainly from the construction of the Healy Building.[5] It seems obvious that fund-raising was at least one of the motives for Doonan's emphasis on the centenary. At the College commencement in 1888, in language usually not associated with celebratory occasions, Doonan admitted that on the eve of Georgetown's Centennial it would be pretentious to claim that the University had become "what we would see her." The main reason for this, he suggested, was the poverty of the Catholic community during most of Georgetown's history. But, he went on, if the University, in its "dowerless existence of a hundred years," had been able to achieve what they were now able to celebrate, they should have every confidence that during the second century they might finally realize the high aims of their founders.[6]

The message was unmistakable. Georgetown's sons were now in a position to change Alma Mater's condition and no better occasion than the centenary to begin. Indeed, Doonan was remarkably successful in raising money from alumni and others. In July 1888, the regional superior of the Society of Jesus, Thomas Campbell, reported to the superior general in Rome that "because of the extremely large gifts given recently to Georgetown College,[7] it no longer has any real financial difficulties."[8] Despite an appeal from the alumni in the summer of 1888 that the general not remove the rector at the completion of his second three-year term, as was customary, but allow him to remain in office until the end of the Centennial celebration, Joseph Havens Richards was chosen to succeed Doonan.[9] When Richards took over in August, Campbell informed him that the debt was between $40,000 and $50,000, a serious one to be sure, but much less than Doonan had inherited. And Richards still had the Centennial to use as an occasion for soliciting gifts. "You will doubtless get something," Campbell assured him.[10]

But if Doonan had left Richards a greatly reduced debt, he had also left a two-story mound of dirt in front of the new building, a painful reminder of the unfinished state of the edifice that Patrick Healy had envisioned as the central symbol of Georgetown University. That fall, Richards hastily made plans to complete the auditorium and library sections of the building.[11] By January of the following year, a month before the celebration, Father Provincial Campbell had to give Richards permission to borrow "a great sum of money in order that the university might be whole and still ours."[12] The mound of earth disappeared and construction resumed. Days before the celebration, Francis Riggs gave $10,000 for the library and promised more, if needed.[13]

If 1789 was weak on historical grounds as a founding date, it had great symbolic value. It marked the beginning of both the federal government and the hierarchical church in America. It also enabled Georgetown to say to The Catholic University of America, just as it was opening its doors: Welcome from a Catholic university that has already completed its first hundred years. These themes surfaced repeatedly in the observance of the centenary.

Euge · Venerabilis · Mater · Sapientum · Nutrix

Tu · Sola · Inter · Omnes

Vixisti · Patriae · Annos

Vivas · Valeas · Vincas.

This inscription on a banner on the west wall of Healy set the theme of Georgetown's unique link with the republic: "Congratulations, venerable mother and nurse of sages! You alone, among the many, have lived since the nation's birth. Live on, prosper, and prevail."[14] Condé Pallen's *Centennial Ode* echoed it, if more floridly:

> Around thy cradle blew the trumpet blast
> Of victory, when Liberty at last
> Burst the chains that held her bound
> And all the land leaped at the glorious sound,
> And a nation sprang to life
> From the dragon jaws of strife,
> Strong-limbed and beautiful in power
> Through mighty wrestling in that heavy hour![15]

The Centennial oration by Martin Morris of the Law Faculty developed it further:

> One hundred years ago . . . when Washington, Franklin, Adams, Hamilton, Jefferson, Madison and Robert Morris, our seven wise men . . . were laying deep and strong the foundations of our Federal Union—in that same year the foundations also were laid of this Republic of the Intellect by one who had participated with the framers of the Federal Constitution in that heroic struggle for human independence—not merely for American independence, but for the independence of mankind . . .
>
> John Carroll, of Maryland, was the Romulus of our University.[16]

Carroll was the link not only to the republic but to the hierarchical church as well, becoming the first bishop in 1789. An inscription on a banner overlooking Washington and the Potomac seemed to bring the three together:

> Behold here the chosen spot of the fathers and of us all! For, on this porch of old there stood that most devoted man, our founder, John Carroll. To high Heaven prayer uplifting, on Heaven's aid relying, and adverse storms facing undismayed, he set his hand with matchless skill to bring to pass that from her very cradle the infant Church of America might be aglow with the love of virtue and of learning.[17]

Carroll had founded Georgetown at the very creation of the institutional American church in order that it might grow in wisdom and truth in a republic that depended for its survival on a free and educated citizenry.

Of the three gold medals that were awarded to mark the event, one went to Grover Cleveland for the United States, one went to Cardinal Gibbons for the Archdiocese of Baltimore (the first See), and one to John Gilmary Shea, for his biography of Archbishop Carroll.

If 1789 was an apt year to choose to stress Georgetown's special republican and Catholic character, 1889 was an opportune time within Catholic America to stress Georgetown's antiquity. Four years earlier, the decision had been made to locate in Washington the university that the hierarchy had agreed to establish at the Third Plenary Council of Baltimore. The Jesuits, through their provincial superior at the time, Robert Fulton, had strenuously opposed the idea of such a national university. When it was proposed to put it in Washington, they objected that it was an insult to Georgetown, as well as to Woodstock College, the Jesuit theologate some thirty miles north.

It seems significant that two of the best known opponents of The Catholic University of America, Archbishop Michael Corrigan of New York, and his vicar-general, Monsignor Thomas Preston, were very visible during the three-day Georgetown celebration. No one was there from Catholic University itself. At the Centennial banquet the toast from "Our Sister Universities" was given by the President of Columbian (George Washington) University. On the last day of the celebration, Father John Murphy, the secretary of the University, read a cablegram from the rector of the new university, Bishop John Keane, who was in Rome:

"Richards, Georgetown: Congratulations and Best wishes. Keane." Terse cablegrams were the stuff of transatlantic communications in the late nineteenth century. Murphy's interpretation was that this effectually answered the suspicions of rivalry between the two institutions.

The strains between Georgetown and Catholic University were already well known. Within a few years, they grew worse with the latter's expansion of its graduate programs from theology to philosophy, and its attempt to appropriate Georgetown's law and medical schools. But the centenary was an occasion to profess magnanimity, as did a student orator, Daniel J. Geary '89, on the last day of the celebration:

> And we, with our hundred years behind us, come forward to-day and take our younger sister by the hand and assure her of our hearty welcome. To-day we bid her God speed, praying for nothing better in her regard than the prospect of as bright a record on the celebration of her centenary as old Georgetown looks back upon to-day.[18]

The Catholic University of America was already a looming presence in the city, even before it had opened its doors; for the next three decades, despite the brave words of the centenary, it continued to cast a cloud over Georgetown.

Much was also made of Georgetown's distinction as the oldest Catholic university in the United States. At the entrance to the Healy Building, a banner heralded "Calverton, 1640; Newtown, 1677; Bohemia, 1740; Georgetown, 1789"—the schools that Jesuits had conducted in Maryland. Two cannon, reputedly from the *Ark* and the *Dove*, the two ships which brought the first Jesuits to Maryland in 1634, guarded the main entrance to Healy as a symbol of Georgetown's connection to the beginnings of Catholicism in British America. Doonan, in fact, the previous June had been responsible for securing the cannon from the Jesuit farm just below St. Mary's City. They played a prominent role in the celebration with endless salutes to the various guests and events.

Still, the planners of the Centennial did not go as far as a later administrator of the University, who in 1934 celebrated "Founders Day" to honor the progenitors of Georgetown University who in 1634 "projected a seat of learning" at Saint Mary's City.[19] This, of course, conveniently made Georgetown, at least *in voto*, two years older than Harvard. Banners and speakers in 1889 praised Georgetown as "the mother of colleges" but they made no attempt to find its real foundation in Cecil

Calvert's Maryland. It was enough to cite the many Jesuit colleges from Worcester to Santa Clara which had followed in Georgetown's wake.

In this regard the speakers made little note of Georgetown's special pluralistic character. Morris, the Centennial orator, did mention the international market from which the University drew its students, "even from the nations of Europe and Asia." But nothing was said of Carroll's provision that Georgetown be open to Catholic and non-Catholic alike. Indeed, the percentage of non-Catholics, at least in the College, had been shrinking steadily since the Civil War. In 1889, of 150 boarders in the College there were fewer than ten non-Catholics, a sharp drop from the prewar years when non-Catholic students occasionally outnumbered Catholic ones.[20]

For most of its first century, Georgetown had been predominantly a southern school. By 1889, blue and gray had become the school colors. The poem of welcome for Cardinal Gibbons on Tuesday evening was entitled "The Blue and Gray," and began:

> Love's welcome from the blue and gray,
> Love's greeting do we sing to-day,
> Between the blue and gray will rest
> The cardinal, for every breast
> That wears the triple colors here
> Hath love for thee whom all revere.
> On battlefields the gray and blue
> Were often dyed a cardinal hue.[21]

At the Alumni Banquet held at Willard's Hotel on Thursday evening, February 21, in response to the toast to "Our Country," a southerner, Hon. Joseph E. Washington of Tennessee, made the following remarks:

> The South put her all to the test, and, by the arbitrament of the sword, she lost! This does not prove that she was wrong—but having lost, she accepts the issues of secession and slavery as settled by the war. She accepts in good faith the war amendments to the Constitution, and, speaking for the young men of the South, I say that she will abide by that settlement. We regret and deplore the loss of life and of property. We revere the memory of our sacred dead, but

> we are heartily glad that the Union and the Constitution were saved, and that they are our common heritage to-day![22]

By 1889, however, Georgetown's student body was becoming more Catholic and more northern.

Much was made of the high value the church had traditionally given to education, especially through the medieval universities. The Society of Jesus had brought that tradition into the modern world and to America. The College senior, Geary, was the only speaker to admit that American Catholics themselves were partly to blame for their institutions of higher education not being all they should be. "There is no going behind the fact," he acknowledged, "that higher education is not as thoroughly insisted upon by American Catholics as it ought to be; but neither is it true that Catholicity in the mass in America here is as illiterate as it is sometimes accused of being."[23] Georgetown, however, was not only the mother of many Catholic colleges but the model for all. "Founded with the Constitution and springing into being side by side with the Government," Geary said, "her progress has been proportionately as phenomenal. . . . She has been the guiding star of Catholic education."[24] That to Geary gave the observance of the Centennial its ultimate importance. It was no mere exercise in filial piety, no sheer wallowing in nostalgia, but a thing of national significance:

> Every Catholic of the land was an interested looker-on. . . . it meant that the children of the Church who are established here in every quarter of this broad, free land had at last waked up to the needs of the hour, and were come together to do honor and service to the cause of the higher education of Catholics in these States. It was like a blessed entry into a later land of promise.[25]

Geary's figures might have been better controlled, but his point was clear. Catholics had the opportunity to respond to the challenges of the age, precisely because they were members of a free society that respected the freedom of religion and religious institutions. He made no bones about the blessing that the separation of church and state constituted, this at a time when such a sentiment still drew unofficial anathemas from Rome:

> Never in the world's history was the Church so regarded by the

> State as she is at this present day and in our own country. I know I am touching on what many are fain to look upon as a dangerous question. But, remember, I am not dealing with theories; I am merely discussing broad and unmistakable facts. We have been allowed to grow up here to the fullness of manhood almost. . . . [The Catholic] beholds the religion he loves so well enjoying all the freedom offered by a free government, he beholds his Church unhampered by any of those inconveniences which are a part of her struggles in other lands, and . . . he sees that not only does she meet with no opposition from government, but that she never can. He sees that with the downfall of the Church's liberty in America must come the downfall of the country's bulwark . . . the Constitution of these United States.[26]

A major theme of the Centennial speakers was John Carroll's appreciation of the unique educational opportunities America afforded. In the Centennial sermon, former President Doonan stressed the repression of American Catholics during the colonial period, which forced the young Carroll to quit his native land for conscience's sake and to go abroad to secure an education. When the suppression of the Society of Jesus drove him from Flanders back to British America, Doonan noted, he quickly became an active supporter of the revolution that shortly followed his return. When the United States became the first colonies to rebel successfully against a motherland, Carroll was as deeply impressed as any of the makers of the revolution with the heaven-given "mission of proving to the world the possibility of a self-governed and self-governing nation." He saw "a land under whose impartial, tolerant government the church of his faith . . . would flourish as a goodly tree planted by the water's edge."[27]

Doonan continued:

> In a republic like ours, wherein each and every citizen must bear not only his share of the nation's burdens, but finds himself charged with an equal share in the responsibility of the nation's government, it becomes of first importance that by the development of his intelligence he be qualified to deliberate with wisdom, and in strengthening his moral character guarantee be given that he will ordain in justice and honesty.[28]

If it is an axiom that the king should be wise and good, Doonan pointed out, in a government where every man is king, should he not be intelligent and upright, wise and good? To make him such was the purpose of Carroll in founding Georgetown.

This did not, however, mean that the government should be involved with education. The state, Martin Morris asserted in his Centennial oration, has no more business controlling education than it does religion.[29] Nor did Georgetown see itself as a people's university, as an institution of higher learning with a special mission to provide education for the immigrant and the poor. It was avowedly elitist, Morris contended in his keynote address:

> [I]t may be that, in the ages which are yet to be unfolded, our increasing knowledge of the secrets of Nature may enable us to escape much of the drudgery that is now the daily fate of the vast majority of mankind, and place the whole race on a higher plane of intelligence. But it is too much to hope that, until the millennium is ushered in, a liberal education will be within reach of more than a small minority.
>
> It is this small minority that is to leaven the mass. All free government, however democratic in theory, is necessarily aristocratic in fact. The few must always administer it; the few must always guide and control it. . . .
>
> The great universities of the Middle Ages were the nurseries of freedom . . . and from them came forth the chosen few whose influence diffused the principles of liberty among the people and kept alive that spirit which enabled the enslaved nations finally to break the fetters of feudalism. Why should it not be to-day as it was in times past? Why should not the university be the conserver as well as the nurse of freedom?[30]

Higher education was not for all, Daniel Geary agreed, but he seemed more expansive in his vision of the potential community of the liberally educated than did Morris:

> Those who have the means and the time—and their number is not so few—should devote themselves to the attainment of all the requisites of liberal and higher education . . . they should become the promoters, the leaders of schools of thought in politics, in

> literature, in art, in all the many walks of life in which men are led to travel; that, above all things, they may endeavor to disseminate genuine Catholic principles, to inspire the masses with reverence for authority, with the spirit of self-control, . . . in a word, toward what is Catholic.[31]

And what was the world they were being educated to engage? Monsignor Preston, in the address that closed the first day of the celebration, unsurprisingly cast it as a battleground in which the church was called to confront error in its many shapes. Preston passed this judgment:

> This is not an intellectual age. In deep and profound studies it can not compare with the glory of the past. It boasts of its progress, and its pride is the evidence of its ignorance. It hath made progress in things material, in the application of scientific truths; but what advance hath it made in serious knowledge? The so-called modern philosophy is the denial of even natural light and the darkening of the understanding with obscure words. . . . We will meet them on the arena of reason and compel them to an inglorious defeat. . . . We will drive them to the sterile regions of utter skepticism, and force those who glory in knowing nothing to confess their folly. . . . By reason we will prove the extrinsic credibility of faith and lead the true intellect to bow before the God who is truth and who can neither deceive nor be deceived. Thus we open the portals of the temple of truth. He that will not enter here shall die in darkness. . . . The mightier the intellect the more fearful the wreck upon the rocks and sands of unbelief. This age can tell us nothing new of God and truth divine. There are no new paths, no new revelations, no elevated heights from which we may look down upon the giants of ages past, the great theologians and philosophers of the Church, who, even now in heaven, are the aids to our feeble efforts and the patrons of our studies. . . . We shall not fall into the snares laid for him who studies without humility and obedience.[32]

Nor could Preston resist attacking, if obliquely, Catholic reformers like Edward McGlynn who were calling for fundamental changes in the social order to achieve economic justice:[33]

> There are always so-called reformers whose avowed purpose is to

> heal the wounds of humanity in its struggle with evil. Dissatisfied with the plans of divine mercy and the guidance of the Church which leads men in safe paths, they would propose remedies which violate every vested or natural right and break to pieces the social bond. Hence communism seeks to bless all by destroying all, giving wealth by taking away. Hence socialism of the most dangerous type lifts its head and talks of natural bounties as the property of all, because, say they, they are the property of none. By such errors they destroy every natural right and would relegate civilized society to the chaos of jarring elements without a principle or bond of union.[34]

For Preston, the key to wisdom was fidelity to the perennial philosophy of the church and "submission to the Vicar of the Lord, the Infallible Pastor . . . to whom God has given the sacred trust of the deposit of the faith. He is the impregnable rock on which rests the whole edifice."[35] Such an ultramontanist stance was not found in the other key speakers, although they echoed Preston in identifying materialism, agnosticism, and socialism as the special challenges of the age.

Martin Morris acknowledged the remarkable progress of the century but found the accompanying unraveling of man's traditional beliefs a steep price to pay:

> The principal religion of our time is Materialism, and Mammon is the chief divinity in its Pantheon. The acquisition of money is the supreme goal of human effort. . . . Even the sciences which are commended to us are chiefly the material sciences. . . . The self-made man, so-called, is the idol of our time; and the self-made man, who is thus held up to us for our admiration, is usually a compound in equal parts of ignorance and self-sufficiency.[36]

In all this ferment of the human mind, what role could the University play in responding to the many complex problems of the modern world? Even those who laud it most do not tell us how education "is to bridge the widening chasm between capital and labor, or to reconcile the growing conflict between cooperative combination and individual freedom, or to fuse radically antagonistic races into one homogeneous people."[37] "There was a time," Morris noted, "when the great universities of Europe were the arbiters of public opinion, and exercised the most potent influence on the social, civil and political life of the world."[38] Despite the prevalence of materialism in the land, Morris saw "remarkable indications of a strong counter-current" in the development of universities such as Georgetown.[39] "Is not all this the harbinger of a newer and better spirit, and of a higher and better appreciation of the culture that is needed to save the social system from impending disaster?"[40]

Intelligence, he warned, was not an adequate remedy. What was needed was not only an education "of the intellect, but equally of the heart." The affective side, "the spiritual and sentimental faculties," had to be nurtured, for "on the combined training of the head and heart depend alike the welfare of the individual and the welfare of the State."[41] This liberal education was the only guarantee of the educated citizenry needed for a republic.

Fortunately, Doonan remarked in his Centennial sermon, this balance was John Carroll's own strength: "His was a conservatism that goes hand in hand with intelligent liberality, a conservatism that holds inviolate the border line which separates positive truth from speculative inquiry," and asserts frankly that its philosophic thought lies "outside the realm of experimental inquiry."[42] Georgetown, Doonan found, had been faithful to Carroll's goal expressed in its motto, *utraque unum.* It continued to balance "religion and learning" by sending forth

> sons, trained in the great principle of moral conduct whose foundation is Christianity . . . sons schooled under a discipline which seeks in all branches of human knowledge the highest development of man's intellectual faculties, but reckons this of lesser worth than the impress of honor, honesty and integrity which the heart is to receive.[43]

The capstone of Georgetown's curriculum, its rigorous system of "intellectual and moral philosophy," provided

> the saving grace that is yet to redeem us from the selfishness of political dishonesty, as well as the ravings of an insane fanaticism. Even if it be only the chosen few that can drink at its Castalian fountains, those chosen few must be the poet-priests, whose anthems are to stir the world and lead it into the newer and better day.[44]

It was the student, Geary, who was least complacent about Catholic higher education. Catholics, to be sure, "find themselves in possession of infallible truth . . . feel the sublimity of their faith . . . see the beauty of its teaching . . . but they neglect the acquirement of that, which, after the grace of God, will alone serve to perpetuate and expand it." Geary argued that the errors of the age needed to be met "in that same fresh and vigorous way, in which the old systems answered the difficulties of the old days." To the assurance that "there is nothing new under the sun," Geary rejoined: "the philosopher that falls back on that disheartening confession, in order to apologize for the old-fashioned ways that the tyranny of custom and habit binds him to, is not a very profound searcher after truth."[45]

Nonetheless, Georgetown's progress, "from the modest academy that Carroll placed upon the banks of the Potomac" to "a university whose schools of arts, science, literature, medicine and law give it place among the foremost institutions of the land,"[46] was the coda of the themes raised during the celebration. Even the dean of the youngest of Georgetown's schools boasted that his school had already "assumed a foremost place among the Law Schools of the country . . ."[47] Not least of its advantages, he noted, was the location in the national capital.

"The Washington connection" was one that several speakers noted in one way or another. Morris recalled George Washington's dream of founding a great university in the federal city:

> But are we not realizing the dream of Washington? . . . Institutions grow; they are not made. They do not spring up in a night, perhaps to vanish like an exhalation before the morning sun. . . . All human institutions that are destined to last must come up from small beginnings. It has taken a century to develop our country into a mighty nation and a united people. The same century has developed the College founded by John Carroll into a great and prosperous university, fully competent to hold her place among the universities of the world. But all is not yet done.[48]

In a utopian peroration, Morris prayed that Georgetown University might

> survive in all her vigor . . . when the second and the fifth and the tenth century shall have rolled away—when all the problems of our day shall have been solved, only to give place, perhaps, to others of deeper and graver import—when from Panama to the Paleocrystic Sea the starry flag of freedom shall float in peace over a hundred

> indestructible sovereign States, component parts of one great indissoluble Union—when our now antagonistic races shall have been gathered together, each in its own local sovereignty, yet bound in the bands of one fraternal Confederacy, into which even the Mongolian may find admission—when, perchance, from yonder observatory hill your astronomers shall flash electric recognition to the denizens of "the star of love and dreams," and convey to the celebrants of future Centennials the congratulations of those who watch by the canals of the red planet Mars.[49]

Georgetown's official historian, John Gilmary Shea, was more measured in his evaluation. He detected as the University's tacit motto "'festina lente'—be in a hurry, but don't break everything you are carrying . . ."[50] In the words of the inscription hanging on Old North during the celebration:

"Proud of her elder children
And having bright hopes in the younger,
The mother hastens towards the goal of her desire."[51]

In that mood the University entered the 1890s and its second century.

Notes

1. Georgetown University Archives (hereafter GUA), 505-14, House Diary, February 22, 1889.

2. Cited in John Gilmary Shea, *History of Georgetown College: Memorial of the First Century* (New York: P. F. Collier, 1891), 339.

3. Carroll to Charles Plowden, 1 March 1788, 12 November 1788, in Thomas O'Brien Hanley, ed., *The John Carroll Papers* (Notre Dame: University of Notre Dame Press, 1976), I, 275, 332.

4. The first evidence of this equation is in a manuscript of an immigrant Jesuit, Anthony Rey, written in the middle 1840s for a European audience. Rey was in residence at the college at the time (Maryland Province Archives, PA 3 B 2, "Notice historique de l'establissement et des progrès de la Religione catholique dans les Etats Unis").

5. The total enrollment in the College and professional schools (law and medicine) was 259 in the 1881-82 academic year, a sharp drop from the peak of 376 in 1867.

6. Cited in Shea, *History of Georgetown College*, 304-05.

7. Many persons, especially Jesuits, continued to refer to Georgetown as "the College" long after it included other schools. Partly, this reflected the loose relationship that the professional schools had with the institution, and partly, the historic precedence of the College. When Cardinal Gibbons addressed the convocation on the last evening of the centenary, he consistently referred to "Georgetown College" in his remarks.

8. Archivum Romanum Societatis Iesu (hereafter ARSI), MD 11, 1, 7, Campbell to A. M. Anderledy, New York, 7 July 1888.

9. Shea, *History of Georgetown College*, 321.

10. GUA, Box 2, Folder 7, Campbell to Richards, New York, August 23, 1888.

11. GUA, 531-1, vol. 2, Consultations Book, Oct. 2, 1888; Oct. 12, 1888.

12. ARSI, MD 11, I, 12, Campbell to Anderledy, Boston, 23 January 1889.

13. GUA, 550-14, House Diary, 1884 to 1892, 173.

14. Shea, *History of Georgetown College*, 339.

15. Ibid., 363.

16. Ibid., 370-71.

17. Ibid., 339-40.

18. Ibid., 417.

19. *Georgetown College Journal* 62 (1933-34), 462.

20. ARSI, Litterae Annuae, Collegii Georgiopolitani, 1886-1889.

21. Shea, *History of Georgetown College*, 344.

22. Ibid., 400.

23. Ibid., 416.

24. Ibid., 417-18.

25. Ibid., 411-12.

26. Ibid., 412-13.

27. Ibid., 350-51.

28. Ibid., 351.

29. Ibid., 382-83.

30. Ibid., 382.

31. Ibid., 416.

32. Ibid., 359-60.

33. Two years before, a professor of ethics at the Law School, Father Holaind, had published a refutation of the agrarian doctrine of McGlynn's mentor, Henry George. Cf. René I. Holaind, S.J., *Ownership and Natural Right* (Baltimore: Hill & Harvey, 1887).

34. Shea, *History of Georgetown College*, 360.

35. Ibid., 359.

36. Ibid., 377.

37. Ibid., 380.

38. Ibid., 374.

39. Cf. ibid., 378: "And have not even misers sought to atone for their hardness of heart to the living," Morris observed in an obvious reference to Cornelius Vanderbilt, "by linking their names, when dead, to the posthumous monuments which they have directed their executors to raise to education?"

40. Ibid., 378.
41. Ibid., 380-81.
42. Ibid., 352.
43. Ibid., 353.
44. Ibid., 386.
45. Ibid., 414-15.
46. Doonan in the Centennial Sermon, ibid., 353.
47. Remarks of George E. Hamilton, Esq., in response to the toast: "The Law Department," ibid., 395.
48. Ibid., 385-86.
49. Ibid., 386-87.
50. Ibid., 340.
51. Ibid., 341.

MONIKA K. HELLWIG
Theology Department

Post-Vatican II Ecclesiology: New Context for a Catholic University

The changing ecclesiology initiated in Catholic thought and practice at the Second Vatican Council in the 1960s[1] is of concern for any institution calling itself Catholic. Educational institutions are more particularly affected by a changing ecclesiology because they play a role in interpreting and implementing the changes. In the case of universities, that role often places the thought and practice of the institution and its members well ahead of the church community at large, including most church officials. Needless to say, this involves tensions and conflicts, both public and intimate, for the Catholic administrators and faculty members of a Catholic institution, and those who do not have a specialized knowledge of the workings of the Catholic Church and its changing ecclesiology may find themselves greatly bewildered by the way these conflicts develop and are resolved. The purpose of this paper is to set out as clearly as possible the changing patterns in the church's self-image, and to suggest the implications for a Catholic university such as ours.

Ecclesiology is theological reflection about the church itself—its nature and purpose, its membership and structure, its relationship to Christ, to the process of redemption and to the ultimate realization of the Reign of God. In other words, it is a reflection on the possibility and actuality of human mediation of divine redeeming grace—a mediation linked with the person of Jesus Christ and expressed in a corporate commitment. The understanding of such mediation varies across a great range of interpretation but in every case it presupposes an established state of disorder or disorientation pervading the lives and values of human individuals and societies—a disorder that can be set right and to which Jesus Christ holds the key.

The far-reaching changes in the Catholic church since Vatican II are best understood in the light of the history, and even of the prehistory, of modern Catholic ecclesiology. By prehistory I mean that span of centuries up to the Council of Trent, 1545-63, during which we have a common past with the Protestant churches of the West, and during the earlier parts of which we have a common past with all the Christian churches. The theological ecclesiology of this long period is largely implicit in the practice of the church and in its traditions of theology of grace, redemption, and sacramental efficacy. Ecclesiology became fully explicit in theology only with the challenges of the fourteenth century to current practices and assumptions, and with the treatises of the fifteenth century defending the practices and assumptions that had been questioned. Nevertheless, the implicit ecclesiology of earlier centuries can be reconstructed in a generally noncontroversial fashion from the extensive documentary evidence available.[2]

The church of apostolic times was, of course, a community gathering and structuring itself experimentally. Key structural features were the assembling for eucharistic celebration (including biblical readings and meditation as well as a fellowship meal), the acknowledged leadership of those who had known Jesus in the flesh, sharing of resources and services with those in need, and a pattern of continuous further outreach or missionary activity, culminating in incorporation of newcomers through baptism. At some early stage, time was structured around the first day of the week as the Lord's Day, rather than the traditional Sabbath.

During the first three centuries the continuing outreach resulted in a loose federation of local churches, each centered around a bishop or overseer, aided by deacons and elders whose functions varied. Relations among the churches were maintained informally, and we have evidence in extant documents both of friendly intervention by leaders of one local church in the affairs of another and of admonition and reproof addressed by representatives of one local church to those causing factions and disturbances in another.[3] Within the local churches the communion and unity of the members were centered upon the guidance and leadership of the bishop and the celebration of the Eucharist. Great store was set by consensus reached through prayer, but when this failed it was the bishop's word that prevailed. It should be noted, however, that the bishops of this time were chosen by their congregations from among their own number either explicitly by popular acclaim or implicitly by tacit consent to the emergence of an unquestioned leader. Moreover, we know the qualities that were sought in a bishop: this should be someone who had close ties with an apostle or with someone who could provide a link with the oral teaching and example of an apostle; the one chosen should be recognizable as one wise according to the gospel of Jesus Christ and a devout practitioner of that gospel; and it was very desirable that such a one should already have raised a family in the ways of Christ. It is abundantly clear that the authority recognized in the bishop at this time is more the authority of expertise than that of command and sanction. So much is this the case that when serious disputes in doctrine or discipline arose it was customary to gather a synod of representatives of the local churches of the region to try to discern the truth of the matter prayerfully.[4]

The definitive change in the mode of structuring local churches and their relations with one another was introduced in the fourth century with the legalization and subsequent official establishment of the Christian churches by the Emperor Constantine and his successors.[5] Under the imperial patronage of the new regime the role of bishops was transformed. In return for privileges allowing them to use public buildings and insignia and ceremonial procedures of officials of the Empire, bishops were expected to function as civil servants in the administration and coordination of the far-flung territories. In the discharge of their civic functions they acquired an authority which was quite distinctively that of command and secular sanction over citizens who were in many cases also Christians and under the spiritual leadership of the same bishops. At the same time, the newly acquired licit and respectable status of the Christians led to churches enlarged in numbers but diminished in fervor. As might be expected, the regulation of these churches became more and more a matter of an external discipline and less and less a matter of spontaneous striving for unity in pursuit of common goals. In the fourth and fifth centuries this discipline included doctrinal control exercised by general councils held at the Emperor's behest and under his patronage and supervision, yielding a number of schisms in which whole clusters of local churches were cut off while the remainder attained a degree of uniformity not previously found necessary.

It is only fairly recently that this pattern of development in the structures and activities of the early church was taken seriously in Catholic circles, though the churches of the radical reform have long pointed to the fourth century establishment and the changes it brought as a betrayal of the ideas and ideals of the gospel. But there is a further development of the early centuries which is of particular importance for Catholic reappraisal of ecclesiology in our own times. The ancient churches, with their rather informal patterns of maintaining unity, had clustered themselves around "patriarchates," that is to say around certain of the oldest sees connected with prominent New Testament figures. Although there were several of these in the East (Alexandria, Antioch, Constantinople, and Jerusalem), the Latin-speaking western empire claimed only one—Rome, which boasted of both Peter and Paul as its founders. While the eastern Christians saw orthodoxy and orthopraxis as resting upon the collegial discernment of the various local churches, expressed through their representatives and explicitly determined by the consensus at least of the patriarchal sees, the western church turned towards more and more monarchic and heavily centralized patterns of authority. This must, of course, be seen in the context of an empire threatened with dissolution from external attack and internal strife, in which the Roman patriarch often played a role as peacemaker, protector of the people, vicar of the distant emperor, and actual if not official administrator of the territories around Rome.

With the expansion into the northern barbarian peoples, and the close liaison with Charlemagne and his successors, followed in the eleventh century by the definitive schism between the eastern and western churches, the monarchic pattern of church administration was well established in the West and was made official and explicit by the reforms of Hildebrand, Pope Gregory VII. At the same time, the church had become a strong conservative force in its alliance with the culture of the Mediterranean past—a trend relieved temporarily by papal chartering and protecting of the rising universities of the thirteenth century, and again (rather problematically) by papal patronage of the arts in the Renaissance period. As is well known, the interest in conserving scholarship and ancient culture among the more privileged was accompanied by great ignorance and superstition among the masses of "Christendom," including many, if not most, of the parish clergy. The self-understanding of the church as implicit in the sacramental and disciplinary practice of the time, and in the power struggles taking place between church and secular leaders, was predominantly that of a divinely mandated structure to take care of the spiritual aspects of life and shepherd individuals through their earthly lives in such a way that they might enter into heavenly happiness at death or beyond it. The notion of church as a countercultural movement in society had been lost except at certain missionary fringes of "Christendom." Likewise lost was any sense of a historical dynamic moving towards the Reign of God in the world of human affairs. There seems to have been an assumption that once a society had been christianized the Reign of God had been established to the extent that was possible in history, and the business of the church was to mark time, maintaining the status quo and "sanctifying," teaching, and in spiritual matters governing the faithful, so as to lead them individually to their salvation. Concerning the "end-time," which for the early Christians was the focus of all their hope, medieval texts speak almost unanimously with unqualified terror.[6]

This changed perception did not go unchallenged. In the twelfth century, for instance, the Waldensians, after reading the New Testament, tried to form themselves into communities of disciples taking the teachings of Jesus and the example of the earliest communities quite literally as though to rebuild the church from the grassroots. But they were excommunicated because they threatened the status and privileges of the clergy. Likewise, Francis of Assisi, in pursuit of the famous vision in which he was bidden to rebuild the church, tried to reinitiate a completely countercultural way of living. But his followers, although they were not excommunicated, were assimilated after his death into the existing structures of the church of the time. Nevertheless, the challenge was not thereby eliminated. Although from the late twelfth century onwards there was a tendency for canon law to be the discipline that defined the church and its purpose and tasks, Thomas Aquinas in the thirteenth century does not seem to consider the legal and governmental aspects theologically significant, for his *Summa Theologica* moves from a consideration of the mysteries of the life of Christ to the gathering of his followers around the Eucharist and the implications of that.[7]

As is generally known, the issues of the nature and functions of the church, its relationship to the society at large, and the proper assignment of church functions among the members all burst wide open in the fourteenth century with the antihierarchic writings and preaching of Marsiglio of Padua, John Wycliffe and John Hus, and were continued in a particularly pointed form in the fifteenth century with the conciliar movement. It is the response to these particular challenges that formulated for the first time explicitly an understanding of the church that was to become the basic pattern for official modern Catholic ecclesiology until

Vatican II. In John of Ragusa's *Tractatus de ecclesia* (1431) and in John of Torquemada's *Summa de Ecclesia* (1486), the church emerges as the complete society (*societas perfecta*) with its complement of governmental, recruitment, and maintenance functions, and with its established hierarchic structure that guarantees these functions. It is this structured and self-maintaining society that was founded and given its essential and unalterable pattern by Jesus Christ himself through the apostles who had direct contact with him.

The sixteenth-century reformers rightly challenged an interpretation flowing from these claims, which identified the entire structure of the institutional church as it existed in their time, along with the details of sacramental practice and the full elaboration of contemporary church teaching, quite simply with what Jesus had envisaged for his followers. It would be false to suppose that the Council of Trent, in establishing the foundation for a Catholic response to the reformers, defended everything in the existing church practice as right or even normative. There was in the strict sense a Catholic counter-reformation in addition to a spontaneous Catholic reform movement spearheaded earlier by such figures as Cardinal Cisneros and later by such as Ignatius Loyola. Yet, while Trent avoided an explicit formulation of ecclesiology, its documents repeatedly assume the extremely legalistic concept and definition of church arising out of the fifteenth-century treatises. Cardinal Bellarmine justified the approach by insisting that it was necessary to speak of the real church that actually existed in the world and not about some ideal church which had no real existence except in the minds of the reformers.

There is no doubt that the ecclesiology which came into play in Catholic circles from the Council of Trent onwards was a defensive one which was to some extent trapped into the categories which the reformers had challenged. The manuals prepared for use in seminaries stressed the divinely sanctioned character of the governmental and administrative structures then in place, the unchangeable character of what were then considered the essential teachings, practices, and rules, and the demonstrable truth of the claim that the Catholic church was the only true church. Key features of this appear in the first draft of the Constitution on the Church of Christ which was presented for discussion to the First Vatican Council which met from 1869 to 1870.[8] This draft was never discussed due to the hasty and unforeseen conclusion of the Council. Nevertheless, the document represents what the theologians of the Council took to be the orthodox Catholic teaching of their time.

This text begins with the observation that because God has placed the whole doctrine and means of salvation in the church it is urgent to show both the faithful and those in error which is the true church, and therefore the document is to "expound the more important articles of the true Catholic doctrine concerning the nature of the Church, her characteristics and her powers, and to condemn contrary errors."[9] With the Pauline image of the mystical body of Christ, the text insists on the compact and clearly defined unity of those joined to the Head in faith, hope and charity,[10] and further states that the church has all the marks of a true and complete (*perfecta*) society whose form and constitution was given it by Christ himself.[11] This church is not simply an invisible community held together by interior bonds; corresponding to these are external and visible bonds. "Whence comes the visible magisterium which publicly lays down what is to be inwardly believed and outwardly confessed . . . the visible ministry which governs and controls [sic] the visible mysteries of God . . . the visible pastorate which orders the unity of the members . . . finally, the whole visible body of the Church . . ."[12] No one separated from any of these visible structures can "in any way be called a part or member of the Church," the reason being that "the Church is so completely bounded and determined in her constitution" by the will of Christ himself.[13] This church is necessary for salvation, though in cases of invincible ignorance God gives special graces for justification and salvation.[14] Moreover, this church, "whether regarded in its existence or in its constitution, is a permanent and indefectible society."[15] It has been given the gift of infallibility "so that the word of God in written and oral tradition shall . . . be maintained and protected from change and innovation."[16] The church "is not a community of equals . . . It is a society of unequals . . . because there is in the Church the power from God whereby to some it is given to sanctify, teach, and govern and to others not."[17]

As is quite generally known, the part of the draft that was discussed, refined, and approved, thus becoming a dogmatic constitution of the First Vatican Council, concerned the special primacy of jurisdiction over the universal church and infallibility of teaching authority in solemn pronouncements claimed for the Roman Pontiff as the direct mandate and gift of Christ.[18] The fact that this was the only part of the original proposal to acquire the explicit approval of the Council resulted in disproportionate emphasis being placed upon it, so that it has often seemed as though all that was summarized in the preceding paragraph primarily, if not even exclusively, concerned the normative functioning of the Roman See, leaving no initiative at all in the local churches, even in the hands of their bishops. Yet, except in the matter of appointments, this may not have been as glaringly obvious then as it is to us, simply because the entire conception of church as depicted above is an extremely static one, so that the main responsibility of those in official positions is to maintain the routine functioning of the "complete society" in its existing, accustomed patterns.

It would be entirely false to suppose that this vision of the church, along with the sense of revelation, redemption, and eschatology that was implicit in it, went unchallenged by Catholic intellectuals exposed to the exciting thrusts of post-Enlightenment scholarship. Although it is not possible here to trace the tempestuous and often tragic course of the more creative Catholic scholars of the nineteenth and early twentieth centuries,[19] their number and persistence is clear from the list of prohibitive and condemnatory statements issued from Rome in response to such scholars: *Qui pluribus*, 1846 (against claims for critical thought and doubt in theological argument); *Singulari quadam*, 1854 (against assertions made for human reason); the "Syllabus of Errors," 1864 (condemning many theses attributed to philosophers and natural scientists); the Letter from the Holy Office to the Bishops of England, also 1864 (reproving Catholics who took part in an ecumenical movement that regarded the Roman, Greek, and Anglican churches as being of equal apostolic continuity); the decree *Lamentabili* and the condemnation of the "Modernist Propositions," 1907 (attacking a very wide range of scholarly theses, for the most part formulated in the document in an exaggerated or distorted way); the prescription of the Oath against Modernism, 1910, etc.[20]

It is true that through the German universities, the Pontifical Biblical Institute, outside pressures, enlightened papal advisors, and other influences, this very autocratic and static image of the church was softened slightly. Yet in spite of papal encyclical letters attempting a more contemporary understanding of the church, such as *Mystici corporis*, 1943, and *Mediator Dei*, 1947, and in spite of a great deal of low-key scholarly writing based on the biblical, patristic and liturgical revival movements, the official understanding of the nature and functions of the church changed very little. Those who understood and exposed the internal inconsistencies of this view also continued to be silenced or persecuted—for instance, Yves Congar, Henri de Lubac, Karl Rahner, and John

Courtney Murray. This continued until their work finally fructified and was vindicated in the Second Vatican Council in 1962-65.

It has been suggested that the Second Vatican Council was such a clear watershed in Catholic history because it was the first council to gather a worldwide church, giving a significant vote to representatives of churches in formerly colonial countries now asserting their indigenous cultures and needs with great vigor and critical perspicuity. In any case, many of the European bishops also came with *periti* who were among the foremost critical scholars in theology and Scripture and in related fields. The conservative *schemata* that were prepared by the Vatican staff were rejected at the first sitting of the council which constituted its own drafting committees of qualified scholars. The first document to be discussed and passed was the Dogmatic Constitution on the Liturgy, which contained an implicit ecclesiology drawn largely from patristic thought because this was the period in the church's historical development of most immediate interest to liturgical scholars. The liturgical constitution envisages a dynamic church that takes a countercultural stance in the world and makes an impact upon the world.[21] Concerned primarily with the church at the moment of public worship, the document nevertheless sees the laity not as passive listeners and onlookers, but as the collective subject of the action that is going on, and as both collectively and individually responsible for the effect of that action in the world.

The documents of Vatican II which address the nature and functions of the church directly are: the Dogmatic Constitution on the Church, the Pastoral Constitution on the Church in the Modern World, the Decree on Ecumenism, the Decree on the Catholic Eastern Churches, the Declaration on the Relation of the Church to Non-Christian Religions, and the Decree on the Church's Missionary Activity. Documents relating to the distribution of tasks within the church include: the Decree on the Apostolate of Lay People, the Declaration on Christian Education, the Decree on the Up-to-Date Renewal of Religious Life, the Decree on the Training of Priests, the Decree on the Ministry and Life of Priests and the Decree on the Pastoral Office of Bishops in the Church. It may also be said that of the remaining three documents two imply a considerable retrenchment of claims made by the post-Tridentine church: the Declaration on Religious Liberty and the Dogmatic Constitution on Divine Revelation.[22]

Most significant of all these documents is the Dogmatic Constitution on the Church, which opens by introducing the church as mystery of salvation linked to the Triune God in a communion of grace. To suggest ways of thinking about what the church essentially is, the first chapter directs the reader to a succession of biblical images and symbols: the seed and beginning of God's reign in the world, growing and reaching towards maturity, a sheepfold, a gateway, a flock whose shepherd is always Christ himself, a tillage, a grafted olive tree joining Jew and gentile, a choice vineyard of God's planting, the true vine in which it is the life of Christ that makes the branches fruitful, a building of God, the dwelling place of God among human persons, a holy temple, a holy city, the new Jerusalem, and yet a spouse of Christ exiled and wandering, but at the same time the very body in which Christ is made present and in which he acts in the world. Out of this plethora of imagery, chapter II selects and develops one—the people of God, people of the Covenant, pilgrim people, priestly people, gathered in sacramental worship but exercising their mission in the whole of their lives, having a prophetic office which makes them a countercultural force in the world. In exploring the implications of this image of the people of God, the text acknowledges the intended ambiguity; all human beings are in some sense God's people, and those who believe in the one God are more specifically so, while those who put their faith in God through the mediation of Jesus have a closer bond as people of the renewed covenant in Christ.[23]

It is clear that when the idea of the church is introduced in this way the juridical structure takes second place. The focus is on the goals of the church as a dynamic force and on the relationship with Christ as an organic bond. The fact that the third chapter of the document develops the understanding of the church as essentially hierarchical does not cancel the established understanding that it is secondarily, not primarily, hierarchical. Moreover, this third chapter stresses the collegial nature of the office of the bishops as successors of the apostles, and therefore implies the collegial nature of the bond that holds the local churches in communion with one another.[24] The further implications of this chapter for local church initiatives and discernment of local pastoral needs and conditions have been far-reaching, and a matter of tension between local churches and Vatican staff clinging to more centralized modes of procedure. In particular, the newly reasserted collegiality of the bishops has led to the effective operation of episcopal conferences which have a strong precedent in the regional synods of the early church but which, nevertheless, due to Roman resistance do not have a clearly defined status in canon law.

Further chapters of this key document deal with the laity, the general call to holiness, members of religious orders, the pilgrim condition of the church (which exists only as a reaching out towards the reign of God), and the role of Mary in the Catholic understanding of the church. Particularly significant in the account given of the role of the laity is the acknowledgment that the laity have an active role to play in the world, reaching into complex matters that are beyond the scope of clerical intervention and which require independent Christian discernment on the part of lay Christians. Any participation of lay Christians in the particular apostolic concerns of the church hierarchy is a special calling to certain people but should not obscure the more basic and general calling of the laity.[25] This principle seems to be very important because earlier Roman teaching had tended to equate "Catholic Action" with the participation of the laity in the apostolate of the hierarchy, implying that judgment and decision lay always with the latter—an assumption which had destructive consequences for the JOCist [Jeunesse Ouvrière Chrétienne] movement in Belgium and France after World War I, and still fuels opposition to the Basic Christian Communities in Third World countries in our time.

Although it is not possible to comment on all the documents of Vatican II which have a bearing on the changing focus and pattern of Catholic ecclesiology, it is necessary to say something about the Pastoral Constitution on the Church in the Modern World, and on the two ecumenical documents. The former does much to redeem the negative impact of the anti-Modernist campaign on the role played by Catholics in the world at large. It recognizes Christian cultural, economic, and political responsibility, sees the church as a service to the world at large in the discernment and welcoming of the reign of God in human affairs, and points in particular to action on behalf of human dignity, social justice, and peace as proper to Christians in worldly affairs.[26] The image here presented of the church suggests multiple initiatives, largely undertaken by lay persons, and implies a dynamic that is dependent on continuing discernment in changing circumstances by those both technically competent and dedicated to gospel values. The document envisages local initiative as well as regional and worldwide collegial action. Moreover, it implies extensive collaboration not only with Christians of the other churches, but also with all persons of good will who acknowledge basic human values which Christians see as belonging to the order of creation. And this relates to the Decree on Ecumenism and the

Declaration on the Relation of the Church to Non-Christian Religions. The former, after commending the acknowledgment of all that is true and good in other Christian traditions, points to the necessity of collaboration with Christians in those other traditions in defense of human dignity, social justice for all, and international peace.[27] In the document concerning the wider ecumenism, collaboration is also urged in pursuit of basic human values.[28]

The cumulative impact of all these documents, and of the means subsequently set in motion to implement them, has been a loosening up of the tightly knit institutional definition of the church of the post-Tridentine era. The new understanding that has been taking shape is more fluid and adaptable, more diversified in roles and functions, more collegial in responsibility, authority and decision making. By this very fact, the church has also become more openly controversial both in the stances taken in the larger society and in its internal relationships. This has consequences for all Catholic institutions. It is no longer quite so clear-cut what are the characteristics that make an institution Catholic. There are particular consequences for Catholic universities and for the roles that they play in relation to the institutional church, in relation to the Catholic community and its tradition, and in relation to the society at large. Particularly helpful in analyzing this is a schema of "models" of the church proposed by theologian Avery Dulles.[29] He suggests six main models as inclusive of most, if not all, of the particular biblical and traditional ones: herald and servant, sacrament and mystical communion, institution and community of disciples. The first couplet expresses the tension between the emphasis on the church's task as primarily that of proclaiming the gospel, and the emphasis on the church's task of *diakonia,* or service in works of mercy, action for social justice and peace, and transformation of structures to welcome the reign of God in the human community. This kind of tension is certainly felt in our times in the definition of the role of a Catholic university. Some are strongly of the opinion that what is most important is clear proclamation of official Catholic teaching through academic courses promoting orthodoxy of doctrine, and policies promoting religious observances and ethical conformity to official moral positions declared by Rome. Others, meanwhile, see much greater urgency in the role a Catholic university can play in challenging unjust and destructive values, assumptions, and structures of the society.

The second couplet, sacrament and mystical communion, expresses the tension between primary emphasis on the visible structures of the church as necessary and effective signs promoting inner conversion and dedication, and an opposing emphasis on the reality of personal and interpersonal commitment as being far more important than ritual and observances. Again, this tension is certainly felt in the experience and definition of a Catholic university in our times. Many feel a strong concern that the visible expression of Catholic life and worship on our campus is so much attenuated that it is in danger of being lost. Others are more concerned whether there is true personal commitment to gospel values among significant numbers of administrators, faculty members and students.

The third couplet, institution and community of disciples, contrasts a predominantly static and formal understanding of the church with one that is more dynamic, unpredictable and personal. It is clear that there is no question of a choice of one in each couplet to the exclusion of the other. Much less is there any question of choosing one model to the exclusion of all others. There are important complementarities of value and function. However, there is little doubt that the choice of emphasis in each case is of vital importance, and that Vatican II and its aftermath have changed the balance of emphasis suggested by the official teaching of the modern Catholic church. It might also be observed that the history of the Jesuits seems to predispose them to greet the change enthusiastically, accepting gratefully the opening that has allowed them to run universities with heavier emphasis on the second member of each couplet. The principle that faith, love, and contemplation are expressed in action suggests a leaning toward the servant model with slightly more emphasis than the herald model. The traditional concern with the formation of the individual for authentic Christian discernment in circumstances that will arise in an unpredictable future suggests a leaning towards mystical communion more heavily than towards the sacramental model of church. Finally, this same focus on discernment, with its traditional modes of implementation, and the commitment to go anywhere and do anything demanded by the gospel in particular contexts, would necessarily point in the direction of community of disciples rather than institution as the primary model.[30]

Of the above, the third couplet is the most consequential, and can profitably be spelt out in more detail. One fundamental polarity in the distinction between an institutional model and one of community of disciples, is that the former is defined with reference to the past and the latter with reference to a goal in the future. The institution is what it is on the basis of predictable patterns already laid down. In the case of the Catholic church there has been a tendency to see those predictable patterns as unchangeable. Community of disciples could conceivably also be defined in terms of unchangeable patterns of observance, but in practice this is not so because the more we know about the person of Jesus and his relations with his disciples and his instructions for their future after his death, the more we are brought to acknowledge that he left no blueprints and that the basis for discipleship is to share his overwhelming concern with the coming reign of God.

A second polarity has to do with which aspects of the church are matters of human responsibility and changeable. Traditionally, we have spoken of a divine element and a human element in the church. In an institutional model there has been a strong inclination to identify the divine element with structures, such as the definition of offices, the determination of patterns of authority, the established patterns of divine worship, and even some points of canon law. The human element was then seen as the way that particular people conducted themselves within these rules and offices. In terms of the model of community of disciples, the distinction comes into focus rather differently. It is precisely the organizational structures and rules that appear as the human element, product of human decisions and subject to change again by human decision. The divine element appears as the foundation in Christ himself, the sustaining breath of the Spirit empowering the freedom of Christians to transcend their limitations, and the call of the transcendent God to whom all is directed.

A third polarity has to do with the patterns of leadership in the church. The institutional model has relied heavily on the assertion that the church is an absolute monarchy by divine institution. Continuing historical research has made this claim more and more problematic. The model of community of disciples does not of itself require a particular pattern of leadership, but it does suggest that there is one master, Christ, and that as all others are disciples they are engaged in a quest together to listen, to try to understand, to discern the way to live and act. This difference is linked immediately with a contrast in the way history is regarded. In the institutional model a continuing quest to discover and interpret the facts of history is not important, because we have the definitive product of the development in the established structures and procedures and rules, as well as in the dogmatic teachings. History may help to explain or justify these, but could never be invoked as a basis for reconsideration. On the other hand, a community of disciples suggests continuing critical self-scrutiny, with a church always still in need of reformation not only in the conduct of individual members but also in the expectations they have of one another, the values and rules they hand on, and the procedures and relationships they observe. History, therefore, plays a vital role: to discover how any feature of the church developed is to learn what value to place on it and what factors justify changes in it.

Another polarity is certainly that the institutional model suggests, and has in fact been used to justify, a monolithic church in which unity means uniformity. Community of disciples suggests plurality, local and grassroots initiative, a certain flexibility allowing for experimental forms and projects. Correspondingly, the institutional church has always had difficulty acknowledging errors in its judgments or decisions and has constantly avoided involvement in situations in which there is risk of being proved wrong. A community of disciples has no cause for a similar attitude. Consequently, to the extent that this model is predominant, Christian people can join forces in difficult conflictual struggles on behalf of social justice and peace, where a predominantly institutional model tends to dissuade Christians from challenge to established power in complex situations. In other words, the institutional model is not well adapted to the prophetic function of the church. It is with the changing emphasis that the prophetic function of the church in the world has been able to come to the fore again.

There are, of course, many other polarities involved, such as the one in interpretation of sacramental efficacy as grace conferred or as relationship of grace established by the quality of the encounter. There is the distinction between the "marks of the church" seen as a guaranteed set of properties inherent in the institutional continuity of the Catholic church or seen as the desirable qualities of the church towards which all Christian communities must strive. There is also the contrast between the church guarding the "deposit of faith" like a sealed package of propositionally formulated revelation and the church as the living tradition of the memory and presence of Christ continuously realized in new people and changing events. And there is the difference between church seen as marking time in history while saving the souls of individuals and church seen as a movement in history to restore all things in Christ that they may be brought fully under the reign of God.

American Catholic universities, like most other Catholic universities in our time, are caught in these tensions in a number of ways. Local expectations tend to be in conflict at present with Roman expectations. Episcopal expectations in some places are in conflict with academic expectations. And within each institution the expectations of Catholic participants who have not been too concerned to study and reflect upon the Vatican II documents and their grounds and consequences tend to be in conflict with the expectations of those who have been deeply involved in the changes. One prominent example concerns the role of the theologian in a Catholic university (most tense at present for moral theologians but in principle the same predicament for all). In a strongly institutional model of church, such as was in effect officially until Vatican II, theology is essentially the explication and rational justification of the orthodox teachings of the church, assumed to be timelessly defined and more or less complete. Therefore, it is entirely logical to keep insisting that none can be considered a Catholic theologian who does not teach what the church teaches. Critical academics will, of course, ask what the difference is between theology and catechetics and will be told that it lies in the philosophical sophistication with which the subject matter is understood. Questions concerning the possibility of research in the field will be answered with examples of critical editing of documents, compilation of texts on particular topics, analysis of writings of classical authors, comparisons of classical authors, etc. In fact, authors who were forbidden to publish in the nineteenth and twentieth centuries were commonly those who drew conclusions from their research which were warranted by the evidence but unacceptable to church authorities because they challenged existing assumptions.

Where a community of disciples model is dominant, there is room for a historical understanding of the formation of doctrine. As formulated by several great contemporary theologians,[31] the development of doctrine always goes through a process of argumentation and this tends to be a continuing spiral. Questions arising from changing cultural experiences of the community of believers prompt theologians and those in related disciplines to consider in the light of Scripture and tradition questions that have not been asked before or to consider old questions in a new light. Most often this discussion arouses debate which is eventually settled on its merits and becomes part of the accepted tradition. Sometimes the debate disturbs the community of believers to the extent that hierarchic authority feels bound to intervene with formal definitions or condemnations of certain formulations. According to this understanding of the way doctrine is shaped, the position of the theologian in the process is different. The theologian is both subsequent to the tradition that has already been shaped and prior to the hierarchic authority in the continuing process of shaping the teaching. In this perception of the role of the theologian scholarly and creative participation is expected, debate among conflicting opinions is welcomed, and the question of who is properly considered a Catholic theologian is necessarily a question for the judgment of peers in the profession. It is not enough to maintain that a Catholic theologian is one who teaches what the church teaches because that is always still in process of formation.

Another important example of the tension for a Catholic university concerns certain institutional controls such as hiring and tenure decisions and administrative policies. In a strictly institutional definition of the church an institution is not to be considered Catholic except to the extent that it is under hierarchic control. This control may not be particularly heavy-handed, especially at times when the institutional model is very generally accepted as the dominant one and there are no major crises in the church. However, it will be understood that any matter of concern will evoke a telephone call from the ordinary of the diocese to the president of the institution, or else a letter directly from Rome, in either case simply calling for conformity to regulations or submission to specific demands made by the hierarchic authority. With the changing emphasis in the self-understanding of the church, combined with the technical, professional, and legal demands of a modern pluralistic society, this kind of institutional subordination is both unworkable and undesirable. In the case of universities as with hospitals, it would quickly lead to civil litigation and professional deterioration. At present, however, this is not evident to all those concerned, and the resultant tensions can be extreme at all levels.

These are not the only examples that could be adduced, but they may be the two most urgent, and they serve to underscore the importance of confronting explicitly the hidden agenda of different basic models of the church with reference to which authority claims and policy decisions will appear as either reasonable or unacceptable and inappropriate.

Notes

1. The official source for the original documents is the Vatican periodical, *Acta Apostolicae Sedis,* for the years 1963-65. Two generally accepted collections in English translation are: *Vatican Council II; the Conciliar and Post-Conciliar Documents,* ed. Austin Flannery (Wilmington, Del.: Scholarly Resources, 1975); and *The Documents of Vatican II,* ed. Walter Abbott (New York: America Press, 1966).

2. A good list of secondary sources is *The Church: A Bibliography*, ed. Avery Dulles and Patrick Granfield (Wilmington, Del.: Michael Glazier, 1985), chaps. 7-12.

3. The Letters of Ignatius of Antioch are an example of friendly intervention. The Letter of Clement of Rome to the church in Corinth, and the admonition of Cyprian of Carthage on the unity of the church, addressed to the leaders of the church of Rome, are examples of admonition and reproof.

4. Unlike the ecumenical councils called solemnly by the emperors later, these local synods were spontaneous, ad hoc gatherings that seem to have been representative of linguistic or cultural clusterings of churches that shared a common church tradition.

5. The changes that this made have been documented many times. A brief and nontechnical account of the ecclesiological shifts of the Constantinian era can be found in Francine Cardman, "The Emperor's New Clothes: Christ and Constantine," in *Above Every Name,* ed. Thomas E. Clarke (New York: Paulist, 1980).

6. A particularly clear liturgical example of this is the sequence, *Dies irae, dies illa.*

7. *Summa Theologica,* IIIa, qq. 50 ff.

8. The critical sections of this text are given in *The Teaching of the Catholic Church,* ed. Josef Neuner, Heinrich Roos, and Karl Rahner (New York: Alba House, 1967), 211-20.

9. Ibid., 211-12.

10. Ibid., 212.

11. Ibid., 213.

12. Ibid., 214-15.

13. Ibid., 215.

14. Ibid., 216-17.

15. Ibid., 217.

16. Ibid., 218.

17. Ibid., 219-20.

18. Cf. ibid., 220-29, for the complete text in English translation; for the Latin text, cf. *Enchiridion Symbolorum,* ed. Denziger-Schönmetzer (Rome: Herder, 1963), 3050-75.

19. This has been done very thoroughly by T. Mark Schoof, *A Survey of Catholic Theology 1800-1970* (New York: Paulist Newman Press, 1970).

20. Cf. Neuner, Roos, and Rahner, *Teaching of the Catholic Church,* for a chronological list of these documents, 442-43, and cross references to texts.

21. Constitution on the Sacred Liturgy (*Sacrosanctum Concilium*), chap. 1, especially nos. 5, 6, 9, and 10.

22. The texts of all these documents are to be found in English translation in the two collections listed in note 1.

23. Dogmatic Constitution on the Church (*Lumen Gentium*), chap. 2, nos. 9-17.

24. How far-reaching a change this was from the thinking in the schema presented at Vatican I may be surmised from the fact that the Roman curial staff of Pope Paul VI insisted on attaching an explanatory note before the document could be

promulgated. The explanatory note insists that "college" applied to the bishops is not to be understood in a juridical sense, as though the one who presides (the pope) had his power derived from or delegated by the group.

25. Dogmatic Constitution on the Church (*Lumen Gentium*), chap. 4, especially no. 33.

26. Pastoral Constitution on the Church in the Modern World (*Gaudium et Spes*), passim.

27. Decree on Ecumenism (*Unitatis Redintegratio*), especially chap. 2, no. 12.

28. Declaration on the Relationship of the Church to Non-Christian Religions (*Nostra Aetate*), nos. 1 and 2.

29. Cf. Avery Dulles, *Models of the Church* (New York: Doubleday, 1975), and *The Reshaping of Catholicism* (New York: Harper & Row, 1988).

30. These principles are drawn primarily from the *Spiritual Exercises* of St. Ignatius Loyola.

31. Especially Bernard Lonergan and Karl Rahner.

R. BRUCE DOUGLASS
Department of Government

The Academic Revolution and the Idea of a Catholic University

One of the most common ways of characterizing the changes that have been afoot in recent years at American Catholic universities like Georgetown is to speak of "pluralism." The term tends to be employed with something less than conceptual precision, but its meaning is usually not difficult to detect. It refers to the increasingly prominent and influential presence in Catholic higher education of faces other than the traditional ones. This usually means non-Catholics, of course, but it also refers to persons of different gender, race, and nationality from those who have formed the traditional constituency of these institutions. For all the talk of Georgetown's tradition of pluralism,[1] there is clearly a much more varied population now being attracted to this university, and the prevailing sense is that this trend is not likely to be reversed.

The question which is usually implied in any such characterization is what is going to happen to the historic identity of the institution as these new faces make their presence felt. There can hardly help but be changes, some of which will be far from minor in their meaning and significance, and, as these take place, the old, familiar institution, beloved to alumni and others who have known it in days gone by, is bound to give way to something new and different. But how different? And in what direction? And with what effect on its capacity to function as a center of learning and scholarship in keeping with its professed Catholic character?

There is no denying, moreover, that there is a sense in which this puts the issue exactly as it needs to be posed. The image it suggests is that of a complex mix of new forces, each with a somewhat different set of interests and aspirations, entering actively into the life of an established institution, and thereby reshaping its character in diverse ways. And in an institution which has gone in the space of a few decades from being a predominantly American, white, male, Catholic enclave to a place where people of different races, faiths, and sexes mingle, that does indeed seem to be exactly what is taking place. The changes in the composition of the student body in recent decades portend, inescapably, a transformation in the character of campus life. The increasing national prominence of the institution and the resulting attraction which it now has for non-Catholics would suggest, too, that the heterogeneity we now see is just the beginning. In the future, it is reasonable to expect that the pool of prospective students and staff from which Georgetown has to choose will increasingly take on a character that is little distinguishable from that available to the rest of the better universities in this country, and the resulting diversity will affect its life even more decisively than it has already done.

Still, for all the obviousness of this, it does not really capture, I think, the real dynamic that is at work in this institution today. Not very precisely, at least. Nor does it identify accurately what is at stake in the changes that are underway. For like other usages of the concept of pluralism, it gives the misleading impression that what is taking place is a refashioning of the character of an established institution through the interplay of a whole series of discrete new forces, each of which can be expected to have about as much influence as the next in determining the eventual outcome. But, in this case, it is obvious that some of the new forces are destined to be much more influential than others. So, the actual situation is much different from how it initially appears. Indeed, so much so, I propose to argue, that the imagery of pluralism is best set aside and replaced by an alternative which, while not altogether different, leads us to think about the whole matter in distinctly different terms.

I.

The image that I have in mind is that of an encounter with what Christopher Jencks and David Riesman characterized some years ago as the "academic revolution."[2] They used this term to refer to a fundamental transformation that had been taking place in the nature and purpose of higher education in this country since the advent of universities (approximately a century ago) and the consequent professionalization of academic life. Before the emergence of graduate schools, they observed, institutions of higher learning on this side of the Atlantic tended to have a very different character from what they have now. Even the better colleges tended to be highly parochial (serving one or another very specialized constituency), with the emphasis almost exclusively on teaching and the faculty having very little sense of professional identity. Control was vested almost entirely in the hands of the president and/or the board of directors, who tended to define the entire enterprise in their own image. Whether public or private, the schools in question were, virtually without exception, forthright attempts to create an instrument for the transmission of one or another particular cultural inheritance to the new generation, and it was taken for granted that almost all of what took place under their auspices would conform to this end.

But, with the rise of universities, all of this began to change. It had to. For universities meant graduate education, which, if it was to be at all credible, had to be accompanied by scholarship. The scholarly professionalization of faculties soon followed, and once this happened, a whole new dynamic was introduced into academic life. Professors who conceived of themselves as active, contributing members of scholarly "disciplines" were a fundamentally different breed from the generalist pedagogues who were the stock and trade of the nineteenth-century liberal arts college, and they were not about to devote themselves unquestioningly to serving the objectives laid down by trustees and administrators. They had their own research interests to pursue, and they were inclined to honor only those institutions which allowed (indeed, encouraged) them to devote themselves actively to the pursuit of such interests. Nor were they willing to go along with functioning as mere hired hands. Precisely because of their professionalism, they wanted—and usually insisted upon—a greater role in academic administration, and, especially in matters pertaining directly to their professional interests (such as faculty hiring), they expected to play a decisive role.

This is not for a moment to suggest, of course, that the professoriate, thus redefined, was the only force responsible for giving the American university its current character. Or that the interests and aspirations of the faculty, even at the more distinguished institutions, in fact conform neatly to a single orientation. If there is anything on which virtually all informed observers of American academic life today (Jencks and Riesman included) agree, it is the fact that the contemporary university is, in its own way, every bit as much a creature of wider social forces as was its predecessor.[3] And precisely because of the relative freedom which they now enjoy, faculty can and do vary in the way that they choose to live out their professional lives. But comparatively speaking, the faculty today at virtually every university of any note are in a fundamentally different position with respect to academic governance from their predecessors in preindustrial America. Their views *have* to be taken into account; indeed, in most matters of genuine academic substance (the hiring and promotion of faculty, particularly), the presumption has to be that they will *prevail* if the institution is to maintain its scholarly standing. And most faculty, in turn, recognize full well that they, too, must conform to the conventional assumptions of their colleagues about their work. In principle, of course, they are free to do as they choose, but if they want to succeed, they know well that they had better invest their time and energy in the favored pursuits of the profession.

The ascendancy of such people cannot help, in turn, but give academic life a very different character. For all of the talk about the multiplicity of different purposes at work in the university today, experience shows that there is a quite identifiable cast given to higher education wherever they congregate. The education of undergraduates, for example, ceases to be the dominant, overriding concern that it once was. With the rise of graduate and professional schools, there are no small number of faculty who have little or no instructional contact with bachelor-level students. Undergraduate education itself, moreover, tends to be directly affected by the value which academic (and other) professionals place on advanced degrees. More and more it takes on the character of a preparation for further study, and even in the liberal arts it ceases to be looked upon as an end in itself. The success of the institution is measured, above all, by the number of students it has "going on" to distinguished graduate and professional schools.

Inescapably, too, there is a strong inclination to make scholarly research the primary business of the institution. Especially as the penchant of scholars to define the quality of educational institutions in terms of the scholarly achievement and eminence of the faculty comes to be institutionalized, there is a natural tendency to give scholarship priority in the making of the decisions that give a university its identity. In everything from the tenor of campus life to the expectations that are brought to bear in evaluating their performance, appropriately socialized academic professionals assume that scholarship ought to be given pride of place, and the administrator who is committed to putting (and keeping) his or her institution on the academic map can hardly afford to think otherwise. So, teaching loads decline, research budgets expand, and the premium in both recruiting and retaining faculty is on scholarly achievement. And more and more, as the research centers and scholars with minimal classroom activity multiply, the campus takes on the appearance of a vast, multifaceted workplace for scholarly projects. A research factory, if you will.

II.

It would be a mistake, I think, to identify this point of view with any particular method or approach to scholarship. It is held, after all, by people engaged in all sorts of different research, with a wide variety of scholarly and practical commitments. Students of Chaucer are just as likely to insist on the prerogatives of academic professionalism as are biochemists. So, too, are deconstructionists and Straussians, feminists and behaviorists, etc. All across the whole vast spectrum of American academic life, it is a rare practicing scholar who does not subscribe to one or another version of it.

But for all of this variety, it is a quite definite point of view, with rather specific implications about how academic life should—and should not—be conducted. It is rarely articulated as such, but that should not blind us to the fact that what it amounts to is little short of a full-blown philosophy of (I hesitate to say) education. It entails, in other words, a definite "idea" (in Newman's sense) of what a university is about, and it is typically held with all of the dogmatic intensity that normally goes along with any principled commitment. Or, more precisely to the point, it is taken for granted as self-evidently true, and any serious challenge to it tends to be greeted with instinctive disbelief.

Aside from the priority which it assigns to scholarship, the thing above all which distinguishes this outlook is the value which it places on the *autonomy* of the scholarly enterprise. It is not autonomy per se that is valued, to be sure. As the very concept of a "discipline" would suggest, the properly trained scholar will as a matter of course submit him/herself to the canons of method and significance laid down by the acknowledged authorities in the field. But within those parameters, the assumption is that research is to proceed wherever the scholar alone thinks it ought to go. It is his or her sense, as an informed professional, of what is worth exploring that ought to govern what goes on, and the only consideration that should enter into evaluation of the results should be the judgment of peers in the profession.

Applied in its pure form, of course, this would mean that it was inappropriate for those responsible for university governance even to indicate a preference for one form of scholarship over another, and hardly anyone is so naïve as to think that, as a practical matter, this is likely. The decisions about disciplinary priorities, which are normally at the heart of academic administration, inescapably involve, after all, the establishment of preferences of just this sort, and it is a rare academician who would question that it is the legitimate prerogative of trustees and administrators to make decisions about which schools, departments, and specializations will be favored and which not. Whether the institution be public or private, it has a right to decide what, broadly, it will and will not set out to accomplish as a center of research. Yale and Harvard, for example, may choose to train lawyers, but there is no requirement that Princeton do so, too. The latter can easily do without a school of law without anyone (even the lawyers) questioning its standing. And, in like manner, Georgetown may choose to invest its resources in ethics in a way that contrasts dramatically with many other comparable institutions, and no one seriously challenges the legitimacy of its doing so.

All across the academic landscape, there are variations of this sort, traceable to quite specific decisions made by the appropriate officials, which are not seen by scholars as posing any illegitimate challenge to the conception they hold of how academic life ought to be ordered. At the same time, however, it is also apparent that there is a line which should not be crossed. Yale may choose to have a school of law, but is it really the business of administrators (much less trustees), the properly socialized academic professional is inclined to ask, to decide what legal education—or scholarship—should be about? And the clear presumption is that it is not. The content of scholarship—and, by extension, education as well—is assumed to be the preserve of trained professionals, and them alone.

Few things are more central today to the professional self-understanding of university faculty than the presumption that such autonomy is essential to the integrity of the scholarly enterprise. Administrators may make all sorts of decisions about the framework within which faculty go about their work, scholarly and otherwise, but they ought not go any further. In a *good* university, at least, it is assumed, what specifically is studied and how it is treated are matters to be left almost entirely to the discretion of the relevant professions. Especially in the face of the high degree of specialization that now characterizes almost all scholarly life, they and they alone are presumed to be competent to make such judgments. And the administrator who thinks anything else soon learns how strongly this conviction typically is held.

III.

The problem which this poses for any university which is founded on some alternative idea is obvious. Especially when the insistence on autonomy in scholarship is combined with a consistent adherence to meritocratic procedures in the recruitment and advancement of faculty, it is difficult to see how there is any room at all for creating and maintaining a scholarly community which would serve any other purpose than the self-conceived priorities of scholars themselves. The idea of Catholic educators that scholarship ought to proceed "from the vision and perspective of faith"[4] simply does not fit. Not as an *institutional* objective, at least. It is perfectly admissible, of course, for the individual scholar, as a matter of personal conviction, to fashion his or her own work in such manner. But to set out, self-consciously, to create a whole company of scholars dedicated to such a purpose is quite another matter.

Predictably, the more the effects of the academic revolution have come to be felt, the more difficult it has become for such institutions to retain their historic identity. Most private colleges in this country with any history to speak of have religious roots, but in the main these institutions have shown themselves to be essentially defenseless in the face of the challenge posed by the rise of the professionalized professoriate.[5] In so far as they have chosen to partake at all of the innovations involved in creating the modern university, they have simply succumbed to the necessity of abandoning their roots. Even many of the better undergraduate colleges with a confessional history have ended up this way.

There are degrees, to be sure. Duke today is surely less removed from its Methodist roots than is Yale from the Congregationalism of its founders, and schools like Davidson and Augustana are even less so. But the broad trend is unmistakable. Clerical control has long since gone by the boards, and the notion that there should be any religious or philosophical identity to the faculty is fast fading. In most cases, any sort of formal tie to a particular ecclesiastical institution is also a thing of the past, and there is no longer even a pretense of looking to a particular confessional tradition for direction in defining the purposes to be served by the institution. The major players in the making of policy, from the president on down, tend to have no real acquaintance with the intellectual substance of the tradition out of which the institution emerged, and even if they do, are inclined to look upon it as an inappropriate basis for making policy.

Lip service is almost always paid, admittedly, to "tradition." Even in this country, it is a rare academic institution which does not make at least a pretense of respect for the past. But as a practical matter, what really counts in the inheritance which church-created colleges and universities claim to preserve has only the vaguest of connections to the original rationale for their existence. Especially with regard to decisions that affect the character of their intellectual life, the effective thrust is in just the opposite direction. They look forward, not backward, seeking to be as up-to-date as possible, and if they are to begin to measure up to the standards that count in the academic world itself, they know that they can hardly afford to do otherwise.

IV.

Catholic institutions have always represented, to be sure, something of an exception to this pattern. The combination of clerical control, members of religious orders in the faculty, and a continuing dedication to serve the needs primarily of Catholics has made them far less susceptible to the influence of the academic revolution than their Protestant counterparts. But it has also made them, at the same time, academically less respectable. Georgetown may have preserved its confessional identity more successfully than Princeton, but hardly to the betterment of its standing in the scholarly world. In fact, even in the eyes of Catholics themselves, the designation "Catholic" hardly ever has signified genuine academic excellence.

But this, too, is now very much in flux. There is clearly a very different mood at work today in American Catholicism from the one that prevailed even at the time (the 1960s) that Jencks and Riesman did their research, and the changed circumstances that it reflects cannot help but affect profoundly the way that Catholic institutions of higher learning go about conceiving and pursuing their mission. In a time when the generation that is now coming of age takes for granted the Catholic penetration of the mainstream of American public life symbolized by Kennedy's accession to the presidency, it is no accident that institutions like

Georgetown aspire to more than just distinction within the Catholic world. The emerging Catholic "moment," as more than one informed observer senses is now beginning to unfold in American life, naturally invites ambitions of a wider role, at least for the more distinguished centers of Catholic education. The more success the Catholic community enjoys in taking advantage of the resulting opportunities, the stronger these ambitions can be expected to become.

Especially is this likely as these schools achieve some measure of prominence and attract significant numbers of people who are drawn to them, not because of any interest in their Catholic character, but rather because of their promise as academic institutions. Much of the pluralism which was our point of departure is directly attributable to the appeal that universities like Georgetown already are beginning to acquire as they seek to establish themselves as serious centers of advanced learning and research, and it can only be expected to grow as they progress in this regard. As they attract faculty whose primary reason for identifying with the institution is its academic standing, not its Catholicity, there will be increasing pressure to redefine its character in terms that conform to the wider society's conception of what a university is meant to be.

Even less distinguished Catholic colleges and universities can be expected to experience increasingly some of the same pressures, albeit for rather different reasons. The declining availability of faculty from religious orders, for example, combined with the increasing availability of other academic professionals, many of whom have no commitment to Catholicism whatsoever, cannot help but alter the dynamics at work in even the least prestigious Catholic schools. Add to this the probability of an increased need, for financial reasons, to appeal to a non-Catholic clientele, and the encounter of Catholic education, even at this level, with the effects of the academic revolution is almost assured. That, almost certainly, is where events are headed.

V.

The obvious question is whether there is any reason to think that the result of this encounter will be any different in the Catholic case from what it has already been in others. And even more to the point, whether there is any reason worthy of consideration to think that it *ought* to be. The two are intimately related, of course, in that the answer to the first is almost a foregone conclusion unless a convincing case can be made that

Catholic particularity is worth preserving. Even if it is, admittedly, there is no guarantee that it can, in fact, be successfully maintained. But in the absence of a clear reason for attempting to achieve something distinctive in their intellectual life, institutions like Georgetown are almost certain to go, in relatively short order, the way of their Protestant counterparts.

This is hardly a fate, to be sure, which is to be despised. Devotees of the enclave conception of Catholic higher education may be nostalgic about its passing, but the fact remains that the secular university as we know it today is by no means an unimpressive institution. It is not for nothing that it is precisely to such institutions that the better Catholic schools now routinely turn for most of their faculty. Or that theirs are the graduate programs to which, in the main, the more talented and ambitious Catholic intellectuals themselves aspire. They represent, unmistakably, most of what is truly distinguished in American scholarship, and it would be no small accomplishment if an institution like Georgetown were to begin to approximate the standard they set.

So, it would hardly be an unmitigated calamity if Georgetown were to become "just" another distinguished center of research. Indeed, it would be an accomplishment of the first magnitude. And it would be a highly important sign, too, of the "coming of age" of Catholicism in this country. What better evidence could there be of the assumption of full responsibility for the fate of the American "experiment" by Catholics than the creation of centers of advanced learning of sufficient quality to attract the very ablest minds, Catholic and non-Catholic alike?

Even so, it is appropriate, I would submit, to raise—and ponder carefully—the question of whether this is *all* that they should aspire to be. For all the achievement that the sort of institution produced by the academic revolution represents, it is by no means the only way of pursuing the goal of academic excellence. Nor is it without its costs. Although most members of the professoriate consider it self-evident that this is the proper way to conduct academic life, there is no reason to think of it as the last word. Higher education, like most other aspects of this society, continues to evolve, and there is every reason to want to encourage the sort of experimentation that a serious commitment on the part of institutions like Georgetown to be *both* Catholic and superior in scholarship would entail.

The point, above all, has to do with pluralism, albeit in a different form from the one with which we began this discussion. For Catholic institutions to accept uncritically the logic of the academic revolution would be to squander the opportunity that is now beginning to open up to them to pursue alternatives—alternatives that could well be in the interests of virtually *all* of the affected parties. For Georgetown to mold itself after, say, Stanford would surely serve well certain worthy purposes. But it would, at the same time, ill serve others. The opportunity, in particular, would be squandered to contribute to the cultivation of a distinctively American Catholic intellectual life, which, as Ellis, Ong, Gleason, and others have insisted, is still very much a task yet to be accomplished.[6] And if this were to happen, it would not be just the church which would be the loser.

VI.

The rub, of course, is that precisely because of the current state of the intellectual life of the Catholic community in this country, such a claim can hardly be much more than the expression of a hope. It would not be fair, I hasten to add, to suggest that there are *no* extant examples of the sort of contribution that a flourishing, self-consciously Catholic intelligentsia might make to the life of both the nation and the church. But they are few and far between, and their significance tends to be measured much more in terms that are internal to the Catholic community than the wider culture and society. The contribution of a figure like John Courtney Murray, for example, would appear to have much more to do with ecclesiastical reform than it does the progress of ideas beyond the confines of the church. And the natural question, in turn, is what reason there is to think that things can be any different in the future. If an institution like Georgetown is truly going to become a distinguished center of research, why should the assumption be made that preoccupation with things Catholic will serve that end? Devotees of the academic revolution will surely argue that abandoning such preoccupations is the price that has to be paid to get on with the business of building a great university.

Given the extraordinary pluralism that characterizes Catholic intellectual life today, it could well be objected that it is difficult even to know what it might mean to pursue an identifiably Catholic agenda. In the days when Neoscholasticism reigned, it was possible to have a reasonably clear idea of what such a project might yield. But no more. In a time when Catholics appear to have almost as many different interests, presuppositions, and methodologies as the rest of the American intelligentsia, it can hardly be said that a Catholic orientation guarantees much. And in the absence of coherence in this regard, it is no wonder that not a few Catholic intellectuals themselves entertain doubts about the point of it all.[7]

These doubts, too, have only been reinforced by what the Curran affair—and related developments—represent.[8] Given the preoccupation with autonomy that has characterized the professoriate in this country ever since the onset of the academic revolution, it was virtually inescapable that the recent initiatives taken by the Vatican would put fresh life into the old prejudice that Catholicism is, at base, anti-intellectual. To the extent that Catholic faculty in this country are themselves caught up in the culture of their respective disciplines, it is understandable that they, too, would draw a similar conclusion. Precisely for the sake of the integrity of the scholarly enterprise, one sees the conclusion being drawn, perhaps it is better that faith and scholarship be kept separate.

All of this, however, is a matter of perspective, and needs to be seen as such. As Ellis acknowledged in his path-breaking statement on the subject, there have been good historical reasons why Catholics in this country have tended not to look upon scholarly pursuits as their natural field of accomplishment. But most of the conditions to which he pointed in making his observations back in the 1950s are passing from the scene, and as they do, it is not unreasonable to expect that the attitude toward cultural and intellectual pursuits will change as well. Indeed, there is ample evidence that this is already beginning to take place. From the new aspirations to academic excellence at institutions like Georgetown to the now routine manner in which Catholics are finding their way, as both students and faculty, into the elite centers of learning, there is unmistakable evidence of the beginning of the "coming of age" of Catholicism in the intellectual life of this nation in much the same way that, a few decades ago, there was comparable evidence of its penetration of the higher reaches of American political life.

This is having, in turn, predictable effects. For all of the confusion—bordering, one sometimes senses, on anarchy—of Catholic intellectual life in this country today, no less obviously is it characterized by a dynamism and vitality that is surely unprecedented. From Charles Curran to David Tracy, Michael Novak to Mary Daly, there is evidence of one serious effort after another to rethink carefully the more fundamental issues of the faith, and one does not need to be Pollyanna to think that this is only the beginning. For every luminary there are dozens (conservatively speaking) of other scholars engaged in comparable, less publicized projects, and countless others in the making. And while there may not yet be any *teaching* of Murrayesque stature available in the work of the present generation of Catholic scholars in this country, what is in the process of formation is something which is arguably of even greater long-term significance: namely, a whole company of independent-minded thinkers dedicated to developing the Catholic tradition in ways that creatively address the more fundamental intellectual challenges of our time.

For all of the controversy generated by the sanctions imposed by the Vatican on Charles Curran, moreover, there is precious little evidence that this incident has anything like the wider significance that has commonly been attributed to it. It would be naïve, to be sure, to overlook the broader message which the action taken against Curran's work is almost surely intended to convey. But, at the same time, I at least have a hard time imagining how this message can have much success beyond the very narrow terms of the sanctions invoked against Curran. There is simply too much momentum in the other direction for the broad course of Catholic intellectual life to be reversed, and every effort to do so, I would predict, will simply prove the point.

VII.

There is, however, a deeper issue at stake here. Quite apart from the inclination or capacity of ecclesiastical authorities to insist on a particular way of fulfilling the vocation of the Catholic intellectual, there remains the prior question of whether such a notion is in principle any longer defensible. In the light of the insistence on autonomy which today routinely characterizes most academic professionals' understanding of the nature and purpose of their work, the question is whether it makes any sense at all to continue acting as though it were still possible for serious scholarship to be done on such terms. It is, after all, not just the demise of Neoscholasticism that pulled the rug out from under the way of conceiving of the vocation of the intellectual that prevailed among Catholics before Vatican II, but the whole process of change that has been under discussion here as well.

Allowances are often made, to be sure, for those scholars whose disciplines require that they focus specifically on things Catholic. Theologians, for example, tend routinely to be treated as a special case. But a university is more than just one school or department, and the obvious question is what relevance the notion of functioning as a self-consciously Catholic intellectual has for the other disciplines. What might it mean with respect to the study of literature or history, sociology or economics (not to speak of physics and chemistry)? We are beyond the time, presumably, when it was possible to take for granted the possibility of a distinctively Catholic sociology. Or even, indeed, of a Catholic philosophy. But what is the alternative? And in view of the premium that has come to be placed on autonomy in most of the scholarly life of this nation, is there even any point in pursuing the matter any longer?

That it does matter is central to everything I have been attempting to argue in this paper, and there is reason to believe, I think, that such an alternative can—and should—be carved out which is intellectually every bit as defensible as the conception of scholarship with which we are now more familiar. Indeed, in some fields, at least, I would be inclined to believe that it is *more* defensible. For it reflects a more realistic understanding of how intellectual life does, in fact, operate and what is the real logic of the progress of scholarly knowledge.

The alternative I have in mind is what might be characterized as the critical indwelling of an established tradition.[9] The criticism in question may well go very deep, and the refusal to accept unquestioningly the inheritance received from the past is an essential part of what makes its appropriation scholarly. It is precisely because the scholar is not disposed to take it for granted that the ground on which he or she stands is the last word that further inquiry is called for. But the need for the ground is recognized, at the same time, and occupied as such. Instead of conceiving of his or her work as nothing but an autonomous project, the scholar operating in this mode quite deliberately chooses to do his or her work as part of what Murray characterized as the "growing edge" of tradition, and defines his or her scholarly agenda accordingly.

I characterize this as a more realistic understanding of how scholarly life operates because this is the way in which most of us actually do go about our work. The more we know about the sociology of intellectual life, the more obvious this becomes. One need only invoke, by now, the notion of the "paradigm" effectively to call into question any suggestion that scholarship really is autonomous. By virtue of our participation in one or another discipline, most of us are, in fact, wedded to one or another organizing framework of inquiry, and we take for granted the necessity of doing so. We would be hard put even to imagine doing without what they provide us with.[10] So we are Humeans or Keynesians, Weberians or Freudians, and for all of the pretense of autonomy, we are more than content to accept the conformity to established criteria of significance and method which participation in such a "tendency" typically entails. And if, for one or another reason, we are not altogether satisfied with the paradigms available to us, we are usually in search of an alternative, a new "home" fit for our habitation as scholars.

To the extent, however, that we are nothing but creatures of our disciplines, the range of acceptable options available to us tends to be limited. What is at stake in seeking to insure that the idea of a self-consciously Catholic intellectual life has a future is the enlargement of these options. It is to establish the possibility of Catholic scholars, in a number of different disciplines, being able to elect to inhabit the traditions cherished by the church as the foundation for their research and writing. And to make it appropriate, in turn, for Catholic universities to constitute themselves as centers for scholarship in this vein. Just as other universities today routinely function, especially in particular schools and departments, as centers for the propagation of one or another specific kind of scholarship, so Catholic institutions would take as their vocation the creation of communities of scholarship united by a common dedication to the creative cultivation of the distinctive concerns and illumination emanating from Catholic tradition.[11]

VIII.

But what, then, of pluralism? What would the embrace of such a purpose mean for the heterogeneity that now increasingly is upon us? I am well aware that the argument I am making here will almost certainly be read by some as an effort to reverse that tendency. Indeed, even as an apology for a return to Catholic insularity. As one who myself has been a beneficiary of the new Catholic openness to the wider society, however, nothing could be further from my mind. I take it for granted that in the new era of their development that now awaits Catholic colleges and universities in this country, such openness will inescapably be an integral part of almost any objective they might pursue that is worth pursuing. Even if it were desirable, it is unlikely that a return to the enclave mentality would be possible. Now that the barriers to their own acceptance in the wider society have fallen, Catholics themselves would almost certainly not want to accept it.

My own conviction is that the challenge that lies ahead is to embrace the tendency toward pluralism as a matter of principle and pursue it even more aggressively. Precisely because of its Catholic character, I would think, it is incumbent on an institution like Georgetown to be more actively inclusive than the law (and other external forces) require. Especially with respect to race, gender, and ethnicity, anything short of this would be a betrayal of what catholicity in its most fundamental sense means, and the sooner this comes to be taken for granted, the better.[12]

But there remains, at the same time, a world of difference between openness with and without a defining center. The one is a recipe for maintaining a distinct identity, while the other is a sure-fire way to lose it. And it is primarily for this reason that I would argue that the former is what the pursuit of lasting pluralism in this society is all about. It is all well and good to break down the barriers that previously have made so many private institutions in this country little more than ghettoes. But unless this is accompanied by comparable efforts to insure that these institutions are able to retain something of their historic identity, the resulting "pluralism" is almost certain to end up functioning as a Trojan horse for homogenization. Even as we congratulate ourselves on our openness to diversity, we shall, in fact, be becoming more and more alike.

The point, above all, that needs to be grasped in this matter is a sociological one. Genuine particularity does not just happen, and it does not exist in a vacuum. It requires institutional support. In our intellectual lives no less than in the rest of our existence, we need communities which have the freedom to dedicate themselves to the cultivation of distinctive beliefs and practices, if we ourselves are to stand a chance of enjoying a comparable freedom. This is something which American Catholics, by virtue of the experience they have already had in this society, are uniquely positioned to appreciate. The whole, vast project of primary and secondary as well as higher education which the church has undertaken on these shores may be understood, in fact, as a direct response to the recognition of this reality. Now that the battle for assimilation has largely been won and the door is beginning to open for Catholic leadership in this society, it is essential that it not be forgotten. And that it be acted on, just as creatively, to meet the new challenge that is now presenting itself. There is a lesson here to be taught to the wider society that could prove to be of enormous long-term value.

Notes

1. Georgetown was, from the beginning, an institution receptive to the presence of non-Catholics, and for this reason it has always had a somewhat distinctive

character among Catholic colleges and universities. Cf. R. Emmett Curran's forthcoming Bicentennial history for a fuller treatment of this point.

2. Christopher Jencks and David Riesman, *The Academic Revolution* (Garden City, N.Y.: Doubleday, 1969).

3. As Jencks and Riesman point out, the professionalization of the professoriate occurred at approximately the same time that professionalization was taking place in other fields as well, and for essentially the same reasons. All of this was intimately related to the creation of a division of labor appropriate for an industrial society.

4. Text of Pope John Paul II's address to leaders of U.S. Catholic colleges, *The Chronicle of Higher Education* 34:4 (23 September 1987), A17.

5. Jencks and Riesman summarize the drift of their analysis as follows: "Over the past century several hundred formerly sectarian Protestant colleges have dropped their church ties and become officially non-sectarian. This has been particularly characteristic of the predominantly Anglo-Saxon colleges, of the predominantly upper-middle class colleges, and of the predominantly 'national' colleges drawing from suburban families. Today, while most leading universities and university colleges can trace their origins to some Protestant denomination, very few can point to any significant current difference between themselves and those private institutions that have always been non-sectarian" (327).

6. Cf. John Tracy Ellis, "American Catholics and the Intellectual Life," *Thought* 30 (1955), 351-88; Walter Ong, S.J., *Frontiers in American Catholicism* (New York: Macmillan, 1957), chap. 6, and *American Catholic Crossroads* (New York: Macmillan, 1959), chap. 5; and Philip Gleason, *Keeping the Faith* (Notre Dame, Ind.: University of Notre Dame Press, 1987), chaps. 3 and 8.

7. Cf. Gleason, *Keeping the Faith*, 87f.

8. I refer, of course, to the Rev. Charles E. Curran's loss of his teaching position as Professor of Moral Theology at the Catholic University of America in August, 1986, when the Vatican Congregation for the Doctrine of the Faith declared that he was no longer "suitable nor eligible to exercise the function of a Professor of Catholic Theology." This came in response to Curran's refusal to retract certain positions he held in dissent from official church teaching.

9. A thoughtful and suggestive amplification of much of what I have in mind is to be found in the keynote address given by Walter J. Burghardt, S.J., under the title "Intellectual and Catholic? Or Catholic Intellectual?" at the 1989 Georgetown faculty conference on the state of American Catholic intellectual life (sponsored by the Committee on Catholic Studies). This address subsequently appeared under the same title in *America* 160:17 (6 May 1989), 420-25. The analysis Burghardt provides is particularly helpful in exploring the conditions necessary for the critical indwelling of Catholic tradition to take place.

10. On this matter, as on so many others, Alasdair MacIntyre speaks an illuminating word in *After Virtue* (Notre Dame, Ind.: University of Notre Dame Press, 1981). "All reasoning takes place," he observes, "within the context of some traditional mode of thought, transcending through criticism and invention the limitations of what had hitherto been reasoned in that tradition; this is as true of modern physics as of medieval logic" (222).

11. The difference in question is almost certain, I would assume, to be a matter of degree. It would not be a matter of departing completely from the pattern of academic life with which we are now familiar, but rather of amending it selectively through the infusion of purposes which would lend to the scholarly enterprise a somewhat different character than it otherwise could be expected to have. It would mean encouraging, where appropriate, a Catholic dimension to the scholarship done in a variety of different disciplines, and insuring that the conditions existed for ongoing cross-fertilization among the projects involved. The point would not be that every member of the faculty should define his or her scholarly agenda along such lines, but rather that within each relevant school or department there should be provision made for the presence of scholars with such interests. From philosophy to physics, there should be a generous "sprinkling" of scholars actively engaged in ongoing research on problems that reflect the direct influence of the Catholic tradition.

12. Another dimension of the composition of the student body that definitely needs to be taken into account is socio-economic class. The last thing a Catholic university should aspire to be is a preserve for the well-to-do. In this respect, much of the rest of elite private higher education in this country presents an example of the course *not* to be taken, and I would think that charting a new direction in this regard is every bit as important as some of the other, more talked about challenges of "openness" that Georgetown now faces.

William V. O'Brien
Department of Government

Georgetown and the Church's Teaching on International Relations

The Catholic Church has developed a body of political, social, and economic thought which provides the foundation for papal, conciliar, episcopal, and other authoritative analyses of contemporary problems and their moral implications. Pronouncements by church authorities carry weight beyond the American Catholic bishops' pastorals on war and peace and on the economy. Naturally, such pronouncements are controversial. Those who disagree with their policy implications or reject their empirical bases and arguments invariably question the competence of the bishops and other church spokesmen to deal with such matters. Others are dissatisfied with the quality of moral reasoning in church pronouncements.

Recognizing their inability definitively to resolve the empirical and moral dilemmas of modern problems, popes, councils, bishops' conferences, and individual Catholic authorities have frequently encouraged further study and debate designed to improve the quality of the church's social teaching both in terms of its foundation in moral precepts and reasoning and in its mastery of empirical facts and concepts.

Thus, in *Pacem in Terris*, John XXIII said:

> In the highest and most authoritative assemblies, let men give serious thought to the problems of peaceful adjustment of relations between political communities on a world level: an adjustment of relations founded on mutual trust, on sincerity in negotiations, on

> faithful fulfillment of obligations assumed. *Let them study the problem* until they find that point of agreement from which it will be possible to commence to go forward towards accords that will be sincere, lasting and fruitful.[1] [Emphasis added.]

The Fathers of Vatican II stated in the Pastoral Constitution on the Church in the Modern World *(Gaudium et Spes)*:

> The problems of peace and disarmament have already been the subject of extensive, strenuous, and relentless examination. Together with international meetings dealing with these problems, such studies should be regarded as the first steps toward solving these serious questions. They should be promoted with even greater urgency in the hope that they will yield practical results in the future.[2]

The American Catholic bishops, having wrestled with the empirical, policy, and moral problems of nuclear deterrence, defense, and arms control, acknowledged the enormous tasks that remained and called for further study and debate. At the end of their analyses and prescriptions concerning deterrence, defense, and arms control they acknowledged that:

> The need to rethink the deterrence policy of our nation, to make the revisions necessary to reduce the possibility of nuclear war, and to move toward a more stable system of national and international security *will demand an intellectual, political, and moral effort.* It will also require, we believe, the willingness to open ourselves to the providential care, power and word of God, which call us to recognize our common humanity and the bonds of mutual responsibility which exist in the international community in spite of political differences and nuclear arsenals.[3] [Emphasis added.]

In the concluding part of *The Challenge of Peace* the American Catholic bishops call upon educators to bring the social teaching of the church into the classrooms. At the same time, they acknowledge throughout the pastoral letter that there are opposing points of view about many issues held by qualified and reasonable people.[4] Similar injunctions and caveats are found in the American Catholic bishops' pastoral on the economy.[5]

All of these appeals for study, reflection, dialogue, teaching, and social action are directed to institutions such as Georgetown. Who is to, in John XXIII's words, "study the problem"? Popes and the Fathers of Vatican II have directed the injunction to statesmen. However, the statesmen who formulate and implement policies depend in large measure on the scholarship and policy debates within their own and other countries. When an American president, secretary of state, director of the Arms Control and Disarmament Agency, or negotiator at Geneva "studies" the great issues of war and peace, of international social and economic justice, he or she relies on a corpus of scholarship in American universities, research centers, and government agencies—as well as on available resources from other countries. The United States alone cannot solve all the material and moral problems of the world but it obviously is in a preeminent position to influence all aspects of international relations. The United States also greatly exceeds the academic resources of the rest of the world when it comes to the study of international relations.

Georgetown University is in the capital of the United States. Georgetown emphasizes studies in international relations, foreign languages and areas, comparative politics, political theory, history, economics, philosophy, and theology, to mention only some of the fields relevant to the concerns of *Pacem in Terris, Gaudium et Spes*, and *The Challenge of Peace*. When the church calls for intensive, expert, and morally motivated and informed study of the great issues of contemporary international relations, it should be evident that Georgetown has a great mission which it dare not decline to pursue.

It is the purpose of this essay to assess the recent record of the Catholic Church in developing its social teaching on international relations and the role of the Catholic universities in contributing to this teaching. It will be contended that the Catholic Church generally and the American Catholic Church have barely scratched the surface of the vast tasks of research, analysis, and prescription which are required to respond to the challenges of pronouncements such as *Pacem in Terris, Gaudium et Spes*, and *The Challenge of Peace*. Without prejudice to other sources of expertise and moral counsel, it will be argued that the time has come for the Catholic Church to marshal its scholarly resources and that a large portion of those resources are in the United States. It will be further argued that a central resource for the church should be Georgetown University. Finally, it will be suggested that the growth of the National Conference of Catholic Bishops and its pioneering efforts to bring in a spectrum of experts and moralists to assist it in drafting pastoral letters on public policy issues means that institutions such as Georgetown can play an important role in developing the social teaching of the church generally. This discussion, however, will be limited to issues of international relations and particularly, to issues of deterrence, defense, and arms control.

Catholic Teaching on International Relations: From Augustine to Suarez

Historically, the Bible has not been employed as a rich resource for those attempting to develop a Christian political theory and guidelines for the conduct of international relations. Most of Christ's teaching concerns individual morality; acceptance of the existing political status quo was enjoined. This is not to say that contemporary and future biblical scholarship may not develop themes relevant to international political theory but only that this did not eventuate in the past. Although there are profound theological elements in Catholic political and social thought, its early development was heavily indebted to Roman philosophy, political theory and practice, and law.[6] This is particularly true with respect to international relations. Greek and Roman philosophic and legal concepts of *jus naturale* and *jus gentium* were adopted by writers such as St. Isidore of Seville and kept alive throughout the Middle Ages to be developed by Scholastic writers such as Vitoria and Suarez,[7] thereby contributing critically to the success of Grotius and the foundation of modern positive international law. Indeed, a continuing characteristic of Catholic thought on international relations has been an emphasis on international law.

A related emphasis has been on international organization. As late as the time of Vitoria this tended to take the form of proposals to revive a Christian (Holy) Roman Empire.[8] While these came in the context of controversial practical problems between the Holy Roman Empire and the emerging sovereign states of Europe as well as the church itself, concepts such as the international common good became accepted as basic elements in Catholic thought.[9]

Of critical importance to modern debates over war and peace is the development of just war doctrine from Augustine to Thomas to Vitoria, Suarez, and other Scholastics. A number of basic concepts were developed in this doctrine which are still the starting point for moral analysis of security measures. The Catholic just war doctrine, particularly from the time of St. Thomas's contributions, started with the concept of political society as natural and necessary for the good life, both material and moral.[10] Political society, properly ordered, was conceived as a good in itself. Accordingly, the right of self-defense existed not just for individuals, families, or groups of people but for the corporate entity of political society.[11]

Acknowledging that evil and injustice, arising from human sin, appeared to be a perennial source of conflict and aggression, the Scholastic just war doctrine granted the right to have recourse to armed force in defense of justice, freedom, and human rights. However, the just war theorists subjected the right of just recourse to force to a number of conditions. They started with a moral presumption against killing in general and war in particular. Just war doctrine was then formulated in terms of conditions that must be met in order to overcome the moral presumption against war.[12]

These conditions came in two parts. The first part, the war-decision law or *jus ad bellum*, laid down the requirements for just recourse to armed coercion: competent authority, just cause, comparative justice, proportionality of the costs of the war to the just ends in the light of probability of success, exhaustion of peaceful remedies, and right intention.[13]

The second part of the just war doctrine, the war-conduct law or *jus in bello*, required proportionality of military means to legitimate military ends and discrimination, i.e., no direct intentional attacks on innocent noncombatants and civilian targets. The war-conduct law also developed a number of specific rules of conduct, many of which became part of positive international law.[14]

Significantly, when the American Catholic bishops drafted their 1983 pastoral letter on war and peace they explicitly reaffirmed the authority and relevance of just war doctrine to the modern issues of deterrence, defense, and arms control.[15] This was possible in part because of the perennial character of just war doctrine but also because of a revival of modern just war scholarship since World War II. However, the history of just war doctrine brings out the problem confronting virtually all parts of Catholic social thought on international relations. The essence of this thought was perfected by the time of Suarez in the early seventeenth century. After that there ensued a long period of inactivity in Catholic social thought which lasted well into the twentieth century. Thus, when interest revived in Catholic thought on international relations it was necessary to adapt concepts developed in the environments of the Middle Ages and the Renaissance to the modern world. As regards just war doctrine, for example, it is obvious that discrimination is considerably more practical with the weapons of the seventeenth century than it is with those of the twentieth century.

Catholic Teaching on International Relations: 1918-1945

When interest in Catholic thought on international relations was aroused by the tragedy of World War I, moralists had to confront the fact that enormous changes had occurred since the early seventeenth century when the development of church doctrine on this subject had virtually ceased. Incredible scientific and technological developments had made life better in many ways but had also made possible modern total war. Modern total war could also be traced to political and ideological development that, given the military capabilities of modern advanced states, led to wars for near-total ends pursued with near-total means.

Thus, the task of church authorities and scholars after World War I was to reformulate the church's social teaching in ways that would be relevant to the challenges of the modern world. In order to meet those challenges it would be necessary to master the empirical disciplines and facts that had contributed to human knowledge since the time of Suarez. Some recognition of the tasks facing Catholic social theorists was already evident in the analyses of issues of domestic economic and social justice as early as 1891, when Pope Leo XIII issued the encyclical *Rerum Novarum*.[16] However, Catholic scholars were slow to undertake the kind of intensive studies of the new facts of international life necessary to deal with the world of the 1920s, 1930s, and 1940s.

The interwar Catholic scholarship on international relations tended to keep the basic principles of the old Scholastic thought and to apply them almost exclusively in terms of support of the League of Nations and international law.[17] These efforts are well illustrated by the 1937 Malines Code of International Ethics, revised in 1947 and 1948. This was a product of cooperation of European Catholics.[18]

The Malines Code is loyal to the traditional Catholic approach to international relations. It builds from concepts of human nature to human societies to "The Natural Society of States."[19] It treats the issues of colonialism with a gentle evolutionary approach that contrasts with the contemporary demands for radical revision of the relations of developed and developing states.[20] The Malines Code is quite clear on the continued validity of just war doctrine.[21] Above all, it puts its hopes squarely in the League of Nations (in the United Nations in the postwar revisions).[22] The authorities cited are twofold: the old Scholastic moralists and modern popes. Altogether, it is a serious attempt to show how Catholic natural law principles could be applied successfully in a world in which an organization like the League of Nations or the United Nations operated more or less in conformity with the ends and means of its charter. Unhappily, by the time that the Malines Code was being revised in 1947 and 1948 the international system it envisaged was already clearly unrealistic.

Catholic Teaching on International Relations: 1945-1965

After World War II world politics continued to be far too conflictual and violent to permit realization of the advances in international organization and law enjoined by Catholic thought as represented by papal pronouncements, documents like the Malines Code, and the writings of eminent theorists such as Jacques Maritain and Heinrich Rommen.[23] A bipolar world wherein the superpowers were locked in cold war and restrained from hot war by the delicate nuclear balance of terror, a world where new nations burning with new ideologies demanded new definitions of justice and took over international organizations, a world where indigenous conflicts were fed by exported revolution and competing interventions, such a world dashed the hopes for world peace, order, and justice.

The post-World War II world posed problems that could not be resolved by exhortations to support the United Nations, work for world government, take risks for peace through disarmament initiatives, and increase aid to the emerging developing nations. Nevertheless, most Catholic thought on international relations from 1945 to 1965 was confined to the study of papal pronouncements. Granting the wisdom and sanctity of Pius XII and John XXIII, there was very little institutional research and debate within the church to provide the popes with the empirical facts and analyses and, even, the normative arguments that were necessary for adequate responses to the problems of a rapidly changing, volatile, dangerous world.

Secular universities and research centers were developing new theories and approaches to the study of international relations, comparative politics (particularly in the Third World), deterrence/defense and arms control, foreign trade and aid, revolution and intervention. American scholars and academic institutions were in the forefront of these efforts. Yet the knowledge and analytical techniques developed in these years were seldom reflected in papal teachings on international relations and at the episcopal level there was a vacuum. Until 1967 the American Catholic Church's social action organization, the National Catholic Welfare Conference (NCWC), had no office, much less research center, concerned with international relations generally. (There were offices manned by small staffs of dedicated people, dealing with relief, refugees, missions, and other humanitarian concerns.) NCWC officials considered the moral issues of international relations not to be "bread and butter" problems for the American Church. The NCWC passed the great issues of war and peace and international justice to a voluntary organization, the Catholic Association for International Peace (CAIP), which was granted one secretary working in the Social Action Department, an office otherwise almost entirely concerned with domestic social issues.

The CAIP, through the efforts of individuals, developed from time to time a core of clergy and laity who had genuine expertise in international relations and who were interested in finding better moral guidelines for debates on international issues. There was no material base for the organization and continuity was fortuitous. Still, at a time when most other American Christian denominations had international relations offices, the volunteers of the CAIP were the main source of studies of the moral issues of international relations directly connected to the American Catholic Church.

The upshot was that by the time that the Second Vatican Council convened in 1962 the tasks of updating Catholic thought relevant to international relations had not been recognized and acted upon by the institutional church in Rome, in America, and, as far as I am aware, throughout the dioceses and Catholic institutions of higher learning around the world.[24]

Vatican II and International Moral Issues

The document called the Pastoral Constitution on the Church in the Modern World was produced late in the proceedings of Vatican II.

Apparently, it developed spontaneously, beyond its original scope, in part because of a broad consensus that the church could not permit the occasion of this great council to pass without speaking to some of the critical issues of the modern world other than those addressed in more particularistic pronouncements.[25] It does not appear that Pope John and his successor Paul VI envisaged the need for a major effort to marshal, coordinate, and synthesize the empirical evidence relevant to this wide-ranging document or to summarize, clarify, and evaluate the principal normative approaches to the critical issues addressed in it. The commission on what was originally schema 17, then schema 13, overlapped the work of other commissions. Members of this commission turned their minds to schema 17 only after completing work on other documents.[26]

Thus, the commission that drafted and presented schema 17 came to its work at the end of hard labor on other matters and hastened to complete the Constitution on the Church in the Modern World before the Council was scheduled to end. The commission followed the general practice of Vatican II and employed experts, *periti*, to draft the document. The choice and employment of the *periti* appear to have followed the traditional Vatican system of bringing in a small number of persons held in high esteem by key bishops and Vatican officials. They were mostly European clerics. The main change in traditional Roman "insider" practice appears to have been the enlargement of the commission drafting the Pastoral Constitution to include more bishops from non-Western countries.[27]

It is not within the scope of this paper to review the Pastoral Constitution's treatment of issues of individual, family, and social morality. These sections appear to be reasonably satisfactory although they contain remarkably few references to the emerging role of women in the modern world. There are only five references to the roles and rights of women in this document of 109 pages. However, this paper will focus on the way Vatican II approached the great issues of international relations in the nuclear age.[28]

If ever there was an opportunity to call upon the scholarly resources of the church, it was present when the commission on schema 17 came to the sections on international relations. In the mid-1960s the United States led the world in practical experience with and responsibility for the problems of deterrence/defense and arms control, and figured prominently among advanced nations in experience with and scholarship related to international economic issues, international law and organization, development and nation-building, and many other salient international issues. Indeed, this was the most active period of scholarship and debate in the United States on what have become the central concepts and themes of nuclear deterrence and defense, arms control, and foreign trade and aid. Yet there were no American *periti* working on the international relations sections of *Gaudium et Spes*. One who could have been of help was John Courtney Murray, S.J., but he was concentrating on the issues of religious freedom to which he had contributed so much.

Moreover, American Catholic bishops were not encouraged to take a leading role in the debates and except for Bishop Philip Hannan, then Auxiliary Bishop of Washington (later Archbishop of New Orleans), none who spoke in the general discussion of what was finally schema 13 challenged the draft on the grounds of insufficient recourse to the vast corpus of scholarly work on subjects such as nuclear deterrence and arms control.[29] To be sure, there were experts and scholars working on the problems of security and arms control in Western Europe and the *periti* employed by the commission may have profited from their writing and counsel. Unfortunately, the evidence of the original draft sections on nuclear deterrence and arms control in schema 17 suggests that the *periti* were not expert by existing American standards.

Fortuitously, I had an opportunity to critique the original draft of schema 17 and organize an effort to suggest improvements to the Council. This experience in itself demonstrates the procedures of Vatican II. In the summer of 1964 there was a conference at Georgetown on the moral issues of intervention, co-sponsored by Georgetown's Institute of World Polity and the Council on Religion and International Affairs. One of the participants was Robert Bosc, S.J., of the Institut Catholique in Paris. Bosc had obtained a copy of schema 17 from his Paris colleague, Jean-Yves Calvez, S.J. During a dinner party at my home, Bosc and others translated the sections on nuclear deterrence and arms control from Latin to English. The guests, all scholars expert in issues of international morality, were struck by the simplistic and imprecise character of the draft treatment of this subject.

At this point, the modest resources of the Catholic Association for International Peace proved helpful. I organized a CAIP committee of Catholic laymen, co-chaired by Professor James E. Dougherty of St. Joseph's College, to prepare a critique of schema 17's treatment of deterrence, defense, and arms control issues. The committee included Alain

Enthoven, one of Secretary of Defense McNamara's key aides, and Charles Herzfeld, then head of the Pentagon's advanced research projects office. We prepared the critique, reflecting the current consensus of American authorities on the subject. When the critique was ready it was submitted through the auspices of Msgr. George Higgins, director of the NCWC's Social Action department, to Bishop (later Cardinal) John Wright of Pittsburgh, who was a member of the Mixed Commission of Bishops working on schema 17. Bishop Wright submitted our critique to the commission and its receipt was acknowledged by Msgr. Higgins in his capacity as spokesman for the American bishops on November 9, 1964.[30]

I do not know what, if any, influence the statement had. Some of its arguments were touched on by Bishop Hannan in his intervention in the debate. In any event, the final version of the sections on nuclear deterrence, defense, and arms control in *Gaudium et Spes* was, from our point of view, a great improvement over the version of schemas 17 and 13.

The point of the preceding account is not to claim that American experts on nuclear deterrence, defense, and arms control had or have all the answers. It is implied that when the church has ready access to expertise, it should take advantage of it. The efforts of Vatican II to deal with the nuclear and other great issues could have been improved had there been semipermanent commissions or panels of experts, reflecting the full range of responsible approaches, to help in the preparation of the drafts. On subjects such as this American Catholic institutions of higher learning in general and Georgetown in particular should have been mobilized by the church in Rome and by the American Catholic bishops at home.

I will not rehearse the imperfections of the treatment of international relations issues in *Gaudium et Spes.* Generally speaking, they flow from a continuation of the tradition of modern Catholic thought to hold out unrealistic hopes and expectations for international law and organization, even for world government, in a time when almost all of the trends in the international system are going in opposite directions with little relief in sight. Unfortunately, these imperfections are perpetuated because of the natural tendency of church documents to rely on the authority of previous church documents. Vatican II documents, in particular, are a highly respected source.[31] However, if an estimate of the situation or a normative prescription does not rest on sound research and reflection, it is not a reliable foundation for further thought and teaching. Indeed, discussions of issues of international relations that are manifestly divorced from contemporary realities are of little or no value as teaching texts. Try, as I have, to get Georgetown students majoring in international relations to take seriously some of the central propositions of *Pacem in Terris* and *Gaudium et Spes* and you will find that not just senior international relations scholars but students educated by Georgetown in the discipline of modern international relations conclude that the church authorities often have noble goals but lack scholarly rigor as well as simple realism.

The American Catholic Bishops and International Relations: 1968-1988

A major result of Vatican II was the growth of national conferences of bishops which from time to time issued pastoral pronouncements on the moral issues of the day, including international relations issues. In the United States the National Catholic Welfare Conference became the United States Catholic Conference (USCC) and for the first time there was an office of International Justice and Peace to deal with general international relations issues. As this new office was being formed with a small staff, the voluntary Catholic Association for International Peace was dropped and had its last annual conference in 1967. This was unfortunate because, despite its small numbers and lack of material support, the CAIP provided a cadre of academicians and moralists from many Catholic institutions, as well as dedicated lay persons who held important positions in government and business. These people now had no formal point of contact with the American Catholic hierarchy.

The office of International Justice and Peace was able to make only modest contributions to the American Catholic bishops until Rev. J. Bryan Hehir joined the USCC. Hehir combined a strong theological/ philosophical formation with a Ph.D. in international relations from Harvard. A man of great imagination, energy, and political skill, he managed—still with a tiny staff—to furnish the USCC and the National Conference of Catholic Bishops with position papers, studies, and testimony for congressional hearings that enabled them to increase substantially their pronouncements on international issues.

However, Father Hehir alone is not a sufficient international relations resource for the American Catholic bishops. Hehir himself tried to broaden his base by convening a series of meetings on international security issues with a group of Catholic academicians and moralists in the early 1970s. When funding was discontinued, this venture ended. It should be remarked that in addition to the problem of funding there was the problem of leadership since Hehir was tremendously overcommitted, constantly moving from one difficult issue area to another and producing drafts for the bishops at a pace determined by their requirements rather than by the standards of scholarly research, reflection, debate, and writing. Having said this, it must be emphasized that the improvement in the character of empirical knowledge and normative arguments that was evident in the pronouncements of American Catholic bishops on international relations in the 1970s and 1980s can be credited largely to the work and influence of Bryan Hehir.

When, in 1981, the American Catholic bishops created a Committee on War and Peace to draft a pastoral letter, Hehir was instrumental in creating a system of consultations whereby experts on the empirical and moral aspects of international security issues could appear before the committee to testify and answer questions. He also arranged for the committee's drafts to be widely circulated and commented on in writing by experts. This process, in turn, meant that the drafts were public and debated in the media.

The consultation arrangements supporting the work of the Committee on War and Peace were far from ideal. The testimony was usually given in half-hour periods. There was no sustained dialogue or debate between the principal consultants and the committee. The only permanent consultant was Bruce Russett, professor of International Relations at Yale. Despite the efforts at outside consultations, many observers had the impression that Hehir's influence on the committee was necessarily critical since he kept the main initiative to himself and his small staff. Naturally, many of us disagreed with Hehir on issues of substance and procedure, and would have preferred to have a more broad-based team providing the bishops with different approaches—much in the way that problems are handled in an organization like the National Security Council or on a major congressional committee. Nevertheless, the experience of the debate over the 1983 pastoral, *The Challenge of Peace*, was a major step forward in the development of the moral issues of Catholic thought on international relations. This process was employed again in 1987-88 as a committee under Cardinal Bernardin conducted a five-year review of the issues raised in the 1983 pastoral and produced a report approved by the bishops in May/June 1988.[32]

It can be concluded that the American Catholic bishops have made significant progress since Vatican II in the formulating of their pronouncements on international relations. In the first place, the quality of the discussion of the political, military, economic, and technological problems of international security and arms control has greatly improved. Second, the quality of the moral arguments advanced has also improved markedly. A major flaw in church pronouncements on security issues since 1945 has been a lack of rigor in moral argument. The just war doctrine was seldom employed. Papal and other church pronouncements were full of broad condemnations of "weapons of mass destruction" and "weapons that escape" control, with no elaboration of the rationale for these condemnations in terms of such traditional precepts as proportionality and discrimination.[33] The American bishops' 1983 pastoral fully restored the just war doctrine to its rightful place as the main vehicle for normative analysis of deterrence/defense policies and preparations. To be sure, the pastoral does not always carry out just war analyses as fully as some of us would like but it is incomparably superior to the generalizations of earlier papal and episcopal documents.

The American Catholic bishops are not alone in tackling the moral issues of international relations. The French and German bishops, for example, have issued pastoral letters comparable to the 1983 American pastoral.[34] Moreover, there is increasing dialogue among some of the principal resource people of the national episcopal conferences. Conferences have been held at Georgetown and in Bonn bringing together the consultants of the American and German Catholic bishops, an enterprise organized by Bryan Hehir and John Langan, S.J., of the Kennedy Institute of Ethics and the Woodstock Theological Center. Finally, almost half a century after World War II, the Catholic Church in the United States and Western Europe is beginning to conduct more or less sustained discussions of the great issues of international relations. This is a good start, but only a start.

How to "Study the Questions" of International Morality

No major institution confronting issues as complex and difficult as those to which the church speaks when it deals with international relations would be content with the level of "study" presently within the capabilities of its office of International Justice and Peace, Bryan Hehir's network of experts, and the knowledge and wisdom of the National Conference of Catholic Bishops. The American Catholic Church does not organize and support occasional commissions like the Scowcroft Commission to study intensively a major problem area.[35] It does not maintain any permanent centers of research, reflection, and writing on the major problem areas of international relations in the manner of Harvard's Center for International Affairs. It is embarrassing to compare the modest staff of its office of International Justice and Peace with the resources of a typical congressional staff. In brief, the American Catholic bishops have progressed from the 1960s when they had no institutional resources for international relations issues to a point where they have the part-time services of one knowledgeable, talented, and tireless priest with a tiny supporting staff and an impressive network of potential consultants operating almost exclusively through him. The American Catholic Church can and should do better.

Yet, would it be desirable for the church to invest vast resources in its own research center for international relations, a center capable of carrying out long-term studies of the major moral issues? It is difficult to imagine the bishops building buildings, developing libraries, drawing scholars and experts away from their academic, government, and other positions. A single episcopal think tank is not a realistic possibility.

However, the American Catholic bishops have resources that have never been seriously tapped. As Theodore Hesburgh points out, virtually all of the major Catholic universities in the world are in the United States. There are very few Catholic universities (as distinguished from religious houses of study) in Western Europe and even fewer in the Third World. Many of the Catholic institutions of higher learning outside the United States are not up to American standards.[36] To be sure, American Catholic universities have yet to equal the resources and standards of Harvard or Berkeley. They are, however, good and some are becoming very good. One of these is Georgetown.

It would make sense for the National Conference of Catholic Bishops to call upon American Catholic universities to make specific commitments to "study the questions" of morality in international relations—as well as a broad spectrum of issues of social ethics that are mainly concerned with domestic problems, e.g., those addressed in the pastoral letter on the economy. It might not be beyond the capabilities of the National Conference of Catholic Bishops to survey the resources of Catholic universities in the United States to determine which institutions or combinations of institutions promised to be most relevant to a serious attempt to marshal the expertise of American Catholic scholars, moralists, and technical experts. At the request of the bishops, Catholic universities could establish interuniversity committees to coordinate research, dialogue, and writing on the kinds of issues to which the American bishops should be speaking in their pronouncements. Given adequate advance notice (a pastoral letter is often several years in the drafting, revision, and promulgation), individual scholars and research centers could prepare background material, position papers, and critiques of proposed episcopal documents in an orderly, scholarly fashion.

With this kind of scholarly infrastructure, the American Catholic bishops, in turn, could make available to Rome the mature product of the best thinking of American Catholics, who on many subjects include some of the leading experts in the world. The day might even come when Rome would summon American *periti* to assist in the drafting and critiquing of church pronouncements—instead of relying solely on the inevitable Roman and Western European insiders. In the near term, however, it should be the purpose of American Catholic institutions such as Georgetown to reach out to the American Catholic hierarchy and offer their resources to the church. In so doing Georgetown will also naturally be serving America and, indeed, the world.

A Georgetown Agenda for the Study of Moral Issues of International Relations

Georgetown in its third century should have an agenda of subjects and issue areas on which it intends to concentrate and excel. The effort to set such an agenda and to establish priorities has already begun. International relations is one of the areas that was identified as a strength to build on in Georgetown's review of its graduate programs in the early 1980s. What has not been done, except for the decision to strengthen further the programs in philosophy and theology, is to identify moral components and issues within the various fields selected for the pursuit of excellence. Georgetown should review systematically all of the programs selected for excellence to see to what extent they include courses, research, and writing directed to the moral dimensions of respective fields. For example, it should not suffice to say that Georgetown wants to excel in the field of economics. Georgetown should go further and specify moral issue areas within economics where resources should be developed.

It happens that Georgetown has, in recent years, had a considerable expansion of courses, conferences, and scholarship relevant to the moral issues of contemporary international relations. Bryan Hehir as a lecturer, Father Francis X. Winters and I as full-time faculty, have taught courses and conducted seminars which emphasize moral issues. A conference on nuclear deterrence/defense and just war doctrine produced a book co-edited by John Langan and myself.[37] Bryan Hehir heads a committee, drawn from many different Main Campus programs and the Law School, which conducted a conference on the future of arms control in March 1989 as part of Georgetown's Bicentennial celebration.

These developments are encouraging. However, they remain ad hoc and somewhat fortuitous. What is needed is an agenda of subjects and issue areas in the broad field of international relations to provide goals for Georgetown's faculty, and programs and rationales for the creation and allocation of resources necessary for serious research, reflection, dialogue, and writing on the agenda items.

A partial agenda is fairly evident:

(1) What is the nature of international politics? Can it be based on "mutual trust alone" (*Pacem in Terris*)? If not, does Catholic thought on international relations have to move in the direction of political realism?

(2) What is the future of international law and organization? Is world law a realistic goal in a badly divided and conflictual international system that lacks an underlying moral consensus? If not, what approaches would make international law effective at least as a self-imposed restraint and the basis for intercourse with nations holding similar values?

(3) What is the nature of the Soviet/communist threat to the liberty and values of what may still be called the free world? Are there other threats, e.g., from fundamentalist Muslim or other sources, to political societies that espouse Christian values? No one can evaluate the proportionality of security measures of deterrence/defense without some working definition of the threats that necessitate such measures.

(4) Can nuclear—or even conventional—deterrence/defense be reconciled with just war doctrine? What would need to be done in terms of strategic doctrine and military capabilities to make possible a just and limited deterrent/defense posture?

(5) Is the goal of total elimination of nuclear weapons realistic in a world wherein nuclear weapons cannot be uninvented and proliferation is increasing in the Third World? Is total nuclear disarmament even desirable? What are its probable consequences?

(6) How much do we know about arms control? How do we assess our progress in arms control to date and our prospects for the near future? Is all arms control necessarily desirable?

(7) What does the church have to say about revolution? What is the future of liberation theology? If liberation theology and Marxist-Leninist-Maoist revolutionary doctrine are not to monopolize the moral debates about revolutionary ends and means, what are the prospects for developing a just revolution doctrine comparable to just war doctrine?

(8) Granted that the distribution of wealth between the advanced and developing nations is unjust, how can the unjust balance be rectified? How much do we know about the ways to improve unfair trade patterns? How much do we know about giving aid effectively? If there is a moral obligation of the rich nations to help the poor nations, there is an obligation to help them effectively. After forty years of foreign aid, what is our assessment of the effort?

(9) How can a realistic approach to advancing human rights be reconciled with the principle of nonintervention and the need to avoid counterproductive destabilizing initiatives?

These are some subjects and issues that should be on Georgetown's agenda for the study of moral issues of international relations.

How should Georgetown marshal the resources to work on this agenda? Above all, people will be needed. Scholars in the faculty should be identified, encouraged, and supported. Additional scholars should be added to the faculty to work on subjects and issue areas where Georgetown lacks people with the competence and interest to do the job. For example, if there is no one particularly qualified or inclined to take on the task of studying the question of effective foreign aid and the University believes that this is something that should be on Georgetown's agenda, an appropriate scholar should be recruited. To be sure, it will not be possible to make large numbers of such appointments. The task of setting the agenda is to achieve consensus as to what tasks Georgetown should take on, their priorities and timing, and the appointments that will be necessary to accomplish those tasks.

Research centers may be desirable but, in my view, they are secondary to the requirement of finding and supporting the right people. If research centers are to be justified, they should maximize direct support to the scholars in them and minimize institutional make-work and empire-building.

Relations with other American Catholic universities, as well as with scholars and centers abroad, will be important. Georgetown cannot alone provide all the research, reflection, dialogue, and writing necessary to advance Catholic thought on international relations. Georgetown should, however, be a major leader in the effort to develop this body of Catholic thought in cooperation with other Catholic institutions.

Georgetown's obligation to serve as a scholarly resource for the church is clear. It is stated in the University's Statement of Goals and Objectives:

> Within the commitment of a Jesuit University, the Graduate School has goals and objectives proper to itself: the establishment among its students of a permanent relationship to learning, the definition and dissemination of existing bodies of knowledge, the extension of present limits of that knowledge and its practical application. A specific mission of the Graduate School, as part of a Catholic university, should be research into the normative and empirical bases for the development and interpretation of Catholic social principles.[38]

Georgetown's mandate to "study the problems" extends to many subjects and issue areas. However, Georgetown's opportunity to contribute to the development of Catholic teaching on international relations is unique because of the University's location in the capital of a superpower and its existing capabilities for international studies.

Scholarship on the moral dimensions of international relations is an enormous undertaking and deserves to be improved and increased on its own merits. Yet there is a further dimension to the challenge of scholarship on international morality. Georgetown has a long tradition of effective teaching. Indeed, initiatives to increase scholarly activities are sometimes viewed as competing with the teaching mission of the University. This should not be the case. Surely, good scholars probing the frontiers of the great questions of modern international relations from moral perspectives will further enhance the quality of international education offered by Georgetown. This should be as true at the graduate as at the undergraduate level. It is just possible that the Suarez of the twenty-first century may have a Ph.D. from Georgetown in international ethics.

Notes

1. *Pacem in Terris, Encyclical Letter of Pope John XXIII* (Washington, D.C.: National Catholic Welfare Conference, 1963), #118, 28 (hereinafter, *Pacem in Terris*).

2. *Pastoral Constitution on the Church in the Modern World* in *The Documents*

of Vatican II, ed. Walter M. Abbott, S.J. (New York: Guild/America/Association Press, 1966), #82, 296 (hereinafter, *Gaudium et Spes*).

3. National Conference of Catholic Bishops, *The Challenge of Peace: God's Promise and Our Response* (Washington, D.C.: United States Catholic Conference, 1983), #196, 62 (hereinafter, *The Challenge of Peace*).

4. Ibid., #304, 92-93.

5. National Conference of Catholic Bishops, *Economic Justice for All: Pastoral Letter on Catholic Social Teaching and the U.S. Economy* (Washington, D.C.: U.S. Catholic Conference, 1986); for a collection of critical essays on this pastoral letter, see *The Deeper Meaning of Economic Life*, ed. R. Bruce Douglass (Washington, D.C.: Georgetown University Press, 1986).

6. Heinrich A. Rommen, *The State in Catholic Thought* (St. Louis: Herder, 1945), e.g., 1-9, 107-11.

7. Ibid., 620-27; Heinrich A. Rommen, *The Natural Law*, trans. M. Hanley (St. Louis: Herder, 1947); James Brown Scott, *The Spanish Origin of International Law* and idem, *The Catholic Conception of International Law* (Oxford: Clarendon Press, 1934).

8. James Brown Scott, *Law, the State and the International Community* (2 vols.; New York: Columbia University Press, 1939), vol. 1, 310-23.

9. On the Catholic concept of the international common good see, for example, John Eppstein, *The Catholic Tradition of the Law of Nations* (Washington, D.C.: Carnegie Endowment for International Peace/Catholic Association for International Peace, 1935), 247-75.

10. Rommen, *The State in Catholic Thought*, 220-28.

11. Ibid., 652-57.

12. Paul Ramsey, *The Just War* (New York: Charles Scribner's Sons, 1968); James T. Johnson, *Ideology, Reason and Limitation of War* (Princeton, N.J.: Princeton University Press, 1975); idem, *Just War Tradition and the Restraint of War* (Princeton, N.J.: Princeton University Press, 1981); Michael Walzer, *Just and Unjust Wars* (New York: Basic, 1977); William V. O'Brien, *The Conduct of Just and Limited War* (New York: Praeger, 1981).

13. Ramsey, *The Just War*, 13-36.

14. Ibid., 37-70.

15. *The Challenge of Peace*, #80-110, 26-34.

16. On *Rerum Novarum* see Richard E. Mulcahy, S.J., *The Economics of Heinrich Pesch* (New York: Holt, 1952); Henry W. Briefs, "Solidarity within the Firm: Principles, Concepts and Reflections," *Review of Social Economy* 42 (1984), 295-317.

17. Eppstein, *The Catholic Tradition of the Law of Nations*; Rommen, *The State and Catholic Thought*, 615-735.

18. The International Union of Social Studies, *Code of International Ethics*, trans. ed. John Eppstein (Westminster, Md.: Newman Press, 1953).

19. Ibid., 48-54.

20. Ibid., 94-105.

21. Ibid., 113-62.

22. Ibid., 201-41.

23. Papal pronouncements on war and peace from Leo XIII to John XXIII are compiled in *Pattern for Peace*, ed. Harry W. Flannery (Westminster, Md: Newman, 1962). See Jacques Maritain, *Man and the State* (Chicago: University of Chicago Press, 1951); Rommen, *The State in Catholic Thought*, 672-735.

24. In the early 1960s a scholarly journal, *World Justice (Justice dans le monde)*, was published in Louvain. Its board of editors was international. I was the U.S. member. The journal collected and published articles on issues of international morality but it had no research base or agenda and a very precarious funding which did not survive the decade.

25. Most Rev. Mark G. McGrath, C.S.C., "The Constitution on the Church in the Modern World," in *Vatican II: An Interfaith Appraisal*, ed. John H. Miller, C.S.C. (Notre Dame, Ind.: University of Notre Dame Press, 1966).

26. Ibid., 399-403.

27. Archbishop McGrath, who was a major figure in the development of *Gaudium et Spes*, reports (ibid., 402):

> The steering committee met twice briefly in Rome before the end of the second session and decided upon the main lines of the work to be done. A handful of theologians were chosen who, under the direction of Bishop Guano, as president, and Father Bernard Häring, as secretary, were to prepare a new draft.
>
> At the end of January, 1964, in Zurich, Switzerland, this small group went over the new text.

My understanding of the processes of Vatican II was greatly enhanced by an interview with Msgr. George Higgins, June 24, 1988.

28. Abbott, ed., *The Documents of Vatican II*, index, 792.

29. *American Participation in the Second Vatican Council*, ed. Msgr. Vincent A. Yzermans (New York: Sheed & Ward, 1967), 231-61. Archbishop Hannan's intervention is on 247-48.

30. James Dougherty reports that the CAIP commentary on schema 17 "was acknowledged by Monsignor Higgins at the U.S. Bishops' press panel on November 9, 1964" in "The Catholic Church, War and Nuclear Weapons," *Orbis* 9 (1966), 881.

31. See, for example, the reliance on the authority of *Gaudium et Spes* by the American Catholic bishops in their 1983 pastoral *The Challenge of Peace*, #104, 33; #147, 46; #148, 47; #81, 52-53.

32. "Building Peace: A Pastoral Reflection on the Response to 'The Challenge of Peace,'" *Origins* 18 (1988), 133-48.

33. For examples, see O'Brien, *The Conduct of Just and Limited War*, 378, n. 17.

34. *Out of Justice Peace: Joint Pastoral Letter of the West German Bishops; Winning the Peace: Joint Pastoral Letter of the French Bishops*, ed. and intro. James V. Schall, S.J. (San Francisco: Ignatius Press, 1984).

35. *President's Commission on Strategic Forces* (Washington, D.C.: United States Government Printing Office, 1983).

36. Theodore M. Hesburgh, "The Vatican and American Higher Education," *America* 155 (1986), 247-50, 263.

37. William V. O'Brien and John Langan, S.J., *The Nuclear Dilemma and the Just War Tradition* (Lexington, Mass.: Lexington Books, 1986).

38. "The Educational Goals and Objectives of the Georgetown University Main Campus," 3. This statement emerged from several years of discussions between faculty and administrators. It was issued by the Office of the Provost in August 1981.

DOROTHY M. BROWN
Department of History

Learning, Faith, Freedom, and Building a Curriculum: Two Hundred Years and Counting

At a faculty convocation in the spring of 1985, President Timothy S. Healy, S.J., reflecting on his ten years at Georgetown University and on the pending arrival of the Bicentennial class of 1989, asserted that our two hundredth year provided "a chance to contemplate Georgetown." Using a poem by Rupert Brooke as his touchstone, he ended: "In my moments of dreaming, [I] see Georgetown, above all in its faculty and students, for what it is and can be, 'a gathered radiance under the night.' To get it ready for its third century is worth the work."[1] The theme Healy set for this Bicentennial work and reflection, "Learning, Faith, and Freedom," is an apt departure point for a study of the crafting of curricula in the contexts of American freedom and Catholic faith in the Jesuit tradition of learning.[2] In each of these contexts there was little that gave early promise of curricular innovation much less "a gathered radiance" in Georgetown's course of studies.

"Born free" Americans generally debate freedom and the nature of the republic only in times of crisis. Until recently, American Catholic leaders have been similarly reticent. As newcomers in an alien land, they and the institutions they built struggled for acceptance while defensively circling the wagons. The colleges they founded to protect the faith of a burgeoning number of immigrants remained throughout the nineteenth century, according to one analyst, "static in educational philosophy, traditional in curriculum and pedagogy, rigid in discipline and student life, clerical in faculty [and] administration, and isolated almost completely from the mainstream of American higher education."[3] Confident in the church's organic "integrity of vision," Catholic administrators and faculty "were not so much concerned with the pushing back of the frontier of truth as with passing on a given tradition of truth in which little in the way of addition or alteration was necessary."[4] In this they were not too unlike their Protestant American brethren who offered "a curriculum and a college life designed not so much to open minds as to fill them—with knowledge and modes of behavior that were fixed, unalterable, not to be questioned."[5]

While freedom and faith prompted little early curricular debate, the Jesuit learning instituted at Georgetown seemed even more resistant to discussion. When John Carroll's school first opened its doors to students, it had a method and curriculum that was tested through two centuries of experience, the celebrated *Ratio Studiorum*. Yale's curricular revision of 1828, with its confident claim that it contained all the common elements of culture needed to educate a citizen, might reverberate through other institutions; Henry Tappan's and Charles Eliot's elective system might transform Michigan and Harvard and much of American higher education; accreditation agencies might set standards and new ways of measuring education through credit hours; Harvard's 1945 report, *General Education in a Free Society*, might dominate the curricular dialogue, but Georgetown's documents continued to articulate the time-tested wisdom, strength, and coherence of the Jesuit tradition of education, the *eloquentia perfecta* of the *Ratio Studiorum*.

Through the mid-twentieth century, when there were major curricular changes in undergraduate education at Georgetown, they did not occur within the College that grew from Carroll's little academy. The Georgetown way of curricular innovation was to create a new school. In the earliest instance, the Nursing School emerged in 1903 to educate young women who might also staff the Georgetown University hospital. In 1919, after the cataclysm of World War I, Edmund A. Walsh, S.J., founded the School of Foreign Service. Like Adam's rib, the Institute (eventually School) of Languages and Linguistics was "taken out" of the School of Foreign Service after World War II. Another offshoot of the School of Foreign Service was the School of Business Administration, which struggled for students and identity through the years of the Eisenhower administration. Each of the four new schools affirmed the commitment to liberal arts education and the Jesuit tradition in addition to their special professional orientation, but the College continued as the "heart" of the University. Only in the College, two hundred years after its founding, is there still an insistence that the academic dean be a Jesuit. It is on the curriculum of the College of Arts and Sciences, then, that this essay will concentrate until considering the challenge of the third century of Learning, Faith, and Freedom.

Ratio Studiorum: The Sheet Anchor of the Curriculum

In its American transplanting at Georgetown, the *Ratio Studiorum* proved a sturdy anchor for the young institution. St. Ignatius Loyola's organizing vision for a university was based on the Roman trivium and quadrivium adapted to places, times, and persons.[6] The course of studies was carefully prescribed, but the major emphasis of the *Ratio* was on method. Strong teaching was central. "With God's grace," the professor was to be diligent and unremitting in his work and eager for the advancement of his students.[7] These students, in the parlance of 1989, were "engaged." At the end of each lecture, students reviewed the material. Latin was declaimed; drama was used as an "educational instrument." There were debates, disputations, repetitions, contests, projects, and above all exercise, exercise, and more exercise. These were, of course, varied, for "nothing slackens youthful diligence more than monotony."[8] The goal of *eloquentia perfecta* was not simply acquiring rhetorical skill. Renaissance educators presupposed that students developed character and intelligence in achieving this eloquence.[9] The wider aim of the early Jesuit training rested on the conviction that "the truly human man must possess both wisdom and eloquence; must know something and be able to say what he knows; must be able to think and to communicate."[10] In its fullest achievement, each student reached his full potential; each learned "to distinguish and to savor all that should charm the imagination and heart."[11] Each student was liberally educated.

In the 1820s, the seven-year program in Carroll's fledgling institution followed the spirit, if not the letter, of the *Ratio* in its American translation. There were heavy doses of Latin and Greek, but while Cicero remained the model of style, students also read Addison, Pope, and Milton in the quest for *eloquentia perfecta*.[12] Spanish was offered, and music and dance could be elected. Chemistry experiments were carried on in the new laboratory. Philosophy brought synthesis and integration. "It was a curriculum," concluded University historian R. Emmett Curran, S.J., "that blended tradition (classics and mathematics) and the new knowledge of the sciences, with a modest recognition of utilitarian needs."[13]

In 1835, following proposals formulated *ad experimentum* by Father General Roothaan in 1832, there were some modest revisions. The first year (called "rudiments") continued the emphasis on Latin and Greek grammar, Cicero, and English grammar, and added the history of the Old Testament, and elements of geography. By the sixth year, the courses in history had moved through the history of Rome and leapt to American history. In the seventh year, students grappled with logic, metaphysics, and ethics—lectures were delivered in Latin—and could elect music and drawing. The prescribed curriculum became the model for Catholic higher education until the first decade of the twentieth century.[14]

The 1905 catalogue of Georgetown College continued to affirm confidence in the classical curriculum and the method of the *Ratio*. To attain a "complete general and liberal education," the course of studies was *not elective* but prescribed. No student would be excused from any requirement, "*not even from Greek*." The curriculum, reflecting some of the suppleness Ignatius had envisioned, insisted on the Latin and Greek classics, but included English, History, Modern Language, Mathematics, Physics, Chemistry, the elements of Geology, Astronomy, Mechanics, and "a very thorough training in Rational Philosophy." Christian Doctrine was offered in the first and fourth year. Summing up, the catalogue proclaimed: "It is believed that its requirements are seldom equalled." Beyond this, Georgetown enjoyed "peculiar advantages," since professors were guided in their teaching by the principles of the famous *Ratio Studiorum*. The student who followed this prescribed course would "have a considerable amount of positive knowledge in every department of learning" and "be possessed of trained and cultivated faculties."[15]

Five years later, as the reforms of the Progressive era were reaching higher education and the state universities of the Midwest were rising to increasing positions of leadership, the College catalogue reasserted Georgetown's commitment to classical languages. In "the experience of a century or more," it had yet to be demonstrated that "an adequate substitute of equal educational power" had emerged.[16]

And yet Robert I. Gannon, S.J., recalled that in 1909 as a Georgetown freshman he was already conscious that "the poor old liberal arts were in strategic retreat," and in the course of the next fifty years "the ancient phalanx of the liberal arts has been steadily giving ground all these years, fighting a rear-guard action, the hardest of all battles to win."[17]

The gradual expansion of the curriculum lamented by Gannon reached almost explosive proportions in the rending aftermath of World War I. In the 1920s the emphasis on organization, efficiency, and standards in American society and American higher education persuaded Georgetown to stand for accreditation by its peers in the Middle States Association of Colleges and Schools. The method of the *Ratio* and the Latin requirement still survived, but the catalogue now listed distribution requirements across seven groups of disciplines. As at every other institution of higher education in the region, 128 credits were required for graduation.[18]

As the golden bowl of classical education was placed on the shelf, there ensued in Catholic discussions, as Philip Gleason has detailed, a massive quest for a new unity and coherence. New terms like "organic unity," "synthetic vision," "integral Catholicism," and "Catholic culture" became buzz words. The Thomistic synthesis provided an integrated vision for life and in the curriculum. By 1935, the National Catholic Educational Association approved a report of its Committee on Educational Policy and Program which noted:

> The Catholic college will not be content with presenting Catholicism as a creed, a code, or a cult. Catholicism must be seen as a culture. . . . graduates of the Catholic college of liberal arts . . . will have before them not merely the facts in the natural order but those in the supernatural order also, those facts which give meaning and coherence to the whole of life.[19]

Coherence within Catholic culture could be articulated in a coherent curriculum in the Catholic colleges. The anchors were in the courses and faculty of the departments of philosophy and the newly emerging departments of theology.

On the eve of American involvement in World War II, the studies and teaching methods were substantially those of the *Ratio* promulgated in 1599 and revised in 1832. The Jesuit system held that "a solid course in Scholastic Philosophy, based on a foundation of Languages, both Ancient and Modern, History, Mathematics and the Natural Sciences has cultural advantages far superior to those offered by other educational systems." For an A.B. degree, the student completed eighteen credits in Latin and twenty-four in Philosophy. Three elective courses were allowed in the four years. Adherence to a fixed program of studies for all students had "stood the test of time." Religion courses were obligatory for all Catholic students, who were also expected to approach the sacraments at least once a month and to attend the three-day retreat held at the beginning of the fall semester. The catalogue noted: "A man of culture without a conscience, is in no sense of the word an educated man, but a menace to society."[20]

Georgetown's 1951 self-study for the Middle States Association of Colleges and Schools reflected its traditions and the changing times. There remained a certitude about its identity and mission. As an American Catholic, Jesuit university, Georgetown "represented certain established principles, specific ideals, and definite traditions through which she seeks to uphold defend, propagate and elucidate the integral Christian and American cultural heritage."[21] These principles included not only philosophical truths about the nature of man, the truths of Christian revelation, but also (at the height of McCarthyism and the Korean War) the truths expressed in the opening paragraphs of the Declaration of Independence and the American Constitution and Bill of Rights. Theological and moral virtues fused with patriotism, loyalty, and social consciousness.

The curriculum described for the visiting accrediting team was a compendium of the old, the changing, and the new. "Traditionally," the self-study noted, "the Jesuit Code of Liberal Education was based on the conviction that the objective of the liberal arts college is best realized through the study of the abiding human values to be found in the Greek and Latin classics." The study of Scholastic Philosophy and the study and practice of Catholic religion integrated those values "toward the harmonious development of the Christian gentleman, informed in intellect, and formed in character." The Georgetown graduate should be ready to make the great decisions by which others are led to action.[22]

While the liberal education of the College of Arts and Sciences remained an education of the whole man, an education for a citizen of this world and the next, the curriculum had "undergone considerable change" in response to technological and social change. Now there were three paths to a degree in the college, A.B., B.S., and a B.S.S.S. (Social Science).

The report of the visiting Middle States accrediting team in 1951 duly noted the changes reported over the past twenty years; the reduction of requirements in Philosophy from thirty-six to twenty-six hours; the increase of electives from eighteen to thirty-six hours. Team members, nevertheless, urged a consideration of a further reduction of the number of hours required in Philosophy, and a somewhat greater choice of subject matter for the student. In spite of the planning on curriculum, the visiting team also reported a certain vagueness by chairmen about how new courses were introduced. And they cautioned about inbreeding in the faculty, noting that almost all were Jesuit-trained.[23] In the hopeful dawn of the 1960s and John F. Kennedy's first year in office, a new reaccrediting team found the curriculum promoting the expressed aims of the College and sound in most areas. Some on the team worried about a "cultural lag." The introduction of new courses was still "somewhat haphazard." While individual syllabi reflected admirable planning, the team questioned, what do they all add up to? Still, they wondered, were there too many required courses? The science facilities (though they noted that the Reiss Building was soon to be completed) were assessed as barely adequate. Much more troubling was the question of whether an undergraduate should earn a bachelor's degree with no exposure to music or art or the aesthetic experiences those fields offered. Did the emphasis on language as a tool work against the cultural interest it might inspire?[24]

Clearly, at the beginning of this tumultuous decade Georgetown's curriculum was moving slowly into the American mainstream of requirements and distributions and responding to the criteria for excellence promulgated by the regional accrediting agency. Yet, there was an obvious tug and pull. How to hold on to the old while engrafting the new?

Earthquakes and a Shattered Synthesis

As the Second Vatican Council opened in the fall of 1962, the catalogue of the College graphically underscored the vitality of the Jesuit traditions while demonstrating simultaneously the changing of the guard. In no previous edition was the mission of an American Catholic, Jesuit university so clearly stated. As American, and true to John Carroll in its pluralism, Georgetown served the country through its well-trained and educated graduates in Congress, the professions, and communities. As Catholic ("not merely a creed but a culture"), Georgetown offered the integration of the Catholic vision as a sturdy counter to the compartmentalization of modern life and the rise of materialism. Every student should have "a philosophy of living, for shaping conduct, for reference in doubt, for challenge, for stimulus, and driving power!"[25] And, finally, Georgetown as a Jesuit university rested on four hundred years of educational experience and the *Ratio Studiorum*, "a method, possessing marvelous adaptability for all times and countries," dedicated to developing the whole man through a curriculum characterized by order and proportion.[26] Yet in the curriculum section, the *Ratio* recedes. The first two years of general education courses introduced the student to three broad areas of human knowledge, the humanities, social sciences, and the natural sciences. Thirteen majors were available; four different paths to the Bachelor of Arts and five to the Bachelor of Science were listed. Twenty hours of philosophy and sixteen of theology were required as well as modern language through the intermediate level.

Georgetown was clearly moving in the direction of increased flexibility and student involvement before the deluge of the 1960s. Then all the dams seemed to burst at once. Academically, the knowledge explosion and the proliferation of fields and specializations challenged the old distribution requirements that still distantly echoed the 1828 Yale confidence that there was a certain body of knowledge that could be transmitted in the undergraduate years and was guaranteed to produce an educated person. By the 1960s there was clear evidence that faculties radically disagreed on how to achieve a distribution that had unity, order, or coherence, or more significantly, produced a shared learning carrying on a Western, Judeo-Christian tradition. There was no longer an accepted canon. Turf battles raged. Reform was easier in upperclass offerings, with seminars and colloquia narrowing the gap between the undergraduate and graduate school and throwing into further imbalance the special and general aspects of the curriculum.[27]

Not surprisingly, it was at the great multiversity of the University of California at Berkeley that the students began to decry the state of their education. The baby-boom generation, scientifically reared and skilled in consumerism, had fought its way into a highly competitive institution, to find absent research professors, a distant, multilayered administration, and a curriculum that did not relate to the real world of civil rights marches and a gathering war in Vietnam. Their cry of rage combined a call for free speech with a denunciation of an education that was irrelevant and a culture that was murderous and obscene. Berkeley's Free Speech Movement attracted pilgrims from Michigan, Wisconsin, Swarthmore and spread to other schools. By 1965, with the Fulbright hearings on Vietnam and the first teach-ins at Michigan, students simultaneously demanded greater attention to their needs and to the nation's ills.

In the crisis, the Carnegie Commission on Higher Education sponsored a major, multivolume study of the complex variety of America's troubled colleges and universities. Lewis Mayhew of Stanford undertook the challenge of chronicling efforts at *Changing the Curriculum*. In the Mayhew report the students moved to the center of the discussion. Reflecting on the generational divide evident on the campus and in society (richly detailed by Kenneth Kenniston, Paul Goodman, and Erik Erikson), Mayhew observed:

> Youth . . . want new kinds of learning which maximize the involvement of the intellect with the individual's experience, rather than dividing the two. They search for new concepts of man in society which acknowledge the unique individuality of each human being, but which also stress social involvement.[28]

They were impatient, he observed, wanting instant poetry, instant psychoanalysis, and instant mysticism, but they must be listened to.[29] To build a curriculum, faculty needed a variety of evidence ranging across students' characteristics, desires, and needs, patterns of progress over four years, graduates' reflections, the expectations of societies, and faculties' interests and abilities. The problem of the curriculum revision attempts of the 1960s, summarized Mayhew, was the problem of "a subject-centered faculty attempting to offer a student-centered curriculum."[30]

Curricular battles were fought out in the midst of a bewildering variety of extraneous agenda. At Georgetown, curricular relevance was discussed while students entered classrooms to summon volunteers to occupy the "Three Sisters" islands in the Potomac in protest of a proposed new bridge; others found recruits to march on the Pentagon or the Justice Department. The momentum for curricular change mounted and collided with the complex forces for continuation. Departments which already had protected turf in the general education distribution requirements were not anxious to make room for others. Yet they were increasingly beleaguered in explaining why their discipline was more central to the education of students than others. While historians argued for roots, psychologists and economists countered that no citizen and no nation could survive without the informing principles of their disciplines. The outcome nationwide and at Georgetown was a reduction in the number of required courses, an expanded advisory system, development of cluster courses, integrating seminars, honors programs, and, in some instances, a change from five courses per semester (5-5) to four per semester (4-4) or a 4-1-4 program to provide more depth and intensity. Brown, Stanford, and Rutgers led the way. Brown retained only a requirement in modern languages and developed a range of new, interdisciplinary courses, seminars, and student-designed majors. Narrative evaluations replaced letter grades. Pass-fail systems were initiated. Stanford developed a series of demanding freshman seminars taught by their faculty stars. Rutgers stood the old curriculum on its head, scheduling surveys in the senior year and seminars in the freshman semesters.[31]

Developments in Catholic colleges and universities were tracked for the Carnegie Commission series by Andrew Greeley in his aptly titled volume, *From Backwater to Mainstream*. Clearly, the 350 Catholic colleges and universities were fully involved in the maelstrom of curriculum discussion of the 1960s, but they had their own further challenges. Surveying the adaptation and acculturation of American Catholicism in its institutions of higher education, Greeley observed: "The Catholic higher educational problems of the United States were initially far more Catholic than they were American, and through the years of acculturation have become more and more American problems and less and less specifically *Catholic* problems."[32] Almost all of these institutions were going through a period of questioning and self-doubt; they strove to emulate Harvard and Berkeley, yet to do that in the Catholic, and in Georgetown's case, in the Jesuit tradition. Greeley cited one Jesuit university president as insisting that his school was distinctive but refusing to focus on any particular element as essential to that distinctiveness. Somehow the catholicity of his institution would survive.[33]

The double-identity question in the 1960s for American Catholic higher education brought a gathering of Catholic university and college leaders of the North American Region of the International Federation of Catholic Universities to Land O' Lakes, Wisconsin, in July of 1967 to grapple with defining their evolving institutions. Hedged in with caveats on its incompleteness and selectivity, the "Statement on the Nature of the Contemporary Catholic University" set forth ten identifying characteristics. The Catholic university had a commitment to excellence and insisted on true autonomy and academic freedom from any external lay or clerical authority. In its community of scholars, Catholicism would be "perceptibly present" and "effectively operative." This presence would be most operative in the teaching and research of the theology faculty, which would engage others interested in cross-disciplinary confrontation in "interdisciplinary dialogue," deepening "an awareness that there is a philosophical and theological dimension to most intellectual subjects." Through these dialogues and in research, the Catholic university would serve society and be the "critical reflective intelligence of the Church."

In the undergraduate curriculum this "effective intellectual presence of the theological disciplines" would translate into a concern for ultimate questions; for the full human and spiritual development of the student, with special emphasis on interpersonal relationships; and a concern with social justice issues of race, peace, and poverty. The Catholic university should build a community, with reorganized governance structures, where students and faculty could find ways to be fully Catholic, to express and witness and share their faith. If all of these objectives were achieved, the Land O' Lakes participants concluded, "the Catholic university of the future will be a true modern university but specifically Catholic in profound and creative ways for the service of society and the people of God."[34] Yet, as Andrew Greeley and others observed, it was not only important that these universities be uniquely Catholic, but somehow or other they must be uniquely in the tradition of their own religious community.[35]

In 1969, the Jesuit Educational Association (JEA) sponsored a workshop at Denver on "Jesuit Universities and Colleges: Their Commitment in a World of Change." Like the delegates at Land O' Lakes, the assembled Jesuits found agreement on the distinctive marks of the special Jesuit "style" of Catholic education:[36] apostolic intent; a lived witness by faculty; pragmatic strategy that placed reflective intelligence at the service of practical action; an emphasis on intellectual development; and a world-affirming spirituality which optimistically proposed the worth of natural and human values, for "God could be found in all things." The Spiritual Exercises of Ignatius Loyola rooted this world-affirming spirituality or "secular mysticism." Jesuit education should be

> distinguished by the way in which a significant number of men, Jesuit and lay, express that secular mysticism in their professional and personal lives, win a consensus on campus, and design an effective educational enterprise aimed at developing all the dimensions of the human person.[37]

Open to experimentation, Jesuit education would accept provisional answers, seek a genuine ecumenism, and

> be able to bear a prophetic testimony to the crises of the times. . . . A great premium should be placed on this world-affirming spirituality, on the Spirit moving in the world, and on the legitimacy behind change. The Jesuit school should not be a center for preserving the old, but rather one for discerning, endorsing, and contributing to the new aspirations and inventions of man. There is a need for conversion, a conversion that results in a grand hopefulness about man's possibilities in the future.[38]

The adaptability to "places, times, and persons" of Ignatius's university remained intact.

The Denver Workshop "Statement on Liberal Aims of Jesuit Higher Education" provided a clear 1969 state-of-the-art definition of liberal education: "one that prepares the free person for a full and fruitful life in a free society." Reflecting on the turmoil of the time, the drafters observed:

> More than ever, society today needs a process of learning appropriate to a world in which profound continuities and radical changes are in dynamic confrontation. . . . liberal education still constitutes the optimum path toward full, rich human development—both personalization and socialization in a world of continuity as well as unceasing change.[39]

To foster such an education, faculty communities committed to "comprehensive human learning and the insights of religion and theology" were essential. The curriculum must place the student at the center. Freshmen should be engaged on issues "of keenest concern to them by the most exciting and creative faculty," but all students should be fully engaged in the shared search for truth and values, a search in which philosophy and theology were still central. The curriculum should balance general and specialized education; it should include non-Western studies, and, responding to the student demand for "relevance, immediacy, and involvement," should work for interactions of scholarly analysis and personal commitment in internships and off-campus programs of social responsibility.[40]

A Denver Workshop "Statement on Innovation in Liberal Education" charted trends for the future: the increasing importance of the verbal-visual aspects of the culture; the ready availability of information banks; the inability of ordinary courses and structures to meet problems in personal growth; the need expressed by students and younger faculty for broadening, noncampus experiences; the importance of noncognitive elements in education. All twenty-eight Jesuit colleges were urged to establish centers of innovation in liberal education.[41]

Georgetown Curriculum Revision—The Reverberations of the 1960s

Three months after the Land O' Lakes meeting and with a new Dean in place in 1967, Georgetown's College of Arts and Sciences began its review of curriculum. Seventeen faculty and three students, appointed by the Dean, met with him from the fall of 1967 through 1970. The committee moved, as the final report noted, with "slow deliberation." Struggling to define liberal education in the Jesuit context and working to transcend departmental territorialism, the committee early agreed on two points: that there was need for reform and that, reflecting the conclusions at the Denver Workshop, in working for this reform, the student would be the "center" of Jesuit education and have a responsible role in charting her/his education.

The first year and a half, the committee went to school, reading reports of the Rutgers, Brown, Smith, and Stanford revisions and reductions in their core curricula. Each member tracked decisions made in his/her discipline at other universities. No single model or program was widely accepted; there was, in brief, no Harvard report of 1945. The nationwide pattern that was emerging favored a retention of some distribution in the humanities, social and natural sciences, and a reduction in the number of required courses; a stress on flexibility and legitimacy or relevance, and an emphasis on a responsible student role. It was this pattern that the curriculum revision committee adapted and recommended to the Executive Council of the College and the general faculty.

The reductions were substantial; the modern language and history requirements were dropped; only ten courses were now required. For A.B. students all of the general education courses, except a second course in philosophy and theology, should be completed in the freshman year: two courses in literature, which could be in either English or a foreign language; two courses in mathematics or physical science; two courses in social science, including history as an option; two courses in theology were required now of all students, and two in philosophy (in 1967 the philosophy requirement had dropped from six courses to four). There was a free elective in the freshman year. To increase further the number of elective opportunities, a maximum of thirty-six semester-hours could be required by departments and a maximum of forty-two semester-hours might be taken in the major. Included with the committee report were recommendations and proposals for a new advising program; an interdisciplinary major in American Studies; and individually crafted interdisciplinary majors.

The most intense committee discussions focused on which disciplines should be in the general education core and why. Committee members agreed that, given the knowledge explosion, the curriculum could not attempt to include everything. The theology and philosophy requirements were considered central. Philosophy in its self-study documents was increasingly emphasizing pluralism; while Theology was developing a program, reflective of the recommendations of Vatican II and the Denver Workshop statements, that was increasingly inclusive of other religious traditions. The members of the curriculum committee outside the disciplines of theology and philosophy consistently stressed the centrality of these two subjects to Georgetown's identity as a Catholic, Jesuit college. Just as insistently, the theologian and philosopher on the committee emphasized that theirs should not be seen as the only synthesizing disciplines, and they should not be expected to bear the full weight of the identity question.

History argued that *it* was the last of the synthesizing disciplines and asserted that it should be included with the humanities rather than the social sciences. The French Department argued against dropping the language requirement in a time of increasing interdependence, but won only the agreement that departments might require language proficiency for their majors. Biology and Chemistry developed new courses for the nonscience majors: in Biology, a team-taught offering, Biological Concepts, and in Chemistry, the Scientific Worldview. Both departments insisted heatedly that a laboratory experience was essential. Physics seeking students outside the premedical orbit, offered nonlaboratory courses to fulfill the requirement and gradually won the majority of A.B. students to the physics option. Physical education, meanwhile, was dropped as a requirement for male students in 1969, though retained for the women students now accepted into the College. It was the only curricular notice initially given to the introduction of women.

There had been several faculty meetings over the two-year span with faculty on specific areas; consequently, when the Dean presented the report of the committee to a meeting of the general faculty, in spite of all of the major changes cited above, the major outcry was over a proposal to move toward a 4-4 curriculum. With the charge led by the scientists who argued that they would not be able to fulfill the requirements for accreditation and that this flew in the face of the aim for greater flexibility, other faculty cited the potential increase in teaching-load from nine to twelve semester-hours (since they did not believe that they would be able to offer only two courses a semester). Some who had come from a 4-4 program insisted that it was viable for Georgetown and that it provided greater coherence in a program and greater intensity for the bright student that Georgetown was increasingly winning. In the ensuing firestorm, the committee finally endorsed a flexible 5-5 option, recommending that the Dean work with departments to gradually develop four-credit options at the upper-division level to eventually enable students to carry only a four-course load and hence to have more time for research and reflection.

The model was a distribution model that was distinctive only for its insistence on philosophy and theology for all students. Its emphasis on the student as center and on flexibility and responsible choice would only work well if there was a strong advisory system in place. The major challenge was in the sophomore year, where the breadth endemic to general education goals was insisted upon (no sophomore could elect more than two courses in any one discipline), but Eliot's concern that students would select from courses spread out as at a bazaar seemed pertinent.

The 1971-72 *Bulletin* reported the program changes. The College, it stated, continued the liberal arts tradition "by seeking to develop the student's ability to make judgments and to see relationships. . . . The new curriculum, however, is very flexible in order to allow the student to assume a greater responsibility and initiative in his own educational growth, yet it is structured enough to give him an introduction to the different areas which reflect the different ways that a man thinks, knows and creates."[42] The emphasis was on the how, the methodology of the disciplines, rather than on broad coverage.

Meanwhile, the other undergraduate schools were also revising their curricula. The School of Business Administration, with a revolving-door experience of Deans, dropped the requirement in science for the entering class of 1971, and gave students an option of either history or sociology. Revised concentrations were introduced in accounting, finance, marketing, international business, public administration, and organizational analysis in 1973. A new Dean in 1975 approved of the stress on the "application of ethics, morality and moral theology to the whole area of business."[43] The School of Languages and Linguistics defined its science requirement as including physical or social sciences for the class of 1974. It retained its formative courses in philosophy, theology, history, and English. Most extensive was the revision in the School of Foreign Service with a new Dean and a newly developed core faculty. The new curriculum was achieved after fierce infighting. A draft agenda of reform proposed that all requirements of this multidisciplinary program be compressed into the first two years. Five structured elective divisions were created for the upper classes. Philosophy, theology, and English remained as requirements. The Dean urged each of these departments to craft specific courses to meet the international interests of his students.

By the end of the 1970s each of the schools had completed a curricular revision; each had reduced requirements in its core program, worked for increased flexibility, and been sensitive to relevance and legitimacy. In each school, the changes were brought to a conclusion by new decanal leadership after strenuous consensus building; in each the faculty, responding to leadership, student pressure, and changes in the core nationally, agreed that some change was necessary. None of the changes called for major resource allocation. All were implemented in a time of change and trauma in higher education, in the church, and in the nation. Learning, Faith, and Freedom were all under challenge and in this instance, crisis and challenge brought curricular change.

Georgetown Curriculum Deliberations: A Pause and Promise, 1989

Preparing for a reaccreditation visit from a Middle States team in 1981, Georgetown once again launched a self-study. The opening passages of its introductory overview were written by its new president, Timothy S. Healy, S.J. He began:

> Saul Bellow's Mr. Sammler tells us that when drawing maps it's a good idea always to put the Mississippi River in the same place. He adds that originality is great, but you have to know where you are. Georgetown's Mississippi is its 192 years as a private Catholic and Jesuit college and university.

> For two centuries Georgetown has been private enough to be master in its own house. All private universities share a growing intricacy of ties to the federal government, both by regulations and by federal aid. Despite this, Georgetown's privacy has not in any way substantially diminished. We still sit on our hilltop where John Carroll put us; we are open to all qualified comers, our thrust is ecumenical; and our being is what its being always was.[44]

The self-study steering committee, reflecting that the last visit had occurred in the wake of the Kent State student strike, the agony of Vietnam, and the insistent questioning of the relevance of programs in American higher education, concluded: "In 1981, after a decade of change and growth, undergraduate education at Georgetown is alive and well, with high selectivity evidenced by a record of 8500 applicants for the class of 1985; the average rank of those admitted is in the top 8% of their high school graduating class."[45]

The focus of the self-study of the 1980s, was on the area where Georgetown's reputation and record were not so clearly evident—in its graduate programs and in the articulation of these programs with the professional programs in the medical and law centers. This graduate focus was also evident in the goals and priorities of the first Main Campus Five-Year Plan, 1982-1986. Of the six major goals in that 1982-1986 plan, the third received major emphasis: "to develop recognized national leadership in selected graduate programs consonant with our resources and our goals and objectives." Acting on that goal, departments with graduate programs targeted areas for excellence and detailed the faculty, fellowship, and fiscal resources necessary to achieve that excellence.

The Provost and a committee of faculty and administrators met and corresponded with departments throughout 1982 and 1983. In May, they announced major and controversial decisions, selecting some departments for augmented resources in response to their programs for achieving excellence (History, Chemistry, Linguistics, Arabic, Spanish, Business Administration, Masters programs in Arab Studies and English); some major departments were asked to resubmit proposals (Government, Economics, Philosophy); some graduate programs were suspended (Physics, the other languages, and Russian and Latin America Area Studies Programs [RASP, LASP]).

Faculty who had believed that this process was a win-win review and that, while some might be marked for excellence, no program would be terminated, protested bitterly; the Faculty Senate asked the Board of Directors to rescind the decisions. In the aftermath, and at the behest of the Board of Directors the governance procedures of the Graduate School were revised. Government, Economics, and Philosophy submitted proposals and were brought into the select group of programs for resource support. RASP and LASP rose from the ashes. The years 1984-1985 were years of readjustment and a major effort to institute new courses and revise graduate programs. The emphasis on graduate work and excellence stressed faculty research more than formerly and standards for promotion and tenure, which had been steadily inching forward, reached new heights.

In the midst of this internal churning, the next Five-Year Plan was completed. It called for a review of the core curriculum. Departments were now asked to respond to a question posed by the Provost and the Council of Deans: Given Georgetown's Jesuit and Catholic tradition, its grounding in the liberal arts, and its commitment to intercultural education, what are the skills, knowledge, and wisdom which every Georgetown graduate should have? Each department submitted its own vision of the ideal core and expanded on the contribution of its discipline to that core. The key challenge of this effort was that the question was posed to the faculty and students of *all* of the undergraduate schools. In 1985, when that challenge was issued, the only courses they had in common were two offerings in theology, in philosophy, and English. Could a Georgetown core be developed? Should it? What would it mean for the moats between the schools? What did it portend for the identity of each? What did it suggest for the identity of Georgetown?

As in the 1960s, these questions were posed in the midst of a larger and urgent national debate on undergraduate education for Americans. Higher education, shaken as all institutions by the attacks on authority, and in the tight money years of the 1970s, was increasingly called to account. Of what value was the education provided for American citizens? It was a questioning that had begun on the elementary level and moved up from *Why Johnny Can't Read*[46] to "A Nation at Risk,"[47] a hard look by a national panel of educators at the weaknesses of the programs and teaching of the nation's high schools. It was obvious that higher education was next.

As in 1945, Harvard issued a report and produced a new core curriculum to begin the decade of the 1980s. Once again there was a "red book," Phyllis Keller's sensitive analysis, *Getting at the Core: Curricular*

Reform at Harvard. She opened her book with a quotation from the 1945 report, *General Education in a Free Society*: "General Education perpetuates itself, if only by seeking endlessly to discover what it itself is." She ended her reflections on "A Century of Change" by concluding:

> By the mid-1970s it was clear that there was a growing disposition—often no more than an unfocused yearning—to restore some degree of purpose and coherence to Harvard undergraduate education, to balance liberty with order.[48]

Three major national reports emerged in 1984 and 1985: "Involvement in Learning: Realizing the Potential of American Higher Education," from the Study Group on the Conditions of Excellence in American Higher Education, in October 1984, was quickly followed in November by "To Reclaim a Legacy," written by the chairman of the National Endowment for the Humanities (NEH), William J. Bennett, based on the reflections of a study group on the State of Learning in the Humanities in Higher Education; three months later the Association of American Colleges (AAC) report, "Integrity in the College Curriculum," was issued. While differing on particulars, they formed a unified chorus that the undergraduate core curriculum needed reform.

The most sweeping indictment of "the decline and devaluation of the undergraduate degree" came from the AAC. Their study team found "pervasive evidence that there is a profound crisis." In creating a college curriculum, they testified, "almost anything goes." The only agreement they discovered was on the length of the education, not its content and purpose. Beyond the chaos of the core, they reported neglect and drift in the major fields. Nationwide, the marketplace mentality was widely evident. It was, they concluded, as if no one cared, so long as the store stayed open. Rehearsing the history of higher education—the early authority of tradition, the development of the professional academicians, the departmental control over curriculum, the demands of technology and industry, the accelerating democratization and market demands of a new, large student population—the committee drew a picture of "the dispersal of authority," "the unhappy disarray" and "the loss of integrity in the bachelor's degree."[49]

Though not as sweeping, the report on Humanities in Education, "To Reclaim a Legacy," was more severe and caustic. William Bennett pungently claimed that "what we have on many of our campuses is an unclaimed legacy, a course of studies in which the humanities have been siphoned off, diluted, or so adulterated that students graduate knowing little of their heritage." Faculty had turned away from the "great task of transmitting a culture to its rightful heirs." Majors in the humanities had plummeted dangerously. There was, the report intoned, no "clear vision of what constitutes an educated person." In many colleges, the thickness of the catalogues substitutes for a philosophy of education.[50]

Other warning signals sounded in the text of "Involvement in Learning," a study of how to meet the "trust" of the citizenry. Members of this study team warned of increasing specialization and the barriers to liberal learning from professional accrediting bodies. While colleges struggled to raise standards for "inputs," the report expressed concern that there was insufficient attention dedicated to "outputs." Increased access to higher education, it concluded, "will mean little to the nation at large if its academic institutions offer fragmented, vocational curricula."[51]

These three reports were only the first major shots fired at colleges and universities. Three years later, Ernest L. Boyer, President of the Carnegie Foundation for the Advancement of Teaching, a member of the AAC study group, completed his best seller, *College: The Undergraduate Experience in America*. The central question, he suggested, "is not whether the curriculum selected is old or new, disciplinary or thematic—but whether students are helped to see integration across the disciplines and discover the shared relationship common to all people."[52] He repeated "the growing concern that the pieces of a college education do not add up to a coherent whole."[53]

Each of the reports and the Boyer study suggested solutions for the academic crisis. For the curriculum, the two central words were coherence and integrity. There were some echoes of the 1960s in the AAC acceptance that not everything could be taught, and the insistence that there were "methods and processes, modes of access to understanding and judgment, that should inform all study." The AAC recommended a curriculum that included nine essential experiences: inquiry, abstract logical thinking, critical analysis; literacy, writing, reading, speaking, listening; understanding numerical data; historical consciousness; science; values; arts; international and multicultural experiences; study in depth (urging a careful review of the majors).[54] The Bennett report on the humanities stressed the centrality of the humanities in a curriculum based on original texts. The "Involvement in Learning" report centered on student involvement, high expectations, assessment and feedback. To this end, colleges and universities should reallocate faculty and fiscal resources to the first- and second-year students. Each of the reports and Boyer worried about the specialization of the professoriate and the increasing institutional demands for publication, emphasized the importance of better teaching and better reward for it.

Clearly, as Georgetown's Core Review Committee began its work in the spring of 1986, it did not lack for advice. Each department and the Educational Affairs Committee of the Faculty Senate had access to the 1984 and 1985 reports; the Core Review Committee reread those reports, reviewed Harvard's report and Keller's *Getting at the Core*; surveyed the core curricula of the COFHE schools;[55] discussed the recommendations of each department, and then worked to respond to the central question posed by the Provost: "Given Georgetown's Jesuit and Catholic tradition, its grounding in the liberal arts, and its commitment to intercultural education, what are the skills, knowledge, and wisdom every Georgetown graduate should have?"

All of the undergraduate schools were represented except the School of Nursing, reflecting the curious fact that this school is under the jurisdiction of the Medical Center rather than the Main Campus. Chaired by a Jesuit professor of German, the eleven-member committee included the chairs of the curriculum revision committees of the College and the School of Foreign Service in 1969-70; the Dean of the College; the chair of the Chemistry department, who had devised the Scientific Worldview course; the chair of Sociology; three former chairs of History, Fine Arts, and Philosophy, American Studies, and faculty from Theology and the School of Business Administration. Meeting from April into October, the committee proved a microcosm of the problems in crafting a vision for Georgetown, while remaining sensitive to the individual identity of each school. Each of the schools articulated a commitment to the liberal arts; each cherished the Jesuit and Catholic traditions; yet how did that translate into a curriculum? The substance of the discussion was further complicated by the continuing strains that the drive for graduate excellence placed on faculty; the trend of reduced teaching responsibilities to meet increased research imperatives; the concern over the challenge of a 5-5 course load for our bright students. As in 1970, the question of 4-4 versus 5-5 generated a heated debate.

The Core Review Committee succeeded in hammering out a report in October 1986, which began with a statement on the enormity and the importance of the work. In the decade and a half since the Denver

Workshop and the curricular reforms of the College, Georgetown had accomplished much. But, the report asserted:

> . . . it is precisely our uniqueness and our success that urge to the surface the realization that Georgetown, as a university which seeks to be Catholic, American, and Jesuit all at once, and to be these things late in the twentieth century, and which in addition prides itself on its pluralistic faculty, faces the most serious issues of identity, purpose, and coherence.[56]

All of the key words of the debates of the 1980s were there. The rationale for the recommended core was an eloquent compendium. It opened with a reflection on a number of topics: on including the foundations of Western and non-Western culture, of basic texts and monuments; on encouraging a reflective and critical approach to fundamental assumptions; on fostering analytic and interpretive skills; on exposing the student to complexity within the framework of an integrated vision. To those ends, the committee, while agreeing on areas of knowledge for inclusion in the core, insisted that the "core" knowledge be "knowledge personally acquired and responsibly applied. . . . To acquire knowledge *personally* and to apply knowledge *responsibly* is to be wise, and to apply it *effectively* is to be skillful."[57]

The core areas included: foundational questions (fundamental philosophical and theological issues); natural sciences; literatures and the arts; historical studies; and the social sciences. The committee proposed that every course (as in the Harvard model) offered in the core be developed specifically for the core. Each core course should be taught with the conscious goal of "the reflective, the critical, the personally engaged and responsible student."[58]

To develop and to monitor this new core, the committee suggested five area subcommittees and then a standing core curriculum committee. It urged that faculty teaching in the core should be tenured or with tenure-track appointments; that faculty in the core be supported by stipends to discuss their work during the summer. It also recommended that a committee be established to finally and fully discuss the feasibility of a 4-4 option for Georgetown. With those specifics behind it, the committee ended its report on a hopeful note and with a measure of *eloquentia perfecta*:

> . . . the core, properly planned and implemented, can offer a coherent introduction to the tradition and issues of the intellectual life. It can shape the imaginations of our students in cultural and intercultural ways. And it can see to it that questions of value and of person are centrally present in the curriculum in the only way that makes sense, namely as questions addressed by the major intellectual enterprises that constitute a university.[59]

The report was discussed in the executive councils of the College and the other undergraduate schools and at three general faculty meetings called by the Provost in the spring of 1987. Faculty from the School of Languages and Linguistics were out in force. Where was the language requirement? With the resources and the traditions of Georgetown in intercultural education, and when Congress was ready to appropriate funds to respond to the scandalous weakness in foreign languages in American society and business, why was there no language requirement in the core? Mathematicians asserted that in a world of technology and computers, Georgetown students could ill afford to be mathematically illiterate. Faculty from English worried about their specific pairing with the language departments. Would there be a decline in the interest in writing that they had worked so hard to promote? The School of Foreign Service and the School of Business Administration manned the barricades to stop any movement to 4-4. There was a brief flurry of declamations followed by an immense silence.

Into the Third Century

In 1985, the Provost of Brooklyn College, Ethyle R. Wolfe, who had led the much acclaimed, NEH-supported revision of the core curriculum at her financially beleaguered campus, addressed the Georgetown faculty and shared her formula for success. Her review of nationwide struggles for curriculum revision revealed three essentials to produce change in the core: leadership, a faculty persuaded that change was necessary, and resources. Brooklyn had all three; in the 1970s, Georgetown had the first two; in 1986 and 1987 all three were missing.

The structure of the curriculum review precluded the leadership of the Deans so evident in the earlier revisions. The 1980s review was a Main Campus effort to build a core across schools. While the Dean of the

College was a member of the review committee, he was present as a colleague, not a decanal leader. The Provost's leadership, given the remaining tensions from the Graduate Review, was limited to process, beyond the posing of the central question for consideration.

Faculty, meeting the demands of teaching and research, unconvinced that service was highly rewarded, and still putting the graduate changes in place, did not respond with alacrity to this new undertaking. The Middle States accrediting team had agreed that undergraduate education at Georgetown was alive and well only five years earlier. What was the imperative for change now? More specifically, faculty in the School of Languages and Linguistics wondered if this were another move to erode the position of languages; the School of Business Administration had just won accreditation from the American Assembly of Collegiate Schools of Business; the School of Foreign Service, with a highly structured multidisciplinary curriculum, was not enthusiastic about change, particularly if it involved new requirements or a 4-4 option. More importantly, the faculty did not have a fully fleshed out proposal for consideration. The Core Review Committee recommended areas of knowledge, but the actual crafting of guidelines for core courses and actual development of core courses would only follow in the next committee phase of development. There was no real target for discussion. The concerns expressed at the three faculty meetings centered on specific turf questions and governance (the power of the core committee) rather than on a coherent vision.

Finally, resources were problematic. More than eighty percent tuition-dependent, the Main Campus had just allocated significant resources to the graduate programs. What money was there for any major change in the core? At Brooklyn College, the revision endeavor was handsomely supported by a planning and implementation grant; at Duquesne, NEH and the Pew Foundation supported the planning and implementation for a new core (across schools) with a half-million dollars. External support, as Provost Wolfe noted, builds credibility in the enterprise, buys faculty time for planning, and helps to fully launch the new program. Georgetown did not seek a planning grant.

Yet, in this Bicentennial year, the three essentials, leadership, faculty readiness, and resources are there ready for the marshalling. The University has a new President; the College has a new Dean. The Provost will have the responsibility of working with administrators and faculty in developing the *next* Five-Year Plan for 1991, which coincides with the *next* Middle States reaccreditation visit. The Goals and Objectives Statement of 1981 will have to be seriously reviewed in preparation for both the plan and the visit. It will focus the community forcefully on vision, and on each constituent part of the vision articulated in that statement: "Georgetown is a Catholic and Jesuit University," "Committed to a Tradition of Liberal Education," "Dedicated to the Service of Others," "Extending the Limits of Knowledge," "Building a Sense of Community and Responsibility," "Preparing Citizens and Leaders to Serve Washington, the Nation," "and the International Community."[60]

While the Vatican and American Catholic university leaders have been tensely discussing mission and governance,[61] the Jesuit voice from Rome, Father General Peter-Hans Kolvenbach arrived in June at Georgetown to address Assembly 89, the largest American gathering of Jesuits (over seven hundred) and lay colleagues in higher education ever assembled. Kolvenbach issued a ringing challenge. The central Jesuit priority of the service of faith and the promotion of justice, he asserted, creates "a pressing commitment to reevaluate our colleges and universities, our teaching priorities, our programs, our research efforts to make them more effective."[62]

In the most far-reaching statement since the 1969 Denver Workshop reports, he suggested priorities and possibilities for the third millennium. Jesuit education, he began, "is value-oriented." Jesuit universities "make their essential contribution . . . by embodying in our educational process a rigorous, probing study of crucial human problems and concerns." The complexity of these problems and concerns demands an "integration of inquiry," an interdisciplinary approach. No one discipline can "legitimately pretend to offer comprehensive solutions to real questions" or provide a holistic point of view on genetic research, homelessness, poverty, human rights, the environment, and artificial intelligence.[63] Curricular means to achieve such integration should be sought in the core and in capstone courses for seniors. In summary, he quoted a 1988 report on lay-Jesuit collaboration in this mission, noting "a need for a new *Ratio Studiorum* . . . so that value-centered education evolving out of the ideals of Ignatian spirituality and the Gospels would continue in Jesuit institutions."[64]

The comprehensiveness of a Jesuit education should include outreach to Jesuits in social ministries, to bring their expertise onto campuses and to send student interns and faculty to share in their work. It should be international and intercultural in preparing its students to be global citizens and in cooperative research. It should be alert to ways in which its research and teaching can serve the church, and be especially committed to the preferential option for the poor. Indeed, he observed, Jesuit education "should challenge all of our students to use the option for the poor as a criterion, making no significant decision without first thinking of how it would impact the least in society." All of these recommendations, he concluded, had "serious implications for curricula, for development of critical thinking and values, for interdisciplinary studies for all, for campus environment, for service and immersion experiences, for community."[65]

While the Jesuit leadership was issuing a clarion call for curricular reassessment and change, it also seemed that the second essential to produce change, faculty receptivity, was more in evidence at Georgetown. Certainly, the Jesuit community was charged with the responsibility by Father Kolvenbach to reflect, pray, and plan on ways, within the structures of the university, to work with colleagues to realize more fully the development of Jesuit vision in program and community.

The time that has elapsed since the graduate review, a concern about a possible imbalance between research and teaching, and a commitment to undergraduate education should provide more readiness in all faculty once again to consider liberal education in a Jesuit university. Georgetown's past propensity for curriculum building by opening a new school provides another possibility for faculty readiness. On campus are unparalleled resources for intercultural education in the School of Languages and Linguistics and the School of Foreign Service. The Business School has a special mission to develop international business. The College has a commitment to "value-oriented" education and deep resources in the liberal arts. The first decade of Georgetown's third century is a propitious time for the trumpets of Jericho finally to blow down the walls which close off the exciting possibilities of joining these resources in the liberal arts and intercultural education. Finally, there is a growing concern, as tuition escalates, that Georgetown will become an enclave for the rich. Faculty worry about heterogeneity and are even more committed to the Jesuit mission of educating leaders for service. If an effort by faculty to combine all of these resources and aspirations were externally funded, this, too, would enhance credibility and win internal commitment.

The question of resources is easily resolved. A grant proposal from the oldest Jesuit, Catholic university in the nation, posed at a position of leadership in both Catholic and American higher education, seeking support for curriculum planning that would bring together such rich resources in the liberal arts, intercultural education, ethics, and the Jesuit tradition of service could not fail. It may not prove "a gathered radiance under the night," but it certainly reflects the Denver Workshop's "grand hopefulness," and it would surely advance learning, faith, and freedom in the next century.

Notes

1. Timothy S. Healy, S.J., Faculty Convocation Address, April 27, 1985.

2. Charles L. Currie, S.J., "The Anatomy of a Bicentennial," position paper for fundraising, fall 1987.

3. Andrew M. Greeley, *From Backwater to Mainstream: A Profile of Catholic Higher Education* (New York: McGraw-Hill, 1969), 13.

4. Ibid., 11.

5. Phyllis Keller, *Getting at the Core: Curricular Reform at Harvard* (Cambridge: Harvard University Press, 1982), 1.

6. According to Ignatius's plan, the pupil began the study of classical languages at age ten; at twelve, he began two years of poetry, rhetoric, and history with the objective of obtaining *eloquentia perfecta*; at fourteen, he began the study of philosophy, physics, and mathematics; at seventeen, he received a Bachelor's degree and entered the faculty of law, theology, or medicine. His course of study was completed at age twenty-one. Cf. George E. Ganss, S.J., *Saint Ignatius' Idea of a Jesuit University* (Milwaukee: Marquette University Press, 1954), 45.

7. *The Jesuit "Ratio Studiorum" of 1599*, trans. Allan P. Farrell, S.J. (Washington: Conference of Major Superiors of Jesuits, 1970), 72.

8. Ibid., 66.

9. See John W. Donohue, *Jesuit Education* (New York: Fordham University Press, 1963), 120, note.

10. Ibid., 70.

11. Georges Gusdorf, "L'avènement des sciences humaines au siècle des lumières," (Paris: Payot, 1973), 97.

12. John M. Daley, S.J., *Georgetown University: Origin and Early Years* (Washington: Georgetown University Press, 1957), 220-21, 234.

13. R. Emmett Curran, S.J., "Of Constellations and Unfledged Bodys," draft of chapter 4 of his forthcoming history of Georgetown University, 18-20.

14. Daley, *Origin and Early Years*, 222-24; Edward J. Power, *A History of Catholic Higher Education in the United States* (Milwaukee: Bruce Publishing Co., 1958), 55.

15. *Catalogue of the College, 1905-1906*, 40-41.

16. *Catalogue of the College, 1910-11*, 30.

17. Robert I. Gannon, S.J., *The Poor Old Liberal Arts* (New York: Farrar, Straus & Cudahy, 1961), 198-99.

18. *Catalogue of the College, 1925-1926.*

19. Philip Gleason, "In Search of Unity: American Catholic Thought, 1920-1960," *The Catholic Historical Review* 55 (1979), 196-98.

20. *Catalogue of the College of Arts & Sciences, 1941-1942,* 20-22.

21. Georgetown University Report to the Middle States Association of Colleges and Schools, February 1, 1951.

22. Ibid.

23. "Report of the Inspection of Georgetown University, Washington, D.C., by the Commission on Institutions of Higher Education of the Middle States Association of Colleges and Secondary Schools, February 28-March 3, 1951." The National Catholic Educational Association believed, however, that to present a Catholic culture to undergraduates required a high level of institutional inbreeding. Cf. Gleason, *In Search of Unity,* 198.

24. "The Competence of Georgetown University, as appraised by An Evaluation Team Representing the Middle States Association of Colleges and Secondary Schools, April 1961."

25. *Catalogue of the College of Arts & Sciences, 1962-63,* 10.

26. Ibid., 14.

27. Frederick Rudolph, *Curriculum: A History of the American Undergraduate Course of Study Since 1636* (San Francisco: Jossey-Bass Publisher, 1977), 245, 254-55. Rudolph, 253, summarized the curricular battles of the 1960s: "Breadth, distribution, and general education were the hobby horses of new presidents, ambitious deans, and well-meaning humanists of the sort who were elected to curriculum committees by colleagues as a gesture of token support for the idea of liberal learning. When that gesture collided with the interests of departments and the major field, only occasionally did the general prevail over the special."

28. Lewis B. Mayhew and Patrick J. Ford, *Changing the Curriculum* (San Francisco: Jossey-Bass, 1976), 35-36.

29. Ibid., 37; cf. 13, where the authors recall a point made by Nevitt Sanford that the students were right in many ways. Studies in education, psychology, and sociology all stressed the need of college freshmen to expand "impulsivity." Their first-year curriculum should include courses in literature, philosophy, and the arts, instead of rhetoric, chemistry, and history.

30. Ibid., 8.

31. Rudolph, *Curriculum,* 272.

32. Greeley, *From Backwater to Mainstream,* 19.

33. Greeley, *From Backwater to Mainstream,* 83. Greeley believed that "as Notre Dame goes, so probably goes American Catholic higher education. If American Catholicism is able to produce a viable form of higher education for the new Catholic upper middle class, then Catholic higher education will survive." Ibid., 23. Georgetown was not one of the institutions he focused on in this 1969 study.

34. "Statement on the Nature of the Contemporary Catholic University," 17. The entire Land O'Lakes Statement is reprinted in *Denver Workshop,* 11-17; see n. 36 below. Georgetown was represented by its president, Gerard J. Campbell, S.J.

35. Greeley, *From Backwater to Mainstream,* 75.

36. "Statement on the Distinctive Characteristics of Jesuit Higher Education," in *Guidelines for Jesuit Higher Education: The Consensus Statements, Recommendations, and Committee Reports of the J. E. A. Denver Workshop on Jesuit Universities and Colleges: Their Commitment in a World of Change*, ed. Eugene E. Grollmes, S.J. (Washington, D.C.: Jesuit Educational Association, 1969), 1-10.

37. Ibid., 9.

38. Ibid., 10.

39. Ibid., 31.

40. Ibid., 33-38.

41. Ibid., 41-43. Other major papers on philosophy, theology, social concerns, the students' needs, and Jesuit-lay collaboration provided guidelines and agenda for the future.

42. The College of Arts and Sciences Revised Curriculum is in the University Archives (GUA), CAS, Box 31. Georgetown University *Bulletin*, Undergraduate Schools, 1971-72, 7.

43. Minutes of the Executive Council of the School of Business Administration, (GUA) Box 4, Henle Administration. The school in 1973-74 initiated an M.S. in Accounting and a summer program in London.

44. Self-study, 1981, 1.

45. Self-study, 1981, 1-2.

46. Rudolf Flesch, *Why Johnny Can't Read* (New York: Harper, 1955).

47. The National Commission on Excellence in Education, "A Nation at Risk: The Imperative for Educational Reform," A Report to the Nation and the Secretary of Education (Washington, D.C.: Government Printing Office, April 1983).

48. Keller, *Getting at the Core*, 33.

49. Association of American Colleges, "Integrity in the College Curriculum, Report of the Project on Redefining the Meaning and Purpose of Baccalaureate Degrees," *The Chronicle of Higher Education* 29 (13 Feb. 1985), 12.

50. William J. Bennett, "To Reclaim a Legacy: Text of Report on Humanities in Education," *The Chronicle of Higher Education* 29 (28 Nov. 1984), 16.

51. Study Group on the Conditions of Excellence in American Higher Education, "Involvement in Learning: Realizing the Potential of American Higher Education." See *The Chronicle of Higher Education* 29 (24 Oct. 1984), 35-49.

52. Ernest L. Boyer, *College: The Undergraduate Experience in America* (Cambridge: Harper and Row, 1987), 100.

53. Ibid., 251-52.

54. See "Integrity in the College Curriculum," 12-30.

55. In 1981 Georgetown was invited to join the Consortium on Funding Higher Education [COFHE], a private, highly selective group of about thirty schools. Georgetown is currently the only Catholic member institution.

56. Report of the Core Review Committee, 1. This report was distributed to all Main Campus faculty members by the Provost, 21 Jan. 1987.

57. Ibid., 2.

58. Ibid., 5.

59. Ibid., 6.

60. "The Educational Goals and Objectives of the Georgetown University

Main Campus," 1-5. This statement was the result of lengthy discussions between faculty and administrators. After being circulated to all the departments for comment, it was issued by the Office of the Provost in August 1981.

61. The recent removal of Charles E. Curran from his position as Professor of Moral Theology at Catholic University; the new oath of fidelity, published by the Congregation for the Doctrine of the Faith, which is to be taken by, among others, university teachers of disciplines dealing with faith or morals; and potential interference because of Canon 812 in university hiring, promotion, and tenuring procedures have all contributed to this tension. The Land O'Lakes Statement insisted that the contemporary Catholic university must have "true autonomy and academic freedom in the face of authority of whatever kind, lay or clerical, external to the academic community itself." See *Denver Workshop*, 13. Participants at the Rome meeting in May 1989 reported some progress between the Vatican and university leaders.

62. Peter-Hans Kolvenbach, Address to the U.S. Jesuit Higher Education Assembly at Georgetown University, June 7, 1989, cited from *Origins* 19:6 (22 June 1989), 83.

63. Ibid., 83-84.

64. Ibid., 86.

65. Ibid., 86.

JOHN B. BROUGH
Philosophy Department

Philosophy at Georgetown University

Philosophy has been a constant and usually robust presence at Georgetown since the University's inception. Indeed, throughout most of Georgetown's two hundred years, philosophy enjoyed pride of place in the curriculum: coming at the end of the student's career, it served as the culminating moment of a carefully structured classical education. Philosophy's place in the curriculum is now comparatively diminished. Most students take it in the first year or two of their education, rarely returning to it later; and most take it in quantity so small that their predecessors of only twenty years ago would be astonished. But philosophy is still wedged firmly in the curriculum and is still honored, in every official way, as centrally important to the liberal education in the Catholic and Jesuit tradition that Georgetown intends to provide.

If a subject has had such stature in the curriculum and in some measure still has it, and if—of more importance—it is said that it *should* have it, then one can reasonably seize on the Bicentennial as an occasion for reflection on that subject's place at Georgetown: on the position it held in the past, on its current state, and what prospects its future might hold. This essay attempts to start that reflection. The first section will focus chiefly on the history of undergraduate philosophy at Georgetown and the second on the history of graduate education in philosophy. The third will offer a few observations about the present and future course of the program.

I. Undergraduate Philosophy at Georgetown

THE EARLY YEARS

It is no secret that Georgetown did not spring full blown into existence in 1789; indeed, its first student did not arrive until 1791. Philosophy's appearance was even more tardy. But philosophy was intended from the beginning to be part of the curriculum, although the moment of its actual introduction seems to have been determined less by intellectual principle than by institutional expediency.

As for the intention, a prospectus for the College from 1798 announced plans "for the introduction 'of the study of the higher sciences, as history, moral and natural philosophy.'"[1] Since Georgetown in its initial years enrolled students who pursued what was basically a secondary school curriculum, it was contemplated that the moment of actual introduction of the "higher sciences" would have to wait for the presence of students (and faculty) sufficiently advanced to manage their study.[2]

But it was concern over competition, perceived as possibly fatal, that seems to have prompted the first offering of a course in philosophy. Bishop John Carroll, the guiding force behind Georgetown's founding, had always entertained a vision of two institutions in his diocese: an academy or college that would educate young men of all faiths but would also precipitate vocations to the clergy, and a seminary that would then provide the clerical training.[3] Carroll was determined to develop an indigenous clergy. The first part of Carroll's vision was realized with the opening of Georgetown. The second was put on the way to realization by members of the Sulpician order who, escaping the French Revolution, arrived in Baltimore and opened a seminary there in the 1790s. In the absence of a sufficient number of seminarians, however, the Sulpicians planned to introduce a course in humanities, including philosophy, into the seminary's curriculum.[4] Since Georgetown at this time relied heavily for its faculty on candidates for the clergy, the school's directors feared that, if philosophy were offered in Baltimore but not at Georgetown, the young clerical candidates might abruptly abandon their teaching responsibilities in order to study philosophy at the Sulpicians' seminary.[5] "Georgetown would steadily decline and the 'sanguine expectations formed by the clergy of Maryland in regard of the College . . . providing a sufficient supply of *operarii* in the vineyard of the Lord' would be frustrated."[6]

John Carroll was not convinced that the time was ripe for philosophy's introduction but said that he would give his approval if two conditions were met, one of which he stated as follows: ". . . if there were amongst us a man fit to undertake a course of philosophy, without disgracing himself and the College."[7] Bishop Leonard Neale, Georgetown's president at the time, attempted to bring one or two ex-Jesuits (the order was suppressed during this period) from England to teach the course, but was unable to do so. Instead, Georgetown's first teacher of philosophy was Ambrose Maréchal, a Sulpician, who lectured on metaphysics, ethics, and logic in the fall of 1801.[8] Those enrolled in Maréchal's course were young clerical candidates who intended to go on to the seminary in Baltimore after completing the course at Georgetown.[9]

That philosophy's introduction into the curriculum was immediately tied to the instruction of young candidates for the clergy could be misleading. In point of fact, philosophy's place in Georgetown's curriculum, particularly the undergraduate curriculum, has not been linked primarily with the preparation of the clergy.[10] Indeed, Maréchal, who had only arrived in 1801, was gone at the end of the next school year, and philosophy presumably left the curriculum for a few years with him. According to the *Classical Journal*, however, philosophy reappeared by 1817 at the latest in the form of logic and metaphysics, enrolling about seven "scholars," as they were called at the time.[11] In 1820, Roger Baxter, S.J., an English Jesuit, appears on the faculty roster as "Professor of Philosophy and Prefect of Studies."[12] With Baxter's appointment, one senses that philosophy gets a firm foothold in the curriculum—a foothold it never relinquishes, despite occasional periods of difficulty over the next few years. The course in logic and metaphysics now seems to be required of all those scholars who have advanced to the "higher schools" and seek a degree. In some years during the 1820s and 1830s, philosophy may not have been offered because there were no advanced scholars to take it; and even when it was offered during this period, course enrollments could be quite low. But there seems to have been no question that philosophy became the crowning course of the curriculum and the final step that anyone who aspired to a Georgetown A.B. would have to take.[13]

By way of illustration, consider that in the fall of 1821 only two students were enrolled in Baxter's philosophy course. Enough is said about them in the *Classical Journal*, however, to tell us a good deal about the status of philosophy and the way in which the subject was taught at the time. The following statement from the "Report of the

Compositions and Examinations" for the fall term, written by Baxter in his capacity as Prefect of Studies and read before the whole community on December 22, 1821, is worth quoting in full for what it tells us about the place of philosophy in particular and about the atmosphere of the school in general early in the nineteenth century:

> In speaking of the philosophers, I could employ the highest terms of approbation, but I feel that they are actuated by nobler motives, than the little official praise which I can give them here. If their future conduct in life correspond with the solid application, which they have given both to moral and natural philosophy during this short term, if they afterwards judge of what is truly honorable for themselves, by the same principles which have lately directed them in the employment of their time, every one in the circle of their future acquaintance will unite in the commendation. . . . The place which I hold forbids flattery, and I must not be conversant in it. These praises will wear well, for they have been dearly earned.[14]

On July 29 of the following year, the two students enrolled in philosophy received their degrees: "On this day Messrs. Jas. F. Faulkner, Va. and Lewis W. Jenkins, having finished their course of natural and moral philosophy, received the degree of A.B. . . . "[15] From the 1820s onward, getting a degree and passing through the "Class of Philosophy" were virtually synonymous at Georgetown, which suggests that philosophy was viewed as something more than one requirement among many.

Faulkner and Jenkins also received awards when they graduated, the character of which tells us something about what was required at the time of students in philosophy. Faulkner won the prize "for the best treatise in natural and moral philosophy," and Jenkins received the award "for the best defense of theses in natural and moral philosophy."[16] The "treatise" and the oral "defense of theses" were standard requirements for decades; oral examinations in philosophy, in fact, would continue to be required of all juniors and seniors in the College until well into the 1960s.

Throughout much of the nineteenth century the "Senior Classes"—that is, the students in the higher school—first pursued humanities, followed in order by poetry, rhetoric, and, in the final year, philosophy. In 1850, students "in philosophy" studied logic, metaphysics, and ethics. Lectures were delivered in Latin, an examination on the lecture was given daily, and once a month the students had "public exercises before the faculty, to test their improvement."[17] This was a taxing regimen, and one senses from the slight changes in requirements that adjustments had to be made to accommodate the ability and stamina of the students. In 1852, for example, the daily examination on the lecture is replaced by "a daily discussion (in Latin) . . . on the lecture."[18] Only a year later we read:

> In order to consult the interests of the students of this class and to prepare them for their future professional career, the exercises have been enlarged and varied by introducing English Dissertations on the various subjects of philosophy, in addition to the regular discussions in Latin.[19]

Such efforts to make the course in philosophy less esoteric and demanding reflected a certain urgency, since during this period the Senior Department (roughly equivalent to undergraduate school) enrolled a fairly small number of students, and few of these persevered through the final year in philosophy and actually obtained a degree—only seven in 1851, for example. Still, the course in philosophy could not be escaped. The catalogue of 1850-51 makes it plain, as Georgetown catalogues will for the next 115 years, that the curriculum for students is laid out in advance and that there will be no deviation from it, "as experience has proved exemptions in this regard to have been a great source of idleness."[20]

What sort of treatises or dissertations did students in philosophy undertake at this time? The announcements of public defenses of dissertations, part of the exercises held immediately before commencement, suggest a rich array of topics. On July 6, 1858, for example, Beverly C. Kennedy of Louisiana defended his dissertation on "The foreknowledge of God Not Incompatible with the Liberty of Man." The titles of the other three dissertations for that year were "The Brute Soul," "The Origin of Evil," and "The Internal Possibility of Things."[21] A year later students were writing on topics such as the principle of causality, space, the origin of language, and the ontological argument for the existence of God. The diversity of topics suggests a course of study that was fairly broad. It also indicates that the curriculum in philosophy was a version of the mix of rationalism and Scholasticism that had prevailed in seminaries and church-related educational institutions since the seventeenth century. Frederick

Copleston describes this "rather wishy-washy eclecticism"[22] as "an emasculated Scholastic Aristotelianism, tinctured with ideas taken from other currents of thought, especially Cartesianism," and largely out of touch with contemporary philosophical and scientific developments.[23]

Thin as it may have been, this philosophical gruel inspired some students to titanic efforts. For example, the announcement of the "Annual Termination of the Course of Rational and Moral Philosophy" for 1863 included the following: "All the main topics of Rational Philosophy, and the Fundamental Principles of Ethics, will be defended in English, or Latin—by William L. Hirst, *Pennsylvania*."[24] Needless to say, Hirst won the philosophy medal that year.

THE RISE OF SYSTEMATIC SCHOLASTICISM

The form of the curriculum in philosophy remained fairly constant until 1900. In the early 1820s the list of philosophical subjects covered was logic, ontology (or metaphysics), and natural theology. In 1868, "the course of RATIONAL PHILOSOPHY includes LOGIC, METAPHYSICS, and ETHICS."[25] It is probable that natural theology was not simply dropped but incorporated into metaphysics when ethics was introduced.

The content of these three courses, however, may have undergone some change around 1870. The catalogue for 1869-70 lists for the first time the textbooks used in "rational philosophy": "Liberatore's Logic and Metaphysics.—Jouin's Ethics."[26] Matteo Liberatore (1820-72) was an Italian Jesuit who taught at the Gregorian University in Rome and was one of the early figures in the Neoscholastic movement in Italy in the nineteenth century, as was Tongiorgi (1820-65), whose texts were used in conjunction with or in place of Liberatore's during this period. Louis Jouin (1818-99) was an American Jesuit writing in the Scholastic tradition. While these textbooks were written in Latin and certainly belonged to the philosophical genre known as the Scholastic "manual," they were probably of higher quality than the eclectic Scholasticism that Copleston found so unsatisfactory. Still, they predated Leo XIII's encyclical *Aeterni Patris* of 1879, which urged that the thought of Thomas Aquinas be taken as a guide by Catholic philosophers, and did not represent fully "Neoscholastic" or "neo-Thomist" texts. Later editions of Jouin, following the encyclical, added references to the works of Aquinas, but one gets the impression that these were basically cosmetic changes laid over what was essentially a Scholastic manual of the sort intended originally for use in seminaries.[27]

The works adopted around 1870 would, therefore, probably be subject to the criticisms of Brother Azarias, F.S.C. (Patrick Francis Mullaney), who wrote in 1888 that courses in Catholic colleges prior to the final year in philosophy had been "carried out upon exclusively seminarian lines," and then "to these is added a course of some text book giving the essentials of scholastic philosophy with or without explanation. The whole trend of modern thought is ignored . . ."[28] Furthermore, the texts continued to be used for an extraordinarily long period of time, leaving one with the impression that for decades philosophy at Georgetown was not so much perennial as simply frozen. The scholastic text by Georgetown professor Nicholas Russo, S.J., for example, in use by 1886, continued to be assigned as late as 1921, almost twenty years after its author's death.[29] Although Russo's two-volume manual was called "probably the most valuable"[30] of the scholastic texts written by Jesuits in the late nineteenth century, its longevity says something about the constancy of the systematic content of the philosophy courses at Georgetown and about their dependence on the manual format.

Against this somewhat bleak picture of the stasis into which philosophy had fallen by the end of the century, one might balance the following pedagogically reasonable statement from the catalogue of 1889:

> The last year of the course serves especially to discipline the reasoning faculties by the study of Logic, Metaphysics, and Ethics, and by higher studies in Mathematics and Natural Sciences. During this year great attention is given to Metaphysics, a thorough knowledge of which is regarded as of the utmost importance, since it serves to arrange systematically all the student's knowledge and to furnish the key to all true science. Whatever is important in Natural Science is made part of the curriculum and is taught with a philosophical analysis intended to guard the student against that confounding of mere information with learning that is the danger of modern education.[31]

In 1900, the philosophy curriculum was revised and expanded to nine courses. Seniors took psychology, natural theology, ethics (general and special), and the history of philosophy; juniors took cosmology, general metaphysics, first principles of knowledge, dialectics, and the history of philosophy.[32] This elaborate set of courses represents systematic Scholastic philosophy in full bloom. It still maintains the spirit of the earlier and simpler curriculum—logic, metaphysics, ethics—that had prevailed throughout most of the century. But it signals by its baroque form that Georgetown has begun to adopt the complex course structure (though without electives) that was becoming increasingly characteristic of the modern college or university, while simultaneously attempting to conform to the church's determined support of Scholastic philosophy following Leo XIII's encyclical of 1879. To be sure, Georgetown's curriculum, like that at other Catholic colleges at the time, remained based on Scholastic manuals and was not leavened by a careful study of the writings of St. Thomas himself, which Leo's encyclical had particularly urged upon Catholic philosophers.

The form the curriculum assumed in 1900 would remain basically the same for the next sixty years. Georgetown had now entered fully into the era of systematic Neoscholasticism. What precisely did this mean in terms of the life of the student and of the College? It meant that each student would take as many as thirty-two credits in philosophy. It meant, too, that philosophy was intended to play an integrating role in the student's educational experience. This aim was already set down in 1889. Although that particular formulation disappears from the catalogues by 1895, there can be no question that the integrating function continues to be a principal reason for philosophy's presence in the curriculum for the next six or seven decades.

The declaration of 1889 certainly had in view a Scholastic approach to philosophy, but it did not directly mention Scholasticism and expressed no self-conscious concern for faithful adherence to a particular kind of philosophy. By the end of the century, however, as we have seen, Scholasticism had clearly begun to assume an official standing: "As Catholic higher education developed, its distinguishing characteristic would be philosophy and by the end of the nineteenth century, this meant scholastic philosophy."[33] And as the twentieth century progressed through its early decades, "neo-Thomistic philosophy became almost synonymous with Catholic thought."[34] Thus in the catalogue of the "Graduate Division" of 1932-33, Scholasticism is mentioned frequently, and there can be found the following description of a set of two courses in the "Fundamentals of Scholastic Philosophy," which might equally serve as a description of the entire undergraduate program at the time. The courses, we are told, are designed to give an overview with emphasis on that trait which is unique in Scholasticism: "its organic unity, as an all embracing rational philosophy of life."[35] The description goes on:

> Care is taken . . . that no lacunae occur, which would blur the lines of the system as a whole and thus impair for the student the cultural value to be gained from contact with the most highly organized body of thought known to the history of philosophy.[36]

No doubt Scholasticism's "organic unity" is stressed because it endows Scholasticism with the capacity to integrate the student's personal and academic experience. But one cannot miss three other elements in this statement: first, a concern that nothing happen in the student's philosophical education that would stand in the way of his absorption of the system in its integrity; second, a conviction that Scholastic philosophy has a unique cultural value; third, an implied assertion of Scholastic philosophy's superiority among philosophical approaches.

The elements of cultural value and philosophical superiority are explicitly confirmed in the College catalogue of 1935-36:

> . . . The goal of a liberal education is culture, mental as well as moral development, and learning as such is a means toward that end. . . . The Jesuit system of education holds that a solid course in Scholastic Philosophy, based on a foundation of languages, both Ancient and Modern, History, Mathematics, and the Natural Sciences, has cultural advantages far superior to those offered by other Educational systems.[37]

Given the conviction that a particular kind of philosophy offers singular educational advantages, it is no surprise that all students were required to pursue a standard curriculum that did not and could not allow electives. Exemptions to the specified course of studies (along with the chewing of tobacco) were explicitly proscribed, as we have seen, as early as 1850,[38] and in 1935 the principle of "adherence to a fixed program of studies [that] . . . excludes the evils attendant on the elective system"[39] is strongly reaffirmed. Scholastic philosophy was the centerpiece and by far the largest portion of this fixed program. Its importance was signaled by the fact that, with rare exceptions, philosophy remained the first subject (or department, when the departmental system is introduced)[40] listed in the catalogue until the mid-thirties. And even when philosophy was relegated to its proper alphabetical position, its preeminent place was unthreatened for at least another twenty years, when the changes began that led to philosophy's current position in the curriculum.

THE DECLINE OF SCHOLASTICISM

The forces leading to philosophy's present situation have a long and complicated history, but events that occurred in the 1950s certainly played a determining role. Chief among these was the influx of lay faculty members. In the early fifties, the College undergraduate faculty in philosophy was composed almost exclusively of Jesuits, most of whom did not have a doctorate in the field. By 1959 they had been joined by a number of lay faculty members, including Wilfrid Desan, Louis Dupré, Germain Grisez, Jesse Mann, Thomas McTighe, and Rocco Porreco.[41] Rudolf Allers and John Callahan are listed only on the graduate faculty at this date, but were important influences in shaping the department. All of these held the doctorate in philosophy. All were Catholic, and most had done their graduate work at Catholic universities (Desan, however, studied at Harvard, Callahan and Grisez at Chicago). Many, but not all, were in one degree or another committed to the philosophy of Thomas Aquinas. What chiefly distinguished them was that they had received a professional graduate education in the field. Whatever their religious commitments and philosophical predilections may have been, they brought new standards of scholarship and professionalism to the department. They also brought interest and expertise in the objective study of the history of philosophy, in contemporary nonscholastic continental thought, in certain areas of American philosophy, and—in the case of those committed to Thomism—in the careful study of the texts of Aquinas himself. It was no surprise, then, that the fixed Scholastic curriculum began to loosen and, after about a decade, disappeared entirely.

The decline of Scholasticism was not a phenomenon unique to Georgetown; it happened, to greater or less degree, in most major Catholic universities and colleges in this country and abroad. There is, it must be said, much that is poignant about it. Frederick Copleston could write in 1955: "Today the philosophy of Aquinas occupies a favored position in the intellectual life of the Catholic Church."[42] And by that he meant more than that Thomism simply enjoyed a kind of official sanction; he meant that it was a vital and developing movement, "deriving its inspiration from Aquinas but conducting its meditation on his writings in the light of subsequent philosophy and of subsequent cultural developments in general."[43] But nineteen years later he writes: "Given the changed situation, it is arguable that the impetus of the Thomist revival is spent."[44] And why? The church no longer seems interested in promoting a particular philosophical approach: ". . . the Second Vatican Council was careful not to make pronouncements in the philosophical area."[45] Furthermore, significant changes have taken place in theology, which have turned it away from Thomism as a source of philosophical support. And then there has been ". . . the natural reaction in Catholic colleges and seminaries to past indoctrination in what amounted to a Thomist party line. . . ."[46]

As the allegiance to Scholasticism as a superior philosophical and educational instrument evaporated, both within the church and within the Jesuit order, philosophy's role and position within the University inevitably underwent change.

The most obvious manifestation of the change was the rapid decline in the number of courses required in the field. In 1962, twenty-five hours of philosophy were required of all undergraduates in the College. Modified Scholastic course titles remained largely in place, although, depending on the instructor, the content of the courses often had little or nothing to do with Scholasticism or the thought of Aquinas. The twenty-five hours required consisted of specified courses; no electives were allowed. All students in the College still sat for oral comprehensive examinations in philosophy at the end of junior and senior years—an ancient practice that came to an end over the next two years. In 1963, the number of required hours was reduced to eighteen, and philosophy was introduced into freshman year for the first time. In 1967, the requirement in philosophy in the College was further reduced to twelve hours. Finally, in the general curriculum revision implemented in 1970, the philosophy requirement was reduced to two three-credit courses, which is where it presently stands. The two courses, Introduction to Philosophy and Problems of Value (now Ethics), would normally be taken in freshman and sophomore years.

In about ten years, then, the grand philosophical edifice that dominated the curriculum for so much of Georgetown's history was dismantled. Philosophy was no longer the crowning moment of the student's undergraduate career, as it had been for Mr. Faulkner and Mr. Jenkins in 1822. It came at the beginning of undergraduate study and constituted only a small fraction of the student's total experience across four years.

The decline of Neoscholasticism did not play the only role in this change—Georgetown's efforts to construct a more modern and comprehensive curriculum were essential factors in it—but it played a key role. Scholastic philosophy enjoyed its dominant position in the curriculum because it was understood to be the force integrating the student's entire education. With the demise of Scholasticism, philosophy at Georgetown effectively abandoned its role—at least its official and exclusive role—as the integrating discipline.[47] The end of its synthesizing function effectively removed the justification for philosophy's dominant place in the curriculum. Its shrinkage to a two-course requirement, located in freshman and sophomore years, should come as no shock, then.

Still, philosophy—and theology as well—were accorded special standing during the curriculum revision of 1970. Even if philosophy no longer performed the function it once did, it is still seen to be an integral part of a Jesuit education. The College continued to affirm its "commitment to liberal knowledge" and to hold that philosophy is among the subjects giving the student "the opportunity to avoid narrowness of mind and intellect."[48] In 1970, when philosophy and theology come to be listed together under "General Education Requirements," the following justification appears:

> Philosophy and Theology
>
> All students will take a year of Philosophy and a year of Theology since Georgetown feels by its commitment to the Jesuit tradition that the modern man and woman should consider seriously their relationship to God and their fellow man.[49]

The changes that have affected the undergraduate program in philosophy over the past twenty-five years have been immense, then, yet the subject itself has survived and, even in diminished form, remains at the center of the curriculum.

Now, to get a more complete sense of what philosophy at Georgetown has become in the "postscholastic" era, it will be helpful to look at the history of the graduate program.

II. Graduate Study in Philosophy

THE EARLY YEARS: BEFORE THE 1930s

Sorting out the origins and early years of graduate education in philosophy at Georgetown is a difficult task. Compared to the steady presence of undergraduate philosophy in the curriculum, graduate education had the quality of an anemic phoenix for well over a century. A thing of fits and starts, it finally settled into a state of modest prosperity only in fairly recent times.

The *Classical Journal* notes that James Faulkner and Lewis Jenkins, who received their bachelor's degrees in 1822, could have received Master of Arts degrees and had the right to ask for them after one year.[50] Given the fact that the final year before the granting of the bachelor's degree was devoted to moral and natural philosophy, the master's degree in question could be considered essentially a degree in philosophy and science. In later catalogues, no mention is made of this early period of graduate education—assuming that it really deserves to be called that—until 1949, when the *Graduate Bulletin* states that "mathematics and philosophy were the first fields opened to higher studies" and that a Master of Arts degree was awarded to the Reverend John Fairclough on July 27, 1821.[51]

The next mention of advanced work in philosophy occurs in the 1850s. The "Catalogue of Students" for 1855-56, for example, includes a new section—"Resident Graduates"—with four names and the notation that their class is the "2d course of Philos'y."[52] The catalogue of 1906-07, in a less ambitious genealogical claim for the graduate program than the one cited above from 1949, refers to these four students in asserting that the Graduate School "was in existence as early as 1856, in which year it comprised four resident graduates. It has continued with varying degrees of success since that time."[53] Since these four students were apparently studying philosophy, it seems only mildly outlandish to claim that the birth of graduate education in philosophy at Georgetown coincided precisely with the birth of the Graduate School itself.

Whatever one thinks of that proposition, however, there is little doubt that the new arrival took its time in maturing. One step along this path seems to have occurred in the 1890s. A distinct "Department of Philosophy" emerged within the Graduate School, and catalogues (in 1897-98, for example) began to publish quite detailed accounts of the contents of graduate courses in philosophy.[54] In addition, *all* graduate students in whatever field were required to take a course in "rational philosophy"[55]—a practice that continued (only the name of the course changing) into the 1960s.

It is unclear how successful the program in philosophy was in the nineties. As a remarkable sketch of the history of the Graduate School indicates, the period from 1891 to 1907 formed sixteen years of effort to build the graduate program as a whole.[56] That the success of these efforts proved to be modest is suggested by some rather startling announcements. We are told first that all scholarships were withdrawn in 1905-06. In the next academic year admissions standards were changed, requiring new graduate students to have an educational background more closely resembling the one received by undergraduates in the College. Furthermore, resident graduate students were made subject to the same strict regulations governing undergraduate students. The result? ". . . In 1907-8, no graduate students have matriculated."[57] Hence, no graduate courses were offered—not just in philosophy but in any field. No doubt the changes in standards and regulations stemmed from a desire to tighten and reform the program—many of the "graduate students" seem in fact to have been imported athletes whose academic credentials and standards of behavior were questionable[58]—but it does seem in this case that the baby was thrown out with the bath water.

For a number of years after the dramatic events recounted above, the Georgetown catalogue assured its readers that if enough eligible students applied for the coming year, graduate courses would be offered. It is not until 1914, however, that the Graduate School actually rises again, this time with its own Dean and professors appointed annually. Of the five departments in the school, philosophy is listed first in the catalogue and has the most lengthy course description.[59] Indeed, during the 1920s, the number of graduate courses in philosophy grows dramatically, reaching eighteen by 1925, including seven courses in ethics.[60] Among these were several that were devoted to specific themes and that we might now term courses in "applied" ethics. The range of topics these sections covered was remarkable: the morality of strikes and lockouts, the family, the press, war, intervention, and so on. These courses, and one offered in international ethics in 1921-22,[61] probably reflect the same institutional concerns that culminated in the founding of the School of Foreign Service in 1919. The emphasis on ethics reached its peak (at least before the present era) when, in the catalogue of 1925-26, a separate "Department of Ethics" with eight courses is listed.[62] By the end of the decade, however, the Department of Ethics has disappeared and only seven graduate philosophy courses are offered.[63] One suspects that the outpouring of activity in the mid-twenties did not meet with much more real success than the flurry of activity just before the turn of the century.

THE 1930s

The graduate curriculum was basically Scholastic during the period before 1930, although there is no explicit statement to that effect until 1932, when students in the program were required to have, or develop the equivalent of, an undergraduate background in Scholastic philosophy.[64] The graduate program itself included two courses in "Fundamentals of Scholastic Philosophy" that were highly and self-consciously systematic, affording the student the opportunity to appreciate Scholasticism's unique "cultural value" as "an all embracing philosophy of life"[65] and as "the most highly organized body of thought known to the history of philosophy."[66] The curriculum of the graduate program in philosophy, therefore, reflects the important role given to Scholasticism as an integrating force in Catholic intellectual and academic life during the 1920s and 1930s.[67] The program did include courses that were not rigidly Scholastic, however, and perhaps even pointed in nonscholastic—although still Catholic—directions. Thus Francis Burke, S.J., offered a seminar with the title "The New Humanism," which considered contemporary Catholic thinkers, such as Blondel, with the immediate purpose of providing "a metaphysical background for a Catholic new humanism."[68]

These statements from the early 1930s suggest that Georgetown had designs on becoming a significant force in graduate philosophy within specifically Catholic circles. Nothing, however, comes of these designs. In fact, graduate philosophy soon disappears entirely from the Georgetown campus. A solitary and cryptic message in the 1935 catalogue under the heading "Department of Philosophy" adumbrates this extraordinary occurrence: "Announcement will be made later."[69] What was later announced—in language so obscure that one wonders whether it was not willful—was that the Graduate Department of Philosophy had moved to Woodstock College in Maryland and that matriculation was restricted to members of the Society of Jesus. This dramatic turn of events occurs only three years after the confident pronouncements concerning the cultural value of Scholasticism and the possibility of building a new Catholic humanism.

THE POSTWAR YEARS

But in 1944 the phoenix rises again—along with the first truly straightforward statement about what had been going on during this period:

> Formerly this Department [Philosophy] was located at Woodstock College and available exclusively to members of the Society of Jesus. . . . It is now proposed to offer [graduate] courses in philosophy on the Georgetown campus and to open them to the general public.[70]

The entrance requirements were made quite stiff, although "special students" were allowed. What is said about the kind of special student the new program had in view indicates that the idea of a department with a self-consciously Catholic thrust, suggested in the early thirties, is still very much alive. Thus the special students the program sought would be those who "wish to deepen their culture or integrate their knowledge with the principles of Catholic thought and action."[71] This kind of declaration illustrates nicely that Georgetown supplied no exception to the general emphasis in American Catholic higher education during the twenties, thirties, and forties on culture integrated through specifically Catholic principles.

But the statement concerning special students, comparatively mild as it is, hardly prepares one for the dramatic and aggressively Catholic description of the graduate program that appears the next year. This description, given in its entirety below, is a fascinating sociological artifact; it also describes one of the ancestors—albeit a most sectarian one—of the contemporary program.

> Founded in 1944 as the Institute of Christian Philosophy, the Department proposes as its special field of research the relationship of philosophy to Christian revelation. Hence in addition to the conventional divisions of systematic philosophy and the history of philosophy, stress is laid upon the history of that relationship, its theoretic justification, the consequences of excluding revealed truths from the realm of rational speculation, and a study of those modern philosophies which stem ultimately from an erroneous interpretation of revelation. The program also includes analyses of modern culture, modern economic, political and social theories, modern art, drama and music, education, the physical sciences and mathematics. The intention will be to discover the force of Christian inspiration in these activities, as well as the philosophic confusions arising from certain interpretations of that inspiration.[72]

The Graduate Department of Philosophy, which was distinct in personnel and even in location from the Undergraduate Department, had three regular members and one visiting professor in 1945. The Chairman, who was also Dean of the Graduate School, was J. Hunter Guthrie, S.J. Joseph Durkin claims that it was only in the mid-forties that the Graduate School finally managed to establish itself on a firm basis, and that this occurred through the efforts of Hunter Guthrie.[73] It may equally be said that it was Guthrie who initiated the evolution of the graduate program in philosophy toward the form it now has. Guthrie did his graduate work at the Sorbonne and was conversant with the main trends of contemporary continental philosophy, including the thought of Nietzsche, Kierkegaard, Husserl, Heidegger, and Scheler, among others. With faculty members such as Guthrie involved in it, the curriculum of the "Institute of Christian Philosophy" was, therefore, not closed to twentieth century influences. On the other hand, course descriptions from the period suggest that contemporary thought was often explicitly related to the Scholastic tradition. For example, in 1946 it is said in the description of a course in the philosophy of science that, when the thought of such contemporaries as Duhem, Cassirer, Carnap, and Whitehead is taken up, "the purpose of the discussion will be to see the vital relation between the teaching of Aristotle and St. Thomas and these new doctrines."[74] One senses in a statement such as this the desire to create a Catholic intellectual culture that is open to the contemporary world but seeks to come to grips with it in terms of a tradition that has its roots in the Middle Ages and classical antiquity.

The strongly Catholic description of the Institute of Christian Philosophy disappears from the catalogue after two years. The fact that the department was founded as the Institute is still mentioned but the project of the Institute—the consideration of contemporary intellectual and cultural issues "in the light of the principles of Christian philosophy"[75]—is now listed together with the history of philosophy and systematic philosophy as things the program aims at doing. The description of the courses in the history of philosophy is particularly interesting, given the role of history in the department's subsequent development: "Courses in the history of philosophy emphasize the reading and interpretation of the texts of the leading philosophers and attempt to show the position of each in the philosophical tradition."[76] The department has five members in 1947, including John Callahan, whose career at Georgetown will extend for thirty years.

The form of the description is revised further in 1949, although its substance remains for the most part unchanged. Four areas are now mentioned. History of philosophy is one of them. The term "systematic" is no longer used in connection with any area. Instead, it is said that "courses in the treatment of the basic problems of philosophy from Hellenism to and including Neo-Scholasticism"[77] are offered. A third area is "applied philosophy," and it is here that "the principles of a Christian humanistic critique" still find a place. The fourth area, psychology and psychiatry, reflects the interests of Rudolf Allers, a philosopher and psychiatrist, who came from Catholic University to join the department at this time.

Over the next few years, the graduate department remained small, numbering three faculty members. In 1954, Professors Thomas McTighe and Rocco Porreco appear. Their arrival signals the beginning of a period of steady growth that leads directly to the present. It is in this year as well that a new and short program description appears that makes no mention of Christian philosophy or Christian humanism. Two areas of courses are cited: the history of philosophy and the problems of philosophy. The latter category continues to tip its hat to the Scholastic tradition: the courses are still described as treating "the basic problems in philosophy from Hellenism to and including Neo-Scholasticism."[78] But even that description goes two years later, when it is said that the department offers "courses on the basic problems of philosophy in systematic presentation and their historical development to our times."[79] One could argue plausibly that with this slight change the department has now become thoroughly "modern." Certainly, the change from the description of the Institute of Christian Philosophy only a decade earlier could hardly be more vivid. There is no immediate clue in the new language to suggest that the program has any sort of Jesuit and Catholic character. But to conclude that it did not would be a mistake. For the most part, members of the faculty continued to have a background in Scholastic philosophy received at other Catholic universities, a fact that was often reflected in the curriculum. And although most members of the graduate faculty were not Jesuits, they were Catholics—something that would continue to be the case into the seventies.

By 1959, the graduate faculty had grown to ten, now including Jesse Mann (who had been on the undergraduate faculty in the School of Foreign Service),[80] Wilfrid Desan, Germain Grisez, and Louis Dupré (George Farre arrived a year later). The Chair was Thomas McTighe. A year before, even the brief statement of the purpose of the graduate program had disappeared from the catalogue; only the listing of courses with their descriptions remained. At the same time, the Undergraduate and Graduate Departments had clearly begun to merge. Although the two departments were still being distinguished in the catalogue as late as 1960, the graduate faculty (with the exception of Rudolf Allers) had begun to be cross-listed in the undergraduate faculty two years before, reflecting the fact that graduate faculty members were also teaching undergraduates. In 1960, Professor McTighe became Chair of both departments, another indication of their merger. Furthermore, the two departments, which had been geographically distinct, now came to be located together in the Nevils Building.

FROM THE SIXTIES TO THE PRESENT

By the early sixties, then, the department had completed a period of considerable growth and evolution. It may be considered as a single unit serving graduate students as well as students from all five undergraduate schools. Its Chair is not a Jesuit. Furthermore, although the merger of graduate and undergraduate departments meant that there was a Jesuit presence in the department at this time, it was not a strong presence, either in terms of numbers or of influence. It would, in fact, be fair to say that the lay faculty, all of whom were Catholics, dominated the department in every respect from the early sixties on. The Jesuit presence became progressively weaker until, during certain periods in the seventies and eighties, the department had no Jesuit faculty members at all. The latter circumstance reflected changing conditions within the Society of Jesus rather than any hostility on the part of the lay members of the department. On the other hand, with the exception of the occasional Jesuit in training, such as Otto Hentz or David Hollenbach, who taught briefly in the department in the sixties, the era was now past in which Jesuits, usually without the doctorate, could simply be assigned to the faculty. (Although the department has what can now best be described as an "affirmative action" program for the hiring of Jesuits, Jesuit candidates must meet the department's standards if they are to be recommended for appointment. The department currently has two Jesuit faculty members out of nineteen, although the primary appointment of one of these is in the Kennedy Institute of Ethics.)

Some Catholic departments of philosophy experienced intense internal conflict during this period over the position and role of scholastic philosophy. Allowing for the influence of the general cultural climate, the issue was decided at Georgetown, as I noted in the last section, largely by the influx of lay faculty members who, while Catholic and often trained in scholastic thought, nonetheless had scholarly interests and standards different from those that had prevailed in earlier decades. On the graduate level, this was reflected in a curriculum in the sixties and seventies that did not stress Scholasticism at all. In fact, the emphases of the department came to settle on two areas: the history of philosophy and continental thought of the nineteenth and twentieth centuries.

As David Tracy has remarked, Catholic scholars tended to turn towards the history of their field following the decline in the hegemony of neo-Thomism.[81] With the passing of Scholasticism, the movement of the department at Georgetown was not towards an embracing of the mainstream of contemporary Anglo-American philosophy, nor was it finally in the direction of a new Catholic humanism suggested in the brave statements of the mid-forties. The "tradition" had now become the tradition of the field itself, its history. At the same time, when contemporary philosophy was taken into account, it was mainly the European line that had run from Hegel through Kierkegaard and Nietzsche and on to the phenomenologists and existentialists of the twentieth century. I do not think that it would be an exaggeration to say that both emphases were viewed as "Catholic" in some sense. This was reasonable enough, given the fact that most American universities at this time—and particularly the best known research institutions, with the exception of the University of Chicago—stressed neither the history of philosophy nor continental thought. Indeed, they were often indifferent to the first and usually openly hostile to the latter.

Furthermore, there was a perception among most of the lay faculty that the dominant trends in Anglo-American philosophy were antimetaphysical and, therefore, implicitly and sometimes explicitly, antireligious, or at least dismissive of questions concerning religion and transcendence as of any relevance to philosophy. Thus, while the most influential thought in Anglo-American philosophical circles barely made its presence felt in the program throughout most of the sixties, the Georgetown curriculum offered a fairly steady array of courses that included continental theistic philosophers, such as Kierkegaard and Marcel, and continental atheistic philosophers, such as Sartre and Nietzsche. That the latter could be included in the curriculum, both undergraduate and graduate, at a Jesuit university no doubt reflected the opening-up of American Catholic higher education that had begun in the fifties; but it also reflected the conviction that the continental philosophers, whether atheist or not, took seriously the great metaphysical questions in a way that the "analytic philosophers," who dominated the American philosophical scene, and who by and large were identified at Georgetown as logical positivists, did not.

The Georgetown department that took shape in the late fifties and sixties, therefore, had a unique form; it did not simply duplicate what was being done elsewhere. It had an openness to the larger philosophical world that it did not have during the years of Scholasticism's triumph, and it certainly had higher standards of scholarly excellence among its faculty members. On the other hand, it took a largely negative stance toward the dominant philosophical culture of the English-speaking world, and this negative stance owed a great deal to Georgetown's sense of identity as a Jesuit and Catholic university. It is probably true to say that the department of this era was trying to build a program of genuine scholarly and philosophical quality that was firmly rooted in tradition but that self-consciously turned away both from what was perceived as the rigidity and narrowness of the old Scholastic way and from what was perceived as the equal rigidity and narrowness of Anglo-American philosophy.

In addition to the emphasis on the history of philosophy and continental thought during this period, there were certain elements of the curriculum that manifested more immediately Georgetown's Catholic tradition. Germain Grisez offered courses in Thomistic ethical theory, which he also explored in his published work, and applied the natural law position to contemporary issues. Louis Dupré offered a series of courses in the philosophy of religion. Dupré's courses were not peculiarly or exclusively Catholic in character; they included Catholic as well as non-Catholic thinkers and did not hesitate to raise the full range of questions associated with religious experience. Dupré and Grisez also engaged in lively debates in the mid-sixties over the Church's position on artificial contraception. These arguments were as much theological as philosophical, but they sprang from the faculty of the Department of Philosophy and from there went on to engage a much larger audience in the Washington area and even nationally. With the departure of Dupré and Grisez in the early seventies, the department lost the two faculty members who were most inclined to write and speak on ethical issues from a specifically Catholic perspective.

Many of the features of the department that developed in the fifties and sixties remain visible today. The department still offers courses in the history of philosophy, and it still has specialists in continental thought. But there have also been profound changes that began in the seventies and accelerated in the eighties. As one would expect, these have to do both with changes in the contemporary philosophical world and with decisions made within the department. As for the changes in the general philosophical climate in America, there is much greater respect for, and activity in, both the history of philosophy and continental thought. Narrow linguistic analysis or positivism is no longer the norm for contemporary American philosophy. This means that the department need not take a defensive—or offensive—view of what it does in the history of philosophy and continental thought; it also means that, to the degree that it still actively promotes itself in these two areas, it can no longer claim the same degree of uniqueness it once did.

As for changes within the department, one must point first at the hiring that has taken place in recent years. If the department earlier experienced a shift in its membership from Jesuit to lay but Catholic, the shift recently has been from lay and Catholic to lay and non-Catholic. Furthermore, while most (though certainly not all) of the lay Catholic faculty members who replaced the Jesuits in the past came from graduate programs in Catholic universities in this country and abroad, our recent appointees received their degrees from some of the most prestigious secular departments in the country (Harvard, Princeton, Stanford, Yale, Pittsburgh). This change in the composition of the faculty has brought to the department an openness to several contemporary currents of American philosophy and an active scholarly participation in them.

The change noted above began in the seventies, which was also the period in which the department first mentioned pluralism as one of its objectives. Soon after Henry Veatch arrived to chair the department in 1973, he drafted a "Statement of the Department's Objectives" (the department had been without such a statement for a number of years). The first objective affirmed the department's dedication to the history of philosophy and to "the sense that philosophy may best be learned . . . through a constant occupation with . . . the major figures in the history of Western philosophy." The second expressed "a concern for philosophic pluralism." And the third renewed the theme, and the question, of the role of a philosophy department in a Catholic institution. This third objective may also be taken as a variation on the theme of pluralism: "A concern for the pursuit of philosophy in the over-all context of a Christian and Catholic university. Although such a concern in no wise manifests as being in any way an actual test for membership in the department, or even as involving curricular requirements of a particular kind, the department nevertheless recognizes the continuing relevance both in its research and its instruction of issues having to do with the import of philosophy for religion and of religion for philosophy."

While the objectives formulated by Henry Veatch and promulgated by the department well into the eighties might still be taken as setting it apart from other departments of philosophy, the department's ongoing evolution and its hiring continued to lead it in another direction. Indeed, although we remain something of a maverick in the field, the department of the eighties has come to resemble more and more closely departments in secular universities. Of the three objectives, only the one concerning pluralism continues to be applied actively in practice, and some would argue that even it is no longer fully honored. The questions of identity raised by this evolution will be discussed in the next section.

In addition to appointments, the single most important development in recent years was the decision to concentrate on ethics in the graduate program. In 1982, the Department of Philosophy, along with all other departments with graduate programs, was asked to submit a proposal outlining an area in which it might be able to achieve excellence and, therefore, national prominence. The department selected ethics as its area. Its initial proposal, submitted in 1983, was found unacceptable by the committee that had made the original request. The much longer proposal, submitted in 1984, was accepted. Basically, the department expressed its intent to offer specializations in ethical theory and the history of ethics and in certain areas of applied ethics, particularly biomedical ethics. It would still maintain a "general program," though with fewer students.

On one level, the department's proposal for attaining graduate excellence reflected certain realities that had made themselves felt a number of years before. The Kennedy Institute of Ethics, an independent research institute located on the campus and administratively under the president, had by the mid-seventies acquired a reputation as an outstanding research facility in the burgeoning field of biomedical ethics. People around the country began to express an interest in studying at the Institute, but the Institute was not a department and had no independent way of offering courses or establishing degree requirements. Furthermore, the scholars at the Institute did not think that a concentration in biomedical ethics without strong philosophical underpinnings would be desirable. In the late seventies, therefore, the department put into place a joint program in biomedical ethics with the Kennedy Institute. Students were enrolled in the Department of Philosophy and met the standard requirements for the advanced degrees. Scholars from the Institute, who in most instances were given appointments in the department, offered graduate courses on a regular basis and participated in administering comprehensive examinations and mentoring theses and dissertations. This aspect of the program was flourishing before 1980, and one could make a convincing case that in a time of declining enrollments in graduate programs in philosophy nationwide, the concentration in biomedical ethics enabled the department's graduate program to survive. Furthermore, our graduates in this specialization were able to find jobs during the driest period of academic employment opportunities in the humanities. The proposal put in place in 1984 formalized the concentration in biomedical ethics and added to it the broader program in ethical theory and the history of ethics. The proposal also cited other fields of applied ethics into which the department hoped eventually to expand (hopes that persist, although nothing tangible has come of them).

The graduate program has been meeting with increasing success as the proposal for graduate excellence has been implemented—success reflected in the quality of admissions, in the recruitment of some first-rate young ethicists for the faculty, and in the growing national recognition the department has received.

This success, of course, should not be taken as a suggestion that either the department's present or its future is free from problems. The strong emphasis on building up the graduate program in recent years has led many in the department to suspect that it is now time to turn our attention and resources, including the hiring process, in the direction of the undergraduate program. This observation leads into the final section, which will look somewhat more closely at the present and at what might be done in the years to come.

III. Where do we come from? What are we? Where are we going?

Where philosophy at Georgetown comes from has been suggested by the previous sections, and something of what we are has been indicated as well. Still, we can afford to say a bit more about the current state of the discipline at Georgetown and about where it might, or should, be going.

One of the things we are is a presence in the curriculum, and not incidentally so. If every undergraduate in every school is required to take two courses in philosophy, and if the graduate program has been selected for "excellence" and for the support that attends such selection, then there must be a reason—or better, a cluster of reasons. These will have to do with the fact that Georgetown is a university, and specifically, a Jesuit and Catholic university. In order to get a grip on these reasons, it might be useful, first, to say a few words about the discipline of philosophy itself, quite apart from the form it may have assumed at Georgetown. I realize that my comments in this respect are controversial and that many of my colleagues would disagree with them. What I hope they would not seriously disagree with are the conclusions to which they lead.

Philosophy is an unusual enterprise. To begin with, it does not have a specific subject matter, at least not in the sense in which chemistry or literary theory or art history or government does. Everything imaginable and conceivable is its subject matter—which, as philosophers are fond of saying in such cases, is tantamount to claiming that nothing is. Suffice it to say that there is no area of human experience that the philosopher cannot think about. On the other hand, the philosopher does not approach the subject of his or her reflection in the same way as the chemist or the art historian does. What distinguishes the philosopher is a matter of attitude or stance, and this is what saves the philosopher from foolishly competing, say, with biologists or sociologists on their own turf.

The philosopher tends to ask the most universal questions, questions aimed at essence and at fundamental distinctions and conflicts—the questions that will reveal the forest and not just the trees. And it is out of the autonomy of reason that the philosopher asks these questions. The philosopher will, therefore, give you no new facts about Gauguin's painting whose title supplied the heading for this section of the paper. The philosopher will ask, however, what the nature of a work of art is, and how works of art differ from other things—perfectly useless questions, to be sure, but hardly ones that could be charged with triviality.

Similarly, the philosopher does not engage in ordinary theory-construction, as it might be found in art history or geology. But the philosopher might tell you how such theories are related to the disciplines in which they are found and to whatever aspect of the world they purport to explain. The philosopher is never directly a player; he or she is always the relentlessly reflective spectator, carefully sifting and analyzing, and, if need be, criticizing.

Now, in any education that claims to be liberal, this approach to reality—not a canon, but an approach—should be present. This, I think, has been the constant reason why philosophy has been in the Georgetown curriculum for most of the University's history. The Jesuit understanding of the intellectual life has recognized and continues to recognize that the way in which philosophy seeks to understand what it is to be human is simply not something optional. Philosophy asks the questions that must be asked in a truly liberal education. In asking these questions, philosophy cannot help but take on an integrating role; and this is true even if philosophy is no longer expected to carry the burden of integrating the whole of the student's experience. This realization may be as old as Plato and may not be unique to the Jesuit vision, but the Jesuits have held on to it, and this tenacity is reflected in the curriculum.

Now, if that is what philosophy is, more or less, and if that is a principal reason why it enjoys a privileged place in the curriculum, what form should it take within the setting of a university that is Jesuit and Catholic? First, since the setting here is that of a *university*, philosophy at Georgetown must meet the demands of the discipline that prevail for any university, whether Catholic and Jesuit or not. This involves among other things the presence in the department of scholars who are actively involved in contemporary philosophical investigation. This is by no means a stipulation that one must slavishly follow what happens to be in vogue in the field at the moment. But the department does have to have members who know from the inside what is being done at the moment and who are capable of engaging it critically on its own terms. The era is long past in which a Catholic department of philosophy that wants to be genuinely faithful to the field can adopt a hostile and defensive attitude towards what is being done in the larger philosophical world around it.

In this respect, the department at Georgetown is in fine shape. To play on Mark Tushnet's distinction,[82] we have become "national," not in opposition to "local," but to "narrowly sectarian." We have first-rate scholars who are actively conversant with the latest developments in the field. But in saying that, one is saying no more (though that may still be quite a bit) than that the department is doing what it must do to be academically respectable. It does not address the issue of whether there is or should or could be anything unique about the philosophy department at

Georgetown—unique, that is, because Georgetown is a Jesuit and Catholic institution.

One should say at the outset that there are probably some members of the department who would argue that there should not be anything unique about philosophy at Georgetown, that philosophy has a universal character that makes it the same everywhere, and that in this respect philosophy differs not at all from the sciences or from mathematics. I believe that one can accept this proposition and still argue that the department of philosophy at Georgetown should be committed to doing certain things precisely because it is *at Georgetown.* In saying this, I am not implying that the things the department might be committed to doing could not be done in non-Jesuit and non-Catholic institutions. They could be, and sometimes are. The point is rather that we have an obligation to do them here if we are to live up to the stated objectives of *this* university.

What are some of these things? Surely among the most obvious is ethics, which, in fact, is one of the two foci, and effectively the dominant one, of the graduate program; and, of course, all undergraduates take a basic course in ethics. To be sure, ethics is currently an immensely fashionable concern of philosophy departments (and of other sorts of departments and schools) across the country. In attempting to develop an excellent graduate program in ethics, we are, therefore, doing no more than many non-Catholic universities are doing. But we are also doing something that as a Catholic and Jesuit institution we should be doing. Furthermore, in our biomedical specialization we are doing something very well that few other institutions are doing at all, and that fewer still are doing at our level of excellence. This, and the other areas of applied ethics that the department would like to see developed in the future, represent the sort of philosophical endeavors that a department such as ours should undertake.

To say that ethics rightly holds a special place in philosophy at Georgetown is not to claim that a particular sort of ethical theory, whether Thomistic or Kantian or Schelerian, should be emphasized because it seems to be particularly in harmony with religious doctrine. The interest in ethics is there both because ethics is a fundamental part of philosophy and because it is part of the Jesuit tradition to recognize that the human being is a free subject, expected to exercise his or her freedom responsibly. In curricular terms, this means, for the undergraduates, courses that help the student to think carefully and rigorously about the moral life and about the intrinsic dignity of every human being. For the graduate program, it means a broadly based and open curriculum that will familiarize the student with the full range of possibilities in ethical theory in its contemporary and historical forms. Finally, one might argue that it is part of the Jesuit tradition that ethical enquiry cannot, in the end, be coherently pursued apart from metaphysics and epistemology, and that the curriculum, both graduate and undergraduate, should reflect that conviction.

Openness in the curriculum is part and parcel of the discipline. But the openness must be authentic. Observers of the Catholic intellectual life, such as James Hitchcock, have noted that with the decline of the Thomistic establishment twenty-five years ago, Catholic philosophers, like scholars in other fields in Catholic institutions, often sought "professional respectability by hewing closely to the prevailing opinion within their disciplines."[83] If the mandarins in the discipline were disinclined to devote thought to such issues as the possibility of divine existence or of an immaterial dimension in the human being or of natural law in the ethical life, or even to major portions of the history of the field, then the curricular concerns in departments of philosophy in Catholic institutions were apt to reflect those disinclinations. Put more positively, the curriculum was likely to evolve in such a way that it mirrored more or less faithfully the dominant interests of the philosophical establishment, which in the English-speaking world was decidedly not located in Catholic universities.

This tendency was strengthened, of course, as departments such as Georgetown's began to hire new faculty in precisely the same way as major departments in non-Catholic institutions do; that is, by selecting the best available candidate in a given area. Georgetown's recent success in this regard has been little short of phenomenal. We have managed to attract to our faculty the very best young scholars from among the finest graduate programs in the current establishment. And we have done this in the face of competition from schools more prestigious and richer than we are. Our programs, both graduate and undergraduate, have benefited greatly from their presence. And certainly they would never have joined the faculty had the department not become open, which it indeed should have become.

Now, this openness, I am convinced, is genuine. It involves no overt and determining prejudices about what is permitted within the department. But as openness, above all, to the "mainstream," it may well allow areas that an institution such as ours should maintain to fall into neglect, or even to become regarded as old-fashioned. The avoidance of these dangers means, in practice, that certain questions should be respected by the faculty at large and should actually be addressed by someone in the department. The question about the possibility of divine existence is one example, already mentioned. The philosophical investigation of religious experience is another. And the department's long-standing strength in the history of philosophy, now in danger of weakening, is yet another. Again, none of these is a uniquely Catholic or Jesuit concern. Indeed, Georgetown was once very strong in the philosophy of religion on both graduate and undergraduate levels, thanks largely to Louis Dupré, who now holds a chair in the philosophy of religion at non-Catholic Yale, which, consequently, now has strength in the philosophy of religion. But they are nonetheless the sorts of concerns that should be actively addressed in a department such as ours.

How can this be brought about? The most obvious and direct way is through hiring. University departments do not achieve excellence simply by declaring that they offer specializations in this area or that. They become excellent by hiring the right people. Similarly, if there are certain areas in which we should raise questions, we will in fact raise them only if we hire people who are willing and equipped to do so. If, in addition, the department needs a core of faculty members acquainted with and in basic sympathy with the Jesuit and Catholic tradition, this again can come about only through a conscious effort to hire such people. Surely, one component of such a core would be members of the Society of Jesus. The prospects for hiring Jesuits are now improved, and it can be said that the department is quite willing to hire as many as are qualified. We will, of course, need the fulfillment of the administration's promises to help us in this respect.

On the whole, however, it remains true that given the University's and the department's thrust for mainstream excellence, hiring in these directions is very difficult to accomplish. If, for example, we need someone in metaphysics, particularly someone well schooled in contemporary metaphysics for the graduate program, the chances are excellent that we will hire a first-rate person who has no interest at all in certain traditional metaphysical questions, including those of divine existence, of "Being," of human nature, and so on.

But there is one way to come to grips with this issue, and one senses that the times are becoming more propitious for doing so. The department must raise, publicly and officially, that is, in committees and in full departmental meetings, the question of its position in the University and its relation to the Jesuit and Catholic tradition. Such a discussion probably cannot be undertaken without active support and encouragement from the administration. In any event, it will be painful and difficult, but it will also be philosophically interesting and centrally important. Otherwise, we will be in even greater danger than we already are "of being passively carried along by the currents affecting American higher education generally."[84] This is not a call for a new Catholic humanism or intellectualism in the style of the department of the thirties and forties. It is not a call to return to or to take up any particular philosophical position or approach. It is certainly not a call to curtail the catholic character of the department in the name of a narrowly Catholic identity. It is simply to say that we have not had a discussion about what we are in the department or about where we are going. We will remain unclear to ourselves, at least collectively, until we have that discussion. For some departments, those that neither claim nor enjoy a special place in the curriculum, such vagueness may be acceptable. But surely in the case of the Philosophy Department it is not.

Notes

I am grateful to R. Emmett Curran, S.J., Jesse Mann, Thomas McTighe, Terry Pinkard, Rocco Porreco, and John Reuscher for their help in preparing this essay.

1. John M. Daley, S.J., *Georgetown University: Origin and Early Years* (Washington, D.C.: Georgetown University Press, 1957), 90.
2. Ibid.
3. Ibid., 73.
4. Ibid., 107.
5. Information supplied by R. Emmett Curran, S.J. In Daley's version the precise motivation for the introduction of philosophy at Georgetown does not emerge clearly. See Daley, *Origin and Early Years,* 105-12.
6. Ibid., 107-08.
7. Ibid., 105.
8. Ibid., 108-09, and note 32.
9. Ibid., 110.
10. Jesuit seminarians did take philosophy at Georgetown until the 1860s, when the seminary moved to Woodstock, Md. Woodstock faculty were often considered to be Georgetown faculty and the advanced seminarians to be graduate students. As late as the 1940s the bachelor's degrees conferred on the seminarians were Georgetown degrees. In 1833, the Holy See empowered Georgetown to grant

pontifical degrees in philosophy and theology. These degrees, called licentiates, could also be earned by the seminarians.

11. *Classical Journal*, 5. This diary of the prefect of studies is in the Georgetown University archives.

12. Ibid., 22.

13. "Philosophy" at this time included "natural" philosophy, that is, various physical sciences, as well as "moral" philosophy, which in the 1820s embraced logic and metaphysics.

14. *Classical Journal*, 60.

15. Ibid., 62.

16. Ibid., 63.

17. *Catalogue of the College, 1850-51*, 5.

18. *Catalogue of the College, 1852-53*, 5.

19. *Catalogue of the College, 1853-54*, 5.

20. *Catalogue of the College, 1850-51*, 5.

21. *Catalogue of the College, 1857-58*, 4.

22. Frederick Copleston, S.J., *A History of Philosophy*, volume 9, part II (Garden City, N.Y.: Image Books, 1977), 43-44.

23. Frederick Copleston, S.J., *Aquinas* (Baltimore, Md.: Penguin Books, 1955), 238.

24. *Catalogue of the College, 1862-63*, 31.

25. *Catalogue of the College, 1868-69*, 7.

26. *Catalogue of the College, 1869-70*, 8.

27. Jesse A. Mann, "Neo-scholastic Philosophy in the United States of America in the Nineteenth Century," *Proceedings of the American Catholic Philosophical Association* (Washington, D.C.: The Catholic University of America, 1959), 132, note 19. A comparison between Jouin's *Compendium Logicae et Metaphysicae* (1869) and his English compendium, *Logic and Metaphysics* (1897), in which references to Aquinas do appear, is interesting in this regard. In the memorial notice for Jouin we read: "There are many who think that his works on logic, metaphysics, and ethics could be introduced with profit to Yale, Harvard, and Columbia, where the study of mental philosophy is so woefully neglected." See *Woodstock Letters* 29 (1900), 6.

28. Brother Azarias, "Lessons of a Century of Catholic Education," *The Catholic World* 50 (Nov. 1889), 151, 152, quoted in Mann, "Neo-Scholastic Philosophy," 131.

29. *Catalogue of the College, 1920-21*, 83.

30. Joseph Louis Perrier, *The Revival of Scholastic Philosophy in the Nineteenth Century* (New York: The Columbia University Press, 1909), 234, quoted in Mann, "Neo-Scholastic Philosophy," 133, note 22.

31. *Catalogue of the College, 1889-90*, 16.

32. *Catalogue of the College, 1899-1900*, 71-72.

33. Gerald P. Fogarty, S.J., "American Freedom and American Catholic Higher Education: An Historical Analysis," *New Catholic World* 231:1385 (1988), 221.

34. Ibid., 222. Timothy S. Healy, S.J., Georgetown's president, suggested that a key reason why the University seemed to become less Catholic in recent years

is to be found in "the reduction of its philosophy requirement (and its moves away from scholasticism in those that remained)." See "Universitas Fidelium" in *Georgetown Annual Report*, 1987, 1.

35. *Catalogue of the Graduate Division, 1932-33*, 33.

36. Ibid., 34.

37. *Catalogue of the College, 1935-36*, 18.

38. *Catalogue of the College, 1850-51*, 5.

39. *Catalogue of the College, 1935-36*, 18. Electives were not allowed in the required curriculum in philosophy until 1966.

40. Although the term "department" is used off and on in University catalogues as early as the nineteenth century, something resembling the modern departmental structure does not appear until the 1920s (see, for example, the *Catalogue of the College, 1921-22*) and does not mature until the 1950s.

41. *Catalogue of the College, 1959-60*, 83.

42. Copleston, *Aquinas*, 235.

43. Ibid., 250.

44. Copleston, *History of Philosophy*, vol. 9, II, 46.

45. Ibid.

46. Ibid., 48.

47. Terry Pinkard of the Department of Philosophy in conversation observed that as the twentieth century progressed, philosophy *generally*—not just in the form of Thomism and not just at Catholic universities such as Georgetown—lost its cultural role as an integrating force.

48. *Catalogue of the College, 1969-70*, 43.

49. *Catalogue of the College, 1970-71*, 8. In the current catalogue, all of the general education requirements are given a brief justification, but in 1970 this was done only for philosophy and theology.

50. *Classical Journal*, 64.

51. *Graduate Bulletin, 1949-50*, 15. The minutes book of the President and Board of Directors says that Fairclough was the first to receive the M.A. degree "in course."

52. *Catalogue of the College, 1855-56*, 13.

53. *Catalogue of the College, 1906-07*, 6.

54. *Catalogue of the College, 1897-98*, 32-33.

55. Ibid., 31.

56. *Catalogue of the College, 1908-09*, 55-56.

57. Ibid., 56.

58. Information supplied by R. Emmett Curran, S.J.

59. *Graduate School Catalogue, 1924-25*, 50-51.

60. Ibid.

61. *Graduate School Catalogue, 1921-22*, 9.

62. *Graduate School Catalogue, 1925-26*, 36-37.

63. *General Catalogue, 1929-30*, 92.

64. *Catalogue of the Graduate Division, 1932-33*, 33.

65. *Catalogue of the Graduate Division, 1932-33*, 33.

66. Ibid.

67. For a thorough discussion of Scholasticism's integrating function in Catholic academic and intellectual life during this period, see Philip Gleason, "The Search for Unity and Its Sequel," *Keeping the Faith. American Catholicism Past and Present* (Notre Dame, Ind.: University of Notre Dame Press, 1987), 136-51.

68. *Graduate School Catalogue, 1932-33*, 34.

69. *Graduate School Catalogue, 1935-36*, 30.

70. *Graduate School Catalogue, 1944-45*, 30.

71. Ibid.

72. *Graduate School Catalogue, 1945-46*, 30.

73. *University Bulletin, 1974-75*, 7. In 1943, Guthrie admitted women to the Graduate School, it was thought, for the first time. During the 1920s, however, nine sisters from Visitation Convent earned advanced degrees from Georgetown. One of them, Sister Jane Francis Leibell, received her Ph.D. in 1923. Three years later she published *Readings in Ethics*, a work which was widely used for many years.

74. *Graduate School Catalogue, 1946-47*, 33.

75. *Graduate School Catalogue, 1947-48*, 34.

76. Ibid.

77. *Graduate School Catalogue, 1949-50*, 38.

78. *Graduate School Catalogue, 1954-55*, 53.

79. *Graduate School Catalogue, 1956-57*, 59.

80. The School of Foreign Service had its own Department of Philosophy until the late 1950s. This school traditionally had far fewer required courses in philosophy than the College.

81. David Tracy, "Catholicism and Religious Pluralism," Address at Georgetown University, January 26, 1989.

82. Cf. Mark Tushnet's essay in this collection, "Catholic Legal Education at a National Law School: Reflections on the Georgetown Experience."

83. James Hitchcock, "[D]ialogue: how has American Catholic intellectual life changed over the past thirty years?" *U.S. Catholic Historian* 4 (1985), 180.

84. Ibid., 179.

William C. McFadden, S.J.
Department of Theology

"Catechism at 4 for all the Schools": Religious Instruction at Georgetown

In 1826, classes at Georgetown College were scheduled to begin on September fifteenth. However, due to the small number of students present, the president decided to postpone the opening of school until the following day. And so it was that on the morning of the sixteenth the president assembled the entire faculty of Georgetown College in his office. According to a giant, leather-bound, hand-written volume in the Georgetown archives, the purpose of the meeting was to plan the course of studies for the academic year.[1]

There is something very appealing about this picture of the president and five or six faculty members gathering the day school began to determine the syllabus the five classes would cover that year. In 1989, faculty members must turn in their fall schedules to the registrar the previous February and their book orders to the bookstore by the first week in April.

The point, of course, is that anything said of Georgetown College in its early years must be understood as referring to an institution only a tiny fraction of its present size. In the 1820s, there was a stable enrollment of thirty to forty-five students, more than half of whom were under fourteen years of age. By its centennial year of 1889, the College had awarded fewer than five hundred Bachelor of Arts degrees. In contrast, on Commencement Day, 1989, the College alone conferred bachelor's degrees on over seven hundred students, and the other four undergraduate schools graduated almost an equal number.

In this essay I am interested in tracing the various forms of religious instruction practiced at Georgetown over the past two hundred years. More precisely, I am interested in seeing if I can determine what rationale, either stated or implied, supports that instruction. If it should turn out that there is more than one such rationale, then I would like to line them up and see if they have something to teach us about how we got to where we are, and perhaps even suggest directions for future growth in religious education at Georgetown.

Stage One

In keeping with this aim, then, I note that the plan of studies drawn up on September 16, 1826, included for each of the five classes (called "schools") catechism lessons. The youngest students studied the *Small Catechism*, the intermediate three years were assigned Fleury's *Catechism*, and the oldest students worked with Hay's *Catechism*.

The final entry on the page reads: "N.B. On Saturdays Catechism at 4 for all the schools."[2] This unenviable position in the school week was established in 1820 by Peter Kenney, an Irish Jesuit sent by Father General in Rome to oversee a reorganization of the College.

One of his proposals was that each master should, as was usual in Jesuit colleges, teach all the languages (Latin, Greek, English, and French) which largely constituted the school's curriculum. In that way he would be able to begin with the lowest class and advance with them each year until graduation. In addition, each master was to teach his class catechism every Saturday "during the last half-hour of the afternoon."[3] There is also mention of a "general catechism" on Sundays, which generally took the form of a lecture or moral exhortation.

From the small amount of time devoted to it and its placement at the tail-end of the week's classes, it is clear that catechism is not really part of the curriculum. It would be better described as a part of the religious life and training of the student, which included close supervision, attendance at Mass and other religious exercises, a yearly retreat, weekly moral exhortations, and for many students membership in the Sodality with its additional pious practices.

This is very much in keeping with the original *Proposals for Establishing an Academy at George-Town*. The school's curriculum as described therein consists of "the several branches of classical learning." In a separate paragraph the issue of "religious worship and instruction" is taken up. Since, "agreeably to the liberal Principle of our Constitution," the school is to be open to students of every religious profession, provision must be made for those who do not profess the Catholic religion. They will be "at liberty to frequent the Places of Worship and Instruction appointed by their parents."[4] The pairing of "Worship and Instruction" certainly reinforces the idea that religious instruction and catechism lessons are considered part of the religious training of the student and not of his academic program.

Providing for freedom of worship, however, resulted in some practical difficulties. In 1798, the only worship services for those living in the College were Roman Catholic, and all students were expected to attend them. On the other hand, the directors of the school did not wish to oblige anyone "to be present at a different worship from that of their first education." The solution was to direct that a separate boardinghouse be established for students "professing other tenets." This boardinghouse was to be put under the care of a "widow-lady of most reputable character, who has lived for many years in a public life."[5]

By 1833, this was no longer judged to be a practical solution. In the *Prospectus* of that year we read that members of other religious denominations are now required to "assist at the public duties of religion with their companions." The reason given is, "were not this enforced, no proper order, such as should be found in large literary institutions, could exist in the College."[6] The intent is clearly not to proselytize but to supervise. If all the prefects were attending Mass with the Catholic students, who would monitor the activities of the others?[7]

The emphasis, then, seems to be very strongly placed on religion's role in *moral training*. In the *Prospectus* of 1798, irreligion and immorality in a youth are said to "portend the most fatal evils to subsequent periods of life, and threaten even to disturb the peace, and corrupt the manners of society at large." The directors of Georgetown, for their part, openly profess that they have "nothing so much at heart as to implant virtue and destroy in their pupils the seeds of vice. Happy in the attainment of this sublime object, they would consider their success in this alone, as an ample reward for their incessant endeavors."[8]

The original rationale, then, for religious education at Georgetown College was clearly stated in the 1787 announcement of the founding of the school. It was to have a twofold aim: "to unite the Means of communicating Science with an effectual Provision for guarding and improving the Morals of Youth."[9] The first aim is achieved through "Science," a term which refers here to the whole academic program. Religious instruction served the second purpose. Together with attendance at Mass and other religious practices, the catechism lessons contributed to the healthy moral development of the student.

That, at least, was the plan. Religious education, however, is a challenging task and does not always meet with success. This clearly was the judgment of the prefect of studies, William Grace, as he reported to the assembled students in February 1834, the results of their first-term examinations:

> Such as had the small Catechism answered very well and orderly with the exception of a few whose countenances indicated clearly their hearty antipathy to Christian things—calling themselves Catholic Christians and manifesting such marked hostility to the essentials of the system they left us instantly in possession of their hearts' movements and the corruption of their souls. Those of the large Catechism knew not a word at all, whether they have consciences to admit of a little remorse is a question to be settled between them and a higher tribunal.[10]

It is perhaps superfluous to add that Father Grace, in addition to being the prefect of studies, was also the professor of rhetoric.

One way of trying to awaken interest in the study of catechism is to have competitions and award prizes. This was done at commencement as early as 1821. In 1825, a silver medal was conferred on the winner. Apparently, late in the spring, there was an optional examination, like signing up for a spelling bee or contesting for the Horace Medal. Beginning in 1831, the boys were divided into two or three age groups and medals were awarded to the winners in each division.

The high point, I think, in this history of rewards for knowing one's catechism was in 1886. That year the Provincial of the Maryland-New York Province put up a prize of $100 for an Intercollegiate Contest in Christian Doctrine. The Georgetown Faculty offered to give an additional $50 to the winner of the $100 prize. The College as usual awarded a Gold Medal in Christian Doctrine at commencement that year. A Georgetown student won all three prizes. To get a sense of the value of $150 at that time, one needs to realize that it was equivalent to the total cost that semester for tuition, board, lodging, and laundry.

This contest was held again in 1887. The following year, the

Provincial declined to repeat the offer and so did the faculty. Someone else did offer a $100 prize in 1888, but by 1889 this righteous but expensive use of mammon to stimulate the acquisition of religious knowledge had come to an end. Still, that Centennial year there *was* a gold medal "of the value of one hundred dollars," but it was offered for the best metrical translation of two odes of Horace.

Stage Two

The program of religious instruction at Georgetown clearly takes on a different shape at the end of the 1860s.[11] It is difficult to say on the available evidence exactly when the changes were introduced. They appear for the first time in the Catalogue of 1868-69. We have seen that in 1826 catechism lessons were scheduled for late Saturday afternoons. In 1868, these lessons are described for the first time as "daily lessons."[12]

The following year there is a major renovation of the catechetical program. A new item appears on the schedule of sophomores and juniors: "Doctrinal Exposition of Religion." This title suggests a move away from the usual catechism. The textbook used was: F.X. Weninger, *A Manual of the Catholic Religion.* Weninger maintains the question-and-answer format, but the answers are quite long, bringing in proofs from Scripture and tradition, and are hardly intended to be memorized. The book is some four hundred pages in length and, as the author notes in his preface, "contains in brief a complete exposition of the whole of the Christian doctrine, so that, whoever has mastered its contents, may be called, and truly is, a perfectly instructed Christian."[13]

The phrase "perfectly instructed Christian" articulates the ideal Georgetown was beginning to incorporate into its *academic* program. We meet in Weninger also the emergence of an interest in *apologetics.* As Weninger says in answer to the first question in his book, every Christian should know Christian doctrine "in order to be able to live according to faith; and to answer the questions proposed to him concerning it."[14]

These two concerns, bringing the teaching of Christian doctrine into the academic curriculum and providing students with a rational defense of the Christian faith, chart the course of religious instruction at Georgetown until 1940.

In 1889, a new introductory sentence is added to the section on religious instruction in the catalogue: "Religious instruction is considered of the first importance in education." Ten years later, "Christian Doctrine" is listed as a subject in the curriculum together with Latin and Greek. But the most important change of all is the tradition-shattering introduction of religious instruction into *senior year*. Until 1899, philosophy had always been the principal, if not the sole, focus of the academic program in senior year.

The stimulus for this departure from tradition may have been the adoption of a new textbook.[15] Wilhelm Wilmers had published some twenty years before a four-volume work in German, which enjoyed such great success that a new edition had just appeared. The text adopted by Georgetown was reduced to a single volume of some five hundred pages by the editor, James Conway. In place of the familiar "questions and answers" there are propositions, 275 of them. The editor designed this book to be used by "advanced students," by which term he means "college students proper, and those of corresponding grades in academies for young ladies."[16]

Relying on his own years of teaching experience, Conway says he believes that with two lectures per week the matter contained in this volume can be mastered in three years. The book is meant also to be kept and used as a reference work, offering the educated layman "the means wherewith he may be ready at all times to give an account of the faith that is in him."[17]

The book has three parts. The logical order is to take up first the apologetic part, then the dogmatic, and finally the moral. Conway, however, recommends the reverse order as more in keeping with the mental development of the student, proceeding from the more familiar to the more difficult. Then, he suggests that the entire book may profitably be reviewed in the fourth year of college.[18] This plan was adopted and Georgetown seniors began to have Christian Doctrine classes in their curriculum.

This new curriculum, with its systematic presentation of the whole of Christian doctrine semester by semester over four years, continues at Georgetown until 1963. The number of hours per week varies somewhat over the years, but it is this format that most people have in mind when they talk about the way Catholic colleges "used to train students in the faith."

The "Religious Instruction" section of the catalogue in 1907 adds a passage which reflects the growing preoccupation with the *rational* presentation of Catholic faith: "The matter is so divided for the different classes that in the four years of college the student will cover the whole ground of Catholic faith in rational fashion."[19]

Five years later, the subject matter is no longer called "Christian Doctrine" but "Evidences of Religion," and at commencement in 1915 the Christian Doctrine prize is referred to as "The Faculty Medal for Evidences of Religion."

In 1919, for the first time, the instruction in Christian doctrine achieves in the catalogue the status of a *department*. It is surprising, and surely significant, that the name chosen for the new department is "Department of Apologetics." Wilmer's *Handbook* continues to be used for the first three years but seniors, instead of reviewing Wilmers, are introduced to Hill's *The Catholic's Ready Answer*.

We now have "Evidences of Religion" and "Ready Answers" being taught in a Department of Apologetics. At commencement the following year, the Christian Doctrine Medal is awarded for the "Best Essay in Apologetics."

This is the high water mark for the focus on apologetics. The next year, the religion medal is awarded to the student who got the highest grade in a fifteen-minute oral examination before three faculty members on selected pages from Wilmers, and this continued to be the practice for many years.

The department changed its name in 1932 to "Department of Religion." It is difficult to see whether this represents a new rationale or direction for the department since all the course titles offered by the department remain the same. This move established a precedent for the next namechange. In 1957, the department acquired its present name, "Department of Theology," while keeping intact all of the course titles and descriptions that had been appearing in the catalogues for the previous fifteen years.

Apologetics continued to be a subject of great importance, and through the 1930s Georgetown adopted as textbooks English translations of the treatises being taught in Latin to the Jesuit seminarians at Woodstock College. And yet in the midst of the reign of the rational and the systematic, Georgetown's catalogue in 1935 echoed the thoughts of the eighteenth-century founders of the school, arguing for the preeminence of the moral dimension in education:

> . . . however important the mental development of a student may be, his moral development is of far greater importance . . .

> Religious instruction, therefore, which alone can develop and strengthen the will and induce good habits, is of prime importance at Georgetown . . .[20]

This goal, of course, was not to be achieved by formal coursework alone but also by other features of campus life such as attendance at Mass, moral exhortations, membership in the Sodality, and the annual retreat.

The rationale, then, of religious instruction during the second stage was to provide college students with a reasoned presentation and defense of the whole of Catholic doctrine. Initially, this was accomplished with the use of more advanced catechisms, but later on Georgetown began to employ the Scholastic theology system in use in seminaries.

Stage Three

In the 1930s, students expressed great dissatisfaction with this college religion program. They complained about having to study the arid abstractions of Scholastic theology in textbooks which were abridged translations of seminary treatises. It was becoming clear to some that a set of courses should be designed specifically for college students.

The Maryland Province in 1940 called upon John Courtney Murray to set new objectives for the college religion course, and the following year a new syllabus was introduced at Georgetown based upon Murray's proposals. Murray continued to develop his ideas and four years later published in *Theological Studies* a rationale for a distinctive college religion course.[21]

The syllabus based on this rationale was commonly referred to as the "Murray Plan," although there were several different versions of it over the years, and Murray himself by the mid-1940s had dissociated himself from the enterprise. This plan in some form was in effect at Georgetown until the early 1960s.

In his *Theological Studies* articles, Murray boldly attempts to devise a new rationale for teaching college theology based upon the fact that clergy and laity have differing roles to play in the life of the church, and therefore each requires its own appropriate theological training.[22]

The clerical course, Murray argued, aims to promote that intelligence of faith which is required in order that the teaching office of the church may be able effectively to preserve, explain, and defend the whole of revealed truth.

The lay course, on the other hand, has its own specific finality:

> That intelligence of faith, especially in its relation to human life and the common good of mankind, which is required in order that the laity of the Church may be able effectively to collaborate with the hierarchy in accomplishing the renewal and reconstruction of the whole of modern social life.[23]

A second distinctive feature of the lay theology course is that it must, according to Murray, play a role in the *religious formation* of the students, and thus its finality lies more in the realm of charity than of intelligence. In Murray's words, the lay course "aims at conveying an intelligence of the Christian life, as a power for personal and social regeneration, especially in its relation to the contemporary culture of human society."[24]

This goal, however, creates what appears to be an insoluble pedagogical problem. How can an academic course communicate charity and form an apostle? How can it not only communicate ideas and form an intelligence but also be an instrument of a religious formation?

This could easily be misunderstood as an undesirable reversion to the previous system in which teachers often presented doctrinal truths in their Scholastic precision, and then would "go off on a *ferverino*," exhorting their students to apply these truths to their lives.[25]

Murray's view is rather that the matter to be presented by the teacher is not the treatises of Scholastic theology but the Sacred Scriptures, the word of God. The task of the teacher is to illuminate this word, to let it be seen not only as true but as demanding an answer in terms of life. To achieve this requires pedagogical gifts of a high order: psychological insight, imagination, rhetorical power, a warmth of personality, a wide knowledge of the contemporary situation of the church and of the world, a sympathy with the mood of present thought, a profound grasp of the problems in the field of religion and culture which currently are vexing people.[26]

Third, a teacher with these gifts needs further to appreciate what Murray calls the law of congruity: "doctrinal instruction will be religiously formative only if the manner of its organization and exposition is adapted to the psychology of the student and to his existent state of mental and spiritual development."[27] In other words, courses in religion must obey the great law of efficacious grace: they must reach students as grace reaches all persons, where they are, just as they are.[28]

Murray, then, provided the rationale for the third stage of religious instruction at Georgetown. In his program, the apologetic concerns of the previous stage receded in importance. The emphasis was no longer on the rational system of Catholic theology, but on that understanding of Catholic faith which would prepare Catholic laity to work with the hierarchy in the social apostolate called "Catholic Action."

In retrospect, Murray's program came on the scene with a lay theology course as various factors were changing the meaning of the term "laity" and removing from the curriculum the possibility of what his plan presupposed: an eight-semester theology program for all Catholic students. Twenty years after the Murray Plan was launched, the old familiar signs of dissatisfaction were widespread in the student body.

A colleague of John Courtney Murray at Woodstock College, Gustave Weigel, was invited to address the Society of Catholic College Teachers of Sacred Doctrine in 1961. In typically blunt fashion, Weigel told the assembled teachers: "The problem of College Theology in America will have to be handled at the College level. You will wait in vain if you expect the professors in our seminaries to solve it for you."[29]

But the college teachers had been hard at work trying to solve this problem. Between 1946 and 1959, there were five workshops for college religion teachers in the Maryland Province alone. In addition, there were two national meetings sponsored by the Jesuit Educational Association, one focused on college religion (1951) and the other on philosophy and theology as academic disciplines (1962). With the benefit of hindsight, we might say that all of these efforts were in service of a particular idea of Catholic culture which flourished until the Second Vatican Council. Philip Gleason argues that the main thrust in Catholicism in the United States from the 1920s to the 1950s was toward "an organically unified Catholic culture in which religious faith constituted the integrating principle that brought all the dimensions of life and thought together in comprehensive and tightly articulated synthesis."[30]

During those years, in any case, theology courses became assimilated to the other courses taught in the school. Instead of eight courses which met twice a week and were valued at one credit each, the theology requirement came to consist of four courses which met three times a week and were valued at three credits each.

A more significant change occurred in the preparation of teachers of college theology. At Georgetown for most of its history, religion was taught by Jesuits whose preparation for this work was their seminary course, and who were also teaching one or more other subjects. This was simply a continuation of the system brought here in 1820 by Peter Kenney, in which one teacher taught his class most of the subjects they studied.

Even after the advent of the departmental system, all the Jesuit teachers of religion had a primary appointment in another department. The first *full-time* teacher of religion was Eugene B. Gallagher, appointed in 1943. It is probable that he was given this appointment because of his close involvement in the development of the Murray Plan.

Over the years, the number of Jesuits teaching religion full time gradually increased, but in a number of ways they did not function as a *department*. In 1948, Gallagher was asked to respond to a questionnaire about departmental needs. He replied, apparently with equanimity, that the department had no office space, no clerical help, no budget, and that "the only equipment needed is library books."[31] When the Maryland Province Prefect of Studies made an official visitation of the department in April 1963, his first recommendation was: "Organize the department as a department. This means giving it the rights, privileges and responsibilities of a department as expressed in clear statute form."[32]

Though the province workshops regularly recommended that college religion teachers receive special training in addition to the seminary program, it was not until the 1960s that Jesuits were sent for doctoral degrees as a preparation to teach in college.

These gains, however, were not able to maintain an integrated program of courses such as the Murray Plan envisaged, and it quietly disappeared in the 1960s due to a combination of factors: the impetus given by Vatican II to theological pluralism, the social and political upheavals in American life, the pressure for change across the entire college curriculum, especially for reduction of the number of required courses, and the opening up of the curriculum to more electives.

Stage Four

A new rationale for college theology was gradually beginning to take shape. The first indication of this at Georgetown may be seen in some reflections voiced by John L. Ryan, Theology Department chairman from 1963 to 1966.

At the first departmental meeting of his chairmanship, Ryan expressed some "personal points of view" he had adopted from his experience teaching theology at Georgetown. It is true, he said, that students rebel against required courses, especially when theology classes seem to repeat matter they have already learned in earlier schooling. On the other hand, there is a tremendous advantage for teachers in dealing with truths which are "existential." In contrast to the more objective "scientific" truth, the truths of theology spring up from the spiritual nature and the inner struggle of the one who possesses them. For such truths someone is willing to live and die.

He also underlined the importance of open discussion of the ideas of authors, both non-Christian and anti-Christian, who have challenged the very possibility of religious belief in the modern world.

Finally, he expressed his conviction that students should be encouraged to exercise their freedom to raise questions and pursue them as questions until they arrived at some conclusion, for they are the ones who are ultimately responsible for their faith.

He quoted Romano Guardini to the effect that "faith is a precarious and vulnerable gift." At every major stage in our life, we face a crisis to our faith. College provides our students with such a crisis. A student's mental horizon is being greatly extended. Former concepts and presuppositions are shaken. With this there naturally comes a disturbance, a shaking of the student's personal faith. Throughout this period open and honest discussion is the best way to enable a student to develop a mature and solid faith.

These reflections led a few years later to a revision of the theology curriculum which signaled the end of the attempt at presenting theology as an organized body of truths to be learned by all Catholic students. The focus now was on the religious education of all *Georgetown* students and what contribution the Theology Department could make to that end.[33] The problem of college theology now became: what is the best way to enable students to develop a mature personal faith?

The foundation of the new rationale taking shape was a commitment to the following proposition: a college student's religious belief (or, for that matter, unbelief) will only develop toward maturity in the context of respectful dialogue with a plurality of religious perspectives.

The practical steps that were taken as a consequence were as follows: (1) the requirement that all students take a new introductory course, "The Problem of God," (2) changing the composition of the Theology faculty to reflect new perspectives, (3) the development of a broad series of elective course offerings, and (4) the initiation of a major program in theology. It would be helpful for our purposes to say something about each of these.

1. THE INTRODUCTORY COURSE

The conviction had been growing among the faculty that it was no longer desirable to *require* college-age students to take coursework in their own religion. It is the responsibility of the department to make such courses available, but it must be the students' responsibility to enroll in them.

It was thought to be desirable, however, on educational grounds to require all Georgetown students to ponder the great religious questions and to study various authors who have wrestled with the profound human problems which religions have historically faced.

In 1966, the department adopted a new introductory course entitled "The Problem of God." It focuses on the phenomena of religious belief operative in human history and culture. It does not presuppose any specific religious faith on the part of the students, but it does assume a willingness on their part to examine their "religious" beliefs, whether theistic, atheistic, or agnostic. It also assumes that in our present world an educated person should acquire an understanding of and sympathy with the beliefs of others.

The introductory course is described as "student-centered." This is not simply a pedagogical strategy but results from a major shift in Catholic theologians' understanding of the enterprise of theology itself.

Prior to Vatican II, it was largely the case that theological truths were systematically expressed in Scholastic categories, rooted in a philosophy considered to be perennial. After Vatican II, this unified system was seen to be only one of many ways of interpreting Catholic faith, and it was a way which seemed unaware of its own historical and therefore time-conditioned character.

In 1968, the Theology Department was asked to submit to the curriculum revision committee of the College a statement of the department's aims. This statement first affirms that the department sees it as its function to aid students in bringing the light of intelligence to bear on their faith, to bring that faith to consciousness and articulation, to expose its inadequacies, and to foster its maturity.

Then the statement turns to a consideration of theology itself, advancing the view that theology is an endless and open-ended search to appropriate a religious tradition which is seen to be historically conditioned in its original expression, historically shaped in its transmission over the centuries, and inevitably affected in its present-day reception by our historical situation. By introducing students to this process of appropriation, the faculty is introducing students to the endless task of theology itself.

Given the fact that there is a historical coefficient at work in the handing on of even the most sacred teaching, the statement concluded:

> Theology, then, is necessarily affected by the growth of other sciences, particularly philosophy, history, hermeneutics, anthropology, sociology, and psychology. Major advances in these fields are continually presenting theology with new questions with which it must grapple.[34]

In a parallel way, students are continually challenged to adjust their beliefs as they learn more and more of life on this earth. Theology courses which introduce students to this process of grappling with new questions and of seeking truth through respectful dialogue and collaboration, or which make students a part of the "conversation" with classic religious texts and current questions, are courses which introduce students to the present method of theological reflection.

In the years since its adoption in 1966, the "Problem of God" course has regularly incorporated new perspectives from current theological thinking, and what is now done in the course is properly described as "foundational theology."[35]

The objective of the course is to foster in the student a critically appreciative awareness of the religious dimension of human existence. The course reflects modern theology's conviction that the mature appropriation of a religious tradition today involves a critical awareness of the various modes of religious expression. Religious life itself is typically spontaneous, "naïve," and not self-critical. However, contemporary theology has been shaped considerably by the critical spirit of modern thought, and sees the need to place "naïve" religious life under critical examination.

Such an examination must avoid reducing religious belief to a mere emotional state or psychological mechanism. When properly carried out, it should encourage the emergence of what Paul Ricoeur has called a "second" or "post-critical naïveté." This is the stance of a mature religious consciousness which has learned with the tools of reason and science to be self-critical without being reductionistic.

A mature religious consciousness adopts an attitude of abiding reverence toward the symbolic and mythic expressions in which religious consciousness and a sense of mystery are "naïvely" embodied. When approached with humility rather than with a spirit of arrogance or mastery, these expressions yield depths of meaning that would otherwise go unnoticed. A mature religious consciousness is at the same time aware of the possibly narrowing and even dehumanizing effects of an uncritical relation to symbol and myth.

The objective of fostering a critically appreciative awareness of the religious dimension of human existence can be achieved in a variety of ways. There are, however, certain shared concerns and themes that cut across the diversity and give an overarching unity to the course. Each version of the course, for example, deals in some fashion with such questions as the following: What is religion and what is its value (socially, psychologically, ethically)? Why are people religious? What is the source of the belief in God? What does the word "God" mean? Will the sense of the sacred disappear in a secular culture? Why are secularism, atheism, and agnosticism so plausible to many thinkers today and implausible to others? What are we to make of suffering and evil?

The aim of the "Problem of God" course, then, is to provide students with the option of choosing for themselves a post-critical interpretation of religious life as an alternative to either uncritical religion on the one hand, or on the other, a reductionism that would explain it away. It provides in many differing ways a "pedagogy into mystery," which is one of the tasks of a foundational approach in religious studies.

2. THE COMPOSITION OF THE FACULTY

Until the 1960s, religious instruction at Georgetown had been carried out, with only an occasional exception, by Jesuit priests. Vatican II, however, had given a great impetus to the ecumenical movement, seeking greater unity among Christian churches, and to serious dialogue with non-Christian religions, in the interest of greater harmony and collaboration in building a better world. Theologians became more and more interested in carrying on their work in an ecumenical setting. Furthermore, the new rationale for Georgetown's theology program placed a high value on bringing students into respectful dialogue with a plurality of religious perspectives. The time had clearly come to introduce this plurality into the composition of the faculty in the Theology Department.

Beginning in 1967, Protestant and Jewish theologians joined the faculty. Over the years, this policy has changed the department from one entirely composed of Jesuits with seminary training in Catholic theology to a faculty composed of men and women from various religious traditions, including a substantial number of Jesuits, all of whom hold doctorates from various universities. Inevitably, this single change has had the most far-reaching consequences for the theology program at Georgetown.

This dramatic change occurred not only at Georgetown but throughout Catholic and Jesuit higher education. In 1967, a group of twenty-six leading Catholic educators participated in a seminar which issued a statement on the nature and role of the contemporary Catholic university. The secretary of this seminar, Neil G. McCluskey, S.J., wrote in the preamble to the statement:

> The group clearly recognized that the presence of and active participation by persons who are not Catholics in the Catholic university community are most desirable and, indeed, even necessary to bring authentic universality to the Catholic university itself. Those of other views, whether students, faculty members, or administrators, bring rich contributions from their own traditions. They also insure by their active participation the seriousness and integrity of the search for understanding and commitment.[36]

In 1969, the Jesuit Educational Association sponsored a Workshop on Jesuit Colleges and Universities. The participants listed as one of the "distinctive characteristics of Jesuit higher education" the following:

> *A Genuine Ecumenism*—Religious belief and behavior are learned and lived within a tradition. Roman Catholicism has been the tradition that has nourished education in Jesuit colleges. A substantial number of educators and students in these colleges have represented and will, in all likelihood, continue to represent that tradition.

> Today, the Roman Catholic Church clearly affirms the values of other religious traditions, Christian and non-Christian, as well as the human concerns expressed by non-believers. It encourages honest dialogue between these traditions. This ecumenical openness must be realized on our campuses, in the classroom, in social and religious activities, and in the makeup of faculty, administration and student body.[37]

The participants in this workshop argue that the theology program in Jesuit colleges should give serious attention to the world's great religions in the conviction that Catholicism does not claim to be the exclusive possessor of revelation, but teaches "an openness to truth wherever it is found."[38]

3. THE DEVELOPMENT OF ELECTIVE COURSE OFFERINGS

The change in composition of the faculty enabled the department to offer a wide variety of courses. The new rationale envisaged that the number of required courses in theology for each student would be reduced from four to two, thus giving the students many more electives in junior and senior years.[39]

It is in keeping with our traditions and the religious backgrounds of our students that the largest number of these elective offerings is in the Christian tradition. The most remarkable development in this area is the rise of interest in biblical courses. After the twenty or so years of the Murray Plan, when the freshman required course consisted of a study of the Gospels and the life of Christ, Georgetown students manifested a strong resistance to coursework in this area and it was dropped from the program in 1966. A few years later (1973), when a new course, "Introduction to Biblical Literature," was introduced, two hundred students enrolled in it as an elective. Interest grew and enrollments rose as the department added more sections of the course. By the 1979-80 school year, registration in the course had reached over four hundred and in 1987-88 there were 650 students electing this course.

There are probably a number of different factors to explain the popularity of this course. Certainly, the faculty members teaching the course are largely responsible. Perhaps the fact that students are free to elect the course or not is also a contributing factor. Finally, the method employed in teaching the course may play a role in the course's success. This method ideally achieves the same goals as the "Problem of God" course in promoting the development in the student of critical consciousness.[40]

In order to understand the Bible, students must develop the skills needed to learn how to grasp the meaning of texts from an ancient culture. These skills turn out to be the same skills needed to understand texts from our own culture, and to interpret reliably what others are saying to us. Ultimately, they are needed if we are to come to an understanding of ourselves.

James P. M. Walsh, who began teaching the "Introduction to Biblical Literature" at Georgetown in 1973, lists certain habits of mind which the student of the biblical tradition should learn: reflectiveness, imaginative capacity, hermeneutical sophistication, and self-critical awareness.[41]

The student should learn to read a text in the light of the world of experience in which it takes shape, as an expression of the self-understanding of the people Israel or the early Christian community.

The student is taught to keep in mind various levels of meaning embedded in the text, as an original story is passed on (and inevitably reinterpreted in the retelling) within a faith community over many generations. Thus, a tension arises between an "original meaning" of a story and later meanings within a tradition.

Finally, the effort made by the student to enter imaginatively into the world of the ancient Near East or early Christianity brings to the surface the student's own biases, presuppositions, and ways of imagining reality.

This description of the methods used in the biblical courses has been presented at some length because it expresses a style of teaching widely shared in the department. The broad range of elective courses currently offered is, of course, a direct result of the new rationale, but it is also due to a growth in the size of the department.[42] Each year there are more than a dozen courses offered in the areas of systematic theology, historical theology, and spirituality. An equally large number explore the ethical implications of Christian faith. About the same number introduce the student to various "world religions": Judaism, Hinduism, Buddhism, Islam, and African religions.

These courses do not form a unified program. What they share is a focus on promoting in the student moral and religious growth in a context of freedom and intellectual challenge.

4. THE MAJOR PROGRAM IN THEOLOGY

What has been described up to now is a fourth stage in religious instruction at Georgetown University. The current two-course requirement, the Theology Department's contribution to the general liberal arts education of the Main Campus schools, is our distinct way of carrying out a task begun two centuries ago. To give a complete picture of this fourth stage of religious instruction, however, a word must be said about the initiation of a major program in theology.

In the fall of 1967, members of the department began to discuss the possibility of beginning a major program. Vatican II had stimulated a great deal of interest in new forms of theological reflection. The lay faculty who had recently joined the department were the precursors of many more to come. Teaching positions in the Theology departments of Catholic schools were no longer filled entirely by clergy and members of religious congregations. A few students had even begun to express interest in such a major.

Benefits to the theology faculty itself were obvious: the opportunity to offer specialized courses to small groups of interested students, the stimulus for research and publication, added incentives for recruiting new faculty and retaining qualified colleagues, and a stronger base for interdisciplinary work with other departments.

The major program began in 1968 with a single track, the Christian Theology concentration. Over the years we have added four additional tracks: Biblical Studies, Christian Ethics, World Religions, and Religious Studies.

In terms of numbers, the major program was quite small at the beginning. The first graduating class in 1970 consisted of four majors. The numbers grew slowly and by the end of the first ten years 82 students had graduated with a major in theology. In the course of the second ten-year period (1980-89), 133 more majored in theology.

Our most recent survey of majors (1986) indicated that roughly one-third had gone on to graduate school, another third had moved into some form of religious ministry or teaching, and the remainder had taken this program as a humanities major for personal enrichment. In a number of cases, students took Theology as a second major and then proceeded to law school or medical school or into the business world.

The introduction of the major program brought the Theology Department to a new level of development. It ceased being simply a service department, staffing required courses for the five undergraduate schools.

Conclusion

So, the conclusion of this study would apparently be this: religious education at Georgetown has proceeded through a series of stages, each with its own distinct rationale. First, there was catechetical instruction, largely for students of grammar-school and high-school age. There followed a more systematic presentation of the Catholic faith, intended for college-age students, which also served as a defense of the faith in an age of rationalism. The third stage was characterized by an attempt to fashion a "theology for the layman," based on a particular understanding of the role of the laity in the Catholic church.

Our current rationale is certainly distinct from each of the three previous ones and so constitutes a fourth stage. This rationale is expressed in a program which seeks to promote critical appropriation of the religious dimension of human existence and encourages thoughtful dialogue with various religious traditions. What began as extracurricular catechetical instruction for Catholic students has become over the years an introduction to theological reflection and religious studies as part of the core curriculum for all students.

IMAGINING THE FUTURE

In the best of all possible worlds, a Bicentennial would arrive as did the infant Jesus, at least according to the Roman martyrology, "when the whole world was at peace." In such circumstances, it would be simple to describe the present and anticipate the future. Our Bicentennial is in that regard poorly timed. Ours is a time of ferment. The changes that have taken place in our world over the last thirty years have been extensive and give promise of greater changes to come. The "modern era," we are told, is over. We are now living in the age of "postmodernity," which David Tracy characterizes as an age of radical plurality and radical ambiguity.[43] In a future book Tracy plans to assess the implications of postmodernity for interpreting the Christian tradition:

> What the "essence of Christianity" might be after Christians seriously acknowledge first, the plurality within their own traditions, second, the import of the many other religious traditions for Christian self-understanding and third, the profound cognitive, moral,

> and religious ambiguity of Christianity itself is, to put it mildly, a very difficult question . . .[44]

It is a challenging time to be a theologian—and an exciting one.

While maintaining our commitment to the Catholic tradition, we wish to continue to grow ecumenically. Georgetown has received a major gift to endow a program in Jewish Studies, which will probably be an interdisciplinary program, but may be located in the Theology Department. Given the Catholic character of this school, this is most appropriate since the Jewish tradition is the olive tree on which Christianity was grafted as a "wild olive shoot" (Rom 11:17). We currently have one position devoted to the Hindu religious tradition and another to the Buddhist religious tradition. We need to increase our coursework in African and African-American religious traditions. When our resources permit, we would like to add a position in the area of Islamic studies.

The department will almost certainly experience a continuing decline in the number of Jesuits teaching theology.[45] As in so many other areas in the Catholic church today, tasks once carried out by clergy and religious congregations are being taken up by the laity. Theological scholarship is increasingly becoming the province of laypersons who are professional theologians.

In terms of the undergraduate program, there is currently much discussion of revising our core curriculum, and perhaps moving from a five-course to a four-course curriculum. In either case, I expect Georgetown to maintain its strong commitment to a liberal arts education which includes theological reflection on the religious dimension of human life. The major program, now twenty years old, is solidly established. The future may bring some rise in the number of students majoring in theology, especially if the size of the undergraduate student body is increased, but I think this program will remain relatively small. The most important issue for the department's future is the inauguration of a graduate program in theology. A graduate program will foster the academic development of its current faculty, providing the stimulus for more research and publication. A graduate program will also strengthen the present faculty by the appointment of additional members.

Out of respect for our ancestors, we should probably speak of the *restoration* of our graduate program since, from its earliest days, Georgetown did have a theological faculty. It was established, not for the purpose of educating lay students, but to provide the seminary courses necessary for members of the Society of Jesus.

The first theology professor was Peter Epinette, S.J., who arrived in 1807 to direct the studies of four Jesuit seminarians. The number of faculty and students was quite small, but the hopes invested in this enterprise were very great.[46] In 1833, the Maryland Mission was made into "the Province of Maryland," and in the same year the Sacred Congregation for the Propagation of the Faith granted Georgetown the power to confer doctoral degrees in theology.[47]

Jesuits continued to make their theological studies at Georgetown until 1869, when the theological faculty was transferred to Woodstock, Maryland. This decision had serious consequences for Georgetown which continue to the present day. Shea in his centennial history loses no opportunity to underscore the point that Woodstock "is really at present the Theological Department of Georgetown University."[48]

In 1897, the president of Georgetown, J. Havens Richards, labeled the decision "a grave error of policy," not only for Georgetown, which lost its highest faculty, but also for Woodstock itself:

> The Professors and students were transported to a semi-wilderness, remote from libraries, from contact with the learned world, and from all those stimulating influences which affect intellectual life in large centers of population and culture.[49]

Woodstock did eventually make its way back to the Georgetown campus in time for the celebration of the Bicentennial, but in a much altered form. After spending a century in this "more retired seat of ecclesiastical learning,"[50] the theological faculty moved to New York City, but after a few years the school was closed and the faculty disbanded. The library, a carefully built-up collection of books and periodicals, including some of the same books which had been carted out to Woodstock, Maryland, in 1869, returned to the campus of Georgetown University in 1975, where it is being given at least a temporary home until its next journey. The Woodstock name continues on, however, in the Woodstock Theological Center, an autonomous research institute which is housed at present on the Georgetown campus.

Through most of the nineteenth century, then, Georgetown regularly conferred doctorates in theology and divinity. These degrees, however, given in virtue of authority received from Rome, are properly referred to as "pontifical degrees." The Theology Department is considering another sort of graduate program, one whose degrees would be granted in virtue of Georgetown University's charter as an American university. This is more in keeping with current university organization in the United States.

Given Georgetown's traditions and its statement of goals and objectives, it is an anomaly that it does not have a graduate program in theology. Georgetown ought to be a university which offers to the church in the United States a place where the riches of the Catholic tradition are continually explored and where there is an ongoing critical evaluation of the Catholic tradition as it faces a very challenging future.

I am uncertain at this writing exactly what shape it will take, but I am fairly certain that a graduate program of some sort will be established in the near future. We cannot, given our resources, do justice to all major theological questions. I believe we will use our resources best if, in the spirit of John Carroll, we set our sights on a worthy goal, establish our own "modest academy," and serenely say, as he did over two hundred years ago: "the difficulties indeed perplex, but do not dishearten me."[51]

Notes

1. *Classical Journal*, 97, Georgetown University Archives (hereafter GUA). This volume, the diary of the prefect of studies, for no known reason is referred to as the "Classical Journal," and I will honor that tradition in this essay.

2. Ibid., 98.

3. Ibid., 29.

4. "Proposals for Establishing an Academy at George-Town, Patowmack-River, Maryland" [1787], Maryland Province Archives (hereafter MPA) 56 R 1.

5. "Prospectus of 1798," GUA.

6. "Prospectus of 1833," GUA.

7. Bernard A. Maguire, while president (1852-58), explained this rule to a Protestant member of Congress from Louisiana and asked what he would think if his son wished to become a Catholic. The Congressman replied immediately that he would have no objection whatever if it would make his son a better boy. On one point, however, he was very particular: "If my son leaves this College anything but a good Democrat, let him not come home to me." Cf. John Gilmary Shea, *History of Georgetown University* (Washington, D.C.: P.F. Collier, 1891), 195-96.

8. "Prospectus of 1798," GUA.

9. "Proposals for Establishing an Academy at George-Town."

10. *Classical Journal*, 150.

11. In 1850, Georgetown College had a seven-year program: four years of

preparatory school and three years of "senior classes." The following year, this was rearranged into three years of preparatory school and four years of senior classes. It seems reasonable to conclude that the division of 1851 gives us for the first time a clearly demarcated four-year program that we may refer to as "college" in our sense of the term. The religious instruction given to the senior classes, beginning in 1851, may then be compared with what today is referred to as "College Theology" or "Religious Studies."

12. *Catalogue of the College, 1868-69*, 8.

13. F.X. Weninger, S.J., *A Manual of the Catholic Religion*, 3d ed. (New York: Benziger Bros., 1872), 4.

14. Ibid., 9.

15. Wilhelm Wilmers, S.J., *Handbook of the Christian Religion for the Use of Advanced Students and the Educated Laity*, ed. Rev. James Conway, S.J. (New York: Benziger Brothers, 1891).

16. Ibid., iv.

17. Ibid., v.

18. Ibid., v.

19. *General Catalogue of the University, 1907-08*, 52.

20. *Catalogue of the College, 1935-36*, 19.

21. John Courtney Murray, "Towards a Theology for the Layman," *Theological Studies* 5 (1944), 43-75; 340-76.

22. This "principle of differentiation" had already been raised at a conference held at Campion College in 1938, and Murray, in fact, took one side of the controversy that arose there and gave it a clear and systematic exposition in his *Theological Studies* articles.

23. Ibid., 75.

24. Ibid., 345.

25. This observation comes from Eugene B. Gallagher, then chairman of Georgetown's Religion Department; cf. *Proceedings of the National Jesuit Institute on College Religion, 1951*, 31 (mimeographed), Theology Department Archives (TDA).

26. Murray, "Towards a Theology for the Layman," 346.

27. Ibid., 347. On the basis of this principle, Murray ruled out the practice of beginning the college religion course with apologetics which, generally speaking, is "of small religious value, and may do positive harm in the direction of rationalism and scepticism to the mentally and religiously amorphous freshman." Ibid., 348.

28. This principle is consistently employed by Ignatius Loyola in his Spiritual Exercises, and, as James P. M. Walsh argues in his contribution to this collection, ought always to be a feature of Jesuit education.

29. Quoted from a report to the College Dean by John F. Devine, Assistant Professor of Theology (March 14, 1962), 7, TDA.

30. Philip Gleason, "The Search for Unity and Its Sequel," in his *Keeping the Faith* (Notre Dame, Ind.: University of Notre Dame Press, 1987), 139. He adds that Catholics who had absorbed this mentality "had about the worst possible preparation for the sixties."

31. "Theology Department" Box, GUA.

32. Letter of Joseph K. Drane (18 April 1963), addressed to the Provincial, John M. Daley (TDA).

33. In 1966, Catholics numbered roughly 83% of the undergraduate student body. Over the next ten years this figure dropped to 61% and has remained at about that level.

34. Minutes of the departmental meeting, March 19, 1968, TDA.

35. The remainder of this section is largely drawn from John F. Haught's contribution to the Theology Department's *Self-Study Report, 1987*, 23-28, TDA.

36. "Statement on the Nature of the Contemporary Catholic University by Members of the North American Region of the International Federation of Catholic Universities," July 23, 1967, TDA. Georgetown's president, Gerard J. Campbell, was one of the signatories. This statement is printed in the report of the Denver Workshop, 12-17. See n. 36 below. McCluskey adds that the group did not attempt to describe how those who are not Catholic can be integrated with the Catholic community of learners so that the Catholic university might become a "Catholic-sponsored pluralistic society." Ibid., 12.

37. *Guidelines for Jesuit Higher Education: The Consensus Statements, Recommendations, and Committee Reports of the J.E.A. Denver Workshop on Jesuit Universities and Colleges: Their Commitment in a World of Change*, ed. Eugene E. Grollmes, S.J. (Washington, D.C.: Jesuit Educational Association, 1969), 6.

38. Ibid., 20.

39. This became, in fact, a feature of the Main Campus curriculum revision which went into effect in 1970. Since then, the theology requirement has been two courses, the "Problem of God" and one other, chosen from some twenty or more elective offerings.

40. For this reason the department approves the substitution of this course for the required introductory course.

41. The following paragraphs are drawn from the Biblical Studies section Walsh wrote for the Theology Department's *Self-Study Report, 1987*, 34-38, TDA.

42. There are currently 22 full-time positions, with authorization for two additional positions over the next two years. In addition, there are six or seven adjunct professors. The department regularly offers between 110-120 courses or sections of courses each year.

43. Cf. David Tracy, *Plurality and Ambiguity* (San Francisco: Harper and Row, 1987), chaps. 3 and 4.

44. Ibid., x.

45. Fifteen years ago, there were fourteen Jesuits in the department. That number has now dropped to nine. More significantly, the department has hired only one Jesuit in the last ten years.

46. Since the Society of Jesus was about to be restored, the Jesuit superior general wrote to John Carroll from Russia in 1805, authorizing him to receive former Jesuits back into the Society. The following year five Fathers were sent to Georgetown from Russia to establish a scholasticate for the training of future Jesuits in America.

47. The Jesuit superior general, John Roothaan, had petitioned for this authority from Pope Gregory XVI. Roothaan argued that this would make

Georgetown the only university in the United States to grant a doctorate in Catholic theology and consequently, "young ecclesiastics allured by the hope of the Doctorate, which is highly esteemed in those States, would gather there from all directions, and thus make thoroughly the course of theology, which they now make superficially in their dioceses." Cf. Shea, *History of Georgetown University*, 107-08.

48. Shea, *History of Georgetown University*, 182.

49. J. Havens Richards, "An Explanation in Reply to Some Recent Strictures," *Woodstock Letters* 26 (1897), 147.

50. Shea, *History of Georgetown University*, 226.

51. John Carroll to Charles Plowden, January 22, 1787; cited in John M. Daley, S.J., *Georgetown University: Origin and Early Years* (Washington, D.C.: Georgetown University Press, 1957), 37.

John F. Haught
Theology Department

Science Education and the Importance of Story

Georgetown University is gifted with excellent scientists and science teachers. Students at the undergraduate level, about whom I am concerned here, give consistently high praise to their professors. The many talented students who major in the natural sciences are well prepared for graduate and medical studies. If our science majors are served well, however, a question remains about the quality of what I shall broadly call "science education" pertaining to the students at large. The extent of interest in serious study of science by nonscientists both at Georgetown and elsewhere is far from desirable.

In his recent Priestly Medal address entitled "Education of the Next Generation of Nonscientists," Frank H. Westheimer emphasizes the "vertical" nature of science education.[1] Science education, he argues, requires that we recognize how one science builds on another, and that without mastering the tools pertaining to one we will not be able to go on to the next. For example, it is impossible to learn much physics without calculus, or chemistry without physics, or biology without chemistry, etc. This verticality means that our students cannot acquire much scientific knowledge with only a scattered requirement or two here and there. Where there are no solid foundations there is little hope for scientific literacy. The only remedy, then, is to increase the number of science requirements.

However, the core curricula in our best universities fail to give science sufficient emphasis, requiring too few two-semester courses.

Compromise courses that dip lightly into science, with titles such as "Physics for Poets," simply will not do, though they are better than nothing at all. In Westheimer's view, only a much heavier load of science, and less emphasis on the core curriculum, will respond to the present crisis in science education.

However, it is worth asking whether such exposure to more and more courses will by itself do very much to address the deeper problems in science education nationwide today. Increasing requirements, without rethinking the whole enterprise of science education in a fundamental way, may actually evoke resentment and even revulsion from many students. No doubt there is a vertical character to mature knowledge of science, but the immediate problem we face today is that of how to get our students interested in science at all. It is a question of how to craft a curriculum in science exciting enough that students will be willing even to begin a journey up the hierarchy of scientific disciplines with enthusiasm rather than fear, uncertainty, or even hostility. Unless they can situate their calculus, physics, chemistry, and biology courses within a larger pattern that gives meaning to the individual branches of the learning tree, students will not likely become genuinely excited about science. Obviously, the present situation of massive resistance to scientific learning will not improve dramatically until students become much more excited about the various scientific disciplines than they are now.

But how can such interest and enthusiasm be generated? And can science teachers alone communicate this fervor by virtue of their own zest, good will, skill, and expertise in the classroom? Perhaps we need to examine more carefully the wider educational matrix in which departments of science do their work. In terms of a broader academic ecology, how may the university as a whole promote awareness and love of the sciences? Scientists all by themselves cannot be expected to provide the motivation for scientific learning. The "simple location" of science education, isolating it and failing to examine its relationship with other aspects of the educational process, may be a major reason why students often fail to see its relevance. Excitement about science can take root in students' minds only if they are able to discern in it a wider meaning than they can generally procure from the science classroom itself.

For a few students the incentive to take up science is already present. In the best of such cases, a natural wonder about the workings of nature is sufficient stimulus for them to master the arduous technical, mathematical, or computer skills needed to do science in depth. In the worst cases, students are willing to meet the academic requirements in chemistry or biology because it is essential preparation for further professional advancement such as medical school (which in turn may be sometimes seen only as instrumental to the goal of having a fashionable and lucrative career). In between these two extremes lie the students with only a scattered and tentative involvement in science at best. It is especially with this body of nonscientists that I am concerned here. For these students the fear of mathematics, an aversion to work, a distaste for the laboratory—these and many other factors may contribute to their scientific lassitude. But even for serious students, commitment to science sometimes seems too difficult. And when science is presented as a vertical series of levels to be mastered only with great difficulty and expenditure of time, students are easily discouraged from becoming involved with it at all.

For science majors, the vertical nature of science is accepted as an inevitable challenge, but for nonscientists it sometimes poses a seemingly insurmountable obstacle. If the latter perceive that the hierarchy of interlocking scientific disciplines requires climbing step by arduous step, the journey will simply seem too long. Many of them will not even want to climb the first step. Standing at the foot of Westheimer's imposing stack of levels, such students will likely be so overwhelmed that they will refuse to embark at all on what could be an exciting journey of discovery.

It is my purpose here to set forth an alternative model that might be placed side by side with the vertical mapping of science education proposed by Westheimer. It is one that may help bring students inside the milieu of science in a way that the vertical approach alone cannot always accomplish. This model is based on the growing persuasion that science, in a carefully qualified sense, may be understood along the lines of "story." This narrative model may serve as the general context for all of our science students, one that they can come back to again and again as they climb the mountain of distinct disciplines. The entire academic community may participate in the development of this model.

In order to be interesting and captivating to nonscience students (and to science majors, for that matter), science education could usefully be linked more closely to the genre of story, not just informally but in a deliberate, formal, and structured way, one that might eventually even be reflected in the shape of the curriculum and the sequence of science offerings (although I cannot develop this idea here). Without doing violence to them, both science itself and the cosmos that science studies might be presented to our students in a more deliberately narrative way than has been the case in the past. In the first place, science itself could be presented more explicitly as the result of an adventurous story of human discovery. And the discoveries of science, in turn, could be arranged and presented according to the format of what might be called "the cosmic story."

Situated within such a narrative framework, science and the cosmos of science may arouse less trepidation in initiates than Westheimer's imposing hierarchy of sciences. The narrative model stands a better chance of drawing nonspecialists into the world of science, especially if they can see immediately that they are part of the story themselves. The narrative form of expression is much more suited to the adventure-seeking spontaneity of students. It is capable of arousing immediate interest since story is inherently more interesting than purely theoretical modes of learning.[2]

I should emphasize, though, that the narrative model is not a substitute for the vertical. Rather, there is a place for both in serious science education. Indeed, quantitatively speaking, the bulk of one's science education will be preoccupied with mastering the various steps in the hierarchy. But in the wider context of science education the vertical model can be adjoined explicitly to, without being dissolved into, a more sweepingly narrative approach. An abiding sense of the narrative dimensions of science and the universe could then nourish the students' consciousness throughout the process of their science education.

From its beginnings, human consciousness has been aroused to enthusiasm for further exploration primarily through what might loosely be called "narrative" modes of expression. It is quite likely that the same is true today, though we educators often seem unaware of it. The function of early myths was to tell about how things began and where they are going so that a sense of purpose and zest for exploring the world would take root in people's lives. Religions have used the form of story as their primary medium. Even though philosophy since Plato has abstracted somewhat from story, one might argue that philosophy has been most able to motivate people when it has preserved its lifeline to a strongly narrative undercurrent. Plato never forgot that myth is what gives rise to theory.[3] Marxism is a good illustration, with its myth of matter evolving dialectically toward freedom. Much of its power consists in its allowing devotees to feel that they are part of a meaningful narrative with the "sense of an ending." Philosophy and theology have been least able to move people when they have strayed far from their mythic matrices and modeled themselves too closely on classical scientific method, reducing themselves to the analysis and clarification of language. Important as such analysis and clarification are in the total context of learning, unless they can be brought back into the narrative mainstream of living purposefully, they remain stranded in irrelevancy.

Is it possible that we have situated science and science education too far from some enlivening narrative framework? Science has rightly been tied explicitly to the detached and impersonal way of knowing that philosophers like Bernard Lonergan refer to as "theory."[4] Classical science and its successes are in part the result of its having learned to leave out or abstract from the personally mythic or narrative aspects that apparently sabotage scientific objectivity. Pure scientific method has to bracket out the soft, personal, affect-arousing aspects of narratives. The ideal of scientific detachment is one of the most significant developments of our intellectual history. The question here is not whether science should back off from its theoretic or detached ways of knowing. Rather, the issue is whether the wider context of science education can afford to ignore the narrative aspects essential for learning.

There is an irrepressible narrative mode of consciousness that exists in humans prior to and alongside the theoretic mode such as we find in scientific method. And while science still correctly adheres to the demands of disinterestedness and dispassionateness inherent in theory, we are now in the peculiar situation where an increasing number of scientific writers and thinkers are expressing their scientific ideas in a more deliberately narrative form. They cannot help doing so, for the cosmos itself is in fact now presenting itself to them more and more as a story. And to leave out this narrative dimension would perhaps itself be unscientific. Yet in framing their ideas in the form of a story, scientists are now introducing ingredients that make it harder for them to be as dispassionate as they might be working in the context of theory alone.

Science *education* has also been tied explicitly to the detached and impersonal way of knowing that we call "theory." But what if it were to take on a more narrative character without at the same time losing its theoretical and vertical aspects? Bernard Lonergan thinks of any theoretical discipline as a departure which intends a return.[5] If it does not return us to the service of life or to a deeper appreciation of life, or to enriched contemplation, then theory has abandoned its proper role and become a dead end. Our students may sense that their scientific education is exclusively a theoretic departure that does not return. Theory is educationally fruitless unless it returns us to life and to the narrative mode of concrete involvement in life. If we leave our students stranded in theory, learning may lose its luster.

Unless its various theoretical aspects can be reconnected to some larger story, the human energy needed to sustain the scientific educational enterprise may eventually sag. Those who still do science with enthusiasm probably indwell some invigorating story, though they may not always be conscious of exactly what it is. At its best it may be the story of the long human struggle for truth, in which the implicit cognizance that one is part of this noble journey provides the tacit basis for further aspiration to scientific knowledge. At its worst it may be the story of a nation's rise to technological supremacy that drives scientific research. In any case, science may become more interesting to our students if it can be connected in some way to the mythic, epic, dramatic, and narrative aspects of consciousness.

Because of our biases about the impersonal nature of science, such a suggestion may at first appear excessively romantic. Many philosophers of science would find it highly suspect. But I am not proposing here that all of science be reduced to story, only that those engaged in teaching it exploit more formally and explicitly its clearly narrative characteristics. For the resources are now becoming more and more available even within the sciences themselves for such an acknowledgment of the connections of science to narrative. Science, almost in spite of itself, is increasingly taking on the features of a story. It is doing so in two ways. First, science itself is now explicitly recognized as the cumulative work of a community of scientists with an identifiable tradition passionately committed over a long period of time to the pursuit of a value, namely, that of scientific truth.[6] In a very concrete sense, science is the heroic story of men and women bound together by a common set of meanings, especially those associated with the value of discovery. If science is what scientists actually do, and not just abstract formulas in textbooks, then science is itself a story, a human epic of discovery in the same general arena with other great human adventures. And second, the universe is increasingly presenting itself to scientists also as a story. This clearly narrative countenance of science has the interesting consequence also of drawing it closer to the other disciplines in the university. We may now look at each of these two narrative aspects of science in more detail.

Science as a Story of Discovery

We know today more clearly than ever that the motivating force behind science is a spirit of discovery, nurtured by a community with its own tradition and authority (not totally unlike that of an ecclesial body). As such, science falls within the area of what Michael Polanyi calls "personal knowledge." But personal knowledge is linked to numerous tacit cognitional elements that are shaped by symbolic and narrative factors explicitly studied and tutored by those disciplines we loosely call the humanities. Though any particular scientific exercise demands that the scientist detach herself from considerations of values, purposes and meanings, the underlying impetus to exploration and the pursuit of knowledge, without which the scientific enterprise would wither away, is deeply personal, social, and communal. As such, the dynamism behind the actual doing of science partakes of a sense of reality given by the stories or "myths" within which persons and communities dwell at the deeper levels of their existence.

It is these "mythic" components that we need to accentuate as we diagnose the failure of science education in recent times. As we examine this failure we cannot profitably bracket out consideration of the stories in which persons, including those in universities, spontaneously dwell. We cannot ignore how these stories function to motivate or discourage exploration. What story or stories might our students' minds "indwell" (to use Polanyi's term) so as to provide them with the spirit of exploration needed for scientific discovery? It seems that for many of our students there is no longer a sense of continuity with the narrative traditions that have sustained the scientific enterprise in the past. We need, more than anything else, then, to reconnect them to some animating story with which they can identify and in which they might immerse themselves.

It may be that classical scientific method itself has provided a thought-form that is now sabotaging its own self-perpetuation by leaving out ingredients essential for education in science. It is not that scientists *qua* scientists have undermined their project. Rather a certain type of philosophical interpretation of scientific method (we may call it "scientism") has enshrined science's allegedly "impersonal" ideal of truth-seeking as the only fully appropriate form of knowing. The scientific method of seeking explanation of all things, including the activity of persons, as far as possible in impersonal terms, has been taken as the only legitimate road to the real. This policy has dismissed, as irrelevant to true knowledge, all those personal and mythic aspects of cognition that we now suspect energize the whole project of scientific pursuing of truth. It has done so by ignoring the personal and narrative aspects needed to sustain any adventure of discovery. It has even led to a "picture of the universe in which we ourselves are absent."[7]

Scientism (and not science itself) eventually upends the process of scientific discovery since it exaggerates science's impersonal, disinterested, dispassionate side and discards as trivial and uninteresting the tacit personal coefficients (such as myths or stories) involved in scientific discovery. In the long run, science education has been victimized by a philosophy of science that has reduced science to the processes of verification and proof, while ignoring the process of discovery.[8] Discovery, Polanyi insists, is the heart and soul of science. And yet writers on science like Karl Popper relegate it to psychology. Popper writes:

> The work of the scientist consists in putting forward and testing theories. The initial stage, the act of conceiving or inventing a theory, seems to me neither to call for logical analysis nor to be susceptible of it. The question how it happens that a new idea occurs to a man . . . may be of great interest to the empirical psychologist but it is irrelevant to the logical analysis of scientific knowledge.[9]

There is something almost puritanical about this refusal to talk about the messy but exciting business of discovery. Drusilla Scott comments that Popper knows there is more to science than questions of validity and verification, but like a Victorian on the subject of sex, he is flustered by the place of discovery in science: "None of that talk in our drawing room please."[10]

Extending the analogy, there is, of course, a place for clinical discussion of sexuality. And without such dispassionate treatment as is provided by the medical profession, the sexual experiences of many might be less fulfilling. It is easy to see in this example how the energy for sustaining such dispassionate "scientific" analyses is really an intense, though momentarily controlled, interest in and passion for sexual enjoyment. In a not entirely dissimilar way the whole scientific enterprise is sustained, as Polanyi and many others have shown, by a perhaps controlled but nonetheless passionate zest for discovery. Ironically, though, theories of science have often virtually ignored this obvious energizing dimension and the narrative soil out of which all passionate commitment grows.

If mainstream philosophy of science cannot make a place for a study of what goes into discovery, however, we can ill afford to neglect this aspect of science as we diagnose the problem of science education today. We must also talk about intellectual passion and focus on what it is that draws out our students' interest. Too often all they see in science is the ideal of impersonality and dispassionateness. In short, science seems sterile to them, whereas in fact it is a long story of discovery by human persons permeated by passion and interest. Here is what Polanyi, a scientist himself, has to say:

> Theories of scientific method which try to explain the establishment of scientific truth by any purely objective formal procedure are doomed to failure. Any process of enquiry unguided by intellectual passions would inevitably spread out into a desert of trivialities. Our vision of reality, to which our sense of scientific beauty responds, must suggest to us the kind of questions that it should be reasonable and interesting to explore.[11]

Science education, in the broad sense at least, has to be concerned with more than the instilling of scientific truths in our students. It has to be concerned with "visions of reality," with what activates our sense of beauty and, perhaps above all, with discerning whatever would be "interesting to explore."

If at all phases of their education our students could envisage science first of all as a story of discovery, and not just a vertical structure of disciplines to be mastered, their interest and personal involvement might be sustained more lastingly. In the larger story of scientific discovery they would meet numerous courageous men and women, knowledge of whose heroic quests would potentially allow them to see themselves as part of a community of explorers with a rich narrative tradition open to new truth. The narrative model seems well equipped to bring such personal aspects of science to the fore.

It is the responsibility of the entire university community to establish a climate in which science, especially in its narrative characteristics, will become personally interesting to our students. Different departments may contribute in various ways. For example, disciplines like philosophy, history, psychology, literature, and theology all have contributions to make in linking our students to the story of science and its significance for the shaping of human consciousness and the modern world. The explicit awareness of science as itself a narrative of exploration and discovery should also allow our students to see its connection with other areas of study.

It is not the task of scientists alone to communicate such a "vague" narrative sense to their students. Strictly speaking, scientists will rightly insist, their discipline typically abstracts from such soft notions. Each distinct scientific discipline deliberately loses itself in the particulars of its own field of inquiry.[12] It is not the job of science to "put it all together" into a cosmological synthesis, nor do we have any right to expect such inspiration from a discipline which quite appropriately prescinds methodologically from consideration of values and meanings. That requires the assistance of poets, artists, philosophers, and theologians. Science and science departments alone simply cannot be expected to give students a feeling for those deeper dimensions of discovery that might arouse in them a personal commitment to exploring the universe. To repeat, this is the task of the entire academic community.

The Universe as Story

The sense of the universe as a story has emerged all by itself from the collective sciences, and not just as a human projection onto nature. Perhaps more pedagogically significant even than the human story of scientific discovery is the story of the universe itself that we can easily see taking shape as the cumulative result of work by the individual sciences themselves. The outlines of a new cosmic story began to appear even in the seventeenth century. But especially after Darwin and modern evolutionary biology, after astronomy's settling on the unitary origin and expanding character of our present universe, and after geology's and quantum physics' detailing of the transformations of earth and matter, natural science has increasingly assumed the explicit form of a cosmic story.

Science, which had formerly presented us with cosmographies of a humanly uninhabitable universe, is now the main stimulus for a new story of the universe. It has increasingly, and almost in spite of itself, taken on the lineaments of a story of the cosmos. Although there have always been mythic and narrative undercurrents in presentations of scientific theory, the past century has brought forth a scientific vision that, starting from the Darwinian account of life on this planet, has moved back in time to embrace the astrophysical origins of the cosmos fifteen or twenty billion years ago. Holmes Rolston states that the most expressive metaphor for what science finds in nature today is no longer *law*, but *story*.[13]

A narrative evolutionary paradigm has come to dominate our scientific ways of thinking about the world. From astronomy and geology at one end of the natural continuum to the study of invisible physical events at the other, science itself has become the story of the universe. Accounts of evolution "from the Big Bang to the Big Brain" clearly tell a story. We need not enter here into disputes as to whether cosmic evolution has always or generally been progressive. All we need to do is notice that since the "Big Bang" occurred fifteen or twenty billion years ago some momentous things have happened, in particular the emergence of life and mind on our planet (and perhaps elsewhere). Both life and mind have generally had the tendency to complicate themselves more and more, for whatever reason. If we think in terms of the epochs of evolution, life and mind made their evolutionary transition into culture and civilization very recently, only a flash of time ago. Yet here too the struggle for complexity continued, and at an alarming rate of speed. The invention of agriculture, civilization, art, and culture, of nations, politics, education, and science—all of these developments exemplify the universe's impatience with monotony and urgent need for subtle shading and more intense modes of being, now that it has reached the human phase of its unfolding.

For nearly uncountable millennia our universe labored before it was in a condition of readiness to bring forth living beings. The heavy chemical elements required for life (carbon, oxygen, nitrogen, phosphorous, etc.) took several billion years of cooking time at the heart of stars before supernovae explosions eventually dispersed them throughout space. Countless more epochs elapsed before these elements began to cluster into planetary bodies like our earth. The chemicals that make up our terrestrial home, having finished their previous careers in some now dead star, finally coalesced five billion years ago into our own planet. Then a billion years or so later, after the Earth's surface had cooled sufficiently to sustain primitive organisms, life began to appear. And following endless more spans of patient waiting and experimentation, it burst forth into the extravagant arrays of higher organisms such as reptiles, birds, and mammals. Finally, perhaps two million years ago, our immediate prehuman ancestors began to appear in abundance and spread out over the face of the earth. That is not very long ago in terms of evolutionary time, and we can safely surmise that much more of the cosmic journey, perhaps the bulk of it, still lies ahead of us.

It is difficult to state these elementary scientific facts without acknowledging the ongoing narrative thread that ties them together and now pulls us into the story itself. The restlessness that launched matter on its pilgrimage toward complexity twenty billion years ago has apparently not yet been quieted.[14] It continues now in our own questioning minds and our spirit of exploration. In the modern development of human consciousness known as science we find one of the clearest illustrations of this exploratory restlessness that has its roots deep down in the cosmos itself. Surely, we could do a better job of grafting our academic curricula onto what may be the most fascinating story ever told.[15] Because of our contemporary awareness of the evolutionary, narrative character of the universe, and the growing sense of our species' continuity with this emergent process, we are now in a position to interpret the "long search" not only of myth, religion, and art, but also of science itself as a protracting of the cosmic struggle toward more intense syntheses. Such a way of looking at science, namely, as an extension of nature's own movement toward complexity, would prevent us from separating it from the story of the cosmos in which it is rooted. It might also make it appear more exciting to our students.[16]

The narrative character of science has enormous implications for integrating science with religious studies and other disciplines in the university. Some of these implications have recently been developed by Holmes Rolston, among others, in his splendid book, *Science and Religion*, and in a Roman Catholic context by Thomas Berry and Brian Swimme.[17] Swimme, a Catholic physicist and student of Berry, emphasizes how the narrative revolution in science is now capable of placing all our religious and other traditions against the more fundamental backdrop of a *cosmic* story. For the first time in our species' history, we now have a single story that can serve as the basis for intercultural and interreligious encounter. I wonder if it might not also serve as the foundation of interdisciplinary studies in which science would be given a prominent role. The physicist Swimme writes:

> . . . the universe, at its most basic level, is not so much matter or energy or information. The universe is story.
>
> Bolstering my conviction that story is the quintessential nature of the universe is the story of how story forced its way into the most anti-story domains of modern science, I mean physics and

> mathematics. For physicists during the modern period, "reality" meant the fundamental interactions in the universe. In a sense, a modern physicist would regard the world's essence as captured by the right group of mathematical equations. The rest of it—the story of the universe in time—was understood as nothing more than an explication of these fundamental laws.[18]

But now, in spite of great resistance to the idea, story has taken over as the dominant horizon of modern scientific knowledge. Swimme recalls how Einstein himself resisted the narrative implications in his own equations. They indicated that the universe is expanding, in which case the cosmos would have had a singular origin and then unfolded sequentially in various phases of a genuine story. But ". . . only when Edwin Hubble later showed him the empirical evidence that the universe was expanding did Einstein realize his failure of nerve. He later came to regard his doctoring of the field equations as the fundamental blunder of his scientific career."[19]

It is common scientific knowledge now that not only life, but the stars, galaxies, planets on the macroscale, and the subatomic layers at the microlevel, are all involved in transformations to which the word "story" seems more and more applicable. Swimme notes that story

> . . . forced its way still further into physics when in recent decades scientists discovered that even the fundamental interactions of the universe were the result of transformations in time. The laws that govern the physical universe today, and that were thought to be immutable and above development of the universe, were themselves the result of the development of the universe. That is, the story—rather than being simply governed by these laws—draws these laws into itself.[20]

But the word "story" is still not quite adequate. We might better characterize the cosmic process as an *adventure* story. Adventure, in the technical meaning given to it by Whitehead and process thought, is the search for ever more intense versions of ordered novelty.[21] The theme of the cosmos as adventure now lies at the center of scientific thought. But have we yet exploited this adventure story sufficiently for educational purposes?

The cosmos is itself an adventure of continual experimentation with novel forms of order, a struggle upward from simplicity toward increasing complexity. This straining for more complexity is not always successful. There are many backwards and sideways movements in the story of the universe's struggle upward from the simplicity of its origins. As in stories of war, there are long periods of waiting punctuated by brief episodes of terror, victory, and defeat. But over the long haul there has clearly been a general trend toward the emergence of more elaborate entities. And it is this generic ascent of the cosmos toward increasing complexity that we may call "adventure."

Adventure is the restlessness that moves a process beyond triviality and monotony toward more highly nuanced forms of order. Any process that seeks to complicate the arrangement of things is adventurous in nature. And such a penchant for more intense complexification seems to be an intrinsic characteristic of our universe. But do our students in their science education acquire a deep feeling for this adventurousness, or of their own participation in it? Or has science education, following the puritanical cautions of modern philosophy of science, abstracted too much from this exploratory fervor, even though science itself is a manifestation of it? With Rolston and Polanyi we have to ask whether, in leaving out of their theories the concretely historical and narrative aspects of nature, scientists and philosophers of science have neglected to feature some of the elements in science that might pull students (and the rest of us) into more intimate encounter with the world of nature.

Out of its abstractions science has conjured up nothing less than a dramatic narrative about the cosmos. It is no longer soft thinking to say quite literally that the universe is a story. But have our universities and their efforts toward promoting interest in science yet taken full educational advantage of science's own emerging narrative character? Ironically, at a time when the humanities are deconstructing stories and challenging narrative consciousness, science is beginning to flesh itself out more and more in the form of a fascinating cosmic saga. It may now be time to ponder ways of restructuring the science curriculum in a manner that makes our students more formally acquainted with the cosmic story from the "Big Bang" up to the present, and in such a way as to make it seem as dramatic and amazing to all of our students as it is to the scientists themselves.

Notes

1. Frank H. Westheimer, "Education of the Next Generation of Nonscientists," *Chemical and Engineering News* (4 July 1988), 32-38.

2. In my courses on science and religion I have often had students who had previously shown little interest in science, for example physics or molecular biology, suddenly developing such an interest after becoming acquainted with the "narrative" cosmological ideas of Whitehead, Polanyi, Teilhard, or even with the opposing cosmologies of soft and hard naturalism. Viewed from within the framework of such cosmological discussion, the more specialized scientific disciplines suddenly take on a new significance. It is especially on the basis of my own classroom experience at Georgetown that I am offering these proposals for a narrative approach to science education.

3. Paul Ricoeur sees philosophical theory as the gift of a symbolic-narrative matrix. See his *The Symbolism of Evil,* trans. E. Buchanan (Boston: Beacon Press, 1967).

4. Bernard J. F. Lonergan, S.J., *Insight: A Study of Human Understanding,* 3rd ed. (New York: Philosophical Library, 1970).

5. Ibid., xiii-xiv; xix.

6. Since it is commitment to values that gives meaning to people's lives, we may say that the pursuit of scientific truth has by itself been sufficiently meaningful to sustain the lives and spiritual health of many an individual in the past three centuries.

7. Michael Polanyi, *Personal Knowledge* (New York: Harper Torchbooks, 1964), 142.

8. Ibid., 14.

9. Karl Popper, *The Logic of Scientific Discovery* (London: Hutchinson, 1959), 31.

10. Drusilla Scott, *Everyman Revived* (Lewes, Sussex: The Book Guild Limited, 1985), 31.

11. Polanyi, *Personal Knowledge,* 135.

12. In a Polanyian way of thinking, any time we attend to such particulars, as happens in science laboratories and classrooms, we are momentarily "alienated" from wider meanings. Polanyi has no objections to such momentary estrangement, for it is a necessary part of scientific knowing. He objects only to our taking what is an essential part of scientific procedure and elevating it to the status of a cultural ideal. Life and education must resituate the alienating moments of science back into a wider and more meaningful context. If not, the motivation for further discovery will itself run dry. See Michael Polanyi, *The Tacit Dimension* (New York: Doubleday Anchor Books, 1967), 18-25.

13. Holmes Rolston, *Science and Religion* (New York: Random House, 1987), 119.

14. See, for example, Louise B. Young, *The Unfinished Universe* (New York: Simon and Schuster, 1986).

15. For example, Fred Hoyle, the astronomer, writes: "No literary genius could have invented a story one-hundredth part as fantastic as the sober facts that have been unearthed by astronomical science." *The Nature of the Universe* (New York: New American Library, 1960), 117-18.

16. Berry notes that our most common scientific terms still retain a highly mythic content. Words like energy, life, matter, form, universe, gravitation, evolution, atom, nucleus, electron, molecule, cell, organism, "each of these spills over into metaphor and mystery as soon as they are taken seriously," in "The Dream of the Earth," *Cross Currents* 37 (1987), 203.

17. See, for example, Anne Lonergan and Caroline Richards, eds., *Thomas Berry and the New Cosmology* (Mystic, Conn.: Twenty-third Publications, 1987); and Thomas Berry, "The New Story," *Cross Currents* 37 (1987), 187-99.

18. Brian Swimme, "The Cosmic Creation Story" (unpublished paper).

19. Ibid.

20. Ibid.

21. For this discussion of adventure, see Alfred North Whitehead, *Adventures of Ideas* (New York: The Free Press, 1967), esp. 252-96.

JOSEPH E. EARLEY
Chemistry Department

Science and Story at Georgetown

The proposal that John Haught has made deserves careful attention.[1] He suggests that we recognize that science is not some mechanical, semi-automatic method of truth-generation but rather that it is an intensely personal quest ("adventure," in Whitehead's sense), influenced by "stories" which individual scientists "indwell." On that basis, however, it seems rash to consider the general science education of undergraduates (Haught's main concern) apart from some attention to the place of science in the overall intellectual culture of the campus. It seems clear that "stories" that are dominant in a university in particular historical periods must strongly influence general education in science. Before considering some aspects of Haught's proposal in detail, I would like to tell a few stories about science at Georgetown.

The Nineteenth Century

At the first meeting of the Directors of Georgetown College in 1797, the main aim of the institution was clearly set out: "the improvement of youth in the three important branches of Physical, Moral, and Literary Education."[2] In this context, "Physical Education" referred to astronomy, chemistry, and "natural philosophy" (that is, mainly, physics). From the beginning, science education was seen as an important part of the function of the University. Continuing a tradition going back to the Renaissance and beyond, classical literature, such as the poetry of

Horace, was a main focus of academic life (at Georgetown as at other American colleges) throughout the nineteenth century. Mastery of Latin (and some knowledge of Greek) was basic to the curriculum, but mathematics and science were highly regarded as well. From 1834 to the end of the century, the first two collegiate years ("Rhetoric" and "Poetry") each included a year-long course (with laboratory) in chemistry for all students, as well as instruction in mathematics.

During the nineteenth century, collections of scientific specimens were proudly displayed and demonstrations in science were frequent. These demonstrations were selected with a view to spectacular effects (color changes, explosions, electrical discharges) and were generally popular, even forming part of graduation festivities. Throughout the nineteenth century, the final year of Georgetown's collegiate program (leading to the A.B.) consisted of two subjects. In 1837, these were "Moral Philosophy" and "Natural Philosophy"; in 1889, the first was called "Philosophy" (including logic, ethics, and metaphysics); the other remained "Natural Philosophy" (including mechanics, electricity and magnetism, astronomy, and geology). When "Philosophy" designated the last portion of Georgetown's curriculum, the name covered much that would now be termed science. Even if relatively few students completed the entire course, it appears that a large fraction of the time and effort of the students of Georgetown College in the nineteenth century was spent on scientific study.

In this collegiate curriculum, science was treated as a "consumer good." In the Georgetown Medical Department (founded 1851), science was taught as a "producer good."[3] Efforts to start a school of applied science were not successful.[4]

From 1831 until 1875, James Curley, S.J., was professor of chemistry, of natural philosophy, and sometimes of botany and of mathematics. He had great energy and a deep interest in conducting and improving laboratory courses for Georgetown students. In 1834, he had persuaded the Rector to spend the substantial sum of one thousand dollars to acquire a fine, small instrument to be used in natural philosophy classes to determine latitude and longitude of particular locations on earth by observing positions of stars. Impressed by the enthusiasm of Curley and his students for the use of this sophisticated device, the Jenkins family of Baltimore donated funds to build and equip the Georgetown College Observatory. When it opened in 1841, this was among the best-equipped astronomical observatories in the United

States.[5] With Curley as director (1841-88), the Observatory concentrated on collegiate instruction rather than on research.[6]

Strong Jesuit involvement in experimental science, as well as in astronomy and in mathematics, goes back to the seventeenth century and earlier. Both experimental and theoretical science held important places in the Jesuit educational tradition alongside moral philosophy and classical literary instruction. Most of the science taught at Georgetown during the nineteenth century could be classed as "natural history." More abstract aspects of science seem to have been reserved for the few students who completed the degree course.

The Twentieth Century

A major change in the pattern of education at Georgetown occurred during the early years of the present century. By 1916, in addition to the traditional classics-based A.B. program, a B.S. program had been introduced for students "who did not have the background required for the A.B. degree or who wished to acquire a training for technological, medical or industrial science careers."[7] The system of academic "major subjects" was developed and special undergraduate study of science had become necessary for admission to medical schools. By 1930 the focus of science education had shifted away from general education for all students toward specialized and preprofessional instruction for some. Separate courses (which had some resemblance to science courses offered in better secondary schools) continued to be offered for students other than those with special interest in science. The development of specialized programs, and the corresponding dilution of classical educational ideals, happened at about the same time as the increase in the emphasis on scholastic philosophy that occurred in the decades following the 1879 encyclical of Leo XIII, *Aeterni Patris*.

An important figure in the transition to specialized science here was George L. Coyle, S.J., who came to Georgetown from Holy Cross in 1923. In 1907 he had earned a Ph.D. in Chemistry at Göttingen, one of the main centers for the development of science education and research and also of the German model of university organization. Until this period, Georgetown courses were generally taught by Jesuits (some holding Ph.D.'s), each of whom remained at Georgetown for only a few years.[8] Coyle recruited laymen as permanent undergraduate faculty members. He also raised money to establish a "Chemo-Medical Research

Institute."[9] For over three decades (1931-63) this research center conducted significant studies in analytical biochemistry.[10] The staff of the Institute generally did not teach undergraduate courses: science faculty members who taught undergraduate courses generally did no research. The Chemistry faculty had been "professionalized," but at two levels, one for undergraduate teaching, one for research. The undergraduate faculty were graduates of Jesuit colleges, some held the Ph.D. when they were hired, others worked on Georgetown doctorates under the mentorship of M. X. Sullivan, Director of the Institute.

Coyle was a modern scientist, familiar with international chemistry and active in national scholarly societies. He deeply appreciated the achievements of nineteenth-century German chemical science in fostering human flourishing. Well ahead of most others, he saw the potential of using chemistry to improve health, and set up the Chemo-Medical Research Institute to achieve that end (and a separate undergraduate faculty for teaching).

In 1932, after decades of quiescence, the Observatory sent an expedition to Maine to photograph a solar eclipse. Subsequent expeditions went to Siberia in 1935 and to the mid-Pacific in 1937, with supervision and financing by the National Geographic Society. These expeditions are reported to have been intended to put Georgetown "on the map," insofar as science was concerned.[11] After the Second World War, large numbers of students enrolled in Georgetown evening graduate programs in astronomy and chemistry. Research at the Chemo-Medical Research Institute and expeditions of the Observatory continued, but most graduate students did their thesis research in government laboratories where they held full-time jobs.

A second major transition in science at Georgetown occurred around 1960. Scientific research on both arts and science and medical campuses benefited from increased public awareness (and government funding) of science. By 1965, the arts and sciences campus of Georgetown was offering Ph.D. degrees in astronomy, biology, chemistry, physics, and mathematics, and Ph.D. programs in several basic sciences (e.g., biochemistry) were in operation on the medical campus. Graduate work in science was now on a full-time (day) basis and B.S. curricula had been broadened away from the preprofessional model, with greater emphasis on pure science and on involving faculty and undergraduate students in research. The system of separate teaching and research faculties had been found to have severe shortcomings both for fostering scientific progress and also for science education, and that system was abandoned. Science departments became integrated, in the sense that faculty members taught both graduate and undergraduate courses and were also expected to conduct research. Somewhat later, some of these developments were partially reversed. By 1988, Ph.D. programs in astronomy, mathematics, and physics had been suspended,[12] and research institutes specializing in neuroscience and in bioethics, somewhat separate from regular academic departments, had been founded.

By 1970, an array of one-semester offerings (usually without laboratory work), on several levels of difficulty and of "relevance," had replaced two-semester survey courses (with laboratory) for nonscience majors. Also during the sixties, required courses in philosophy were drastically reduced in number, and became more diverse in approach.

There has been a consistent long-term trend in development of science and science education at Georgetown. Science was a main component of general education, along with philosophy and literature, throughout the nineteenth century. Although the Observatory was founded in 1841, scientific research at Georgetown operated at a low level of activity until the 1930s, when new beginnings were made in both chemistry and astronomy with private funding. Between (roughly) 1910 and 1960, science teaching shifted away from general education to more advanced instruction (primarily preprofessional in emphasis on the undergraduate level and mainly part-time on the graduate level). A further shift to generalized high-level undergraduate science curricula and to full-time graduate work had occurred by 1970. Throughout this period, scientific research became an increasingly important function both on the arts and science campus and on the medical campus. Georgetown is now an active (if relatively small) center of research in mainstream science, a "research university." On both campuses, science faculty are recruited from graduates of leading laboratories worldwide, with attention to research potential as well as to promise in teaching.

Science and Narrative

In order to engender student interest (asserted now to be largely lacking), Professor Haught recommends that science be taught using "narrative" rather than "theoretical" teaching methods. Undoubtedly, some students would prefer to ignore science, but many students, including humanities students, find science highly interesting. The attendance of students at the science-related activities of the Georgetown Bicentennial year compared quite favorably with attendance at events in other fields that would be expected to be more popular (such as political theory). A large fraction of the students that now come to Georgetown have had superb secondary-school preparation in science. In my experience, few of these well-prepared students display the science aversion Haught describes.

Professor Haught holds that lack of interest in science among arts and humanities students is a symptom of excessive emphasis on "theory," and insufficient attention to "narrative" in science instruction. If this is indeed the case, it is not because science lacks, or has lacked, its own mythic narrative. What yarn of the noble founder of the tribe, in his struggle with titanic forces, can match the saga of Galileo Galilei's encounters with Cardinal Bellarmine and the Holy Office? Mythic tales like this are regarded with proper reverence by scientists and generally passed on "as received." Science does not lack stories, but at least some of the stories of science clash with other highly valued parts of culture.[13] Among the results of such tensions may be that young people can be warned away (sometimes subconsciously) from science. For instance,

> Seek, then,
> No learning from the starry men,
> Who follow with the optic glass
> The whirling ways of stars that pass—
> Seek, then, for this is also sooth,
> No word of theirs—the cold star-bane
> Has cloven and rent their hearts in twain,
> And dead is all their human truth.[14]

But no matter what the root cause or exact extent of the problem of alienation of some students from science, we ought to consider carefully the remedy that Haught suggests.

To begin, let us take the words "narrative" and "theoretical" at face value. Several customary approaches to science teaching might qualify as "narrative," in the usual meaning of that word. A "history of ideas" organization is used in many science courses. The ideas are usually selected for philosophical or technological importance, as judged by the instructor, and inspiring stories of colorful personalities are included.[15] One problem with such an approach is that it may show what science was, but that may give quite a false impression of what science is. It is rarely possible to follow history very far towards the present (which is when "science," as modern scientists understand the term, exists). Conversely, if a course focuses on problems of present philosophic, scientific, or technological interest, then time pressures will cause history to be reduced to caricature.

A second standard technique emphasizes "natural history" (descriptive astronomy, biology, chemistry, and geology). This accounted for much of science in the 1800s, and has an important place today, particularly in elementary and secondary science education. When relatively little was understood, a "stamp collector's" attitude to nature had more intellectual interest than it does now. I know of no evidence that students are attracted by large doses of descriptive science.

"Relevant" science courses (e.g., "Physics of Energy and the Environment," and "Emerging Technologies") constitute a third methodology that might be termed "narrative." This approach is supported by a considerable movement ("Science, Technology and Society") generally based in engineering schools. Although the question should be regarded as open, I know of no evidence that this approach engenders the student enthusiasm that Haught seeks.

But to take Haught's suggestion so literally may be to trivialize it. It seems that Haught often uses "theoretical" with a meaning akin to "objective." Also, he sometimes seems to use "narrative" with a meaning related to self-involvement, close to the usual meaning of "intuitive." He has used these words as technical terms with similar meanings in an earlier work.[16]

To the extent that such meanings are intended, we can understand his proposal to mean that science courses for nonscience majors ought to be taught by persons who are genuinely interested in what they teach, and in a way that will engender personal involvement of the students with the subject. This is a suggestion that every science teacher would endorse, but following it may entail unintended consequences.

Active scientists, in general, are not able to spare time for much interest in the history of ideas, or for acquiring and retaining wide knowledge of descriptive material outside their specialty. They are, however, often passionately involved in current controversies in their own fields, and in the theoretical areas related to their work. An active scientist is much more likely to teach a course in a "narrative" (i.e., self-involved) rather than a "theoretical" (i.e., abstract) way if that course is rather closely related to her area of special interest. Science survey courses, whether cast in historical form or not, have usually been found to degenerate quite quickly into pedantry. An array of clearly focused courses taught by active scientists (narrative in the second sense) is better than an integrated survey of surveys of science, especially if the integrated course is taught by pedagogues (theoretical in the second sense) employed mainly for that purpose. The Georgetown "undergraduate faculty" of 1930-60 were primarily "teachers" who had little personal interest in the science they were retailing. It is better if the faculty are personally involved in what they teach.

Now, Georgetown science faculty are active in research, each sharing the "adventure" of his or her field with colleagues worldwide; they also have a major commitment to educating undergraduate and graduate students to be able to join the scientific quest, if they should decide to do so.[17]

The Cosmic Story

In what seems to be a second main point, Haught asserts that scientific advances have resulted in the emergence, during the past few decades, of a more or less integrated saga of the evolution of the world, which should be the organizing principle for science instruction. With regard to this suggestion, three questions arise. Is there indeed a new "story"? How important is it that our students be aware of it? Should this story, as such, be the focus of general science education?

Most scientists would gladly agree that there is an impressive breadth and coherence to current science-based accounts of the origin of the universe, of the evolution of life on earth, and of the development of human societies. What has happened recently, aided by the development and dissemination of computational power, is that it is now possible to treat dynamic processes, in which new entities emerge from simpler constituents, in much more satisfying ways. The evolution through time of many physical, chemical, biological, and social systems can now be understood fairly well. By this means, previously separate scientific areas have been connected, and important new relationships discovered. Haught's enthusiasm for this relatively new integrative movement is neither misplaced nor unusual.

That each educated person should be aware of the sweep and power of this account would also meet with general approval. But the proposal that scientists should adopt the propagation of this story as the organizing principle of general education in science would be less widely acceptable. Many would agree that there are important cases in which this organization works well. For instance, starting in 1989 the introductory biology course at Georgetown will be organized on an evolutionary, rather than a taxonomic, basis. But this format should not be used as a Procrustean bed for all general education in science.

Later, I will agree with Haught that it would be well if poets, teachers of religion, and others paid careful attention to the new story emerging from modern science because it offers the possibility of achieving much-needed intellectual integration on a mythic level. But there are major differences between scientific and mythic consciousness. Whitehead wrote in 1925 that the growth of science has produced "a new mentality that has altered the metaphysical presuppositions and the imaginative contents of our minds."[18] It manifests itself as "a vehement and passionate interest in the relation of general principles to irreducible and stubborn facts."[19] Whitehead concludes:

> It is this union of passionate interest in the detailed facts with equal devotion to abstract generalisation which forms the novelty in our present society. . . . This balance of mind has now become part of the tradition which infects cultivated thought. . . . The main business of universities is to transmit this tradition as a widespread inheritance from generation to generation.[20]

Scientists should teach the scientific attitude insofar as they can. Mythmongers are necessary, especially in universities, but their activity is distinguishable from science.

Mythic symbols and "stories" clearly are "energy-evoking and -directing agents."[21] The stories of peoples have always been connected with their cosmologies and their technologies.[22] The stories we tell our students must be coherent with the cosmology deriving from modern science. Symbol systems incoherent with the results and attitudes of science should not be foisted on our students. Conceptual and technological changes of recent decades must be taken into account in selecting, revising, and telling stories.[23] Narrative (mythic) activity must take into account results of science, but myth-generation and -propagation, itself, is not science.

Biologist François Jacob states:

> . . . the beginning of modern science can be dated from the time when such general questions as "How was the universe created?", "What is matter made of?", "What is the essence of Life?" were replaced by such limited questions as "How does a stone fall?", "How does water flow in a tube?", "How does blood circulate in vessels?". . . This substitution had an amazing result. While asking general questions led us to limited answers, asking limited questions turned out to provide more and more general answers.[24]

In a recent piece the eminent evolutionist John Maynard Smith writes:

> The function of science is to account for experience, . . . the function of myth is to provide a source and justification of values. . . . Normative science will be bad morality and bad science, and most probably both. . . . [We] need both myths and scientific theories, but we must be as clear as we can about which is which.[25]

I agree with Maynard Smith in resisting the suggestion (made by Haught, if I understand him correctly) that the teaching of science should generally be done in a mythic mode.

Teaching about science, speculation about how and why scientists work, and instruction about the consequences of scientific work and understanding, may often be better done by scholars who are not scientists than by practicing scientists.[26] What these scholars cannot do, but science faculty can, is to provide first-hand examples ("narrative" in the second sense) for arts and humanities students of what it is to be a working scientist and also to provide samples of rigorous scientific reasoning applied to particular questions. Sustained contact (e.g., two one-semester courses, one with laboratory) of each student with an actual practitioner of science is a useful counterpart and complement to the large amount of talk about (and sometimes, at least implicitly, against) science that occurs on every university campus.

Scientists, like other intellectuals, have a duty to participate in what Robert M. Hutchins called "The Great Conversation," but it should not be the function of scientists as such, or as science teachers, to provide mythic initiation. They have their hands full in teaching the methods and conclusions of science and in preparing some students to contribute to human flourishing through science or quasi-scientific work (an essential function of a modern university).

Integrating Visions

Haught also makes a third point that is less extensively developed but at least as important as the other two. He argues that increasing student enthusiasm for science, and for the evolutionary epic, is somehow the responsibility of the entire academic community. I would like to concur with this point and then extend it in a way that goes beyond what he has suggested.

The new cosmic saga starts with the fluctuation in the vacuum that gave rise to the "big bang," to coalescence of galaxies and to genesis of heavy elements. This is what astronomers call "cosmology." It extends on through the concrescence of the earth, to the origin of life and evolution of biological species. It continues through developments that social archeologists discuss and on into areas of interest to historians, sociologists, managers, and futurists. The saga has profound implications for "cosmology" (in the sense that used to be common in philosophy) and also for epistemology, metaphysics, and even politics.[27] If the new vision were to be taken seriously (as Haught recommends), no area of inquiry would remain uninfluenced. The new tinge to thought would be a different way of looking at temporal change and the generation of things. Adoption of an evolutionary cosmology would have more profound effect in other areas than it would have in physical and biological science, where it is already widely accepted.

Dominant scientific visions of past centuries had deep impact on the theology, art, social structures, and philosophy of those ages. We may expect that aspects of the new cosmic story will affect all areas of thought and practice. For instance, much remains to be done in exploring the implications for literature, for fundamental theology, and for social science, of the contemporary understanding of the evolution of coherences. In addition to being a place where specialized studies are possible, universities should also be a place of synthesis. (If not here, then where?) Exploring and interpreting the new vision of the universe will be a long-term task of the entire academic community.

In retrospect, we can distinguish two major evolutionary transitions that have occurred during Georgetown's two centuries. During the nineteenth century, the Renaissance ideal of *eloquentia perfecta* provided the focus for education here. Philosophy and science were important, but the stories of classical learning provided the mythic background and intellectual tone. The first major shift occurred around the turn of the century: Scholastic philosophy grew to dominance and the classics went into partial eclipse. Coincidentally, specialized schools and departments developed. The dominant mythic symbol-system during the first half of the century on this campus was that of Thomism. The notion that whatever God did was reasonably done had a deep impact on generations of students, and provided a framework within which intellectual work could be done, both for its own sake and for utilitarian and professional ends. This vision was strong enough at Georgetown and other Catholic schools to hold off the "scientism" that set the tone at some institutions.

A sublime confidence in the possibility and usefulness of a single coherent understanding of the world was a fundamental part of the Thomistic intellectual outlook but it seems that some aspects of modern science were regarded as somewhat suspect. By 1970, the neo-Scholastic story had largely lost its dominance and a second major change occurred that reduced the curricular and mythic difference between Georgetown and non-Catholic schools. Religious ideals of personal service have remained powerful and beneficial here, and the Scholastic ambition of unification of knowledge is fondly remembered, but it is not obvious that there is now any clear intellectual focus or dominant story on the campus.

The past century has been marked by continual differentiation within the University (departments, programs, specialized faculty). This has been consonant with intellectual, social, and technological changes in the larger society. It would be unwise to try to turn back the clock to times in which Georgetown was an undifferentiated undergraduate college. Georgetown is and ought to be a leading American university, not merely a collection of undergraduate and professional schools. The continental strategy of rather separate teaching and research faculties has been tried here (Chemo-Medical Research Institute, Astronomy Department) with quite limited success. In the future, research and teaching functions of the University ought to be kept closely together.

We may expect (or hope) that in the last tenth of this century Georgetown will gradually adopt some new intellectual vision (by evolutionary development of symbol-systems effective in the past) that will foster the coordination of research and teaching that will be needed. The legacy of the neo-Scholastic confidence that a comprehensive worldview was possible may still be strong enough to help. What are possible candidates to provide the main story of the campus? Evolutionary ideas, related to the new "story" emerging from science, and from recent studies of how science works, have already been involved with major intellectual changes, as several papers in this volume demonstrate. Georgetown's organization is still flexible enough that centripetal influences may be able to counter the disintegrating effects of academic specialism. If ways can be found to engage Georgetown's energies (in humanities and social science departments as well as in the sciences) with the saga of cosmic and human development that is now unfolding, could it provide a suitable integrating vision for Georgetown's third century? Perhaps it is possible that a vision can emerge that would connect Georgetown's religious and social service commitments more closely with the intellectual work (and professional-training function) of the University.

Notes

1. John F. Haught, "Science Education and the Importance of Story," in this volume.

2. Quoted in a paper on science at Georgetown during the nineteenth century by Liam Donahue, College '89, to be published in the student Bicentennial volume.

3. Thomas Antisell, M.D., a political refugee from Ireland, was for many years professor of Chemistry and Toxicology in the Medical Department. He was also the first President of the Chemical Society of Washington. Science instruction in the Medical School has generally been, quite properly, more utilitarian in emphasis than most courses taught on the main campus. For instance, in 1888 prospective students were assured that "the whole field of Chemistry will be considered in a general way, and only such chemistry dealt with in detail as may be of utility to the scientific practitioner of medicine." See *Catalogue of the College, 1888-89*, 76.

4. The ground floor of the Main (now Healy) Building was devoted to scientific teaching laboratories built "on a scale that may be termed munificent." In 1890, Georgetown's president, J. Havens Richards, S.J., included the following appeal in the College catalogue: "Chief among the wants of the College are the following: A Scientific School which would include the present classes of Natural Science, and would add to them the technical courses long contemplated. For the Establishment of such classes, particularly in *Engineering*, the present time is particularly opportune. Applications are constantly received from students who desire instruction in these branches; professors of the highest degree of competence are ready to undertake the task. What is needed is someone possessed of sufficient means and impressed with the value of scientific education who should make this exalted purpose his own. A suitable structure could be erected for a sum not less than $30000 or $40000. For apparatus and equipment, a like sum would be required." This appeal was repeated for ten years, but no scientific school was founded at Georgetown.

5. Francis J. Heyden, S.J., *The Beginning and End of a Jesuit Observatory (1841-1972)* (Quezon City, P.I.: Manila Observatory, [1985]), 3. Georgetown University Archives.

6. During the Italian revolution in the middle of the nineteenth century, Angelo Secchi, S.J., later head of the observatory of the Jesuit *Collegio Romano* (predecessor of the Vatican Observatory) spent some time at Georgetown. Rather than working at the Georgetown Observatory, however, he frequented the new Smithsonian Institution, and was author of one of the earliest research publications of that laboratory. Secchi later made significant contributions to stellar spectroscopy (Martin McCarthy, S.J., Jesuit Chair Lecture, Georgetown University, February 24, 1988).

7. A paper by Antoinette Wannebo, College '91, in the student Bicentennial volume, discusses Chemistry at Georgetown in the period between the two World Wars.

8. Curley, as founder and director of the Observatory, was probably an exception to this generalization.

9. Coyle was quite active in the American Chemical Society (ACS). The ACS appointed him as its representative to the National Research Council (NRC); he became chairman of the NRC committee on "Construction and Design of Chemical Laboratories," and editor of the committee's publication. (Not coincidentally, a new science building was being planned at Georgetown.) The ACS appointed a committee to consider the establishment of a laboratory for research in medicinal chemistry at Georgetown. That committee strongly endorsed the project and recommended an endowment of $10,400,000. The brochure that Georgetown distributed to publicize the project estimated that an adequate start could be made with an endowment of only $3,680,000. By 1931 over a quarter-million dollars had been raised. A staff of three, headed by Michael Xavier Sullivan (1875-1963, A.B., Harvard; Ph.D., Brown), a senior government-laboratory chemist, was recruited and lodged in temporary quarters in the Georgetown University Hospital. Coyle died suddenly in New York in 1932, while fundraising for the Institute. The new building (White-Gravenor) was ready in 1933 and the Institute moved into its laboratories.

10. Including work on the disease pellagra, on toxemia of pregnancy, on developing diagnostic tests for cancer, and on sulfur metabolism.

11. Heyden, "Jesuit Observatory," 11.

12. The Astronomy Department closed in 1972. Georgetown's Ph.D. program in mathematics was suspended in 1976, and the Ph.D. program in physics was suspended in 1985.

13. For example, Joseph Ratzinger, *Eschatology, Death and Eternal Life*, trans. Michael Waldstein, ed. Aidan Nichols, O.P. (Washington, D.C.: Catholic University of America Press, 1988).

14. W.B. Yeats, "The Song of the Happy Shepherd," in *W. B. Yeats: The Poems*, ed. Richard J. Finneran (New York: Macmillan, 1983), 7-8.

15. A well-known program of this sort, associated with the name of James Bryant Conant, involved students repeating classic laboratory experiments.

16. John F. Haught, *Religion and Self-Acceptance* (Washington, D.C.: University Press of America, 1980).

17. Major programs in science are consciously, and effectively, crafted to entice students into the adventure of scientific inquiry. Since they hold that the best way to appreciate the excitement of scientific research is to do science, all science

departments at Georgetown encourage undergraduate majors to do original research. Science majors have full programs in their first two years so that more leisurely research may be possible for juniors and seniors. Whatever may be true in other scholarly fields, a strong on-campus research culture is now necessary for high-quality undergraduate university education in science.

Science faculty generally hold that the motivations of scientific research are similar to those for humanistic or artistic creativity; they feel that an experience in substantial creative work (scientific research, historical inquiry, artistic production, etc.) should be part of every college student's curriculum. Just as Haught would prefer to see "narrative" more prominent in science courses, so also many scientists would be happy if they could be persuaded that a spirit of "inquiry" ("narrative" in the more technical sense) was actively fostered in students throughout the University.

18. Alfred North Whitehead, *Science and the Modern World* (New York: Macmillan, 1946), 3.

19. Ibid.

20. Ibid., 4.

21. Joseph Campbell, *The Flight of the Wild Gander* (New York: Viking Press, 1951), 178.

22. Joseph Campbell discusses how the stories of the Sioux changed when the tribe shifted from agriculture along the Mississippi to buffalo hunting on the prairies, ibid., chap. 4.

23. See, for example, recent works by one of Georgetown's distinguished poets and literary scholars, O. B. Hardison, Jr.: *Entering the Maze: Identity and Change in Modern Culture* (New York: Oxford University Press, 1982) and *Disappearing through the Skylight: Identity in a Technological Culture*, forthcoming.

24. François Jacob, "Evolution and Tinkering," *Science* 196 (1979), 1161.

25. John Maynard Smith, "Science and Myth" in *The Natural History Reader in Evolution*, ed. Niles Eldredge (New York: Columbia University Press, 1987), 222.

26. There are now philosophers, historians, sociologists, and theologians (as well as faculty in area studies and politics) who concentrate on studies about science and about technology. These scholars, both through research and through teaching, are valuable resources for increasing our students' awareness of science and of the cosmic story. The fact that Georgetown lacks schools of engineering and applied science (other than medicine, nursing, and linguistics) should not be taken to indicate that such scholars are not needed here. On the contrary, they are more necessary here than at technical schools where practical science is more prominent.

27. See *New Essays in Metaphysics*, ed. Robert C. Neville (Albany, N.Y.: State University of New York Press, 1987); *Evolution and Creation*, ed. Ernan McMullin (Notre Dame, Ind.: University of Notre Dame Press, 1985).

ANNE D. SULLIVAN

Assistant Dean
College of Arts and Sciences

Interracial and Intercultural Education at Georgetown University

I

The history of interracial education at Georgetown University—if that is defined simply as the presence of minority students and faculty here—is a recent and vulnerable history. It is a twenty-year history, not a two-hundred-year history. As such, the University has barely begun to untangle and "see" all the issues which must be faced if we are to achieve an interracial education of which we can be proud. Though most of this essay will discuss securing the presence of minority degree candidates on campus, I acknowledge at the outset that this is merely a beginning. However difficult it has been to achieve this minority presence (and however continuously vulnerable to erosion that presence is), a genuine interracial education must mean something more substantial, and it will be harder yet to achieve.

Before I turn to the ways in which we must push ourselves as an institution to enrich the interracial education here, let me discuss the admissions world and the dramatic changes which began to take place only twenty years ago at Georgetown and at literally hundreds of now white-majority (no longer exclusively white) colleges and universities across America. Georgetown changed in response to the historic upheavals of the civil rights movement, as all American individuals and institutions were changed by that movement.

The impetus for change at Georgetown came perhaps most directly from these national forces—an America attempting to reform itself, to enact the transforming call of Dr. Martin Luther King, Jr., to reorder the relationships between racial groups within the society in the name of justice and in the name of love. But Georgetown also found reinforcement for the impetus to change from within the Catholic church as the church renewed its commitment through the Second Vatican Council to act upon all questions of social justice. American Catholic education had a double reason to try to enact in its own institutional structures the racial harmony and racial justice demanded now by the nation and always by the gospel.

The most immediate response (and the easiest way to make quick and visible change happen) was to seek minority student applicants and to admit minority students to the University.

In just about twenty years, Georgetown University has succeeded in admitting a stronger-each-year group of minority degree candidates at the undergraduate level.[1] I must concentrate my discussion on the undergraduate admissions picture because it is the one I know best. From initial moves in the late sixties and early seventies to recruit students from the District of Columbia schools, the Office of Undergraduate Admissions has expanded the pool of minority applicants so that we now are admitting minority students from all over the country, from all sorts of high schools with a wide mixture of economic backgrounds, and with continuously stronger credentials. I do not want this essay to bog down in statistics, but in the fall semester of 1988, Georgetown University's undergraduate student body was roughly 17% minority in ethnic background, of whom 7.4% are black American, 4.5% are Hispanic American, and 4.6% are Asian American.[2] Twenty years of hard work on the part of the Office of Undergraduate Admissions has yielded these changes in the mix of students we enroll here.

Problems remain, however, in this admissions picture. In expanding the pool of candidates, we have many choices to make, and can shape our student body so as to eliminate all "risks." The review and rating of minority candidates can become a middle-class exercise unless policy continues to stress that we should be concerned about admitting less advantaged, therefore less credentialed, less well-prepared minority candidates. The Community Scholars' Liberal Studies Program (a program of academic support for minority freshman degree candidates administered through the Center for Minority Student Affairs and serving all five undergraduate schools) has an excellent and well-established track record for helping such "risky" students achieve academic success at the University.[3] I think it is important to reiterate our commitment to enrolling a portion of our students from the ranks of the least advantaged in our American society. We will need to work very hard as an institution to keep this commitment from eroding, and we will need to build in new directions as well.

Nationally, though the number of black American high school students going on to college climbed throughout the seventies, the numbers have started to fall again.[4] Neither as a nation nor as a single institution should we be indifferent to such a drop. We must work constantly to secure large numbers of black applicants of all economic backgrounds. We must be vigilant in our efforts to attract top applicants from the inner city school systems, and to give those applicants careful and sensitive review, even as we seek applicants from black students in many other educational settings who may come to us with stronger academic preparation. The admissions review must always attempt to identify desire and potential to learn, and to adjust its reading of a student's past accomplishments against past resources.

The numbers of new immigrant Hispanic Americans in our nation now going on to higher education is scandalously low. This is the fastest growing ethnic group among children in the United States, and both currently and potentially in the decades ahead, the biggest untapped "market" of eighteen-year-olds for colleges. One would think that Georgetown University, as one of the better known Catholic institutions of higher education in America, would have a natural connection to this constituency—these students, by and large, are reared in the Catholic faith. Indeed, the Catholic church in America may be one of the most important continuities for these new immigrants, serving as a bridge between their former countries, their former culture, and their newly adopted homeland.

To date, this "Catholic connection" has not resulted in any measurable flow of applicants to Georgetown from this constituency. Equally alarming, some of the most attractive applicants we have accepted have chosen not to come. I remember, for example, several compelling applicants in last year's admissions review—two from California's central valley, sons and daughters of agricultural workers, outstanding students in their tiny (probably weak) high schools. We accepted these students, but these students did not accept us. I do not know the reasons, but I can name many possible ones—money, distance, and fear come quickly to mind. In the Community Scholars Liberal Studies Program this year, we had a promising Hispanic-American student from Texas who enrolled in the three-week summer component of that year-long program. The student did not return in late August, homesickness, lack of confidence, and culture shock leading him to enroll in a state university campus in El Paso.

We have much to ponder in these "defections," if you will. We must do more to establish a flow of applications from the new immigrant Hispanic population—new contacts through our admissions officers to critical areas of the country and key high schools and high school counselors and so on—all the hard work that the Admissions Office does without our ever properly crediting them. But we need to do much more.

We need admissions officers of the University to be recruited and hired from our own alumni and alumnae who are of Hispanic-American background to be our emissaries to potential high school applicants. We need, somehow, to extend our welcome to *accepted* candidates all the way to Salinas, California, if you will, so that the parents and the son or daughter who dreamed of applying to a "premier" Catholic university on the other side of the country might risk accepting us. We need to be perceived by such a family as *affordable*, undoubtedly scary but not too scary; as Catholic, too, in the sense of caring about educating all Catholic Americans, and as knowing something about new immigrants' experiences and acculturation problems and tensions; and, finally, as remembering that Catholic education has been a key institution in this country for all the previous waves of immigration from European nations.

We need to make clear that Georgetown wants to play a role in the current and future waves of Catholic immigration from South and Central America and from the western Pacific. I fear that we are so busy being upscale and preening ourselves as a "hot" school in COFHE [Council on Funding in Higher Education] circles (i.e., "mainstreaming" Georgetown, trying to shake off our institutional insecurities as the only Catholic university among the Harvards/Yales/Stanfords and so on that compose the "highly selective" schools in the COFHE list) that we may want to play down this more traditional and far more valuable purpose for ourselves.

The University is doing good things in the whole area of immigration: Harold Bradley's Center for Immigration Policy and Refugee Assistance (a think-tank on immigration studies and problems, which also includes many opportunities for practical service to which Georgetown students commit themselves, such as teaching English and tutoring new immigrant children and adults in the local area, or six-month and one-year postdegree volunteer internships working in international immigration); Otto Hentz's programs in Nicaragua and Peru for a postdegree one-year service commitment; and so on. Unlike the case with black American history and culture (where course offerings are few and hard to find), we offer many courses across many departments that examine Latin American history, culture, language, literature, and economics. But do we convey this picture of Georgetown to the nation's high schools? My point is that we need an analysis and a strategy to penetrate the new immigrant Hispanic population. We need to discover what works.

II

In keeping with all that I have said so far about the twenty-year history of interracial education at Georgetown—the progress we have made in securing the presence of a significant number of minority students here, and the vulnerability of that progress—I want to take up Timothy Healy's invitation that these bicentennial essays "identify questions for internal debate in the next ten years." I want to discuss two such areas that I believe need care and feeding in the next decade: financial aid/ admissions structures and policies with regard to minority candidates.

No matter how strongly we may want to enroll students from among the least advantaged in our society, we will see the numbers of serious applicants and actual matriculation drop off if we continue to raise tuition and keep financial aid policies set so that students with high need must accept maximum loans as an automatic part of their aid. When a poor family must decide where a talented, high-achieving son or daughter will go to college, and the family must choose between a "name," private, huge-tuition university of the highest academic standards, and a big and anonymous but nonetheless academically strong and dizzyingly cheap state university, what would you advise? Georgetown says it will meet full need, but it does so at present with maximum loan and work-study aid first, and then with a grant calculated to close the remaining gap.

The tuition charges at Georgetown (and its competitors—one of the reasons cited as to why we can justify our own increases) have risen every year over the last two decades. There seem to be *no brakes whatsoever* to this process. The arguments which support these tuition hikes are compelling: reduce faculty teaching load to support faculty research, expand the number of faculty to keep class size down, keep faculty salaries abreast and perhaps an inch ahead of inflation, build needed classrooms and faculty offices, etc., etc. Most of these expenditures are *quality* issues.

But we must remember the dangers involved. More and more we make ourselves dependent upon admitting the bright and capable students of the well-heeled in LARGE numbers—students whose families can pay the whole cost of their education straight up, so that some of their tuition dollars can be rolled over into financial aid for those students whose families cannot afford the full cost. This is a vicious and scary spiral.

We cannot be complacent about the future indebtedness of our poorest students. We cannot continue to let the federal government set loan limits, and then, when all the other high-cost private institutions adopt the same limits, feel free to do likewise. First, we must be certain that the loan ceilings we set for students are realistic with regard to projected postdegree earnings (and do not represent crippling debts that will continue for ten and twenty years and mean inevitable postponement of such standards of the American dream as buying a house, for example). Then, our financial aid counseling must be extraordinarily good right from the moment we put freshman aid offers in the mail and students are in that month of decision making about where to commit themselves and their educational future. I think we are in trouble unless we offer aid which working-class and lower-middle-class families *perceive* as representing a future indebtedness a young person can risk assuming.

In the next decade, I think we also need a high-level (President, Provost, Council of Deans) policy review to look again at admissions structures put in place in the late sixties and early seventies. At that time at the undergraduate level, the five standing school committees, which review all applications to their respective schools, extended admission review authority to a sixth Minority Admissions Committee to review minority applicants to all five schools, with the goal (remember, it was starting virtually at zero) of enrolling 10% of the student body from all minorities. This means in practice that the Minority Admissions Committee reads all black American applications (regardless of economic background) and all other minorities (Hispanic, Asian, American Indian) where economic background is judged to warrant extra consideration (so sons and daughters of the wealthy, the well-established third and fourth generation, and so on, go to the school committees, while the son of the Korean family owning the mom-and-pop grocery store, and the daughter of the

Ecuadorean restaurant worker and teacher's aide, go to the Minority Admissions Committee).

This structure has worked well for a good long time. The Minority Admissions Committee in particular has built up years of expertise in reading applications with a sensitive eye for indicators of success among minority candidates, and also has built up confidence in taking all statistics under skeptical advisement. This committee's readers, for example, know that heavy involvement in church activities, especially in leadership roles (with perhaps scant activities in the high school), should be taken seriously. This may be a student of substance. Scores in the four hundreds on the Scholastic Aptitude Test are not to be feared if the student is taking the very best courses the high school has to offer and ranks very high. Those scores may say more about the high school and the family's economic resources than about the student's ability to learn, to set high standards, and to reflect sound values taught within the family.

This six-committee structure creates procedural hurdles. The 10% "goal" was never meant to be a ceiling. In theory, it is not a ceiling now. What happens now is that the "very best" minority applicants, who would have been referred to the sixth committee (as identified by initial review within the Admissions Office), are referred to the five standing school committees to compete for spaces allotted to those committees. If the applicants are accepted there, they go in above the 10% of spaces allotted the sixth committee. If they are not admitted by the school committee, they come back to the sixth committee and are accepted within the 10% (i.e., other applicants at the bottom of the acceptances of the sixth committee get lopped off, and the "very best" are assured an offer of admission).

I do not know how well the five school committees understand how the referral of the "very best" minority applicants fits into all the other agendas those committees are asked to focus on. I have sat on both kinds of committees. I know that school committees want to admit the strongest academic talent, however that might be defined for any given reader. But school committees are also hit with other agendas: geographic distribution, special high school relationships (those lifelines so carefully built and nurtured by good admissions officers), Catholic concerns, and male/female ratios. In this context, it is very hard to fight for working-class applicants. The application is thin, unsophisticated, the high school counselor writes a *pro forma* three sentences, the school is a public unknown, the testing is just okay. No prep school applicant ever receives less than two pages of glowing prose from the school. We must make ourselves "deaf" to such inflated praise, and must "hear" what is not said in the blue-collar application.

In such a welter of contending interests, and in the ratings that drive all admit decisions, it is difficult for readers to know the final outcome of the process, and to know how minority candidates fare in the school committee competition. The detailed breakdown of admissions decisions as they fall across these "jurisdictional" lines is unknown to me. Undergraduate Dean of Admissions Charles Deacon believes that school committees are enthusiastic about admitting the "best and brightest" minority candidates referred to their review, but he argues that we are not particularly successful in securing a strong yield of these students. These same students are being accepted by our strongest competitors and are being heavily recruited with better financial aid packages and sophisticated outreach programs during the admissions cycle (some universities, for example, offer a travel subsidy to enable their most promising minority candidates to fly in for a campus visit).

An admissions policy review might decide some changes in structure or emphasis are in order. The goal of such a review must be toward ensuring that minority proportions within our student body continue to grow. Demographic projections about the characteristics and numbers of American eighteen-year-olds in the next ten, twenty, thirty years tell us that the percentage of white-majority teenagers is dropping, and minorities of all stripes are growing. By the year 2020 the racial mix in the country for eighteen-year-olds is expected to be roughly three-quarters white, one-quarter minorities.[5] Therefore, both for moral and for pragmatic reasons, Georgetown needs to examine and refine its admissions strategies.

Structured attention needs to be paid to the less advantaged, therefore less credentialed students. The sensitivity to read such applications and to weigh them as essential to admit in responsible numbers (responsible to financial aid resources and to space in the Liberal Studies Program, for example, if it is recognized the applicant would benefit from the academic support of that program) has been developed in the admissions review, and must be sustained in the years ahead. Class issues intersect racial and minority issues, but are not one and the same.

Twenty years have taught us that we can find academic talent in every layer of our society, in every racial group, in every geographic pocket, if we can cast a very wide net in pulling in applications, and then sit and read them with imagination. The expertise that has been developed within the Minority Admissions Committee needs to be shared more broadly and the responsibility for racial mix and class mix needs to be assumed by every reader of applications. If we could achieve such a broadly discerning eye in the admissions review process, then we could expect percentages of minority and white acceptances to float up and down from year to year within a reasonable range, driven by the compelling attributes of individual applicants.

III

I have concentrated in this discussion on the presence of minority *students* here at Georgetown. The related issue of minority *faculty* is treated in Professor Mikell's contribution to these pages. I would simply note that this subject is even more complex and more troubling for an institution like Georgetown. Only in very recent years has the University made any significant progress in hiring minority faculty on the Main Campus. This was a direct result of a stipulation in the five-year plan in 1985 to hire five black faculty members by 1990. It has been heartening to see the University move from simple compliance with federal affirmative action regulations to the adoption of our own goals in faculty hiring—to say to ourselves for the first time that we seek minority faculty members not because the federal government is telling us we must but because we know we are an incomplete academic community without the presence of minorities at all levels within the institution—faculty, professional staff, and administrative hierarchies. Still, we stand at the very beginning of making this kind of change.

IV

I wrote at the start of this essay that the presence of minorities does not guarantee a true interracial education. The interracial education we must work toward will move beyond mere presence—putting students and faculty of various racial and ethnic backgrounds side by side on the campus. A genuine interracial education would mean that majority and minority students, majority and minority faculty members were truly "at home" with one another. Such a level of human intimacy—being "at home"—would mean that personal friendships would cross the lines between groups without requiring the individuals to sacrifice their group identities. Racial differences in background would be acknowledged, would be the subject of exploration and exchange, rather than artificially omitted, as though race does not matter and should not be valued. We omit the subject now out of awkwardness, embarrassment, or ignorance. We must do better than this.

The key to transforming the curriculum is, of course, the faculty. A genuine interracial education will have to be pioneered by a faculty which undertakes its own re-education. Faculty members need to recognize that their professional training, as good as it may have been, did not prepare them for interracial education. Depending on what is their field of study, faculty members should be willing to give a critical assessment of it, looking to uncover and eliminate biases of the past and to highlight the contributions to their disciplines of other races and cultures.

Further, this rich interracial education of the future should see white faculty as well as (hopefully) a growing number of minority faculty mentoring minority students, seeking out for special attention and nurture those particularly capable and alert black and Hispanic students, for example, to push these students to even greater excellence in their academic work, to inquire of their career plans, to encourage them to consider university teaching (do not go to law school! do a Ph.D. in Government instead!), to share with them the rewards and excitement our faculty finds in such a calling.

We know we need minority faculty to teach at the university level across the nation. Georgetown admits among its minority degree candidates some of the best and brightest minority undergraduates in the nation. There is no reason why we should not be inspiring a handful of minority students each year to go on to straight academic Ph.D. work. This will not happen, however, unless our own faculty is well read in areas where black American culture, for example, intersects and reformulates their specific discipline, and unless our own faculty is receptive to (and can give critical guidance to) research topics that explore aspects of these intersections. (This is not to suggest for even one minute that minority students have no interest in "pure" philosophy or "pure" chemistry, for example, but only to recognize the powerful attraction we all find in scholarship which connects to our own experience and which illuminates our own culture.)

And so, I come full circle. We cannot get *beyond* mere presence until white faculty members respond to the challenge of providing for interracial education in their teaching and their scholarship, which in turn will create more occasions in the classroom where issues of race and racial heritage are given serious examination, which in turn will sanction for students talk among their peers across racial lines in ways that get them beyond careless stereotyping and hurtful silences, which in turn will prompt a demand to know more about areas of minority culture and history, which in turn will come back to the classroom in the form of proposed paper topics and research.

We have on campus the necessary mix of students and faculty to begin this richer interracial education. I see hesitant initiatives across campus—a particular lecture series, a new course, a faculty member reading in new directions, students open to serious reflection when they are challenged to dig deeper into sensitive and complex material. We can make this education happen if we are courageous and if we stretch ourselves. If we remain content with who we are now, we will fail. The University has much to do in its third one hundred years.

Notes

1. I imagine the number of minority graduate-level degree candidates is more problematic, except at the Law School, which has been a national leader in transforming its student body in terms of race and gender, undoubtedly helped by the decision of administrators to hire a black man as Director of Law School Admissions early in the 1970s and to give him full backing.

2. Stuart Rich, Director of the University's Office of Institutional Research, gave me the following ethnic breakdown of the undergraduate student body in 1988-89:

74.7%	white American
7.4%	black American
4.6%	Asian American
4.5%	Hispanic American
0.2%	Native American
8.7%	Foreign students

3. See Paul Cardaci's "Reading, Writing, and Critical Thinking: A Seven Year Assessment of the Liberal Studies Program for Community Scholars" (Center for Minority Student Affairs, October 1988). "Of the 102 (LSP) students who matriculated between 1981 and 1984, 65 (64%) have graduated and 20 (20%) are still in school. Of the 122 admitted between 1985 and 1987, 115 (94%) are currently enrolled. Thus, the combined retention rate of 89% for all LSP participants compares favorably with the rate for ALL Georgetown Undergraduates, who have an attrition rate of 14% . . ." (from the "Executive Summary" to that report).

4. Numbers of American High School Students Going to College, Eighteen- to Twenty-four-Year-Olds (in Thousands):

	High School Graduates	Enrolled in College	% of 18-24-Yr.-Olds who are H.S. Grads.	% of 18-24-Yr.-Olds who enroll in Coll.
White				
1970	15,960	5,305	81.4	33.2
1975	18,883	6,116	83.2	32.4
1980	20,214	6,423	82.6	31.8
1985	18,916	6,500	83.6	34.4
Black				
1970	1,602	416	59.5	25.9
1975	2,081	665	64.8	31.9
1980	2,592	715	69.7	27.5
1985	2,810	734	75.6	26.1
Hispanic				
1970	n/a	n/a	n/a	n/a
1975	832	295	57.5	35.5
1980	1,099	327	54.1	29.8
1985	1,396	375	62.9	26.9

Source: Rosalind R. Bruno, "School Enrollment-Social and Economic Characteristics of Students. October 1986" (U.S. Department of Commerce, Bureau of Census, P-20, no. 429, August 1988), Table A-5.

Note that black and Hispanic enrollments in college as a percentage of high school graduates peaked in 1975 at 31.9% and 35.5%, respectively. The absolute number of enrolling students has continued to climb as the population has grown, but the percentage of high school graduates has dropped.

5. Demographic projections on eighteen-year-olds show that in 1990 American eighteen-year-olds will be 81.5% white, in 2020 they will be only 77.2% white:

Year	All 18-Yr.-Olds	White 18-Yr.-Olds	White % of Total
1990	3431	2797	81.5
2000	3751	2978	79.3
2010	3877	3069	79.1
2020	3584	2768	77.2

Source: Gregory Spence, "Projections of the Population of the U.S. by Age, Sex, and Race 1983-2080" (U.S. Department of Commerce, Bureau of Census, P-25, no. 955, May 1984), Table 6.

I was surprised to see the seeming "stability" in these projections. It is my impression from press treatments of this topic that one-third of all school-aged children in the U.S. will be nonwhite by the year 2000. I discussed with Stuart Rich the contrast between this "popular" impression and the above projections. He says there is much controversy among demographers about the accuracy of census figures in counting minorities, particularly Hispanics, where illegal immigration is a factor. So, these figures may be regarded as conservative.

GWENDOLYN MIKELL
Department of Sociology

Catholic Diversity, Pluralism, and Interracial/Intercultural Education

Catholics and their educational institutions have both absorbed and challenged the philosophical and social tendencies of American society over the past two hundred years. The legacy of this interaction is indelibly imprinted on the fabric of institutions such as Georgetown University. Although it was clear that Catholic schools and colleges nurtured and trained the offspring of those in the church and helped to sustain the Catholic constituency, it is also clear that during the American revolutionary period these institutions shouldered many of the social and educational burdens of "Americanizing" the society, as did Protestant institutions. While confronting the prejudices and sociocultural hierarchies of Anglo-Saxon Protestant American society,[1] Catholics have attempted to carve out their own social institutions reflecting their concerns for Christianity and service. Recognizing the advantages of pluralism in the emerging American society, the Catholic institutions have been important refuges for European immigrants over the past century, and more recently for urban nonwhite children.

Today, the Catholic educational legacy, which was strengthened by those early challenges, is being tested again. It faces a new type of pluralism: the demands for inclusion made by many Afro-American and Hispanic students who seek to enter Catholic universities.[2] It is this difficult task of balancing religious mission, openness, and pluralism which forces one to reassess the relative success of Catholic institutions such as Georgetown.

The relationship of Catholic higher educational institutions to the church has shifted during the twentieth century, and the newer developments often raise questions about the religious versus the secular role of these schools and about the kind of students they are really intended to serve. Seen in this light, it was fascinating to reflect on the new challenge which former Education Secretary William J. Bennett issued to the Catholic elementary and secondary schools to take on "the poor, the disadvantaged, the disruptive, the drop-out" and set a goal of educational change for urban minority and ethnic groups.[3] Representatives of the National Catholic Educational Association stated that they did not find it appropriate to take that as their sole mission because "We have a commitment to serve our [Catholic] constituency."

The debate evoked memories of another earlier one about the mission of Catholic educational institutions—a debate which took place during the societal retreat from "melting-pot" ideologies of the late nineteenth/early twentieth century. The issue of diversity and how it meshes with the Catholic mission again assumes monumental proportions as large numbers of Afro-Americans and Hispanics raise questions about how their presence as well as their educational needs, cultural traditions, and values could be dealt with by institutions such as Georgetown.

Background to the Catholic Educational Tradition

From a social science perspective, one can understand better the intertwined issues of "mission" and "pluralism" which undergird the Catholic educational experience by adopting a sociohistorical and social structural viewpoint.[4] As groups meet and seek accommodation with each other, social hierarchies may be constructed which, unless aggressively countered, may continue to provide a challenge to the goal of achieving diversity within American life and institutions. Within the United States, various groups have struggled to realize themselves and their goals within a competitive and often difficult Anglo-Saxon Protestant social environment. Catholics were no exception. However, Catholics have a history of a long and determined challenge to Anglo-conformity, even though this challenge has been opposed and occasionally transformed by the configuration of social forces at various times.

Indeed, from the initial presence of the Catholic church in this predominantly Protestant country, its central religious aims of gaining "a doctrinal foothold" and "ensuring the allegiance of Catholic people to their Church"[5] were opposed by white Protestants. Although there was an early expansion of the Catholic church in the distant Southwest, the lengthy persecution of the tiny Catholic population ensured that it was the Anglo-Saxon Protestants who would develop and interpret the national mission of these United States, and who would control its fortune.[6] The Catholic mission faced the problem of the American national goals which separated church and state and advocated the possibility of all men achieving economic and political freedom, even while securing the North American soil for the expansion of Calvinist Protestantism by encouraging the immigration of northern European peoples.

Catholics, for their part, in responding to the discrimination they faced, made a major contribution to the development of the American mission by forcing a broader reinterpretation of democracy and freedom. The historically unique American mission was limited by the fact that Blacks, Catholics, women, and non-Caucasian immigrants were not usually considered qualified to participate, and so were not among those intended as democracy's major beneficiaries. The American mission, grand yet flawed, demanded a priori, unquestioning allegiance—and it was this mission with which Catholics had to come to terms. The Catholic decision to adopt the American stance toward the Old World and its institutions was the kind of liberal position which enabled it to participate in the evolving secular American national culture. True, it was a small elite group which possessed the education and the social means to achieve this level of social participation. Nevertheless, this group implemented the emerging Catholic choice, which was to play a national role; and they hoped that by participating in American thought and social conditions they would win the ordinary working people to the church.[7]

Since it was the religious/ideological and cultural characteristics which fed American discrimination against immigrant white ethnics, religious assimilation was sometimes chosen by upwardly mobile persons. The Presbyterian Scotch-Irish who immigrated between 1717 and 1725 faced little resistance to cultural assimilation after the first generation since they largely conformed to the already existing Anglo norms,[8] but their marital assimilation occurred at a much slower pace. The German Protestants and Mennonites who arrived between 1680 and the mid-1700s faced greater resistance than the Scotch-Irish, not because their cultural features were different, but primarily because they were perceived as posing a greater political threat of being disloyal. In contrast, the early Irish Catholics were branded "Papists" because they were considered the emissaries of the pope, and initially encountered considerable opposition to cultural as well as marital assimilation.[9]

The poor among Irish Catholics, sensitive to Protestant English overlordship in Ireland, tended to consolidate as a community around religion when faced with cultural and economic discrimination in the United States. Even when Irish Catholics made major accommodations to the Anglo cultural norms, this did not always guarantee them equitable treatment. Faced with continuation of the discriminatory ethnic/religious hierarchies that Protestants had established, Catholics leaders took liberal as well as defensive approaches. In addition to the visionary concessions to "nativism" made by John Carroll and his contemporaries, Catholics improved their position by following the educational tendencies of the period. They established schools whose major functions were preparatory work for the seminary, missionary activity, and moral development. This decidedly liberal and ecumenical stance was epitomized in 1787 when Carroll announced that his new academy at Georgetown would be "open to Students of every religious Profession."[10] Consequently, Catholic colleges attracted a more diverse student body than existed in most other institutions of the period.

The short-lived but vicious anglophile nativist notion of the Know-Nothing Party in 1850, "America for the Americans," symbolized the continued Protestant hostility toward paupers, immigrants, and Catholics.[11] But it was primarily the Civil War and the issues of slavery which terminated much of the opposition to the first wave of Catholics. Nevertheless, this did not lessen the Catholic resolve to build educational institutions which would protect them from discrimination and favor pluralism. To take but one example, Patrick Healy, son of an Irish immigrant and a former slave, became president of Georgetown University in 1874 and directed such an ambitious expansion of its academic programs and facilities that he became known as the school's second founder.[12]

This is not to say that Catholics insisted upon racial or class equality in all things—in fact, many supported as well as fought against the social and legal conventions of the period. The church owned slaves but it endeavored to treat them humanely and it converted a number of them to Catholicism.[13] In Louisiana and North Carolina it also succeeded in educating a very small black constituency. During the Civil War, Catholic young men in Washington and Georgetown University fought on both sides of the conflict.[14] Even before the war and afterwards, Catholic immigrants saw Negroes as threats and disliked working beside them.[15] Indeed, when a growing Catholic urban immigrant population met migrating newly emancipated Negroes in the 1860s and 1870s in places like Cincinnati, there was also sporadic violence and demonstrations as labor union members protested against the hiring of Blacks.[16] These overt conflicts subsided as institutionalized obstacles to black employment were constructed in northern urban areas. The immigrant Catholics, for their part, organized themselves and began to use ethnic-community cohesion to consolidate their positions in jobs and politics during the early twentieth century.[17]

The major problem which Catholics and their educational institutions have continued to face is the greater liberalism of American society and the tendency on the part of their elite toward assimilation into the Protestant institutions. While some members of the elite were accepted into prestigious Protestant colleges and universities, others were ambivalent and suspicious about sending their children to schools which might "Protestantize" them. Reacting to this tension, Catholic clergy expended a great deal of effort on improving institutions through which they could maintain their values, and were uniquely placed to receive the second wave of Catholic immigrants, especially the Italians who arrived in the 1880s and 1890s. These *catadini*, poor uneducated peasants who fled the economic and social chaos of southern Italy, tended to remain in the cities despite their lack of industrial skills.[18] Their poverty and solidarity in the attempt to get ahead, no matter what methods were used, resulted in their being charged with being *mafiosi*, and they were further rejected by Anglos. In the face of these problems, Catholic educators and lay people mobilized to deal with the social needs of immigrants and to stem the rising anti-Catholic sentiment.

Ironically, in responding to the anti-Catholicism and the popular resentment that the Catholics were not "melting" into the American mainstream, many Catholics increasingly adopted the image of "super-Americans." This dramatic evidence of the Catholic desire for Americanization was to leave its imprint on their churches and schools, and to further fuel the ethnic, language, and political schisms within their communities. The issue of ethnicity and Catholicism against acculturation and Protestantism or secularism lay at the root of several plans which involved state funding of education in parochial schools.[19] Archbishop John Ireland, for example, began an experiment in which St. Paul-area

Catholic schools were leased for a token amount to local school boards, which then funded the entire operation of the schools. Catholic teachers, including nuns and clergy, submitted their credentials to the school board and were hired to teach the regular public school curriculum. Religion was taught after regular school hours. Although this experiment was "tolerated" by Rome in 1892, it stirred up a major debate among Catholics and was shortly discontinued.[20] Despite this temporary victory for the church in maintaining Catholic schools using public funds, the majority of Catholics made the decision to emulate the Protestant majority by sending their children to public schools.[21] On the other hand, many local communities which feared ethnic and religious assimilation adopted the language of their worshippers as the medium of discourse in the church while helping to build the largest Catholic school system in the world.

In the early twentieth century the Catholic schools were primarily the institutions through which the church nurtured and reinforced itself. However, in the period from 1900 to the 1930s, as the church gained control over its expanding mission to the immigrant Catholic community, it was sometimes engaged in a balancing act as to how to achieve its goal of expanding among nonwhite groups. The large, free, but impoverished rural southern black community posed some of the greatest dilemmas for the church because of its need for literacy and the restrictions posed by the recently erected Jim Crow laws. Certainly the complex of Catholic schools in the Northeast, Southeast, and Southwest stood as testament to the liberal tradition of the church, yet leaders such as W.E.B. DuBois were extremely critical of what they claimed was the Catholic accommodation to segregation in educational facilities in the twentieth century, the lack of available Catholic high schools for Blacks, and their inability to produce a black Catholic clergy.[22] Only in places such as the Louisiana area, where Catholicism merged with the former French, Acadian, and slave background, did a significant black clergy and an early black Catholic educational movement emerge.

The sentiment toward Catholic pluralism was advanced as the diverse and enlarging immigrant community increasingly sought the right to achieve upward mobility as bona fide Americans even while being intensely interested in their Irish, Italian, Polish, and Czechoslovakian homelands. Their concern for foreign affairs was not unrelated to the repression which Catholics had experienced in their homelands as national pressures increased during World War II and as Russian socialism expanded. To social scientists, it is not surprising to see that, given the overt discrimination and the pressures toward religious assimilation which Catholics faced in the United States, the battle for ethnic preservation was fought in the churches as well as the schools. Indeed, for many subordinate groups, that aspect of culture which has been most oppressed tends to become the focal point of cultural identity and self-definition—even a tool for ultimate liberation.

The new international and political concern of Catholics was no different from the patterns which Protestant ethnic Americans had demonstrated as they acculturated and assimilated. Nor, in its interest to preserve and strengthen the ethnic "nation," was it different from the intense unity which Jews in the European and American diaspora were experiencing during the early and mid-twentieth century.[23] Georgetown demonstrated these concerns for patriotism and ethnicity as it developed its School of Foreign Service. By so doing, this institution opened up new routes toward Americanization, foreign service and State Department careers. While the legitimacy of an international focus on the part of Catholic ethnic groups was often questioned by Anglo-Saxon Protestant Americans, this focus naturally permitted these newer ethnic-Americans to influence American foreign policy as they articulated the position of their homelands in the world.[24]

The collapse of the melting pot thesis in the wake of persistent ethnic discrimination as well as ethnicity, developed in Catholics a new concern for speeding the process of acculturation while utilizing *democratic-pluralist* tactics. This approach to life implied recognition and acceptance of their unique cultural backgrounds,[25] while participating in institutions which were composed primarily of Caucasian Catholics who were members of several ethnic groups. The Irish and the Italians were the majority within the church, but their roles reflected their length of residence in the United States, their closeness to Anglo-Saxon cultural norms, and their Old World attitudes toward the clergy. The Irish were especially well placed to socialize later Catholic newcomers. The English language and educational advantages possessed by the Irish elite permitted them to staff the urban private schools, and they ultimately spilled over into the urban public school systems. As emphasis on education and upward mobility increased, both Irish and Italian Catholics moved out of blue collar occupations into jobs as policemen and lower-level civil servants, and upwards to higher-status occupations. Their children were becoming members of the stable middleclass.

With the increased acculturation and Americanization of Catholics, their institutions experienced new challenges from the mainstream society. Not only did Catholic colleges experience the need for broader academic professionalization, but the children of Catholic families were encouraged to attempt greater participation in the American educational arena.[26] Georgetown, like many other Catholic colleges, followed secular schools in developing the technical and professional branches.

Reflecting those earlier periods when they had been denied access to mainstream institutions such as Harvard, Yale, and Princeton, Catholics during the 1940s and 1950s developed a protectiveness toward Catholic institutions which is still discernible today. They were trained by Jesuits who proclaimed that "an S.J. is good enough for me," and many had little sympathy for the younger Jesuits who, in the aftermath of Vatican II, desired to be trained at Harvard, Yale, and Chicago. Many of the older generation had acquired their professional degrees in the new departments of Catholic institutions. They were (as most new middleclasses are) lawyers, doctors, businessmen—and consequently, many had ambivalence about intellectualism for its own sake. They willingly sacrificed to send sons and daughters to Georgetown and Notre Dame, anticipating the active sense of Catholic community and commitment to values which they had found as college students. Because these institutions offered security to second- and third-generation middle-class Catholic students, they were strongly defended by their graduates.

The New Diversity in Catholic Institutions

From the 1960s onward, the internal complexion of Catholic institutions has been changing, bringing about a new relationship between church and school, and raising new issues in education and pluralism. A number of factors have conspired to alter the constituency which fed into Catholic higher educational institutions. The most notable of these was the changing social and economic environment within the United States between 1945 and the 1960s. Following World War II, a sizeable Eastern European immigration continued, a massive black migration from South to North occurred, and a steady migration from Puerto Rico and Central America began. With prosperity flowing from industrial, technical, and service jobs during the post-World War II period, residential relocation was pronounced. As a result of the economic mobility combined with the liberalism following the Second Vatican Council, Catholic elementary and secondary school attendance peaked at 5.6 million in the 1960s, but declined to 3.6 million in the 1970s, and to 2.7 million in the 1980s as middle-class white ethnics moved out to suburban areas.[27] Although this has been less analyzed by social scientists, it appears that Catholics also benefited from the civil rights and affirmative action emphases of the 1960s, thus gaining new access to higher educational institutions and high-status jobs. As they moved to the suburbs, they sometimes established new churches there, but they seldom had the wherewithal to replicate the Catholic schools there, and they did not feel the cultural pressures to do so. As products of public schools, many of their children began to aspire toward and to attend mainstream colleges and universities, thereby achieving the desired Americanism while remaining Catholic.

The flight of the Catholic middleclass to the suburbs had drastic implications for urban Catholic education. The poorer Catholic ethnics who remained in the city had a difficult time meeting the educational budgets for the archdiocese. Therefore, it was not surprising that the closure of a number of urban Catholic schools began in the late 1960s, and continues even today. Given the pressures for desegregation which accompanied and followed the Civil Rights Movement, many urban Catholics soon came to feel that the demise of their close-knit community and their private schools could be traced to the demands being made by Blacks and Hispanics. This lingering sensitivity over issues of Catholicism, race, and pluralism was temporarily overshadowed by other national and theological developments, but it remained a significant influence within Catholic institutions. More importantly, during the 1960s the emphasis on social justice by the Catholic clergy, which occurred after Vatican II, strengthened the focus of Catholic educators on seeking a liaison with the urban schools. Thus, a new "educational accommodation," born of the shifting Catholic demographics and the new Catholic agenda, came into being in urban areas.[28]

The new "accommodation" was occurring just as rates of black high school graduation had climbed to an all-time high and black enrollments in predominantly white colleges were increasing. In the 1970s, the gap between black and white high school attainment was disappearing, although gaps remained in outcomes of education and salaries for these two groups.[29] Nevertheless, the increased migration of poor southern Blacks and of Puerto Ricans, Chicanos, and other Latin Americans, combined with the decline in the national economy, was beginning to produce problems for northern urban neighborhoods. The black middleclass had been moving toward the suburbs since the early 1960s, integrating suburban schools but further increasing the concentrations of poor Blacks and Hispanics in central city schools.[30] Then, in the 1970s, the shifting national political mood and fiscal conservatism about scholarships and grants resulted in a dramatic slowing down of black educational opportunity and gains.[31] Nationally, the negative socioeconomic climate was bringing about falling black college enrollments during the late 1970s and the 1980s,[32] although this was not true of Catholic institutions like Georgetown.

In the 1960s, when the urban elementary schools were facing crisis due to the demographic shift, economic recessions, and the declining urban tax base, the new Catholic/urban accommodation provided educational support at the weakest link in the educational chain. True, the majority of black and Hispanic students still faced declining academic quality and the disruption caused by gangs in public schools, but solid working-class families often found the resources to send children to Catholic schools. Many schools in Catholic dioceses shifted completely from white to black and Hispanic, although the nuns and clergy remained. In the 1970s, over 22% of Catholic elementary and secondary school students were nonwhite, over half of these students were also non-Catholic, and their parents were more concerned with educational quality and discipline than with religious education.[33]

By establishing this new educational accommodation, the church was quite conscious that it was attempting to build "the living Cathedral of the Church and the Nation of tomorrow."[34] However, the conversion to Catholicism of many black students proved problematic, given that they were so deeply entrenched in Protestant traditions and church memberships, and that conversion was often opposed by parents. Further increasing the skepticism of many black parents was the emphasis on finances and fund-raising. Since the economic base of these urban schools remained fragile, many of them fell victim to fiscal stringencies in the 1980s and were constantly on the verge of closure. However, from the point of view of students and parents in the black community the issue was "why not mergers, rather than closures?" and it raised questions about Catholic commitment to black, urban elementary and secondary education.[35]

After high school graduation, many of these students have indeed made the choice to enter universities such as Georgetown, bringing about a new representation of urban areas and minority populations in these institutions. Although a few have come as Catholics, having converted while in secondary school, the majority simply thought that they would be comfortable with the discipline, values, and environment of the Catholic schools. Many of the suburban middle-class Blacks who now sought increased "Americanization" through education into politics, languages, and government service, also sought a Georgetown education for their children. Thus, despite the fact that the growing minority population was predominantly middleclass, Georgetown's record for diversity in college admissions sets it apart from other competitive, predominantly white institutions.

The new Blacks and Hispanics had the same desires for American inclusion as well as preservation of their ethnic-cultural traditions as did earlier Catholics. Thus, despite the new socialization to the Catholic environment, many of these students remain deeply involved in the black/Protestant or Hispanic traditions of their home communities. Increasingly, athletes from poor urban communities and minorities from urban working-class homes are gaining admission. They, too, seek to acquire or consolidate middle-class status and achieve the type of cultural synthesis that Catholics are already realizing, but the entire process is still quite new for them. It is this diversity of orientation which marks black and Hispanic students as quite different from the earlier white ethnic constituency,[36] and which has often generated ambiguity in social interaction when they arrive in the Catholic environment.

There is a question as to how much we have recognized and come to grips with the implications of the earlier urban educational accommodation and social agenda which has helped generate some of the new constituencies present within the Catholic university community. While the numbers of Blacks and Hispanics provide an index of the University's commitment, the response of children of the earlier generation of Catholic-educated professionals who come to Georgetown indicates remaining tasks for the University. White Catholic students now face a quite complex educational environment because there are large numbers of white and nonwhite Protestants present, a small but significant Jewish student population, and a sprinkling of Muslims and those of other religious traditions. While the white students (Catholic and non-Catholic) are solidly middleclass and share many normative behaviors and attitudes, they are frequently uncertain as to what to make of the new black and Hispanic diversity and their persisting emphasis on their unique identities.

Although some of the students are interacting with Blacks and Hispanics for the first time, most white undergraduates of today are more comfortable with nonwhites in their midst than their counterparts of ten years ago. They have little or no memory of the Black Power period and the Civil Rights battles which stirred emotions a generation ago; nor do many of them have any guilt or sensitivity about eradicating racial discrimination. It appears to them that there are lots of Blacks, Asians, and Hispanics at Georgetown—certainly enough. While they often harbor suspicions about the need for racial affirmative action in college admissions, such discomfort is now seldom verbalized except by the bolder and more politically conservative students. The major American problems, they would say, are with social inequality—with social injustice which produces hunger, homelessness, and family abuse.

Georgetown students often have real ambivalence about seeing the new diversity extend from student enrollment to the entire Georgetown environment, particularly to faculty recruitment, and this is often accompanied by faculty ambivalence about diversity. Between 1976 and 1981, only one black female faculty member occupied a full-time tenure-track position and the number increased to two between 1981 and 1986, although a few other black faculty were recruited and remained for two-year periods. In December 1984, twenty-five faculty and administrators attended a conference on "White Faculty and Black Students at Georgetown." They unanimously endorsed a recommendation that the University immediately set aside funds to provide tenure-track positions for three black faculty. The Provost, J. Donald Freeze, put this plan into effect, but at that time there were few departments ready and able to take him up on his offer.[37] In 1985, faced with the continued inability of various departments to hire any minority faculty, Freeze announced a five-year plan for "affirmative action" in the hiring of faculty.[38] The plan called for adding three new positions each year for the next five years. At least one-third of these new positions were to be filled by black faculty.[39]

That pockets of student resistance to diversity also continue, and that this diversity is occasionally seen as potentially threatening, was reflected in the strongly negative student reaction to Freeze's proposal. In a futile attempt to derail the proposal, the Georgetown University

Student Association (GUSA) passed a resolution opposing the plan, alleging it "would seriously undermine the academic integrity and prestige of the university."[40] One major problem was that while faculty and administrators who had strongly favored the plan pointed to the cultural enrichment which minority faculty could bring to the University, many students and other faculty saw diversity as diminishing rather than enhancing the quality of the institution.

The two significant issues are that Catholic students, faculty, and administrators must be assisted in working out ways of recognizing, accommodating, and valuing diversity within the Catholic community; and that while the diversity is modifying the social dynamics within institutions such as Georgetown, it should not challenge the Catholic character of the institution. Today's diversity, which is racial and cultural, is considerably different from that of forty years ago, which was ethnic but not racial. In 1957, for example, Blacks were only 2.7% of the student body in Catholic colleges and 5.1% of the national student body, while today they are approximately 7.1% of the student body in Catholic colleges but only 4.4% of the national student body.[41] Although minority numbers are still small, this new situation implies the potential for real change in the internal dynamics of the institution. American Catholics have historically strengthened their communities as they created more open environment into which others could come, and there is no reason why this should not remain so today as Blacks and Hispanics enter. Therefore, the present challenge gives the Catholic community the opportunity to seize relevant educational and justice issues and give them a truly pluralist interpretation.

Georgetown's Catholic character gives it an advantage in working to accommodate diversity, but it is indeed a difficult task to establish pluralism, not just in Catholic environments but anywhere in the United States. True pluralism requires acceptance of the cultural features of the other groups, and a neutral or positive attitude toward their values. Indeed, universal values are best achieved within groups whose members appreciate their own particularistic goals and the importance of the particularistic goals of others. This emphasis on achieving the universal would make it possible for minority groups to assess where their own particular cultural experiences and values actually intersect with those of the larger Catholic community.

Understanding and Creating Interracial/ Intercultural Pluralism

Even with Georgetown's demonstrated commitment to diversity, as evidenced by the growing black and Hispanic student population, the demanding task of creating a pluralist community composed of Catholics and new nontraditional members needs to be approached in a concerted fashion on several different fronts—*academic* (curricular and faculty), *extracurricular* (social and values), and *resource allocation* (scholarships, hiring, research released time). Because the university community exists primarily because of its commitment to conveying knowledge, i.e., to training and educating students, this tripartite task of creating a pluralist "community" is best begun by confronting the realities of who these students are and assessing what their needs might be.

The new black students are disproportionately female, primarily middleclass, either suburban or urban, and predominantly Protestant. Increasingly present is a small working-class group of males on athletic scholarships. All these Afro-American students struggle to overcome their experiences of racial discrimination to some degree, whether they be of Caribbean-American or African background as well. In general, these black students value education intensely because historically it has been the vehicle for upward mobility and because their parents have reinforced these values through personal sacrifice so that they could complete secondary school and now college.[42] Their parents have largely been white-collar workers as opposed to professionals and businesspersons, and only recently have a significant number of these black students come from backgrounds which give them sophistication about the tactics of educational choices. Georgetown is likely to differ from many other Catholic or secular colleges in having a predominantly middle-class and perhaps second-generation black college student constituency. Nevertheless, these students, while exceptionally bright, are seldom encouraged to make imaginative career choices and to venture off into mathematics, the sciences, or engineering. They may also be uncomfortable with intense intellectual discourse because it is new to them, but they can easily overcome this with the encouragement that they, too, can master any of these disciplines.

Black students, for example, have an intense commitment to family as they define it, but that mother-centered family is often different from the cohesive father-controlled nuclear family that Catholics expect to see.

Whether as single parents, divorcées, or part of a two-parent household, their mothers have generally always worked and been strong role models. Therefore, these students sometimes have difficulty adjusting to the Catholic community in which mothers have been well educated but play predominantly supportive roles. In addition, women in the Afro-American community have been central to community maintenance and stability, interacting with schools and churches or establishing networks; and this contrasts with Catholic environments which are more male-centered and where female public roles have been more controversial.

Black Protestant culture encourages outgoing personal involvement and community service, but this is always interpreted as service compatible with one's class background. For the urban poor, this service may involve work in clothing distribution, homeless shelters, and soup kitchens, but for the black middle-class students, whose families have had to keep their distance from the urban ghetto in order to maintain upward mobility, service among the urban poor is fearful. Instead, middle-class black students may volunteer in hospitals and urban reading programs, or in family life centers within the Baptist and Methodist churches—another type of activity which is consonant with Catholic concerns. In short, although Blacks and Hispanics share many common values with the larger Catholic community, they need to see a more expansive interpretation of how these value commitments can be developed and acted upon, and how they can be the bridge between Catholics and non-Catholics.

On the academic front, black and Hispanic students need the mentoring which will allow them to better realize their individual potentials and to enter into new and visionary careers which will make them of service to the national black and Hispanic communities. Then, in terms of values, they need to be engaged as Blacks or Hispanics, in playing roles that harmonize with and expand their concerns. They need to be actively engaged in a dialogue about how their values can be realized within Georgetown's activities so that real diversity and pluralism are created.

As important as all three above-mentioned fronts are, it is the academic front which is given priority here. In the curricular arena, what has often gone unrecognized is that both Afro-American and Hispanic populations share interests in politics and international affairs—areas which have historically been important to Catholic students at Georgetown. Because of their historical experiences of domination and discrimination, Afro-American and Hispanic students are prepared to challenge as well as advance American values related to democracy and liberalism, and this concern unites them with Catholics.

Nevertheless, each constituency is likely to approach Georgetown's international orientation from different angles. The ethnic Catholics brought with them into the universities a concern with different languages, and with the traditions of the areas from which their ancestors had come. For their own status as Americans, they seemingly bought into the American emphasis on pluralism, and worked to elevate the status of their countries of origin. Perhaps because of the discrimination that Catholics have faced in entering foreign affairs fields, traditionally the preserve of white Anglo-Saxon Protestants, many of them were even more determined to become international affairs experts, using ability in European languages, history, and government, to penetrate the foreign service.

In like fashion, Blacks approach international affairs conscious of racism, colonialism, and apartheid, and seeking answers to questions about the interlocked and sometimes conflicting destinies of black and white populations in various parts of the world. The newer working-class Hispanic students are often rediscovering a cultural and linguistic legacy which existed prior to Americanization and territorial expansion, and they are concerned to see recognition of the legitimacy of early indigenous cultures as well as an intellectual focus on resolving problems in Latin America and in relations between that area and the United States. Both Blacks and Hispanics expect that these concerns should be important to any Catholic institution which has committed itself to ethical and moral values within education.

While the number of Latin American-related courses has indeed increased, black students are often concerned when black history/culture courses have difficulty being generated within the various academic departments. Indeed, they share another reasonable expectation that each academic department should seek to integrate concerns about their Afro-American history and culture into its own curriculum, making it an integral part of their concerns and of many courses. Likewise, Blacks are hostile to suggestions that such cultural traits, interests, and values might prevent them from being objective foreign affairs experts. What many of them seek is recognition from the university faculty and staff and from course content, that what they have to offer will make them valuable alumni and future professionals.

This kind of reinforcement must grow from a community which really is convinced of the value of what its new members have to offer.

Thus, within the classroom the persona of the faculty member is significant. It is often the new groups who feel that their needs have not been addressed, because they are aware of the tensions which many faculty members feel when talking about Afro-American history and culture, or Caribbean and African cultures. The new students give a cynical ear to faculty claims to know little about these areas of the world. The presence of black American faculty members (particularly males) and Hispanic female faculty members would encourage intellectual role-modelling and also carry subtle messages that these persons are qualified; that they are appropriate intercultural or international affairs experts; and that the areas of the world they represent are highly valued. As these culture areas are included in the curriculum, it then becomes crucial to ensure that Afro-Americans born in the United States as well as Hispanic faculty are represented in respected roles and positions;[43] and it is important to understand that the perspectives they bring expand the horizons of white as well as nonwhite students.

Only on Georgetown's Law faculty was there a consistent and aggressive attempt to hire highly qualified Blacks.[44] Admittedly, the numbers of Blacks and Hispanics receiving graduate degrees has declined over the past decade and not nearly enough are in the educational pipeline, but a pool of fairly accomplished thirty- to forty-five-year-old academic candidates still exists and should be wooed. Many other universities that are serious about achieving diversity are beginning to take steps to "grow their own minority faculty" by encouraging the brightest black students to attend graduate programs in their institutions, then providing the scholarship money necessary to ensure their completion, and providing them with teaching experience as they move toward completion of graduate degrees.[45] Although Georgetown does have a limited number of graduate programs, they can provide the B.A. and M.A. support which would encourage those who achieve Ph.D.'s at other institutions to return to Georgetown to teach at a later point. In fact, President Healy's May 23, 1989, pledge before the Georgetown-American Council on Education sponsored conference included a commitment to identifying and supporting three Georgetown black graduates so that they could attend graduate programs of their choice, in the expectation that they would return to Georgetown to teach.

If the College and the School of Foreign Service have proven to be especially significant to Georgetown's continued success, then here is where faculty diversity is most important. For example, it is important to hire Blacks and Hispanics within each and every department as opposed to hiring only within International Affairs, because the core of intellectual life and of continuity for University programs comes from the departments. It is likewise important that they be hired in tenure-track positions, and given every encouragement for scholarly productivity. Given the demands which they will face in student advising and administrative responsibility, this encouragement should also include research funding and released time that will allow them to be academically secure as they move toward tenure.

Nevertheless, the recent possibility of altering the faculty composition has been troubling to some departments within the University. Whether because of skepticism about increasing the Protestant cohort among the faculty, or skepticism of their "liberal" social philosophies, or claims that they produced only poor scholarship, many faculty opposed Freeze's 1985 minority hiring plans. Some of this skepticism can be traced to the lingering concerns within Catholic universities for achieving the mainstream of the disciplines as they are reflected in secular universities, and to the perception that the research interests of minorities are peripheral. However, an accompanying problem may be the narrow interpretation of academic interests which has resulted from the insular nature of the Catholic community of the past. A major task for the University would seem to be making departments comfortable with the new approaches in the disciplines as well as with the type of approaches and specializations that stellar black and Hispanic candidates emphasize in their work. This means encouraging department members to take a more expansive view of what is becoming important within their fields—a process which should allow them to see the potential contributions that black and Hispanic candidates can make to the institution.

Hopefully, once hired, Blacks and Hispanics will find the way open to pursuing leadership within their respective fields, their departments, and their programs. It is imperative that once on the road to diversity, Catholic universities not fall victim to those problems which have plagued American academia over the past century—that of placing roadblocks in the path of promising black academics and stymieing their leadership roles through questions about their objectivity and abilities. While black and Hispanic candidates can and should be recruited in a variety of fields, there are definitely stellar candidates in the social and political sciences, in area studies and in the languages. Since the 1940s, some classic examples of racism in academia have been provided as black scholars in African Studies programs have faced virtual "black-balling" by whites who feared that Blacks might be able to oust them from control.[46] In the postaffirmative action environment which has descended upon many academic institutions, "not seeing race" is often the pretext for racist exclusion.

While only a brief word is possible here about the extracurricular and resource-allocation fronts, these should not be deemed unimportant. When the concerns of Georgetown's component groups meet outside the classroom, the new diversity of the campus is evident. In a 1986 student survey administered by the Office of Student Affairs, a large number of white students were concerned about requests of nonwhite students for international forums and groups, for discussions about South Africa and other international developments. Some of them saw these issues as having little relevance to the University and its educational mission, and others thought such issues posed a challenge to the moral and religious environment of Georgetown.

As the Catholic university community becomes more diverse, there will be demands to accommodate the cultural traditions of new members. For example, from time to time issues of support for a Protestant chaplain and for a gospel choir have become explosive and have divided black Georgetown students from their counterparts or the administration. While these demands appear on the surface to challenge the Catholic character of the institution, they need not. Black Protestant students can, in fact, provide the bridge between the wider black and religious communities and Catholics who share these concerns within Georgetown. However, if their demands are forcefully resisted rather than engaged, this reinforces the perception of racist exclusion and exaggerates the movement toward separatism. Recently, one rather extreme example was the development of the Imani Temple in Washington by the black priest, Reverend George Augustus Stallings, Jr., who railed against what he called racism within the Catholic church.[47] Faced with what he called "insensitivity to the cultural, social, and spiritual needs of black parishioners," he decided to break with the diocese and establish a church in which Afro-American rites could be performed.

In the case of the University, support for black and Hispanic forums, groups, and extracurricular activities heads off cataclysmic confrontation by making a symbolic statement that these groups and their concerns are important to Georgetown. Thus, the continuation of such efforts at support as are now being undertaken particularly in Student Affairs and in the Center for Minority Student Affairs can help create an environment in which Blacks and Hispanics realize that they can potentially have a stake in the Georgetown community, and that they can participate in shaping its future. Now that the Georgetown community is becoming diverse, support for pluralism demands greater emphasis on creating understanding and tolerance between Catholics and white as well as nonwhite newcomers to Catholic institutions, so that they come to share each other's goals to a significant extent.

Notes

Thanks are due to my colleagues at Georgetown, especially R. Emmett Curran and Anne D. Sullivan, to the members of the Bicentennial Faculty Seminar, and to friends who either read drafts or commented on issues within the text, particularly Elliott P. Skinner of Columbia University.

1. Donald L. Noel, "A Theory of the Origin of Ethnic Stratification," in Norman R. Yetman and C. Hoy Steele, eds., *Majority and Minority: The Dynamics of Racial and Ethnic Relations*, 2d ed. (Boston: Allyn and Bacon, 1975). See also Robert E. Park, *Race and Culture* (Glencoe, Ill.: The Free Press, 1950).

2. Although originally "Afro-American" replaced the term "negro," which referred to black Americans born in the United States, it eventually came to be an inclusive term referring to all people of African ancestry born in the Americas. Therefore, it increasingly came to include those of Caribbean parentage or ancestry, whether in the United States, the Caribbean, or Latin America. One can argue about whether this has been positive or negative for achieving pluralism in American higher education. From a sentimental as well as political perspective, use of the term "African-American," which has recently been introduced by leaders such as Jesse Jackson, makes considerable sense. However, this term may allow institutions to overlook the extreme and continuing discrimination against those with a slave background here in the United States.

3. "Bennett Urges Catholic Schools to Aid Public School Students," *Washington Post*, 8 April 1988, A5, referring to Secretary Bennett's April 7th talk to the National Catholic Educational Association (NCEA).

4. Milton M. Gordon, "Assimilation in America: Theory and Reality," in Yetman and Steele, *Majority and Minority*, 237-51. For a more contemporary view of the attempt at upward mobility and cultural distinctiveness, see Lawrence Levine, *Highbrow/Lowbrow: The Emergence of Cultural Hierarchy in America* (Cambridge, Mass.: Harvard University Press, 1988).

5. Edward J. Power, *Catholic Higher Education in America* (New York: Appleton-Century-Crofts, 1972), 3.

6. Catholic expansion was more easily accomplished in the Southwest, where inspired men like Father Junipero Serra acquired territory and brought thousands of Native Americans, Hispanics, and others into the church, but it was more difficult to accomplish in the colonies of the Northeast and Southeast.

7. Robert D. Cross, *The Emergence of Liberal Catholicism in America* (Cambridge, Mass.: Harvard University Press, 1958), 8-13.

8. Leonard Dinerstein and Frederic Cople Jaher, eds., *The Aliens* (New York: Appleton-Century-Crofts, 1970).

9. Louis Adamic, *A Nation of Nations* (New York: Harper and Brothers, 1944), 316. For an explanation of the "three-generation assimilation hypothesis" as applied to the Scotch-Irish and the Irish Catholics, see S. Dale McLemore, *Racial and Ethnic Relations in America* (Boston: Allyn and Bacon, 1980), 35-39 and 53-56.

10. "Proposals for Establishing an Academy at George-Town, Patowmack-River, Maryland," Maryland Province Archives 56 R 1.

11. Harold Faulkner, *American Political and Social History*, 5th ed. (New York: Appleton-Century-Crofts, 1948). The Know-Nothing Party elected some state governors and members of Congress in 1854, but it collapsed after its presidential candidate, Millard Fillmore, was defeated in 1856.

12. Patrick's brother, James Augustine Healy, graduated from Holy Cross, was ordained a priest in 1854, and served the church in Boston till 1875, when he was consecrated bishop of Portland, Maine, the first black bishop in the United States. For more on this remarkable racially-mixed family, see Thomas J. O'Donnell, S.J., "For Bread and Wine," *Woodstock Letters* 80 (1951):99-142.

13. Melvin Drimmer, in *Issues in Black History: Reflections and Commentaries on the Black Historical Experience* (Dubuque, Iowa: Kendall-Hunt Publishing Co., 1987), 55, describes the role of the Capuchin, Ursuline, and "Negro Nuns" in insisting upon marriage among slaves and in educating girls on Louisiana plantations. See also the comments of Timothy S. Healy, S.J., in "Conference on Religion and Education," *Daedalus* 117:2 (Spring 1988), 73-74.

14. Michael Larkin, "When Blue Fought Grey: Georgetown's Battle for Survival," *The Hoya* 69:25 (8 April 1988), 10.

15. Benjamin Quarles, *The Negro in the Making of America* (London: Collier-Macmillan Ltd., 1964), 93-94.

16. J. G. Randall and David Donald, *The Civil War and Reconstruction*, 2d ed. (Boston: D. C. Heath & Co., 1961), 483-85. Randall and Donald report that "The use of Negroes as strikebreakers was an element in the ugly race riots which occurred in New York, Brooklyn and Cincinnati" (485).

17. John Bodnar, *Workers' World: Kinship, Community, and Protest in an Industrial Society, 1900-1940* (Baltimore: Johns Hopkins University Press, 1982).

18. For a coverage of this process in Newark, N.J., see G. Mikell Remy, "Class and Ethnic Political Relations in Newark NJ: Blacks and Italians," in Leith Mullings, ed., *Cities of the United States: Studies in Urban Anthropology* (New York: Columbia University Press, 1987), 71-99.

19. See James F. McLoughlin, "The School Controversy in the United States," *American Ecclesiastical Review* 6 (1892):119-22. See also John Tracy Ellis, "Cardinal Gibbons and Philadelphia," *Records of the American Catholic Historical Society of Philadelphia* 58 (1947), 99; and Zachary Montgomery, "Contemplated Educational Alliance Between Church and State," *American Ecclesiastical Review* 7 (1892):341-54.

20. Cross, *Emergence of Liberal Catholicism*, 142-45.

21. The issue of marital assimilation and its impact on the possible challenge to the continuity of the Catholic community was also significant because of the mixture of northern Europeans and Catholics in the St. Paul area.

22. See the exchange of communications between W.E.B. DuBois and Joseph B. Glenn, priest in charge of St. Joseph's Mission in Richmond, Virginia, in 1925, in Herbert Aptheker, ed., *The Correspondence of W.E.B. DuBois, Selections, 1877-1934*, vol. 1 (Amherst: University of Massachusetts Press, 1973), 308-11.

23. Color emerges as a factor in the slowed assimilation pattern of the second-wave immigrants. While Italians and Jews were usually considered Caucasian, the Mediterranean background and the evidence of racial mixture caused Anglo responses to these groups to be more intense. Thus race/color prejudice sometimes combined with religious discrimination to make their adjustment experiences difficult. Obviously, race/color rejection was greatest for still later African-American and Hispanic urban migrants.

24. Elliott P. Skinner, "Race and Ethnicity as Factors in the Formation of Foreign Policy: Theoretical and Practical Considerations," in Michael P. Hamilton, ed., *American Character and the Formation of United States Foreign Policy* (Grand Rapids, Mich.: Eerdmans, 1986), 89-136.

25. Pluralism refers to the existence of distinct but equivalent, separately organized ethnic communities having their own cultures and structure. This term, as it was originally used by F.J. Furnivall, referred to the tendency of groups within colonial societies to organize within their own ethnic segments. Each ethnic segment was seen as having different institutional structures and relationships, and the economy was identified as the main (sometimes the only) point of interaction with other groups. Since the 1960s this concept has undergone severe criticism. See F. J. Furnivall, *Colonial Policy and Practice* (Cambridge: Cambridge University Press, 1948); and Burton Benedict, "Stratification in Plural Societies," *American Anthropologist* 64 (1962):1235-46.

26. Andrew M. Greeley, *From Backwater to Mainstream: A Profile of Catholic Higher Education* (New York: McGraw-Hill, 1969).

27. Deirdre Carmody, "Catholic Schools Facing New Issues," *New York Times*, 7 April 1988, D1.

28. Charles V. Willie and Jerome Baker, *Race Mixing in the Public Schools* (New York: Praeger Publishers, 1973).

29. Gwendolyn Mikell Remy, *The Brown Decision—25 Years Later: Indicators of Desegregation and Equal Educational Opportunity*. Washington, D.C.: Institute for Educational Leadership, George Washington University, 1979.

30. William Julius Wilson, *The Truly Disadvantaged* (Chicago: University of Chicago Press, 1987).

31. Bart Landry, *The New Black Middle Class* (Berkeley: University of California Press, 1987), 205-09.

32. Predominantly white institutions had experienced a spurt in black enrollments between 1965 and 1975 in response to the legislation and educational grants resulting from the Civil Rights Movement. Historically, black colleges and universities had also experienced a spurt in attendance between 1954 and 1976, and managed to retain a stable black enrollment between 1976 and 1980. However, during

the decade 1976-1985, the percentage of black eighteen- to twenty-four-year-olds entering college dropped from 33.5% to 26.1% (College Entrance Examination Board, "Equality and Excellence: The Educational Status of Black Americans," New York: CEEB, 1985; "Share of Blacks, Hispanics Entering College Continues Decline," *Washington Post,* 23 October 1987, A15).

Although this decline was most reflected in black enrollments within predominantly white institutions, the proportion of black students who were enrolled in black colleges and universities has also declined, reflecting severe economic problems with financing education. See Samuel Myers "Blacks in College: NAFEO Trend Analysis," *American Visions: The Magazine of Afro-American Culture,* 2:5 (October 1987), 44-46; and Niara Sudarkasa, "Black Enrollment in Higher Education: The Unfulfilled Promise of Equality," in *The State of Black America 1988* (New York: National Urban League, 1988).

33. Mary von Euler and Sister Gail Lambers, C.H.S., eds., *The Catholic Community and the Integration of Public and Catholic Schools* (Washington, D.C.: National Institute of Education, 1979).

34. Ibid., 16.

35. "A Good School about to Die," *Washington Post,* 28 February 1989, A23.

36. See Sara Lawrence Lightfoot, *Worlds Apart: Relationships between Families and Schools* (New York: Basic Books, 1978); and Myers, "Blacks in College," 44-46.

37. For national statistics on Blacks in higher education and a discussion of the difficulties which institutions face in implementing affirmative action plans, see Niara Sudarkasa, "A Precarious Estate, Minorities in Academe: Affirmative Action or Affirmation of the Status Quo?" *American Association of Higher Education Bulletin* 39:6 (February 1987).

38. "Five Year Plan Calls For Minority Faculty Hiring Quotas," *The Hoya* 66:15 (13 September 1985), 1; "Making Racial Progress," ibid., 8; Paul Cardaci, "Inching to Dr. King's Vision," *The Hoya* 66:16 (20 September 1985), 9; and Lisa Stenson, "Georgetown's Ethnic Education," ibid., 9.

39. The following chart gives the number of minority faculty, as of 30 September 1988:

	Tenured		
	Main Campus	Medical School	Law School
Black	2	1	4
Hispanic	9	5	0
	Nontenured (but in tenure-track positions)		
	Main Campus	Medical School	Law School
Black	5	2	2
Hispanic	3	3	0

40. The resolution is printed in *The Hoya* 66:18 (4 October 1985), 1. GUSA President Mark Ouweleen stated that the plan represented reverse discrimination, and that the University "just can't hire unqualified professors." The mover of the resolution, Kevin McGrath, said, "We are not here to right previous wrongs." See "Assembly Acts on Quotas and Constitution: Minority Plan Condemned," ibid., 1; see also the editorial, "The Quota Resolution," ibid., 6; and Sean Leman, "GUSA

Continues Debate on Quotas," *The Hoya* 66:19 (11 October 1985), 7. See also Mark Ouweleen, "Free the Five-Year Plan" and Starla Williams and Barry Hargrove, "Affirmative Uproar," *The Hoya* 66:21 (25 October 1985), 7; and "Students, Faculty Divided on Minority Quotas," *The Hoya* 66:23 (8 November 1985), 1.

41. See Georgetown University Student Profile Information, Admissions Office, Spring 1988.

42. Andrew Billingsley, *Black Families in White America* (Englewood Cliffs, N.J.: Prentice-Hall, 1968).

43. While many universities manage to find African-born and Caribbean-born or Latin American faculty members, there are often questionable claims of difficulty in identifying available U.S.-born Afro-American faculty members or Puerto Rican faculty members.

44. In the Law School, there are six black tenure-track faculty members, most of whom have joined the faculty since 1974.

45. Here, the recommendations of the Conference on Increasing the Numbers of Blacks in International Affairs Careers become relevant. Georgetown's School of Foreign Service sponsored this conference in April 1988, and the recommendations of the panel on undergraduate education specifically called for creating links with historically black colleges and universities. The goal would be to provide promising seniors the languages, international affairs summer courses, and internships which would encourage them to come to Georgetown for graduate work.

46. One of the major controversies here concerned Melville Herskovits, who initiated the African Studies Department at Northwestern University, but who questioned the ability of Blacks to conduct objective research in Africa. Although Herskovits's position grew out of his dispute with black scholars such as E. Franklin Frazier at Howard University, this position was to indelibly mark African Studies by denying training and leadership to many black graduate students until the 1960s. See the proceedings of the Conference inaugurating the Herskovits Collection at the Schomberg Museum, New York Public Library, April 1988.

47. "Maverick Priest Says He is No Luther but a Man of Ethnic and Religious Soul," *New York Times*, July 9, 1989, A22. See also "The Rev. Stallings, Right and Wrong," editorial in the *Washington Post*, 20 July 1989, A20.

Leona M. Fisher
Department of English
Coordinator of Women's Studies

The Challenge of Women's Studies: Questions for a Transformed Future at Georgetown

Preface

While I understand that these Bicentennial papers are supposed to look at Georgetown's history, as well as to pose questions for the future, I have chosen to focus on the issue of coeducation as it relates to the undergraduate curriculum now and in the future. As a result of this rather narrow (albeit central) consideration, it has not seemed necessary to probe widely in the earlier presence of "women at Georgetown," replicating as it did (in the Nursing and Language Schools) the general definition of women in American society. Instead, I have confined myself to an exploration of women's Catholic higher education and theoretical studies of curriculum transformation in the 1980s. I hope that this approach will generate discussions not only about women's place here at Georgetown, but also about the University's opportunities to create an enriched environment for all people.

In the conclusion to Jane Austen's *Persuasion* (1818), Anne Elliot responds to Captain Harville's claim that "Songs and proverbs all talk of woman's fickleness. But perhaps you will say, these were all written by men," with:

> Perhaps I shall.—Yes, yes, if you please, no reference to examples in books. Men have had every advantage of us in telling their own story. Education has been theirs in so much higher a degree; the pen has been in their hands. I will not allow books to prove anything.[1]

My first response when asked to participate in this seminar and write this paper was that like Anne Elliot and the women of her day, I could not talk about education because the pen had not been in my hands. But Women's Studies had, and it was there that I decided to take up the controversy of education for women at Georgetown and, in turn, women's contribution to the University.

I realize that there are many faculty members who would denigrate Women's Studies as ideological and polemical, rejecting its influence on their own disciplines though perhaps tolerating its interdisciplinary presence as "a sop to the girls." The point I hope to make in this paper is that this new field is both rigorous and legitimate, as concerned with free inquiry and the pursuit of "truth" as any academic discipline. Righting the wrongs and omissions of the past and invigorating the academy with new questions and paradigms of knowledge, Women's Studies both questions the entrenched biases and assumptions that we live with and "defamiliarizes" them, and raises the crucial question of freedom—i.e., power—in the academy. As Carol Gilligan has stated in a book on the difference between male and female moral development: "In relationships of temporary inequality, such as parent and child or teacher and student, power ideally is used to foster the development that removes the initial disparity."[2] Women's Studies acknowledges that temporary inequality and seeks to empower students to proceed beyond gender disparity to intellectual and personal independence.

In other words, a university education should fit the student to encounter the world; empower her to enter the structures of power and question their validity; enable her to undertake the transformation of those structures. An education cannot do that if it is narrow, compartmentalized, passive, authoritarian; if it does not include both the techniques for survival (the preprofessional or practical component) and the critical tools for deconstructing the patriarchal paradigms. In the words of Adrienne Rich, feminist theorist and poet, Women's Studies offers women "a new intellectual grasp on their lives, new understanding of our history, a fresh vision of the human experience, and also a critical basis for evaluating what they hear and read in other courses, and in the society at large."[3]

This notion of a balanced curriculum will not be achieved by mere "consciousness raising" nor can a lowering of academic standards accompany such critical questioning. Indeed, the reconstruction of courses, critical discourse, and pedagogical methods to include women who have had no "story" cannot be accomplished without scholarship, training in writing, logical scrutiny, and a lot of hard work.

I would like to include men and male-identified women (who enter the university "with the innocent assumption that sexism is no longer a problem")[4] as the beneficiaries of these ideas. An incident which occurred several years ago at Georgetown helped point out both that much so-called objective knowledge is ideological and biased and that all students need some strong (perhaps even required) lessons in tolerance, generosity, and the perception of "difference" among people. The conservative student magazine, *The Guardian* (which has since ceased publication) ran an editorial comment "comically" linking homosexuality, affirmative action hiring of black faculty, a lowering of academic standards, Women's Studies, and "Lithuanian Pole Climbing"—all presumably in an appeal for "rigor" and as a critique of the University's encroaching liberalism.[5] The tone of the editorial was smug and self-satisfied, its information proudly ignorant. If we as a University community had acted responsibly toward the student who wrote it, we would have made him aware of the "politics of knowledge" and he would (at least) have been embarrassed to demonstrate his ignorance of Women's Studies and its historical component as well as its interdisciplinary analysis of power and cultural difference. A serious exposure to this area of intellectual research might have allowed the student to confront his own racism and sexism, as well as to articulate the bases of his conservatism.

We as an institution have failed if we have not exposed this student to enough variety in the content and methods of his courses that he is equipped to analyze his opinions from the position of knowledge rather than prejudice. We have further failed if we do not inspire students to a higher standard of journalism. Purporting to be a reputable intellectual forum for conservative truth, the publication instead identified itself, in my mind, with that group of unreflective Georgetown students who, several years ago, reenacted a gang rape as part of a senior talent show and were cheered on enthusiastically by their peers. Aspiring to serious analysis, the journal instead sided with those who recite AIDS jokes and write nasty antigay graffiti in the campus restrooms.

"One of the goals of women's studies is to insure that education becomes democratic . . . Case studies from universities that have had inclusive curriculum projects show that students do learn through women's studies to enlarge their worldviews and to integrate academic learning into their personal experience even though the process by which this occurs is full of conflict, resistance, and anger."[6] I believe that such an enlargement of view is worth the risks.

I

The prevailing liberal "postfeminist" myth in the media and among the population as a whole is that women have arrived. They can attend coeducational colleges (and learn to enter a "man's world"), they can hold jobs (as if working-class women had not always done so!), they can have babies when they choose to do so (if they succeed in marrying before their biological clocks run out), they can hire women to rear their children and clean their homes (at exploitative wages and with little consciousness of contradiction). In short, they "have it all."

But they are still in the singular position of needing to "keep it all clean" as well. In other words, they are required to be "superwomen"—not "equal" in the sense that early activists for women's rights had meant, but somehow superior to the men with whom they had wanted the right to compete. And, to add insult to irony, college-educated women are only able to earn the equivalent of a male high school graduate's salary; they are discriminated against for promotions in the corporate and academic worlds; they are forced either to conform to male standards of attire and competitiveness or be described (by popular economist George Gilder, sociobiologist E. O. Wilson, and others) as "by nature" unable to behave in the rational and competitive ways that will insure their rise on the ladder.[7]

Despite all the high-flown rhetoric about women's equal opportunities, therefore, American and Western European culture still has not directly confronted the need to transform its attitudes toward women's education and capabilities. We have adopted an "add-on" philosophy of women's rights, based partly on economic need, but have retained the older myths that women's nature and aptitudes still peculiarly fit them for the home sphere, not the marketplace or the sphere of ideas. If women wish to participate in the male sphere, they are permitted to do so, but only if they are willing to add that accomplishment to their other "rightful" duties. It is no wonder, therefore, that the women who returned to Georgetown in the spring of 1986 to celebrate the fifteenth anniversary of full coeducation complained almost universally that their university years had not prepared them for the anger, frustration, and guilt that accompanied their careers. As a commentator in the *Chronicle of Higher*

Education recently put it, "When the enemy was obvious we knew how to fight. Now, when sexism is hidden by rhetoric about egalitarian principles, women can be caught unawares."[8]

The answer to this complaint would seem to lie in the progress that Georgetown has recently made in regard to women. We have had an "Introduction to Women's Studies" course since 1983, and a program that offers a minor in the College of Arts and Sciences since 1987. In that same year, the Office of Student Affairs sponsored a year-long feminist lecture series and a group of undergraduate women started *The New Press*, devoted to writing by and about women. The recent Bicentennial conference on "Women in America: Legacies of Race and Ethnicity" drew more than six hundred conference participants from all over the country. Father Healy has delegated Father Freeze to appoint a Women's Commission to examine the status of women faculty, staff, and students at Georgetown over the next few years. The President has also expressed pleasure that the rates of hiring and retention of women faculty have improved over the past few years.[9]

All of this visibility and attention masks the fact that Georgetown has relied almost entirely on the volunteer efforts of a handful of women and men who have been willing to work slowly, patiently, and tirelessly for change. Very little official support and almost no money have been committed to the projects, and their continuation and future are in considerable doubt. Given the recent history of the University in matters of governance, one has to conclude that policies and programs (as well as persons) survive at Georgetown *only* if they are initiated or approved of by the administration; a top-down ethos means that one must work within, not against, the administrative hierarchy in order to achieve longevity and success—no matter how strong the grassroots efforts may be. As most of us would acknowledge, that hierarchy has had little to say about women, except reactively when pressed. Additionally, the necessarily male, Jesuit administration (at the top levels) complicates women's responses to this environment; both faculty and undergraduate women complain of a kind of low-grade chronic alienation, but for undergraduate women this absence of "ego ideals" at the top ought to have been addressed concretely, from the beginning of coeducation, and has not been.[10] It is my belief, therefore, that women have had no systematically recorded "history" here, that their present visibility is accidental, and that their future in the institution will depend on conscious and articulated efforts—at every level—to examine our position and contributions and to discover ways to improve both.

That this effort is being conducted nationally probably will hold little weight at Georgetown, priding itself as it does on its difference from other institutions of higher learning. Indeed, "trends" hold little weight with me as well, unless they can demonstrably improve the quality of learning and life for our student and faculty populations. In this Bicentennial year it strikes me, however, that Georgetown is more worried about its "identity" than it is complacent about it; in other words, we are in process of discovering who we are as a major Catholic (yet also American and pluralistic) university and what unique contributions we can make to education in the future. This is a healthy process and one which depends both on our strong history and on our collective and diverse visions for the future.

For the purposes of this paper and in the interests of space, I will confine my reflections on the future of women and Women's Studies to suggestions about the undergraduate curriculum, with the conviction that "*The center of consciousness in an educational institution is the curriculum*."[11] Since no major curricular changes have taken place since the late 1960s, except by the action of individual departments, it is crucial that we reactivate the discussions about the Core Curriculum, as well as expand our conversations to include cross-cultural and interdisciplinary considerations—avowedly included in Georgetown's goals. Women's Studies, as both a discipline and an interdisciplinary methodology, can contribute both to a transformation of disciplinary activity and to a reconsideration of the goals of a so-called humanistic education.

This restriction does not mean that I am not concerned about the paucity of women faculty, their relatively low status and pay, the quality of extracurricular life for all students, the existence of sexual harassment, the lack of a day-care center or parental leave policies, the absence of a women's center on campus, the lack of counselors and psychologists trained to deal with eating disorders and rape, the prevalence of acquaintance rape and other violence against women, the general disregard of women's health concerns, or the alienation from the church hierarchy and university leadership that undergraduate women feel.[12] It simply means that I had to choose and that I believe that the valorization of women in the curriculum would lead to a campus "climate" much more favorable to change in other areas.[13]

There are compelling reasons, both external and internal, to add women to an enlivening discourse about the curriculum. Across the country the debate about women's studies is lively: major universities as well as small campuses are discussing the relative merits of isolated Women's Studies Programs and the integration of feminist methodology into the disciplines (what is called, somewhat erroneously, "mainstreaming"), with most institutions choosing an uneasy if creative combination of the two, leading toward what is popularly called "a balanced curriculum."[14] There are now approximately five hundred Women's Studies Programs and more than twenty thousand women's studies courses, with universities like Stanford and Harvard offering a major.[15] Debates about the "canon" and marginality have resulted in curriculum transformation projects across the country.[16] In scholarship—encompassing both the recovery of lost texts and history and the transformation of intellectual paradigms—the last ten years have seen the yearly publication of thousands of books and articles on women and feminist perspectives in history, philosophy, literature, theology, psychology, biology, etc. So many women and men are engaged in women's studies and related research that this field is arguably the most dynamic and prolific in the world at this point, affecting the scholarship even of those who do not acknowledge its importance. The "omissions, trivializations, and distortions"[17] of twenty years ago have given way to a renewed energy in the academy and the acknowledgment that women's studies scholars are in the vanguard of this intellectual regeneration. As one converted male professor has written:

> Ultimately, I respond to women's studies not because it is right (although I think it is) and not because it is wise (although I think it is), but because it is exciting. Teachers and administrators concerned about burn-out should take note: transforming courses can entail a stirring transformation of the self.[18]

Within Georgetown, the recuperation of women's contributions to history and culture may seem less revitalizing, its relevance and importance less compelling, because of a conservative Catholic orientation toward women and the family[19] and the comparatively recent (and perhaps financially motivated) addition of undergraduate women to the campus community, with full coeducation coming in 1969. An examination of undergraduate catalogues from the late sixties and early seventies reveals no new courses (with the exception of "Gender Roles" in Sociology in 1971) created in response to the new presence of women in all five undergraduate schools for the first time in Georgetown's history. A course in "Women Writers" did not appear until 1975 and was offered only in the Summer School. A team-taught interdisciplinary seminar on "Women in the Arts and Sciences" was offered through the College of Arts and Sciences in Spring 1976, but never repeated because the guest lecturer format seemed a bit discontinuous and unwieldy. A women's history course was not offered until 1981—by an adjunct professor. Even with the initiation of plans for a Women's Studies Program (which began informally with a faculty group in 1981), the disciplines responded very slowly to the new research: courses on women and philosophy, art, government, health, and theology are appearing for the first time this year; psychology, economics, biology, and most of the foreign languages have yet to develop such courses.

The addition of women to the College of Arts and Sciences therefore seems to have been chiefly a matter of "add women and stir," with little fundamental examination of what full coeducation might mean, how the women's needs might be served, or how women might change the educational experience of the University. As Florence Howe has written in her *Myths of Coeducation*, "one of the central ideas of coeducation provides a central myth: that if women are admitted to men's education and treated exactly as men are, then all problems of sexual equity will be solved. The myth assumes that the major problem for women is 'access' to what men have, and it continues to ignore the *content* and *quality* of what it is women may gain access to."[20] Until quite recently, affirmative action hiring was left up to the individual departments' discretion (and is still not supported by financial commitments except in the case of minority hiring). Administrators worried about where to house the "girls," but in the early years it was left to the newly formed undergraduate Women's Caucus and ad hoc campus groups to make the new presence felt on the Main Campus.[21] These organizations brought feminist speakers to campus and discussed the current issues raised by the nonacademic Women's Movement, but as the hilltop became more accustomed to women's presence, these efforts died down.

Instead of guiding the unformed students to consider their new coeducational condition, the University either responded minimally to student agitation or sought to fill the gap by reasserting that women students had the same opportunities as the men—and to prove it by allowing them to enroll in the same classes and sign up with the same recruiters. As the linguists would put it, men remained the "unmarked case"; women were the special, the "marked" exception (have you ever heard of a male "coed"?). With the benefit of hindsight, Howe has written what seems to be a description of women's place at Georgetown and beyond: "We know now that education per se does not change the status of women with regard to men, but merely the status of women with regard to other women."[22]

There is, however, an older tradition in Catholic education for women in this country to which we might look for wisdom and inspiration. In the late nineteenth century, at a time when many Catholics still considered it immoral to educate girls in the same institutions as boys, there nevertheless developed a solid educational philosophy which justified the special educational needs of young women. In doing so, these educators (most of them members of female religious orders) defended their enterprise by insisting that reason and virtue belonged to all persons, that the church had a venerable tradition of strong women and scholars, and that a higher education of the right sort would not jeopardize women's "gentleness" or their ability to bear children (myths still prevalent, even among gynecologists, at the turn of the century).[23] As Thomas I. Gasson, S.J., said in 1899, in a speech delivered on the occasion of the founding of Trinity College here in Washington, D.C., Christianity had actually improved the condition of women and a good Catholic education would continue to do so:

> . . . who would bring back to earth the degrading principles concerning women that ruled the Hellenic nation, even in the days of its most splendid culture? What need to refer to the position of women under Roman rule, Persian tyranny, or Hindoo mysticism? Under all she was looked upon as the patient drudge, the obedient slave, the willing vassal, fit for household burdens but utterly incapable of ascending the mountains of knowledge.
>
> Christianity changed all this. It gave woman a new position in the world; it brought out her hidden strength. Even in the earliest days of the Christian religion, we find maidens rivalling youths in the eager quest after knowledge. St. Jerome, a literary churchman in the highest sense of the term, was ably assisted in his great work by that illustrious Roman lady, St. Paula.[24]

Having placed the education of women on the firmest foundation, he goes on to cite other examples of learned women in the early church, not all of them cloistered, then proceeds to address the Victorian myths:

> Just as all men are not fitted for a college career, so neither are all women destined for Trinity College. But what we want is that the woman *with a college head* shall be given the opportunities and the instructors for higher studies. It is true that some who have enjoyed these blessings have lost the gentleness and refinement belonging to female manners. But they have lost these charming qualities in spite of their education, and not because of it. It is not in the nature of education to produce such a result, but this sad effect is the outgrowth of the pride and arrogance that spring from superficial knowledge.[25]

While St. Ignatius Loyola and his followers were generally regarded as not favoring the education or equality of women,[26] other church leaders, like St. Francis de Sales, established a scholarly tradition for women. It was not, however, a part of the Enlightenment philosophy which informed the establishment of Georgetown at the end of the eighteenth century. As Cardinal Eugène Tisserant wrote in 1947,

> . . . Jean-Jacques Rousseau . . . advised mothers strongly against having their daughters educated in a system of studies similar to the one in use for boys: for girls, no college ought to exist, and no classical studies. Fortunately, the influence of Jean-Jacques Rousseau, which was great on Thomas Jefferson and through him on the system of American education, did not prevent the American girls from receiving college training.[27]

This idea that girls were differently constituted "by nature" from boys yet had received similar college training sounds positive, but is not entirely borne out by an examination of curricula in the nineteenth century.[28] While boys were studying Greek and Latin, girls were given a smattering of French; while boys studied the humanities, girls were taught to housekeep and to paint flowers; while boys were considered rational and objective, girls were emotional and narrowly subjective; while boys were inclined to sexual peccadilloes and should be indulged, girls were still undergoing clitoridectomies to restrain their sexuality and control hysteria; while men were understandably corruptible because of their places in the world, women were by nature "moral" and pure and hence responsible for the maintenance of morality in the home.

These Victorian notions of the rigid separation of the spheres and the different biological natures of the sexes would die hard. Even when Oberlin opened as the first coeducational college in 1833, the curricula for the two sexes were considerably different and the women were expected to do the men's wash on Mondays.[29] Early feminists complained that "petty 'female colleges'" did not meet "the demand of the age, and so will eventually perish. Oberlin and Antioch Colleges in Ohio . . . admit women on terms *nearly equal with men*" (emphasis mine).[30]

Catholic colleges for women did not exist until the turn of the twentieth century and when they opened, their curricula in part copied those of secular girls' academies and were designed specifically to cater to the special needs and natures of women—with courses in "domestic economy" (later to develop into the "home economics" programs of the 1930s and 1940s), elementary education, and nursing, all regarded as appropriate extensions of a woman's innate nurturing capacity and motherly vocation. Yet their teachers and role models were strong, unmarried women (as were professors in the elite Seven Sisters schools) who believed in the power of reason and were ready to challenge their protégées intellectually as well as morally.[31] In 1910 Mother Pauline O'Neill, C.S.C., issued "A Word to Parents and Guardians Who Are Seeking an Ideal School for Their Girls," describing St. Mary's College and Academy, Notre Dame, Indiana. In it she explained the curriculum of this college preparatory academy, which of course included "domestic science," "physical culture" and music, but its "College courses—English, Classical and Scientific—lead to regular Degrees"[32] and clearly were intended to replicate the best courses of study at boys' schools. There is nothing to indicate that the sexual or moral "double standard" prevailed in such an institution. While women's "manners" might be superior to (or more refined than) men's, there seems to be no fear in Mother O'Neill's mind that women would be corrupted by learning mathematics and logic.

What I am suggesting that we recuperate in our own discussions of the place of women and Women's Studies in the curriculum is the double perspective of these early female educators: (1) women *are* different from men (and from one another), but that does not mean that they cannot study the same subjects and achieve the same levels of competence; (2) since women are different from men, they can bring unique questions and perspectives to those subjects and actually help to transform the institutions they enter. As we proceed in the discussion, we will discover that women who work specifically on Women's Studies can also create new materials and methods for learning, but as a starting point and a tradition, we can at least begin with a sense that many generations of women have benefited from the care, respect, and concern that went into the Catholic women's college curriculum.

To bring the discussion closer to home once more, Georgetown itself has articulated theoretical values that imply ethical as well as intellectual concern for all of its members: specifically, commitments to diversity, intercultural education, and interdisciplinary studies—all of which are central tenets of a Women's Studies curriculum. The Jesuit tradition itself values inclusiveness and broad humanistic goals in its training of young people. As an order, the Society of Jesus has seen specialization as insufficient education for life in the active world. As multiple outsiders (in the church and in Protestant American society) themselves, their educational philosophy necessarily had to be externally empowering as well as internally superior. Georgetown was conceived in that spirit. Students had to be taught to reason *and* to imagine, to arrive at independent judgments, to draw ethical conclusions in complex and ambiguous situations, to take their places in the power structures of the new republic (to "know the enemy," as it were), even if they were perceived as upstarts and outsiders.

This process of independence could once be seen as "universal" if the subjects were all men and the curriculum only included Homer, Aristotle, Virgil, Aquinas, Dante, Shakespeare, etc. (We all know the requirements for "cultural literacy": the list reprinted by William Bennett's office and rearticulated by E.D. Hirsch and Alan Bloom for all to see.) "Western Civilization"'s content and methodologies were immutable; one could not be a "Renaissance man" without an acquisition of the classics. The 1960s threw them out in a burst of relevancy, then guiltily reinstated them at such institutions as Harvard and Stanford as optional parts of the core curriculum. Now many institutions are trying to construct a new model, one which balances the teachers' and students' needs for pluralism and a more global flexibility with the departments' and the institution's need for order and legitimacy.[33]

This new, more inclusive, approach to curriculum development requires that we acknowledge the contributions of the traditional "outsider" in academic discourse. Part of my belief that we must incorporate diverse perspectives results from the perception that unless we radically reexamine our educational philosophy (which has in some cases grown up rather haphazardly, a bit like Topsy), Georgetown risks losing itself in pragmatism or in empty and rigid standards of "excellence" and the unexamined ideals of the secular nineteenth century (such as Matthew Arnold's rather naïve notion of "the best that is known and thought in the world"—i.e., the white, western, patriarchal world). Both ethically and intellectually, we have missed an opportunity if we do not confront academic movements like Women's Studies and their scholarly challenge to complacency. If we remember that Catholic women educators once considered seriously the academic needs of women,[34] that women were once seen as having special educational needs, that Jesuits have traditionally considered education to be empowering, and that the Society of Jesus has important roots in this country as a body of radical intellectuals and religious outsiders, it should be theoretically and philosophically defensible to undertake this new project with a sense of historical consistency.

Before I go on to analyze the place of the outsider and to articulate specific suggestions, I would like to make my premises clear, acknowledging that many will not agree with them (I would not have accepted them myself ten years ago) because we all have a serious stake in protecting our areas of expertise as complete and inclusive:

(1) That all courses not named "Women's Studies" or conceived to be feminist in methodology or woman-centered in content are not "universal" but "men's studies."[35]

(2) That all courses not self-defined as "African-American [or Other] Studies" or as racially or ethnically pluralistic are not "colorblind" but white-defined, ethnocentric, implicitly racist.

(3) That all courses not naming themselves as concerned with class differences are implicitly biased toward the middle class.

(4) That history is not a "given," but an almost infinitely redefinable, revisable, re-visible entity—and that we have a responsibility to redefine it over and over again in the interests of accuracy and honesty.

> (5) That all intellectual discourse and interpretations are "political"—that is, ideological and powerful—if only unconsciously. Those who would deny this do so because theirs is the place of the secure insider in the discourse; their so-called "objectivity," merely the subjectivity of the privileged group.[36]

In summary, I assert that it can be demonstrated (though I do not have time to do so) that courses are not genuinely inclusive simply because they may generalize about "human nature" or "man's identity" or "universal human consciousness" or even though they may describe themselves as "objective." Even the sciences, as Evelyn Fox Keller and Ruth Bleier have shown, begin their inquiries with a priori assumptions governed by ideology.[37]

II

The *Oxford English Dictionary* defines the "outsider" as "One who is outside any enclosure, barrier, or boundary, material or figurative; especially one who is outside of or does not belong to a specified company, set, or party, a non-member; hence, one unconnected or unacquainted with a matter, uninitiated into a profession or body having special knowledge, or the like." Ironically, one of the quotations used to illustrate the word is the 1886 comment from Jerome K. Jerome: "Outsiders, you know, often see most of the game." Without insisting that the education business is indeed a game or that I (and others who can be defined as "outsiders") see most of it, I will suggest that those who have been variously called "other," "deviant," or "deficient," and who have seen themselves as looking-glasses (Virginia Woolf's term for women), invisible, absent, marginal, or trivialized, may have a valuable perspective to offer the rethinking of our enterprise. Moreover, if the institution is itself bounded, barricaded, enclosed, then it is tempting to think that those *inside* are being imprisoned, protected from (because frightened by?) some potential truth which may invade them from the *outside*.

As I see the University's duty to pluralism (in the abstract) as well as to quality and to the needs of its diverse student population, it is our moral and intellectual responsibility to challenge the structures, the invisible paradigms of knowledge—if only to keep those of us working within it, honest and truthful. Without new formulations of questions and support from an intellectual community, it is very difficult to revitalize one's conception of academic "coverage" (for example) and to re-imagine the parameters of a discipline. But once I am able to conceive of new questions, I might be able to imagine a differently defined discipline, even an area of inquiry which is genuinely cross-disciplinary, overtly gendered, and ethnically concrete. For the literary profession, we might take the suggestions of critic Annette Kolodny as a starting point:

> (1) to see literary history as a "fiction" constructed by human beings in power;
>
> (2) to acknowledge that we are taught to read paradigms, not texts; and
>
> (3) to look for the "biases and assumptions informing the critical methods" we use.[38]

This process could, in Kolodny's words, "breathe new life into now moribund areas of our profession."[39]

While all of us in the ivory tower may be considered privileged to one degree or another, it is important to define the "insider" in this discourse as one who either does not *know* there is a problem, in Kolodny's terms, or who does not *care*. As Catharine Stimpson has put it, we must acknowledge that there have been "omissions, distortions, and trivializations" of women's (and Blacks' and Hispanics' and homosexuals' and working class people's) experiences before we can begin to supplement, correct, and respect them. I know that there is a problem with correcting each of these three defects, often articulated in terms of "time": there are those teachers who either do not see or who, seeing the *omissions*, do not have time to fill in the gaps ("I have to cover my field, the one for which I was hired."); there are those who, recognizing the *distortions*, do not choose to correct them in their scholarship or in the classroom ("I do not know anything about feminist theory and besides, if I treated women as a facet of my study, I'd never get through the material."); there are those who, acknowledging the *trivializations*, accept, as given, the devaluation of women's traditional work or art forms or psychology as written by men ("That stuff just is not art, there *are* no women Shakespeares, and how would I justify teaching Elizabeth Gaskell instead of Thackeray, or Harriet Beecher Stowe instead of Melville?").

Some professors have addressed this challenge by declaring that Women's Studies is all well and good, but their own disciplines do not necessitate the inclusion of marginalized groups' experiences or are uninflected by gender questions. Others are afraid that their tenure will be jeopardized by focus on "radical" topics. Still others simply feel comfortable in their defined areas of research and would just as soon leave this research to others. The effect of these excuses (some of them quite genuine) is that those of us who do consider gender, race, and class issues important are tokenized, tolerated, and teased about our interests, even when our approaches are as measured, logical, and "gentlemanly" as the next person's; the omissions, distortions, and trivializations are perpetuated, as we are relegated to the margins of "special interests."

Yet I am talking about over half of the undergraduate population, speaking even for those female outsiders who do not wish to face these issues during their four years here (but who will have to do so once they enter the business world and experience their limitations). Unless we begin to name their differences for them and help them to explore their past and to identify their cultural construction as "feminine," their years at Georgetown will begin to ring false for them. Here they are largely regarded as genderless, able to excel as men do, unburdened by the contradictions of "having it all" but needing to be superwomen in order to negotiate the complex demands of family and career. They will feel betrayed by their undergraduate education, as did many of the returning women at the College celebration three years ago. Rather than leave their education to the media or to future experience, we should seriously consider providing them with the tools of analysis and the intellectual content of a revised historical perspective. We can give women back their own "stories."

The first requirement in this process is that we deconstruct the dichotomy outsider/insider and recognize that there is another kind of "insider" in this discourse: one who, through interest or accident of birth, consciousness or conscience, special skills or qualifications, inhabits the margins and can educate all of us from the *inside out*. As Marilyn Schuster and Susan Van Dyne have written of the African-American "insider" in *Woman's Place in the Academy: Transforming the Liberal Arts Curriculum*,

> We have learned from black studies that slavery was the most salient feature of black experience only from the narrow perspective of

> the dominant group and in a North American context. To study black experience in its own terms it was necessary to step outside the paradigms of the dominant group or the framework of the androcentric, white, Western syllabus, and attempt to adopt an "insider's" perspective. . . . Rather than focusing on cultural subordination, the evolution of black studies demonstrated that the multicultural realities of black experience could be articulated on their own terms.[40]

In my own discipline, literature, as we have seen in the Austen text, the issue of women has been formulated as an absence of "story": men have told their own stories—and women's. As feminist theologian Carol P. Christ has claimed, "We women have not told our own stories"; we have "inhabited" the stories of men.[41] Critic of American literature Judith Fetterley takes the analysis to the next level, claiming not that women have not told their own stories, but that men's "refusal to recognize women as having stories denies women the experience it ensures for men—namely, reading as a validation of one's reality and reinforcement of one's identity."[42] She posits "inimical texts," stories written by men that distort and falsify women's truth and may exhibit overt misogyny. In their important ground-breaking study of nineteenth century women writers, Sandra Gilbert and Susan Gubar make even clearer this connection between women and misinterpreted/misinterpreting texts: for them, the woman writer's battle "is not against her (male) precursor's reading of the world but against his reading of *her*."[43]

III

Intellectually as well as ethically, then, it seems a wasted opportunity not to be a part of the creation of new knowledge, not to admit the outsider into the institution with enthusiasm—at least as a more frequent visitor. Discovering the writing of the past, rediscovering the familiar texts, asking different questions of these stories, constructing new knowledge, breaking the pedagogical hold of authoritarianism: these are the goals of feminist criticism and the presence of Women's Studies in the University. As Adrienne Rich has phrased it, "We need to know the writing of the past, and know it differently than we have ever known it; not to pass on a tradition but to break its hold over us."[44]

The National Women's Studies Association has articulated its goals in terms of the ending of women's "oppression" and it would be pleasant to think that Women's Studies in the University could accomplish that social ideal. But I would prefer to see the transformation of curriculum, in Catharine Stimpson's words, "spring from a desire to be of general service to a college or university." At the center of that service, she believes, must be a research agenda:

> Hard questions continue to demand the accumulation of facts and the construction of theory. The intellectual agenda of women's studies now includes:
>
> (1) brain organization and sex differences in cognition;
>
> (2) the ways in which we perceive differences among people—between sexes, among races, across classes, across generations—and ways in which we then organize those perceptions into psychological patterns and social structures built on domination and submission, superiority and inferiority, violence and victimization;
>
> (3) motherhood and child care;
>
> (4) the feminization of poverty;
>
> (5) equal pay for work of comparable worth;
>
> (6) the conditions that lead to gender change and the relationship of change to equality;
>
> (7) feminist theory and its connections to other philosophical and political concepts.[45]

Numbers (2), (6), and (7) can be applied to most disciplines; number (1) applies to biology and psychology; some of the others are sociological or historical. While the direction of research must depend on the inclinations and skills of individual scholars, the university could make a financial and intellectual commitment to such research—by stating its overt support for such projects, encouraging noted scholars to pursue them, granting released time, increasing the number of summer grants, and earmarking some of them for feminist and "minority" research.

The application of this new knowledge to the classroom presents greater difficulty. Summer research grants in curriculum development have seldom been awarded in the past five years. I see this trend as the result of the University's new focus on becoming a major research institution. But the naïve notion that teaching and research do not go together belies Georgetown's more responsible articulation of its primary commitment to undergraduate education. Few of us have the financial or temporal luxury to prepare an entirely new class that is wholly unrelated to our current area of research. I have spoken with at least ten women in the past five years who have indicated enthusiasm for developing feminist courses in their disciplines; each of them has postponed the project because the demands of publication (and tenure and promotion) must take precedence over curriculum development. If curriculum grants were taken seriously by the Graduate School (or the five undergraduate schools were given control of these grants, as they logically should be), we would see the burgeoning of team-taught, cross-cultural, feminist courses, as well as the integration of feminist research into traditional courses. (It might also be possible to reward those scholars who make efforts to develop courses that grow directly out of their publishing; the side benefit of this policy would be a faculty that felt less fragmented and taught with more enthusiasm.)

As faculty members involved in curriculum change, we would also be faced with giving up certain privileges: for example, our received standards of "excellence," our assumed authority and objectivity, our notions of coverage, any easy assumptions about universality, and what one theorist has called "disciplinary solipsism." Another way to look at this need to give up cherished notions is to imagine a system in which entropy has replaced energy—in other words, a closed environment. As we work on the new curriculum I envision, energy (and with it, intellectual excitement, flexibility, cooperation, and a much broader realization of differences) will be released. As Rich has described a similar process, "It's exhilarating to be alive in a time of awakening consciousness; it can also be confusing, disorienting, and painful."[46] The ultimate trade-off for this sacrifice of the old ways is a genuinely revitalized environment in which respect and challenge coexist.

To help the process along and legitimate it, the University could provide retreats, faculty seminars, informal symposia in which faculty members share their research within and across departments. Visiting experts could offer concrete suggestions and inspiration. Released time for the participants in these activities would help stave off exhaustion and speed up the process. Finally, the University might seriously consider a major curriculum transformation project like the four-year, cross-disciplinary one sponsored by the National Endowment for the Humanities at the University of Arizona.[47] By the conclusion of that project, forty-five faculty members representing thirteen departments had prepared revised syllabi for approximately eighty courses and discovered that their own research had been "profoundly affected" in the process.[48] The ACE Commission on Women in Higher Education recommends "that each campus have both a women's studies program and a transformation of the curriculum project which includes women and minority women and men. . . . Strong institutional priority should be reflected in level of funding and faculty/administrative support."[49]

In terms of individual departments, the efforts have begun, with new courses to be offered in Fall 1989 in "Feminist Theology," "Women and Philosophy," and "Women in Government" (adding significantly to the "Gender Roles," "Women Writers," and "Women and Art" offerings that have become staples). In order of increasing complexity, professors can begin by adding women and the study of women to existing courses, proceed to develop specialized courses, and then begin to imagine interdisciplinary projects. Beyond these individual efforts, departments might be encouraged to examine their offerings in more comprehensive and theoretical ways, engaging in a self-analysis and conceiving of "coverage" in new ways.

It is difficult to transform the canon, or radically to rethink the curriculum, without also examining our methods of imparting information and ideas. Recently, I encountered in Catherine Belsey's *Critical Practice* a definition of three kinds of texts that I would like to convert into a description of three kinds of pedagogy: the *declarative* text imparts "'knowledge' to a reader whose position is thereby stabilized, through a privileged discourse which is to varying degrees invisible. The *imperative* text, giving orders to its reader, is what is commonly thought of as 'propaganda.' . . . The *interrogative* text . . . disrupts the unity of the reader by discouraging identification with a unified subject of the enunciation. . . . it does literally invite the reader to produce answers to the questions it implicitly or explicitly raises."[50] Like these three kinds of texts (corresponding to the classical humanist, the propagandist, and the postmodernist), we can see (at least) three kinds of pedagogy in the university, each of them corresponding roughly to different moments in the education process and to different goals for education:

(1) a *declarative pedagogy* is "objective," professing its universalist, scientific truth as self-evident to a rational listener; it believes that its ideas and information are apolitical and centrally important; its method is lecturing, with some room for the novice student to question and be informed of the correct answer;

(2) an *imperative pedagogy* is absolutist and urgent, seeing its listeners as in need of exhortation and conversion; it may acknowledge its political content and see itself as oppositional to a general loosening of morals or educational standards; its method is preaching;

(3) an *interrogative pedagogy* is exploratory and questioning, regarding its students as fellow inquirers; it believes in declaring its political stance and in deconstructing traditional hierarchies of power; its method is discussion, the integration of experience and scholarship, student research and conduct of discussions.

While I have created and named these three types of teaching, I do not see them as at all times mutually exclusive. It should be clear by now that though many would place feminist pedagogy in the second category, I consider it to be in the vanguard of the interrogative approach. This is not always a simple methodology to achieve, especially if the professor seeks to maintain "certain standards" and reserves the right to guide and judge the student. In this model, the teacher achieves respect and authority by what she knows and the relationship she establishes to the class, rather than by arbitrary methods; this may be a lot to ask, particularly of a new teacher, since it involves the risk of being disrespected and disregarded. But I believe that this collaborative method of learning has always had wide currency at Georgetown and that a discussion of it would only be foregrounding and refining what many of us already practice.[51]

We might actually get to the point of rethinking the whole nature of the university education—of envisioning not only "Men's Studies Modified" but academic life transformed by this productive and revitalizing pluralism. Of the many new "isms" that have developed in the past twenty years, feminism is arguably the most value-centered, the least tied to relativism and overturning the humanist tradition. While there are many feminists who define themselves as "cultural materialist" or "postmodernist," and while "Feminist theory has affinities with post-structuralism's undermining of the major humanist narratives, the unity of the subject and meaning, the 'objectivity' of science and knowledge, the Eurocentric world view," yet:

> many feminist projects in the university are indebted to liberal humanist beliefs about knowledge, experience, and the subject. This is because the recovery of the female experience across the disciplines, the attempt to establish countercanons of a female tradition of texts, represents a valid and important struggle to include women's experiences in our knowledge of culture and history: in our work of tradition-making as humanists.[52]

In other words, Women's Studies is interested in values and the empowered subject; hence its relationship to the traditional humanist project is problematic and even paradoxical. Its value systems are pluralistic and inclusionary, but *not* relativistic or destructive. As literary critic Nancy K. Miller has phrased the dilemma:

> the postmodernist decision that the Author is dead, and subjective agency along with him, does not necessarily work for women and prematurely forecloses the question of identity for them. Because women have not had the same historical relation of identity to origin, institution, production, that men have had, women have not, I think, (collectively) felt burdened by too much Self, Ego, Cogito, etc. Because the female subject has juridically been excluded from the polis, and hence decentered, "disoriginated," deinstitutionalized, etc., her relation to integrity and textuality, desire and authority, is structurally different.[53]

The goal of all this talk of inclusion and transformation is not, therefore, the destruction of the University or its humanistic base. Instead, I would like to see an achievement of wholeness: a more integrated, pluralistic, nonlinear and less privileged approach to learning and scholarship. The genuine implementation of feminist methodology (and more student-centered pedagogy); the challenge to traditional inquiry; and the inclusion of women's history, experiences, and accomplishments into previously male-centered preserves might actually serve the subversive purpose of jolting our students and us into reflection—into "claiming an education" rather than passively absorbing it.

Notes

1. Jane Austen, *Persuasion* (New York: New American Library, Signet edition, 1964), 223.

2. Carol Gilligan, *In a Different Voice: Psychological Theory and Women's Development* (Cambridge, Mass.: Harvard University Press, 1982), 168.

3. Adrienne Rich, "Claiming an Education," in *On Lies, Secrets, and Silence: Selected Prose 1966-1978* (New York: W. W. Norton and Co., 1979), 233.

4. Barbara Brown Zikmund, "The Well-Being of Academic Women Is Still Being Sabotaged—by Colleagues, by Students, and by Themselves," *Chronicle of Higher Education,* 1 Sept. 1988, A44.

5. This is a rather common charge leveled against Women's and Ethnic Studies programs. Cf. Margaret L. Andersen, "Changing the Curriculum in Higher Education," in Elizabeth Minnich, Jean O'Barr, and Rachel Rosenfeld, eds., *Reconstructing the Academy: Women's Education and Women's Studies* (Chicago and London: The University of Chicago Press, 1988), 46: "Various national reports conclude that there is a crisis in education defined as the erosion of academic standards and the collapse of traditional values in education. In all of these appeals, the decline of academic standards is clearly linked to the proliferation of scholarship and educational programs in women's studies and black studies. And, though seemingly different in tone and intent, conservative academic arguments about the need to 'return to the basics' and to reclaim the legacy of 'the classics' are actually attempts to reinstate patriarchal authority."

6. Ibid., 47.

7. Interviewing thirty-seven women who were off the normal academic career track and twenty-five tenured women, over a period of years, Nadya Aisenberg and Mona Harrington discovered that "there is nothing the matter with women, nor are they peculiarly dependent by nature. Rather they enter competitive professional worlds from different starting points and with heavier burdens than their male peers. The starting point is different because women still face questions as to *why* they are entering a professional domain and whether they are prepared to pay the price it exacts, whereas for a man such entry is accepted as natural." Cf. Nadya Aisenberg and Mona Harrington, *Women of Academe: Outsiders in the Sacred Grove* (Amherst: The University of Massachusetts Press, 1988), 50.

8. Zikmund, "The Well-Being of Academic Women," A44.

9. Letter from Father Healy to the Steering Committee of a Retreat on Women's Issues and Concerns, which had made specific recommendations, 21 Oct. 1988: "you will note that the hiring rates for women have consistently been higher than their presence in the faculty already employed over the last five years. I think this is a very encouraging statistic and an important fact. I think this is the direction in

which Georgetown needs to move and I am very happy that our hiring practices over the last five years have resulted in this statistic."

10. Virginia Sapiro writes of the distortions that political scientists have perpetuated by not acknowledging this absence of public ego-ideals for young women, in "The Political Socialization of People," in Christie Farnham, ed., *The Impact of Feminist Research in the Academy* (Bloomington: Indiana University Press, 1987), 152: "one common and often reported finding [in early analyses of political socialization] was that girls were less likely than boys to identify public or political figures as an ego-ideal, and more likely to pick people in their immediate environment. . . None of these reports noted that other than Eleanor Roosevelt, there were precious few female figures that would have been presented to girls as realistic ego ideals with the force that boys are offered hosts of presidents, generals, or Founding Fathers. Log cabin myths aside, the dictum that 'any little boy can grow up to become president' might raise some skepticism in the minds of little boys; the best girls could do was hope to marry one."

11. Florence Howe, "The Future of Women's Colleges" (1974), in *Myths of Coeducation: Selected Essays, 1964-1983* (Bloomington: Indiana University Press, 1984), 130.

12. "Survey of Women at Georgetown University on 'Church-Related Issues,'" sponsored by the Office of Campus Ministry, Spring 1986: "The overwhelming majority of women believes that dialogue would lead to greater appreciation and understanding of women through greater opportunities for study and dialogue with men, as well as among women, concerning issues which pertain to women. The areas most commonly mentioned were SEXUALITY (as pertaining to both self and family); THEOLOGY (women who have contributed to the life of the Church in the areas of theology, prayer, spirituality and ministry); SCRIPTURE (women who have had particular impact in both the Jewish and Christian Scriptures); LIFE ISSUES (economics, employment/child care, legal matters)," 26-27.

13. The term "chilly climate" was coined by Roberta M. Hall and Bernice R. Sandler in their 1982 pamphlet, *The Classroom Climate: A Chilly One for Women?*, Project on the Status and Education of Women (Washington, D.C.: Association of American Colleges, 1982) and has been repeatedly used since that time to name the unfavorable conditions for learning that undergraduate women encounter.

14. This "trend" has not been unaccompanied by the attendant fear that feminist principles and Women's Studies goals would be diluted in the process, "coopted" in some way by the "liberal" mainstream. As Catherine E. Hutchison has put it: "As I discovered in my research of women's studies programs in 1985, in the meeting of feminism and academia, the purported changer itself has been greatly changed. . . . Does the entrance of feminism into the academy give us another case of an institution deflecting radical resistance and recuperating it as liberal opposition? What happens in the move from margin to center?" "Feminist Theory and the Humanities: The Changer and the Changed," in *Humanities in the South: Newsletter of the Southern Humanities Council* 68 (Fall 1988), 1. While I acknowledge the problem, Georgetown is so far from effecting a general curriculum transformation that I cannot see this question as pressing for us at this time.

15. Among Jesuit schools, both Boston College and Loyola of Chicago have organized minors in Women's Studies (the latter for almost fifteen years), and Marquette has an individualized B.A.

16. The *University of Maryland at College Park Report of the Committee on Undergraduate Women's Education*, "Making a Difference for Women" (Fall 1988), Appendix B, reports that most academic professional associations have sponsored projects to assist faculty members in incorporating the new scholarship on women into introductory courses.

In addition, there are centers for research on women at major universities across the country. Several college and university consortia have projects which sponsor faculty development activities, sharing resources among institutions: the Great Lakes Colleges Association, the Five Colleges Consortium (Massachusetts), the Sixteen College Consortium (Georgia), Colgate University (eleven newly coed institutions), and the Western States Project on Women in the Curriculum.

Major faculty development projects of the scope proposed in this report have been conducted at the University of Arizona, Montana State University, Towson State University, Duke University, Rutgers University, and Yale University.

17. This three-part categorization of the inadequacies of male-centered education was first stated, to the best of my knowledge, by Catharine Stimpson, first editor of *Signs*, Dean of Douglass College, Rutgers, and Professor of English.

18. John Schilb, "Transforming a Course in American Literary Realism," in Marilyn R. Schuster and Susan R. Van Dyne, eds., *Women's Place in the Academy: Transforming the Liberal Arts Curriculum* (Totowa, N.J.: Rowman and Allanheld, 1985), 217.

19. A reverence for women is certainly part of Catholicism, with its traditional devotion to Mary. But the difficulty with this celebration of the Virgin-Mother paradox is that women are doomed to failure in trying to live up to such a standard. Even if young Catholic women like their place on the pedestal, it is a precarious perch. In relation to the intellectual life, I would ask them to consider the feasibility of having an equal conversation (let alone relationship) with a man whose eyes are approximately at knee-level.

20. Howe, *Myths of Coeducation*, x.

21. I am grateful to Peg Dowley and Jesica Seacor (College '89) for sharing with me their Bicentennial Archival Project, "Women at Georgetown: An Emerging Tradition," which examines the early problems of coeducation, 13-15; I would also like to thank Susan L. Poulson, Ph.D. candidate in history, Georgetown, for sharing her unpublished paper on "Georgetown Coeducation." In this informative study of those early years, Ms. Poulson includes a discussion of the first feminist groups on campus, the Georgetown Women's Liberation Movement (1969) and the Women's Caucus (1971), and their early consciousness-raising and policy-changing activities, 32-33.

22. Howe, "Women's Studies and Social Change" (1972), in *Myths of Coeducation*, 81.

23. See Barbara Miller Solomon, *In the Company of Educated Women* (New Haven and London: Yale University Press, 1985), 56: "Even though the educability of women was obvious in the 1870s, new arguments emerged from scientific

thinking to endanger female higher education. Darwinian evolution relegated women to a permanently inferior condition, physically and mentally . . . The most famous attack came from Dr. Edward Clarke's *Sex in Education* (1873). This retired Harvard Medical School professor was alarmed by the increasing presence of women in high schools, normal schools, and colleges. After studying the cases of seven Vassar students, Clarke concluded that if women used up their 'limited energy' on studying, they would endanger their 'female apparatus.' Although a girl could study and learn, Clarke noted, she could not 'do all this, and retain uninjured health and a future secure from neuralgia, uterine disease, hysteria, and other derangements of the nervous system.'"

24. Thomas I. Gasson, S.J., "Women and the Higher Intellectual Life," in Mary J. Oates, ed., *Higher Education for Catholic Women: An Historical Anthology* (New York and London: Garland Publishing, Inc.), 1987, 62.

25. Ibid., 65.

26. Cardinal Eugène Tisserant, "The Value of the Humanities in the Education of Woman," from *Catholic Educational Review* (Dec. 1947), in Oates, *Higher Education for Catholic Women*, 267-68: "As a matter of fact, St. Ignatius Loyola had lived seven years amidst the humanists who composed the court of the learned Queen of Navarre, Marguerite of Valois. But it does not seem that he favored the education of women, nor did his followers."

27. Ibid., 268.

28. See Solomon, *Educated Women*, passim, for a thorough history of women's education in America; see particularly chapter 3, "The Utility of Their Educations, 1800-1860," and chapter 6, "Women and the Modernizing of Liberal Education, 1860-1920."

29. As Solomon puts this idea, "Even though coeducation seemed an aberration to those who believed in maintaining the separate male and female spheres of society, Oberlin's academic community operated as a religious family in which both sexes retained their distinctive roles," *Educated Women*, 21.

30. Lucy Stone, "Address to the 7th National Women's Rights Convention," New York, 25-26 Nov. 1856, as quoted in Solomon, *Educated Women*, 43.

31. Solomon, *Educated Women*, 25: "The thought, even more than the curriculum and the techniques of the first great female educators, shaped the spirit of women's education. These pioneering instructors [like Catharine Beecher at the Hartford Seminary and Emma Willard at Troy] attempted to balance their aspirations for students with society's claim of the traditional female sphere . . . Among the values of these educators, piety came first, but learning was also essential."

32. Mother Pauline O'Neill, C.S.C., "A Word to Parents and Guardians Who Are Seeking an Ideal School for Their Girls," *Fifty-Sixth Yearbook of Saint Mary's College and Academy, 1910-1911*, in Oates, *Higher Education for Catholic Women*, 325.

33. It might be interesting to note that the condition of the humanities in colleges and universities across the country is not healthy, in part one suspects because of an increased emphasis on pre-professionalism. "A 1988 survey found that one can graduate from almost 80 percent of the four-year colleges and universities without a course in Western civilization, 37 percent without any course in history, 45 percent

without a course in either English or American literature, 62 percent without a course in philosophy, and 77 percent without a foreign language," reported Reed Sanderlin, Executive Director of the Southern Humanities Council, in *Humanities in the South* 68 (Fall 1988), 11. It is tempting to speculate that the injection of new (feminist and cross-cultural) life into these subjects could only lead to an improvement in the condition.

34. For a recent discussion of a similar topic, compare Adrienne Rich, "Taking Women Students Seriously," in *On Lies, Secrets, and Silence,* 237-45.

35. See Dale Spender, in her Introduction to *Men's Studies Modified: The Impact of Feminism on the Academic Disciplines* (Oxford: Pergamon Press, 1981), 1: "Most of the knowledge produced in our society has been produced by men; they have usually generated the explanations and the schemata and have then checked with each other and vouched for the accuracy and adequacy of their view of the world. They have created *men's studies* (the academic curriculum), for, by not acknowledging that they are presenting only the explanations of *men,* they have 'passed off' this knowledge as human knowledge."

36. See Spender, *Men's Studies Modified,* 1: "Analysing the power base and power relations which are inherent in the codification of knowledge is still—understandably—not always viewed as a laudable or legitimate activity. But in recent years there has been a shift towards the recognition that knowledge is socially constructed, that it is invented by human beings with limited access to explanations and limited claims to infallibility. While all human beings may generate 'explanations' of the world, may devise schemata for organising the objects and events of the world, not all of them become the legitimated and acceptable explanations; there is a selection process at work and it has a power dimension. It can also be a self-perpetuating power dimension, for those who have the power to validate their own models of the world can validate their own power in the process."

37. For an excellent deconstruction of sexist premises and methodology in cognitive processing research, see Ruth Bleier, "Lab Coat: Robe of Innocence or Klansman's Sheet," in Teresa de Lauretis, ed., *Feminist Studies/Critical Studies* (Bloomington: Indiana University Press, 1986), 59.

38. Annette Kolodny, "Dancing through the Minefield: Some Observations on the Theory, Practice, and Politics of Feminist Literary Criticism," in Elaine Showalter, ed., *The New Feminist Criticism: Essays on Women, Literature, and Theory* (New York: Pantheon Books, 1985), 151-57.

39. Ibid., 151.

40. Schuster and Van Dyne, *Women's Place in the Academy,* 22-23.

41. Carol P. Christ, "Spiritual Quest and Women's Experience," in *Womanspirit Rising: A Feminist Reader in Religion* (San Francisco: Harper and Row, 1979), 229.

42. Judith Fetterley, "Reading about Reading," in Elizabeth A. Flynn and Patrocinio P. Schweickart, *Gender and Reading: Essays on Readers, Texts, and Contexts* (Baltimore and London: The Johns Hopkins University Press, 1986), 149.

43. Sandra M. Gilbert and Susan Gubar, *The Madwoman in the Attic: The Woman Writer and the Nineteenth-Century Literary Imagination* (New Haven and London: Yale University Press, 1979), 49.

44. Rich, "When We Dead Awaken: Writing as Re-vision," in *On Lies, Secrets, and Silence,* 35.

45. Catharine Stimpson, "The Future of Women's Studies," in *Women's Studies in the United States: A Report to the Ford Foundation* (New York: Ford Foundation, 1986), 55.

46. Rich, "When We Dead Awaken: Writing as Re-Vision," in *On Lies, Secrets, and Silence,* 34.

47. Papers which emerged from this project are printed in Susan Aiken, Karen Anderson, Myra Dinnerstein, Judy Nolte Lensink, and Patricia MacCorquodale, eds., *Changing Our Minds: Feminist Transformations of Knowledge* (Albany: State University of New York Press, 1988).

48. Ibid., xv.

49. *The New Agenda of Women in Higher Education: A Report of the American Commission on Education Commission on Women in Higher Education,* 1988, 8-9.

50. Catherine Belsey, *Critical Practice* (London and New York: Methuen, 1980), 91; Belsey borrows these terms from Emile Benveniste, *Problems in General Linguistics* (Miami: University of Miami Press, 1971), who uses them to describe three kinds of "discourse."

51. Sometimes teachers confuse what I call a "fill-in-the-blanks" type of discussion with genuinely interrogative teaching. This search for the "right word" or answer to complete the professor's own train of thought is merely a variant on the declarative approach.

52. Hutchison, "Feminist Theory and the Humanities," 3.

53. Nancy K. Miller, "Changing the Subject: Authorship, Writing, and the Reader," in de Lauretis, *Feminist Studies/Critical Studies,* 106.

J.P.M. Walsh, S.J.
Department of Theology

Saint Ignatius's Way of Proceeding: The Spiritual Exercises and Education

As teachers, we probably all have given essay questions of the good old standby "compare and contrast" format. This essay is meant to do that: to discuss an *x* and a *y*, and then show the relationships between *x* and *y*. The *x* is the Spiritual Exercises of Ignatius Loyola. The *y* is the mysterious process we call teaching and its correlate, learning. I will argue that the two terms of the discussion are analogous to each other, and, further, that the Exercises have many and fruitful implications for the task of education.

I think the most useful way of proceeding is for me to describe not so much what the Spiritual Exercises are as what goes on in a retreat made according to the Spiritual Exercises. The other term of the comparison, so familiar to us as educators, might then take on a new configuration in our minds. I hope that, if we can see teaching and learning against the background of the Ignatian Exercises, we may be in a position to understand what it is that people mean when they speak of "Jesuit education."

But What Do You *Do* on a Retreat?

One answer to this question is to say that you try, for a certain period of time—a week, a month—to live in the real world: to let distractions clear away, to focus on your life and your choices, to let God get through to you.

Another, more specific answer to the question is that the retreatant gets together with a *director* in some out-of-the-way *place* and over a number of days follows a program of *exercises,* especially periods of prayer, suggested by the director. Let me spell this out, in reverse order.

Exercises: think of a Jane Fonda workout, or a writers' workshop, or acting classes. The way of proceeding Ignatius suggests is to use the imagination. The exercises are meant to engage one's imagination (in ways I will describe below). So the basic structure is that the director offers a series of suggestions which the retreatant puts into practice. "Try this, see what happens." "OK." That is the way a retreat goes.

The context for doing this series of exercises is a *place* and what might be called a rhythm of life. Ideally, the place is a place apart. Nowadays, it is usually a retreat house. Originally, Ignatius would find a house or apartment where the retreatant could spend the time of retreat in solitude. The point is that one is away from one's ordinary context of life, where quotidian demands on one's time and attention can move away from center stage of consciousness. The voices, memories, regrets, anxieties, and little one-act plays inside the head that constitute our ordinary waking consciousness fade away. Silence is crucial in this retreat-context. Silence is the exterior and interior precondition for the freeing of the imagination. It allows us to focus on giving ourselves to the exercises, to live in the here and now of what we are at any moment doing. It allows certain memories, images, and feelings to surface—memories, images, feelings that are present within us but which we ordinarily do not attend to. It allows us to become listeners. Hence, the rhythm of the day is one conducive to silence. Typically, a retreatant will be encouraged to sleep a lot, to take leisurely walks, to look at trees and study the veins in leaves or the texture of rocks, to listen to the song of birds, to "daydream" (more on this below)—to fill up the day by keeping it empty, to create a kind of vacuum by paying attention to what is around us (clouds, trees, birds). After an initial couple days of restlessness, you settle in to this rhythm and begin to enjoy the silence. And, as we shall see below, interesting things begin to happen. Silence and solitude are central in the dynamic of the Exercises.

What goes on between the retreatant and the *director*? How does the director know what precisely to suggest when he or she says "Try this"? How does the director know what would be a useful follow-up to what the retreatant has just done? It's simple. The retreatant tells the director how it went. "How it went": a central phrase in Ignatius's thought. Particulars will be described more in detail below, but in general the retreat follows this pattern: director suggests praying about such and such, using such and such an approach; retreatant tries it; retreatant gets together with director and recounts "how it went"—what happened in the period of prayer. The director gets a sense of what might be suggested next. So it goes.

As the retreatant generously tries what the director suggests for particular periods of prayer, and in other exercises, so—overall—the retreatant follows the format of the retreat: the rhythm of the day, the embracing of silence, and so on.

So Much for Generalities: How about Some Particulars?

The Spiritual Exercises in their classic, or unadapted, form take thirty days to get through. Hence, the Exercises fall into four "weeks." (So, people refer to the "exercises of the first week," or "Ignatius's focus for the third week," etc.) The content of each "week" can be summarized, simplistically, this way. The *first week* focuses on one's existential situation before God. I am God's creation; I am loved by God; I am called to a relationship of love; and I reject that relationship through sin. The *second week* goes through the life of Christ: incarnation, birth, "hidden life" in Nazareth, public life. The *third week* continues this focus on Christ, attending to the events from the Last Supper through his passion and death. The *fourth week* is centered on Christ's resurrection and risen life.

This bare-bones description is a bit misleading. Though it is accurate so far as it goes, the point is not the content of each week, or even the sequence of topics, areas, considerations, and so on, through which the retreatant is led, but rather *what happens* in the heart and mind, imagination and feelings, of the retreatant.

This "what happens" can best be indicated by sketching Ignatius's directives for the time of prayer: his *method.* This is how it goes.

(Please note that what follows is *one* form of the exercises. Different directors direct differently, while following the method, sequence, and shape of the Exercises. The Exercises are meant to be adapted to the retreatant. That is their genius. One example: in the sketch below the retreatant prays for an hour. Some directors might suggest thirty minutes. There might be four daily periods of prayer, or five, or two. One retreatant might move quickly—say, in five days—through the material of the first week, another might spend twelve days there. It all depends on "how it goes." That said, this is how it might go.)

Your Retreat

You are starting the retreat. The director gives you some material to pray over, and a way to go about praying. Go to your room. Take an hour. Put yourself in the presence of God. Ask for the grace of realizing that God loves you. Ask for that grace calmly and persistently. Be listening as you ask. At the end of the hour, sit down and write in a notebook: put down what happened in the previous hour, answering the following questions. What did you do first? How did that go? How did you feel? What did you do next? How did that go? How did you feel? Then what did you do? . . . After fifteen minutes, stop writing.

Then you go for a walk, or take a nap. Watch the birds. Clear your mind.

At a time agreed on, you see the director. "How did it go?" You tell her how it went, most usefully just by reading what you wrote in those fifteen minutes. The director listens, maybe makes some jottings, and then suggests something for the next hour of prayer.

You do this again, only this time you are asking for a different grace: say, the grace of realization that God wants to give you the gift of loving him. Another hour. Another write-up. Another meeting with the director, in which you acquaint her with how the prayer went. This time the director might suggest you do a "repetition." Go over the previous hour's prayer. Then write that up.

The days go by. Between times of prayer, you are following other suggestions of the director, other exercises. Daydreaming, for example. Imagine your best friend receiving the grace you have been asking for. What if she were suddenly to receive an overwhelming sense of being loved by God? Let your imagination go. The silence must be getting to you, because you have a vivid picture of her happy and serene, free of those awful moods you find so painful. Hmmm. Another daydream is: what if *you* had that realization? You imagine yourself getting up in the morning, and having coffee, and going to work, and going through your day: what would your day be like?

The days go by. You find yourself a bit restless, annoyed, bored. Fine, that's natural. The silence and solitude, the vacuum, is having its effect. (It is, after all, most artificial, as any program of exercises is artificial. The director has stressed this, while encouraging you to try out what she is suggesting.) A magnificent tree on the front lawn suddenly appears to you. You hadn't noticed it till now. A painful memory suddenly surfaces. That happened years ago, it hadn't crossed your mind once since then. The memory brings a rush of feeling. It's been there all along. You wonder if your friends have been aware of it. "I didn't know I felt that way towards so-and-so." In prayer, those feelings are surfacing, too. Some feelings you have for God. You feel bored and restless. You put that in your write-up. The director urges you not to brush those feelings aside: focus on them, let yourself have the problem, be listening. Other feelings emerge in prayer. You have a powerful sense of God's presence, and feel consoled. Or you feel no sense of God's presence whatever. You are stuck there. You feel empty, phony, angry, desolate. It all goes in the write-up. The director urges you to pray from where you find yourself at any given moment. You're bored? Fine, say (in effect), God here I am, immensely bored. You find yourself tending to force things, to act as if you really want to be there, but the director's suggestion is to pray from where you are, not where you "should" be. So you choose to follow that suggestion, and allow yourself to be someone who just now would rather not be in God's presence. With a start, you realize that you don't trust God very much. You tend to look away. If you choose to follow the director's suggestion, you don't look away. Maybe then you find yourself shouting at God. Then God is vividly present. You have emerged into the light of truth. You experience what Ignatius called "consolation."

You put this all down in the write-up. The director says, "It sounds as if it's going well," and suggests a repetition.

The days go by. You've gone through a lot of emotional storms. The material and the method suddenly change. You are in the second week. Now the hour of prayer follows a different format, what Ignatius calls "contemplation." After putting yourself in God's presence (better, recalling that you are in God's presence), you ask for the grace to be given a knowledge and love of Christ, and a desire to be his follower. Then you read a story from the gospels. The nativity, or the multiplication of the loaves, say, or the story where Peter protests, "Depart from me, for I am a sinful man." You are to allow your imagination to go to work on the scene, putting yourself into it. (In the nativity scene, for example, Ignatius says to imagine yourself as a servant, helping in the stable.) Interact, in your imagination, with the characters and the events. Let the imagination flow. Don't "stage" the scenes. Don't manufacture. It's an exercise. After forty-five or fifty minutes (in a one-hour exercise), enter into a "colloquy" with God. Be listening. You have just spent some time, in your imagination, with Jesus and the crowds and the disciples. You have put yourself into a position where you might brush up against the figure of Christ and what God is up to in Christ's ministry. Be listening. At the end of the hour, write up how it went. The director will suggest the next step.

For the next three "weeks" of the Exercises, this is how it goes. Ignatius suggests different forms of imagining, but the focus is the same. Let yourself, in your imagination, enter the story of Jesus. Dwell in that world for the hour. As memories and feelings from your own life have been surfacing, powerfully, they will become entwined with your "contemplation." There is a "you" that finds it easy to explain away, or simply ignore, the choices and patterns of choices that make up your life—especially the resentments, the dismissiveness, the readiness to judge others that typically we are hardly aware of. That "you" comes to the fore, unedited, in those imaginings, and you find yourself echoing Peter's cry, or seeing in the pharisees people very much like yourself. You begin to experience Christ as a figure who, in his eagerness to share God's good news, makes you aware of the bad news that you very much need the good news. But the awareness is freeing. You are blindsided by it, and are filled with alarm, but the context in which it comes is one of salvation, of God's intense desire to free you of those self-imposed burdens and to fill you with joy, so the awareness of your need leads to an awareness of God's purpose, as the other side of the coin, and you are consoled.

From time to time you are given other exercises of the imagination. One is: Put yourself in a refugee camp, or a cancer ward, or an inner-city neighborhood. Watch the people, smell the smells, listen to the voices. Where is God in all this? Does he care? Note the apparent absence of God. Dwell in this world, in your imagination. At the end of the hour, enter into colloquy with God.

In your imagination there are meeting three worlds: your own (as memories and faces and feelings keep popping into your consciousness), the world of the Gospels, and the world of those refugees and prisoners and suffering people. In the gospel stories you are contemplating, Jesus keeps talking about God's concern, the concern of an intensely involved and loving parent. But the other worlds keep intruding, and you find that his invitation to believe in God's good news—in the absence of any proofs or evidence for it, in the disturbing face of a world full of injustice and suffering, in the awareness that in significant ways you are part of the problem—comes into greater and greater prominence. That choice, to believe, is central. But you keep on putting yourself into the gospel world, imaginatively experiencing being a disciple, asking to know, love, and follow Christ more and more. In your imagining, you are making choices, so you have a kinesthetic image, as it were, of being a disciple, and also of the ways in which you resist the call to discipleship.

There are eight days left, of the thirty. You have entered the third week. You follow Jesus through his abandonment by your fellow disciples, and as it seems by God. You watch him choosing to continue to believe in God's intense involvement, despite the absence of proofs. You huddle in the upper room. The fourth week. You ask (this is Ignatius's suggestion for the contemplations on the resurrection and risen life) for the grace to rejoice with Christ: to rejoice in his joy. That is not natural to us, but you enter into the asking, and the contemplation. The days go by quickly but in some ways not quickly enough. You begin to worry about the letdown that will come after the retreat. Is this all going to build up unrealistic hopes? The director urges you to face that anxiety in prayer. Pray from that anxiety. Allow yourself to be someone filled with anxiety. You enter into the feelings. You are filled with assurance: you hear ("hear") something like, "I will be there for you." You find God in and through that anxiety (that is, reluctance to believe). The hope and joy focused in the fourth week come through to you.

A concluding exercise invites you to consider how God conducts himself as one who labors for us, as a working God. His gifts of creation and redemption, his father's care for a needy world: the choices God made and makes on our behalf. The world as the arena of God's costly involvement. You as his beloved, on whom he so desires to shower his gifts. You as you are, invited to share his very life. Your fellow human beings, so vulnerable and full of pain, whom God wants to make it possible for you to love and live with in friendship, and serve. A world being transformed.

After the Retreat

You feel a bit like Scrooge after his three visitations. The world looks different and you feel, if not giddy as a child, somehow serene. You have acquired a new way of looking at reality and at yourself. You have reimagined reality.

This has happened by your own choices. You chose to enter generously into the silence, the praying, the daydreaming, the imagining. You didn't know what would happen but you were willing to "try it and see what happens." That started a chain reaction. The part of you resistant to change drew back, but at the director's urging you chose to confront your unwillingness to face things. You were willing to let yourself be who you were, not yourself as you would wish to think of yourself, with a richly deserved sense of self-esteem, at your very best. And through that choice—to be ruthlessly honest, not to "fake it"—you found God again and again. Or God found you: you let yourself be found. You freely entered into the unknown, again and again, especially in the unmappable bourne of the imagination. It is not surprising that you found God in the unknown. What is surprising is that you found God in the areas of your selfhood and your life where you would least expect him to be.

As you get back into your quotidian world, you find the vividness of the retreat experience fading. What doesn't fade, but becomes stronger, is the habit of finding God in all things. It has become, or started to become, second nature to focus on your unfaith and unlove: that is where you find God, where your need is greatest and he is accordingly most present, at work. When you pray, you take your cue from the publican in the parable, not the pharisee who prayed from his strengths. You are able to look steadfastly at scenes of seeming hopelessness, not taking a detour away from the ghetto to avoid them. You have acquired an instinct for God's whereabouts. He is present, at work, in the situations and human choices that most challenge faith. "The world is charged with the grandeur of God." "Love has pitched his mansion in / The place of excrement."

Part of you wants to go back over those retreat experiences, but the director left you with the counsel of a seventeenth-century Jesuit retreat-giver and spiritual writer, Louis Lallemant. It goes something like this. When you have experienced consolation, do not go over your notes, or read the Scripture passage you associate with it, or try to retrieve it in any way. Let it lie there, and walk on in nakedness of spirit. After all, two things came through in the thirty days. When it comes to knowing God, we are always at square one: there is no accumulated spiritual capital we can draw on. And the converse of that: God is always there, finding us, eager to be found.

Um—Weren't We Going to be Talking about Education?

Yes. Notice what I have done in the pages above. I did not simply list the approaches, techniques, and methods Ignatius uses in the Exercises (though I will be touching on that now). I got into the *content* of the retreat: the kinds of experiences a retreatant goes through in the course of the thirty days. For our purposes, that is not really so useful, precisely because it is content. The specific content of the Exercises is not where their pedagogical value lies. But the "transfer" that I think is possible from the Exercises to the classroom cannot be understood apart from *some* sense of how the Exercises go. The tricky thing is to extrapolate from the process of directing the exercises to the process of teaching. Or, the other side of the coin: to extrapolate from the choices a retreatant might be invited to make to what a student might be invited to try.

One thing, though, about the way of proceeding I have chosen in these pages. I did not describe the retreatant's experience in the third person. I presented it as something that happens to a more or less generalized "you." I hope it did not make you acutely uncomfortable, but I suspect you had *some* reaction to the account of the thirty days. Maybe you were uncomfortable; maybe you were put off by it; maybe you found it accorded with your own experience in life; maybe you found it utterly foreign to your experience. But you generously kept on reading, and certain feelings probably surfaced. Precisely what sorts of feelings they were depended entirely on you. That is the point. I confronted you with a story, which (because of the generalized "you") you perhaps found yourself drawn into or perhaps distanced from. The story interacted with *your* story.

Let this vignette, then, serve to introduce, and illustrate, the first of my conclusions.

The student is a person with a history of choices and with a life to shape by future choices. In presenting material to the student, the teacher should consider that it can be pedagogically and humanly useful to address the material to him or her as he or she is. If that is what is aimed at, then the best way of drawing the student into the material is to engage the imagination, and even the student's experience.

(I think of the technique one of our colleagues in Philosophy uses, as I have heard it described by students. He treats the question whether right and wrong are purely subjective matters or matters about which objective standards can be set. To get them to the point of at least preliminary insight about this question—to get them into the question—he gives a true-false exam which poses the question, "Right and wrong are purely subjective." If they answer True, they flunk. Then when they complain that that is outrageously unfair, he invites them to attend to the fact that their reaction is based on quite another conviction than the one they had assented to. It gets them thinking.)

In a way, I have come round to the old liberal-arts bromide that we teach the whole person—that teaching engages the student *qua* human subject, and is not just the imparting of information and skills.

The second point is a corrective to the first. Ignatius tells the director not to get in the way of the Holy Spirit: don't be too directive. Respect—reverence—the freedom of the retreatant. Make suggestions, yes. "Try this, see how it goes." But do not have a hidden agenda, or a specific outcome in mind. Ignatius's premise is that the retreatant's individuality is what shapes the process, in the dialectic between the suggestions and what the retreatant does with them. The only thing the director does is to invite the retreatant to lend his or her imagination to the work of the retreat—to make that choice. (Indeed, for the director the specific reactions of the retreatant are not so important as that there *are* reactions.) Say "Try this" and back off.

So too the teacher. We should take the students where and as they are, not where we think they "should" be. We should have reverence for their selfhood, especially where matters humanly important, intersecting with their own life experience and choices, come into the dialectic.

The third point follows from this. If, out of reverence for the integrity of the student, the teacher is to back off from anything that could be manipulative, it follows that a certain "playfulness" should characterize the way we present material. Try this, see what happens. Here's a story, how does it strike you? Who do you identify with in the story? What would it be like to be Gatsby? Do you know anyone like him? Just as an exercise in imagination, put yourself in the following situation. . . . That sort of thing.

The teacher can engage the imagination—and to that extent the selfhood—of the student through these sorts of exercises. If the students are encouraged to keep a journal, by the end of the semester they have a record of what they thought and how they reacted to this and that. As with the retreat write-up, there is an ongoing chronicle of their reactions, and the changes the dialectic may have wrought. They have a basis for further reflection, and a sometimes (to them) startling portrait of their own growth in insight. But I hold that the teacher should merely start the process, not presume to monitor it.

Still, exercising the imagination is not something that can happen without results. The student invited to enter into the imagination learns to think concretely. Abstractions can come to be seen to mask, or at least gloss over, human realities. "Supply and demand," "balance of power," "geopolitical strategy," and similar terms of analysis can come to be translated into vivid images—the "cash value" such terms have in the real world of human choices and action and passion. In studying history, economics, international affairs, and so on, the student can develop an instinct for focusing on the telling image, the objective correlative. Corpses in shallow graves, the sullen sidelong look in the eyes of captive populations, the swollen bellies of starving children—images like these can give point and immediacy to what otherwise can be abstractions, terms of art, even shibboleths. The context Ignatius suggests for the imaginative exercises he calls contemplations is

> the persons [on] the face of the earth, in such diversity, in what they wear and in what they do; some white, some black; some in peace, others at war; some mourning, others laughing; some healthy, others sick; some being born, and others dying.
>
> (*Spiritual Exercises*, 106)

To the extent that the use of the imagination in teaching and learning would accord with this Ignatian orientation, Jesuit education would indeed be "different" or "distinctive." The rhetoric used in Jesuit documents, in recent years, about "education for justice" is in my view an attempt to call Jesuits back to this orientation to the real world. The path to developing such an instinct or habit of mind is giving the imagination free rein.

Fourth, though the suggestions the teacher makes have about them the playfulness proper to exercises, the suggestions should be specific and structured; and they should, overall, build on what has gone before. That is, *method* is crucial. It is a historical commonplace, and I suppose it is true, that what distinguished Jesuit education from previous educational practice was its methodical character. The counterpart of method in the presentation of material (the pacing and sequence of material, how it is set forth, the way the student is drawn into it) is the ongoing development of the student through the semester and throughout his or her education. I say "development." I mean that a student can develop new habits of mind, new instincts, even a deepened self-awareness as the semester goes on, and that these can grow organically. In the courses I teach, on biblical literature, that is my aim. In September, I entertain the hope that by December my students will have developed certain habits of thought: at least the beginnings of hermeneutical sophistication, a historical consciousness, and especially a certain playfulness in dealing with a text, wedded to the habit of imaginative representation of texts in the theatre of their minds (not just "reading the words"). I hope that by the end of the semester they will be different in certain ways from the way they are at the beginning of the semester, and I set about inviting them into a series of exercises that will, all things being equal, at least get them started on that process. Things never are equal, of course: each semester differs from the one before, as the students are different. Method is dialectical.

If Jesuit education was notable for being methodical, surely it was at least in part because Jesuit teachers had been shaped by the Exercises. Certain things had become instinctive, habitual, second nature. "Certain things": namely, a way of proceeding (Ignatius's phrase, as you have surely guessed). Students of the Exercises have singled out two elements as defining of the Ignatian method: the use of the imagination, and the repetition. I sketched above how challenging the imagination—giving it free rein—might lead to a certain instinctual habit of mind. So for repetition. Does the prominence of *repetitio* in Jesuit education manuals and practice derive from the habits of mind formed in the Exercises? It is a subsidiary question, so I move on.

Fifth, pity the student caught up in all this. Students crave security. They want to know exactly where they are at every moment—and where they stand grade-wise (or grade-foolish)! The playfulness-cum-method, the dialectic that I am suggesting makes for good educational results, is something they might very naturally resist. They want to control their own destiny. My own experience, in making the Exercises as in life, has been that the best things come out of *not* knowing where I am going. If the students can make the choice to try things and see where it leads, that educational experience can be most valuable for life. They will have a kinesthetic image not only of what it is to learn, but of a new possibility of being human. They will have a taste of freedom.

Summary

What I do when I direct the Spiritual Exercises has influenced my approach to teaching. What I have experienced as a retreatant, myself, has shaped my sense of what learning is. In both contexts, the whole person is the focus. The person goes through a process marked by both playfulness (especially in the use of the imagination) and method; the integrity of the individual person is an absolute, so that one is taken "where he is," not where he "should" be; one is invited to choose to be led beyond where he is comfortable and "in control"; those choices move one beyond the known, and there is an experience of freedom that is formative of the self; there is a piling up, as the process goes on, of "evidence" about what one resonates with and what one finds off-putting; there is, therefore, concomitant with the dialectical growth in skills and understanding and habits of mind, a dialectical growth in interior freedom and in self-appropriation. In both processes, one is led to reimagine oneself and the world. One begins to become able to walk in nakedness of spirit, to become comfortable in always being a beginner, to allow one's imagination to take in an ever larger world of human need and potentiality, and to respond to that world in the engagement of one's freedom.

Some Particular Applications

The pedagogical "transfer" from the Spiritual Exercises to what goes on in the classroom can happen easily and, as it were, of itself when the teacher has interiorized the Ignatian way of proceeding outlined above. Still, even in that case, there is one obvious difference between the retreat and the classroom. The retreat director has the book of the Exercises to follow. The teacher, however, has to work out (usually from scratch) materials and methods that will follow the Ignatian pedagogical approach. Some comments on this problem, then, are in order.

Part of the teacher's task is to expound basic informational content. The temptation is to simply lecture: put it out there, lay it out, say it. This way of proceeding has many disadvantages. If a lecture consists of information that could easily be read in articles and books, indeed if the lecture itself could simply be printed and distributed to the student, lecturing seems pedagogically unsound, and an inefficient use of class time. More importantly, that way of imparting information tacitly gives the students the impression that, as they are, without more, they are able to process the information—without having to learn new *ways* of thinking, acquiring new habits of mind, interiorizing a previously unfamiliar "feel" for the material. Hence, it seems to me, the temptation to lecture is to be resisted.

Instead, the early practice of the Jesuit schools offers a model. It is true that their students were of tender years (as were students at Georgetown in the early decades), but beginners are beginners no matter what their age, and the ways of teaching reflected in the early documents are still suggestive. Drills, "repetitions," games, contests, teams, and prizes appealed to, and engaged the energies of, those youthful students. The underlying reality of what was going on in the classroom, though, was clearly based on a method of teaching that (to lapse into jargon) might be called "interactive." Material was presented in manageable chunks, and the students made it their own by responding to tasks set: exercises. When they had made it their own, the teacher led them to the next stage, and the same process took place. But they did not come to each stage "cold." Crucial to the method was the *praelectio.* A text, an idea, a theorem was sketched or mapped before it was studied. Then the presentation. Then the exercises—the drills and repetitions and contests—that helped make it one's own. All was methodical. In the "prelection," the explication, the exercises, in the systematic unfolding of the material, with give and take and surprising turns and fancy footwork, the student learned *both* the subject matter *and* the habits of mind necessary to interiorize it.

Mutatis mutandis, especially, of course, taking into account the difference in age and attainments of college students, that same sort of methodical, "interactive" approach to presentation of material still stands as a pedagogical model, no matter what the academic subject is.

Some of the contributions to this volume suggest that this sort of pedagogical inventiveness is still at work. John Haught's "story" method for the teaching of science exhibits the pedagogical qualities I have been trying to sketch. It would be possible, for example, for students to recapitulate Mendeleyev's discovery of the periodic table, or to be led to share in Kepler's experience in reimagining planetary motion. (My classes can invent the Documentary Hypothesis for themselves each semester, and in so doing, not incidentally, learn to attend to what is and what is not in the text.)

Leona Fisher's five premises suggest exciting possibilities for the study of literature. They can set up a dialectic by which students are led to come face to face with a whole range of presuppositions, attitudes, and convictions that they bring to texts—and that determine their reading of texts—yet are unaware of. They can learn to reimagine the world of texts and the reading of texts, and their own world as well, and indeed their very selves.

Bruce Douglass's critique of the professoriat seems to me particularly Ignatian, in its careful attention to the ways in which academics imagine and understand themselves and their work—ways of imagining that are operative in and determinative of the substance and style of the academy. The same kind of critique, based on attention to praxis, could be brought to bear on the study of governmental or economic policies, of the conduct of foreign relations, of historiography, of a church in the process of reimagining itself, or of a school that wanted to learn what is genuine intercultural and interracial education.

Finally, though legal education and medical education aim at imparting knowledge and shaping skills necessary for professional practice, their use of the case method, clinics, and "hands-on" experience has much in common with the "interactive" approach to teaching sketched above. Would it not be possible, and appropriate, for a law school and a medical school to take a page out of the Ignatian book in other respects as well? Could students not be invited to reflect on the presuppositions and practices of medicine or law that they are being initiated into? Or better: to reflect on what sort of human being that process of initiation is shaping them into; on the ways legal or medical practice affect real human beings in the real world; on the possibilities of reimagining the profession, of critiquing it and its axioms and procedures, in the light of that larger world of human potentiality and need—

> the persons [on] the face of the earth, in such diversity, in what they wear and in what they do; some white, some black; some in peace, others at war; some mourning, others laughing; some healthy, others sick; some being born, and others dying.
>
> (*Spiritual Exercises*, 106)

In "covering the material" in a course or in a discipline, then, the Ignatian way of proceeding can be pedagogically most useful. To the extent that learning has to do with the learner, and the process of learning, as much as it has to do with subject matter, the Ignatian way of proceeding, in its infinite adaptability, seems to me pedagogically indispensable.

Suggestions for Reading

David L. Fleming, S.J., *The Spiritual Exercises of St. Ignatius: A Literal Translation and a Contemporary Reading*. St. Louis: The Institute of Jesuit Sources, 1978.

William A. M. Peters, S.J., *The Spiritual Exercises of St. Ignatius: Exposition and Interpretation*. 3d ed. Rome: Centrum Ignatianum Spiritualitatis, 1978.

George E. Ganss, S.J., "Authentic Spiritual Exercises of St. Ignatius: A Brief History of Their Practice and Terminology" (*Studies in the Spirituality of Jesuits*, I/2). St. Louis: American Assistancy Seminar on Jesuit Spirituality, 1969; repr. 1983.

International Commission on the Apostolate of Jesuit Education, *The Characteristics of Jesuit Education*. Washington, D.C.: Jesuit Secondary Education Association, 1987.

Arthur F. McGovern, S.J., "Jesuit Education and Jesuit Spirituality" (*Studies in the Spirituality of Jesuits*, XX/4). St. Louis: American Assistancy Seminar on Jesuit Spirituality, 1988.

RICHARD B. SCHWARTZ
Dean, Graduate School

The Georgetown Graduate School in 1989

Graduate schools are evaluated according to several measures, some generally accepted, some less so. The Associated Research Councils' survey of 1982—the most recent assessment—looked at the following:

(1) number of faculty per program;
(2) number of graduates per program;
(3) program enrollments;
(4) percent of graduates receiving some national fellowship or training grant;
(5) median time for degree completion;
(6) employment commitments of graduates;
(7) employment commitments in Ph.D.-granting universities;
(8) scholarly quality of faculty;
(9) program effectiveness;
(10) program improvement in last five years;
(11) assessors' familiarity with faculty work;
(12) library size;
(13) faculty grant support;
(14) research and development expenditures by field;
(15) number of published articles per program;
(16) "overall influence" of program publications.

Some of these measures are quite vague or subjective, but evaluation is irreducibly subjective. All programs are at the mercy of their colleagues' ignorance or awareness. Whether those colleagues are "correct" or not, they are still the individuals who recommend graduate schools to their students. In general, two measures are particularly important: (8) the scholarly quality of the faculty, and (10) changes over the last five years. To the extent that the evaluators themselves are reliable, these categories point to faculty reputation and the extent to which a university is building and growing or contracting and slipping.

There is, in such assessments, a clear prejudice toward size. A department of seventy-five faculty has obvious comparative advantages over a department of fifteen. The large department has a better chance statistically of possessing a higher number of visible, research-active faculty; it has more room for deadwood. It has more opportunity for coverage and for specialization; it has a higher likelihood of financial aid opportunities, and so on. Distinguished small programs always have an uphill battle. Thus, they have traditionally attempted to offer specialized programming or special emphases within programs which will make them more competitive with larger institutions.

Location is not usually a measure in assessment studies, but it is a crucial factor in student decision making. Students are balancing lives with careers, and the location of the institution, its job opportunities, proximity to family, friends, significant others, migration routes, etc., is extremely important. Location is Georgetown's key comparative advantage; and while location carries some debits (e.g., cost of living), there are still many benefits. The city's 250 libraries, for example, obviate the need for deep library investments on the University's part, while offering intellectual sustenance for the specialized curiosity of its graduate students. The presence of national laboratories and various government installations reduces the need for some scientific equipment, and opens up numerous opportunities for students. Internship opportunities are rich, particularly in areas related to certain programming, and there is a strong local appetite for the graduates of several professional programs. If we were located in Ames, Fargo, or Laramie, we might be struggling rather than prospering, but we are not.

That we are prospering does not mean that we are necessarily triumphing. Most of the large graduate schools have either lower tuition or larger endowments than we have. Both of these situations will continue. There will be flutters and fluctuations, but Berkeley will always be bigger and Stanford will always be richer. Neither, however, will be in Washington, neither will be Catholic/Jesuit, and neither will have been founded in the eighteenth century. It does not hurt us to remind the populace of those facts, but it will not be enough to rest on those facts alone. We are the beneficiaries of significant fringe benefits; for example, our faculty are continually interviewed on the evening network news, and the requests we receive for information and commentary, with resulting citations, are disproportionate to the size and stature of that faculty. That is a simple fact. The Stanford and Berkeley faculty are thousands of miles away, and there is a three-hour time difference between them and us. When we are at work, they are in bed. We are a local call or a three-dollar cab ride away. This gives us excellent visibility and free publicity. It heightens the public's awareness of our existence and presence. As a way-station for those in and out of public life, we also reap a great deal of national and international publicity. It is not enough to build a graduate school upon, but it makes us attractive to students and that is very important.

For all of our sense of tradition, our actual traditions are quite young. The Graduate School may be Georgetown's second oldest school, but its prominence is of recent vintage. It has been larger than most would expect it to be, but it has still, in many ways, been invisible. With eighty percent of its programming at the master's level and much of its programming until very recently part-time, few would suspect that twenty-five percent of the Main Campus (in 1986-87) consisted of graduate students. The library is predominantly an undergraduate library, and there are virtually no offices for graduate assistants nor common rooms within departments. This is not to suggest that the students and programs have not been of quality, but that, despite its age and size, the school has not enjoyed the place within the University's consciousness and its physical plant that one might expect.

The situation with regard to research is similar. Despite the fact that a great deal of excellent research has been conducted at Georgetown, comparatively little has been made of it until recently. It was certainly more than tolerated, and in many quarters it was actively encouraged, but the teaching "versus" research argument is still sometimes heard, despite the fact that all experience (and all presidential addresses) have affirmed the obvious interrelationship of the two activities.

Indeed, the University is in transition. Some historians argue that we are always in transition, but Georgetown is in dramatic transition. In the Graduate School in 1981 research proposals were signed without being closely read. Admissions were processed but not monitored. There was no system for advising the faculty on research opportunities and no journal or newsletter focusing on faculty research. Internal faculty development resources were allocated from the Provost's office rather than from the Graduate School. The financial aid budget was expended haphazardly; an additional ten percent of its funds were not available for allocation because of the monitoring system employed. The school catalogue, which had not been seriously updated for years, was being edited by the receptionist rather than a member of the decanal staff. No systematic records were kept of admissions applicants; no recruiting plan was in place; and an extremely labor-intensive admissions system was used, despite the fact that the staff was small.

These things have all changed, and they parallel the larger developments within the University. Until very recently, the University's endowment and physical plant bore no relationship to the size and quality of its operations. This has changed, and—as in the Graduate School—it has changed quickly.

The Graduate School has also undergone a planning exercise intended to identify its opportunities for excellence and fit its resource allocations to its priorities. This has resulted in the suspension of a few programs on the Main Campus and the strengthening—sometimes significant strengthening—of the programs said to be "targeted for excellence." The exercise was more successful than many expected, but it is not yet as far along as we all might wish. The changes have been more than cosmetic, but the most significant changes are yet to come, with the expected implementation of a plan to reduce the faculty teaching load systematically and enlarge the physical plant to accommodate the attendant increases in staff. Until those steps are taken, the incremental improvements that have already been made will not have their full effect.

The inevitable question that must be asked is "just how good are we?" Although the answer will vary with each respondent and be subject to a great deal of qualification, some general statements can be made. In the Associated Research Councils' survey of 1982, those Georgetown programs which were rated tended to fall beneath, sometimes just slightly beneath, the mean for the existing programs in the field. That does not mean that we are mediocre. It means, generally, that we are just beneath the middle of the top programs in the country. For example, the 1982 survey looked at 101 Physiology programs. The mean rating of the scholarly quality of program faculty was 50; Georgetown was given a 48, the top score being 70 (University of California-San Francisco). "Comparable" schools included Emory (46), Florida (48), Illinois—University Medical Center (49), Indiana (44), State University of New York—Upstate Medical Center (47), Tennessee—Center for Health Sciences (47), Vermont (49), and Wisconsin (50).

In a nation of over three thousand colleges and universities a program that ranks at just below the mean for all doctoral degree granting programs will be in the top 2-3% of programs. Granted, some nongraduate departments are excellent, many far better than some doctoral degree-granting departments, but while we compete with those departments for faculty in some cases, we do not compete with them for students.

A recent study of our programming in science estimated that we are between 50th and 70th among universities nationwide (i.e. the top 2-3%). Here again, our size puts us at a comparative disadvantage. In total research expenditures in Chemistry, for example, the National Science Foundation places us 95th, but in funding per faculty member we are 37th. Using the latter measure (for 1983-85), we rank above Virginia, Michigan, California-San Diego, Johns Hopkins, Michigan State, Emory, Duke, Arizona, Brown, Washington University, Florida, Iowa, Carnegie-Mellon, and other distinguished institutions. That does not, of course, mean that students will routinely choose us first. What it means is that we have worked hard to secure funding from the National Science Foundation in our Chemistry Department, and that all rankings and ratings have to be taken with a grain of salt.

The crunch for Georgetown comes in the traditional arts and sciences fields that are usually the center of graduate education. In many of these fields the number of students is small (e.g., the sciences, Economics) or the size of the job market is small (e.g., History, German). The very best students can pick and choose among the top ten to fifteen programs in the country, and in the tight-market fields many students will feel that they must attend one of the top five to ten programs, if they are ever to secure a satisfactory academic appointment. The real competition is at the very top, not among the very good.

Our protection in such a situation must be specialization, for our tuition is high and our financial aid only barely adequate. Thus, we do very well in Ethics, in International Relations, in Sociolinguistics, in Neuropharmacology, in Russian and Eastern European history, and other areas where we have carved out and built a specialty, for example, Hispanic Linguistics. We must do much more of this.

In our professional programs, where our locational advantages are clear and our programming is often distinct, we do very well, indeed. In International Affairs and Security Studies, for example, there are only a handful of competitors. In Public Policy our locational advantages are overwhelming. Striplings straight from college come to us and immediately find internships in the Office of Management and Budget—not a bad beginning for those so inclined.

Our plan for the school is to have our professional programs generate the tuition revenue that will make financial aid possible in our doctoral programs, and that plan is generally succeeding. However, in most cases we have the opportunity to build programs enjoying very high quality as well as offering career possibilities for graduates. The program in Russian Area Studies, for example, fits the pattern well, for it is nationally and internationally recognized for its academic strengths, it has received considerable extramural research support, and it serves as both a professional program and a feeder for doctoral programs in Government, History, and Economics. It is an excellent example of how we hope to see our programs mutually support one another.

One of the key problems in American higher education is its tendency toward mimicry. Each student is different and has different needs and aspirations, while nearly every institution is trying to be Berkeley, Harvard, or Williams. Uniqueness enriches education and America has too little of it. In graduate education, institutions tend to mimic the multiversity: more is better, big is better, breadth is better. If Georgetown attempts such a course, it will never be better than average, for we have neither the size nor the endowment to compete with a 30,000-40,000-student state university or a billion dollar-endowment private university.

We must, in short, be unique, and that means special programs and special emphases within traditional programs. Our array of programs need not be symmetrical. Our model cannot be Berkeley or Harvard; it should be an institution that has limited, focused excellence in a variety of fields that are not necessarily closely related to one another, for example, Carnegie-Mellon. We would not, of course, have strengths (as they do) in drama and engineering, but our pattern could be similar to theirs in that we would attempt to do everything we do well.

In certain respects, we already follow a separate pattern. Despite our small size, we have huge programs in Law and Medicine and a giant program in Linguistics. Our offerings in Middle Eastern Studies are more numerous than those of the University of California at Los Angeles. We do not do doctoral programming in English, but we do operate a writing program that sometimes attracts M.A. students who already hold Ph.D.'s. We have made serious commitments to research in the neurosciences and in the cure of cancer. We have pared back doctoral work in regional studies, and have never instituted a doctoral program in International Affairs, despite the reputation and visibility of our foreign service program. We have a tutorial Ph.D. program in Psychology and discussions underway to strengthen the ties between our scientific efforts on the Main Campus and the Medical Center.

If our traditional arts and sciences programs are to survive and prosper, they will have to continue to sharpen their foci and concentrate their resources, a step that departments tend to resist, since their model is often the wide-coverage megadepartment, and their great fear is that, if one area is stressed rather than others, individual faculty members will be marginalized and forced to operate in what is largely a service capacity.

However, certain areas will always command less student interest than others, and an institution that begins with the twin disadvantages of high tuition and low endowment will have to make itself attractive by stressing its strengths and differences. Those strengths will have to come from concentrations of faculty in specific areas, and the number of such faculty will perforce be a "disproportionate" number, since the multiversities will have far higher numbers to begin with. For example, a small History or English department such as ours will seldom have more than a handful of individuals per field. If a particular area is increased "disproportionately," political strife might result. However, with a "disproportionate" number of specialists in a given field, the small or medium-sized institution will just begin to compete with the multiversities, which have departments of seventy and eighty. One alternative is to have an array of superstars structured in a graduate-faculty vs. undergraduate-faculty configuration, but that is equally expensive and, to many, equally unappetizing politically. Some hard choices must be made. Professional program students will always flock to us because of our reputation and location, but economists and historians, biologists and political scientists, philosophers, chemists, and literature students have dozens of schools from which to choose, many with lower tuition or more generous aid. If we are to attract the best, we will have to have concentrations of strong faculty and rich curricula that are capable of competing with those at institutions which enjoy a number of comparative advantages.

This point becomes crystal clear when we speak to potential graduate students. At any given fair or function, the Georgetown table will be among the busiest, usually the second busiest after Berkeley. However, the interest in our programs always centers around a handful of offerings: Foreign Service, Law, International Relations, International Business, International Economics, Public Policy, Latin American Studies, and Russian Area Studies. We see other students, of course, but these are the kinds of programs that students inevitably associate with Georgetown. They will not come to our other programs in serious numbers unless we make those programs distinctive. This situation increases dramatically as we recruit at more selective institutions, where the number of our distinctive programs is viewed more narrowly. The best informed students know our strengths and tend to focus on a small handful of programs. We are a social science school with an international flavor; that is our reputation and that is our foundation. On the Main Campus, for example, in the fall of 1987, we had 104 students in the Natural Sciences, 210 in the Humanities, 301 in Languages and Linguistics (two-thirds in Linguistics) and 896 in our Social Science and special Master's programs. The Medical Center had 311 students. The picture is clear.

The reality is also clear. In those fields where we have not just reputational but also locational advantages, we can compete with anyone. Students choose our Public Policy program, for example, over many of the best programs in the nation. We can attract students to such programs with comparatively little effort, while our traditional arts and sciences programs must work far harder. This is not something that all are prepared to face. Most of us wish that students would come to college with a consuming desire to read Greek, do mathematics, and study Kant. Our prejudice is for pure education, education that is disinterested, at least initially, with students driven by curiosity rather than careerism, but the fact is that we cannot control American education and American society. We value pluralism and choice, but that does not always translate into the kind of institutions or curricula that we might like. They are, however, the curricula and institutions with which we all must compete.

American education is radically heterogeneous. A bachelor's degree means nothing more in terms of commonality than that the recipient has spent four years in college after high school. A "major" often means nothing more in terms of commonality than that a student has had a single course (Shakespeare, e.g., for English "majors").

Some institutions are virtually free, others very expensive. Some incur massive overhead costs, others are very inexpensive to operate. However, all of those that matter compete for the same students and the same faculty, and the field on which we operate is not level.

When a large state system dramatically increases faculty salaries, we must somehow respond or take second and third choices. When a private institution dramatically increases tuition in order to secure the best faculty, that becomes a fact of life with which we all must conjure. We do not want class sizes comparable to those of some of our competition, but those class sizes enable that competition to pay higher salaries and often attract the best faculty. We cannot react by ravaging our students' pocketbooks and destroying our traditions, but we have to do something. That means that we must know what we are about and what we are trying to do. That means we must develop and stress our differences.

That is not easy in an academic ethos driven by mimicry. Actually, Georgetown has done far better than most institutions in preserving its heritage and retaining the integrity of its curriculum and, while we must deal with the actions of our competition, we can often respond most effectively by going our own way. That is difficult, however, in an academic world where allegiance is increasingly to one's discipline rather than one's school, a phenomenon that has a levelling effect that can be positive (particularly in weak institutions) but all too often is not.

I am one who believes that this problem has been exaggerated and that many professional societies and associations are now so chaotic and silly in their drive for pluralism (often translating, of course, into plentiful membership dues and high attendance at money-making conventions) that their laughing-stock status in the popular press is more and more justified. Prospective faculty and prospective students are often struck by the existence of an institution that knows what it is about and what it expects and needs from the members of its community. After all, many individuals have turned to professional societies and associations out of a sense of alienation from their work and their community. Those institutions which offer a sense of mission and common goals, as we attempt to do, will be attractive as a result. That does not mean that we can ignore the realities of the market, but it does mean that we need not be swept away by them.

One lesson that the academy has had trouble learning is that meeting institutional goals successfully is potentially far more gratifying than trying to do something one sees others doing. To the extent that one's personal goals square with those of the institution, there is a greater likelihood of personal satisfaction in one's work. Those that see themselves as undergraduate teachers alone are not usually very happy in aggressive research universities. Similarly, those who wish to teach and do research endlessly in an extremely narrow area are not usually very happy at Georgetown, where many members of the faculty teach both undergraduates and graduate students—both research graduate students and professional graduate students. They relate to members of the policy community, the academic community, and the general public. They are interviewed by the national media, they consult, and they do focused scholarly research. Georgetown appeals to those who wish to move in varied circles and deal with varied constituencies.

This must always be made clear to potential faculty so that they can join us with a clear sense of what to expect, and so that we can attract those individuals for whom we will be a good fit.

Universities do only two crucially important things: admit students and hire faculty. I believe that we do a reasonably good job at both of those tasks, though some departments and schools are obviously more effective than others. Effective recruiting and mentoring results in a favorable ratio of tenure successes. Here again we have done rather well, for, though some departments have been softer than others in their tenure and promotion recommendations, the University rank and tenure committee has helped considerably in the raising of standards and the enforcement of minima which are impressive, considering our teaching load and our levels of institutional support for research.

On most of these fronts we are in a happy phase of transition, but one fact will have to be faced and that is the question of increased levels of tenure density. A small institution cannot tolerate a high proportion of tenured faculty in tight age-cohorts unless those individuals are demonstrably superior. Not just deserving, but superior. Thus, we are likely to see more stringent standards applied as the overall percentage of tenured faculty increases.

Finally, the only real decision that Georgetown must make is one concerning the degree of excellence it seeks to attain. Survival alone is simple. The Graduate School can generate ample revenue simply by opening its programs to part-time students and admitting students with passable, but not distinguished, records. The Washington location and the University's overall reputation are sufficient to guarantee viability. I believe that we want and need much more than that.

With competitive offers and competitive financial aid awards we can attract the finest faculty and students to those programs which have positioned and structured themselves in such a way as to develop comparative advantages. There is no question of our ability to do this; the only question concerns our will to do it. We need three things, the first, of course, being the willingness to commit resources. In my experience, this is not a problem if the other two are present:

(a) A commitment from the departments and programs to sharpen their foci and concentrate their resources in areas where there is either palpable excellence already or the strong likelihood of it.

(b) A realization on the part of administrators that there are no great American universities without great research and great graduate education. A schizophrenic undergraduate-versus-graduate view is simply not possible in an institution aspiring to excellence. Every hire must count. Every promotion must count. We cannot accommodate poor teachers or poor researchers. Each individual must be able to do both very, very well. Departments of eighty or ninety individuals have a flexibility which we do not enjoy. If each member of a department of fifteen is superb, we are still at a significant disadvantage, when compared with a department of eighty, where thirty are superb.

In most of our graduate departments the faculty (or the vast majority of the faculty) are prepared for significant change and development. Indeed, many feel we are moving too slowly. This is the perfect time to match those aspirations with both high expectations and adequate resources. The key is to maintain the fine balance in our programming between responding to the competitive pressures of the market and preserving a uniqueness which is distinctively Georgetown.

MILTON CORN, M.D.
Professor of Medicine

Medical Education at Georgetown: A Historical Overview

Background

> When Boerhaave, the most accomplished and celebrated physician of the 18th century, died, he left behind him an elegant volume, the titlepage of which declared that it contained all the secrets of medicine. On opening the volume every page, except one, was blank. On that one was written, "keep the head cool, the feet warm, and the bowels open."[1]

In the early years of the nineteenth century, it was still possible for Laennec, a brilliant physician justly honored for the introduction into medicine of the stethoscope, to be embroiled with his French colleagues in a host of bitter professional disputes replete with arguments about vitalism, the life force, and the soul, arguments aggravated by widespread distrust of his devout Catholicism.[2]

By the time Georgetown embarked on the education of physicians, those who dedicated themselves to *Heilkunst* did not concern themselves with vitalism, life force, and the soul. "Medicine in the present day," said the great pathologist Virchow in Vienna in 1845, "designates its viewpoint mechanistic, its goal the foundation of the physics of organisms. It asserts that life is only an expression for an array of phenomena, each one of which takes place in accordance with ordinary physical and chemical, i.e., mechanical laws. It denies the existence of an autocratic life force and natural healing force."[3]

In short, the nineteenth century saw the single most important development in the intellectual history of medicine: the marriage of medicine with science. And so, it was in this milieu, not so much antireligious as not interested in the problem of God, that Georgetown's School of Medicine was born.

Some milestones of Georgetown medicine are listed below. As an aid to understanding medical education at Georgetown in the context of the state of medical knowledge, a few selected developments in the familiar areas of surgery and in management of infection are included, set off in brackets.

[1846: Ether used to provide general anesthesia during an operation at the Massachusetts General Hospital, pointing the way to realization of the age-old dream of controlling pain during surgery.]

1849: Georgetown College authorizes establishment of a medical department (later called the School of Medicine), which begins operations in rented quarters on F and Twelfth Streets, N.W.

1851: The first three students graduate.

1863: Surgeon General William L. Hammond establishes at Georgetown a Chair of Military Surgery and Hygiene, the first in the United States.

[1865: Joseph, Lord Lister, pioneers sterilization of the operating room to reduce wound infections, heretofore the cause of dreadful rates of morbidity and death after surgery.]

1869: School moves to larger quarters leased at Tenth and E Streets, N.W.

1878: Georgetown becomes second American school to extend the medical course from two years to three years.

[1880: The theory that germs are responsible for many infections achieves general currency.]

[1881: Ferdinand Kehrer in Germany performs successful Caesarean section, laying the basis for techniques which lead to the present controversy over "abortion on demand."]

1886: School of Medicine moves into its own building, constructed for the School at 920 H Street, N.W.

1893: Georgetown becomes the third medical school in the United States to adopt a four-year course.

[1902: The discovery that human blood can be divided into four or more blood groups lays the basis for transfusion therapy, thus providing a means of compensating for blood loss during surgery.]

1905: Georgetown's curriculum of 4,400 hours adopted as a standard by Association of American Medical Colleges.

1930: School of Medicine moves into its present quarters on the campus on Reservoir Road.

[1930s: The sulfas and penicillin usher in the age of antibiotics.]

1946: Georgetown University Medical Center is established when the University Hospital joins the School on Reservoir Road.

1947: First woman admitted to the School's freshman class.

1952: Georgetown University Hospital is the site of the first implantation of an artificial heart valve.

[1954: First successful kidney transplantation is performed.]

The Early Years

In 1849, James Ryder, S.J., president of Georgetown College, received a letter from four Washington physicians addressed to the President and Faculty of Georgetown College:

> Gentlemen:
> The undersigned are about to establish a Medical College in the

District of Columbia, and respectfully ask that the right to confer the Degree of M.D granted to you by your Charter, may be extended to them; they desire it to be understood as their object to constitute the Medical Department of Georgetown College, claiming the usual privilege of nominating the professors of their Department.
(SIGNED)
Noble Young, M.D.
Charles H. Lieberman, M.D.
Johnson Eliot, M.D.
Flodoardo Howard, M.D.

District of Columbia, October 12, 1849[4]

The language clearly implied that if Georgetown said no, the physicians would go elsewhere, which may explain why within a week the request was approved, and on November 5, 1849, Ryder appointed the four petitioners to professorships: Noble Young as Professor of Theory and Practice of Medicine, Johnson Eliot as Professor of Anatomy and Physiology, Flodoardo Howard as Professor of Obstetrics and Diseases of Women and Children, and Charles H. Lieberman as Professor of Principles and Practice of Surgery. Several weeks later, Dr. Joshua H. Richie was appointed as Professor of Materia Medica and Therapeutics. Dr. Young was named president of the faculty.

Most American physicians of that time and for decades thereafter received their training through an apprentice system or by proprietary lecture courses. By creating a Medical Department, Georgetown joined the dozen or so American institutions of higher learning which had developed medical faculties for the purpose of providing a medical education closer to the European system. (The University of Pennsylvania, which initiated a medical program in 1765, was the first such.)

However, schools of medicine (or of anything) are rarely created with the casual ease implied by the founding fable. Men, medicine, and academic politics were surely no less complicated in the nineteenth century than in the twentieth. The springs of Ryder's expeditious cooperation are speculative. Georgetown College, then sixty years old, had a student body of 150, but no professional or graduate schools, and was vigorously attempting to upgrade itself with the help of a recent influx of Italian Jesuits, and some peer recognition it had received for its new observatory. Perhaps Ryder perceived the establishment of a medical school as a windfall adornment during a period of aggressive development for the College.

The president was prudent as well as prompt. The risk to Georgetown College was modest. The four founding physicians were men of reputation in Washington, and the College accepted no responsibility for expenses of the Medical Department. All costs were to be borne by the members of the medical faculty, who were expected to pay back as loans any funds they might receive from time to time from the College. The president of the College, nevertheless, retained a final say about all appointments in the Medical Department, all important policy decisions, and in theory could determine the nature of the curriculum.[5] This original allocation of authorities and responsibilities has continued to the present.

More is known about the motivations of the petitioners. They have been described as men of courage and determined character who had the common interest of furthering medical knowledge,[6] all of which is doubtless true, but some enlightened self-interest was another element in the tale.[7] Washington at the time had one medical school, the Medical Department of Columbian College (later to become the National Medical School, and then the Medical School of George Washington University), which had been founded in 1825 and which controlled the city's only hospital. Use of the National Hospital (a grand name bestowed by Congress on a rather modest edifice) was restricted to members of the Columbian faculty, which did not include Drs. Young, Eliot, Johnson, or Lieberman. Georgetown's medical pioneers, therefore, were not only advancing the cause of medical education, but also improving their own position locally by setting up a school and dispensary of their own.

That an olio of nobility, self-advancement, and trust-busting underlies the genesis of Georgetown's School of Medicine is more plausible than pure idealism, and rather endearing. More interesting perhaps is the question of how much value the petitioners attached to Georgetown's Catholic Jesuit heritage when they drafted their letter to Ryder. The founders themselves were an ecumenical lot, including a Roman Catholic (Young), an Episcopalian (Eliot), a Methodist (Howard), and a Jew (Lieberman), but Georgetown's identification with Catholicism evoked trepidation rather than yearning.

As Eliot's son later recounted the story, there had been opposition to the idea of applying to Georgetown, which "arose from the fear that as it was a Catholic College, the newly formed Medical Department would through such affiliation fall under the control of the Jesuit Fathers."[8] It seemed more prudent to make their application to the faculty of the University of Virginia. At this fateful moment, the loyalty of an alumnus influenced this issue, as it has so many others in the history of the University. John Carroll Brent, Georgetown College graduate and benefactor, convinced his friend, Dr. Eliot, that there was no reason to fear the Jesuits. Reassured by Brent, Eliot overcame the dark fears of his colleagues, who finally decided to table Virginia, and to approach Georgetown as their first choice.

It was location, the prestige of the College, and above all, the school's power to award degrees, rather than the Catholic nature of Georgetown, which attracted the attention of the founding physicians, nor, indeed, is there any indication that Ryder, in creating the Medical Department, envisioned any particularly Catholic mission, or articulated any goals which were distinguishable from those extant at any of the other American medical schools.

Pragmatism, then, rather than religious or moral concerns, engendered Georgetown's School of Medicine, in sharp contrast to the clearly enunciated spiritual and ethical considerations underlying the creation of Georgetown College, sixty years earlier. Nor is this surprising. Those who are beginning to think of the physician as a scientist do not look to religion or philosophy for solutions to medical problems.

The new faculty wasted little time (perhaps because there were as yet no committees). Sufficient space was rented on F Street near the corner of Twelfth Street, N.W., to provide two lecture rooms, one room for practical anatomy, and an infirmary. In 1850, eight students were enrolled. It would be charitable to characterize the early admission requirements as lenient. Presumably, the applicant would have to be literate (graduation from high school was desirable but not mandatory), of good moral character, and, it can be inferred, a white male. There was no religious test. That most of the medical students were from the South for many years probably reflects the cultural ambiance of Washington rather than any regional bias.

American medical education in the nineteenth century was no paragon. In 1889, Puschmann of Vienna described American medical degrees as being "regarded with distrust in Europe, and placed in the same category as those amiable, but meaningless distinctions which are conferred on people dancing the cotillion."[9] The course of study in Georgetown's new medical school, like that of all other American schools of the period, was "sundown medicine," i.e., lectures were given during the evening, an arrangement which permitted faculty to earn a living from practice during the day, and, of course, thoughtfully allowed the students to earn the income necessary to pay the tuition. The students were admitted by ticket to two courses of lectures of four months each. The second course was a repeat of the first, a curricular tactic which reflects the depth of the period's concept of a core curriculum as well as some pedagogic theory of reinforcement. In 1851, Dr. Young presented three M.D. degrees at a day-long commencement ceremony. (What befell the other five who matriculated in that first historic class is not known.) Warwick Evans, first alphabetically in the list of that early trio of graduates, has ever since been considered to be the School's equivalent of William Gaston.

The new school prospered with gradually increasing enrollment, faculty, and clinical facilities, stimulated in part by the need for physicians to treat the casualties of the Civil War. Georgetown was particularly affected because of its location in Washington, and because the only other school in Washington was closed when the War Department commandeered the Columbian School and its hospital to provide care for the wounded.

Enrollment reached a plateau during Reconstruction (whether by design or lack of applicants is not clear), and in no year between 1870 and 1900 were more than thirty M.D. degrees awarded at a graduation. The original quarters were outgrown, and in 1869 the School moved to another leased building at the corner of Tenth and E Streets, N.W. In 1886, a new building was constructed on H Street between Ninth and Tenth Streets, N.W., and the School finally acquired a home of its own. Despite the relative stability in student numbers, the increasing demand for laboratories soon exceeded the available space in the new two-story building, and, in 1893, the School was nearly doubled in size by addition of another story and extension of the walls.

Most of the patient-care pearls strewn before the students by the early faculty would be declared paste today, but those who taught the Georgetown medical students were conscientious practitioners who took their teaching responsibilities seriously. We have no better advice to give now than that given by Dr. Montgomery Johns, who told the students in 1868 that "there is *no one* universal method either of teaching or of study . . . Master a little daily . . . let your progress be real, into solid learning." He anticipated by over a century the current goal of preparing students for a lifetime of learning by noting that the diploma "only places you in more favorable conditions to pursue these studies, and testifies that you have mastered the rudiments of the art and the elements of our science." Perhaps anticipating the danger of worshipping the calf of science, he went on to caution that "judgment and tact, rather than encyclopedic learning, are the characteristics of every successful practitioner."[10]

A major curricular improvement took place in 1878 when the course was lengthened from two years to three, and each annual term was extended to cover seven months, an increase in rigor which placed Georgetown among the leaders in American medical schools. Of equal importance was a new emphasis on review, examinations, and more time in dissection room, laboratories, and affiliated hospitals. The increased attention to practical experience represented a genuine educational advance, and was accompanied, appropriately, by a decrease in lectures.[11] More attention was paid to maintaining records of student progress and to standards for graduation. Stricter standards took their toll, of course. The *College Journal* of 1891 reported with apt metaphor that "the [Medical School] examinations were very rigorous this year. Some men were so thoroughly dissected that they succumbed under the operation."[12]

In tandem with the rapidly expanding knowledge base, the course was extended to four years of seven months each in 1895, and all-day attendance was required. *Sayonara,* sundown medicine. By 1900, the curriculum contained twenty-seven courses covering subject matter very similar to that of today's curriculum (radiology was yet to become an element of clinical medicine). The six basic sciences were taught during the first two years, and the last two years were used largely for clinical experience, as is done today.

A scant forty years after the School was founded, therefore, many of the principles which underlie the modern American system were in place at Georgetown. At a time when total hours of instruction at American schools ranged from two thousand to five thousand, the Georgetown curriculum required about four thousand hours, and was sufficiently respected to enable Dean Kober to persuade the Association of American Medical Colleges (AAMC) that a curriculum modeled after Georgetown's should be adopted as the national standard (although attention to minimal requirements rather than a prescribed curriculum was then and remains AAMC policy).

Mid-life Crisis

By the turn of the century, Georgetown's School of Medicine had improved significantly, and was better than most of its peers. Was it, however, an excellent or even a good medical school? Probably not, if compared with the era's "gold standard," the Johns Hopkins School of Medicine. Almost immediately after it opened in 1893, Hopkins transformed the face of medical education by insisting on scrupulous entrance requirements, bedside clinical teaching, postgraduate hospital training, and the goal of a full-time faculty dedicated to teaching and research.

None of these concepts in itself was new under the sun, but never before had such an ambitious and idealistic view of physicians and of medical education provided the very foundation of a school of medicine, its curriculum, and its associated hospital. No other American school was the equal of Hopkins, and only a few were close. Compared to Hopkins, the curriculum of most schools appeared pale and halfhearted, peripheral exercises tacked on to the activities of a group of practicing physicians (however august their professorial titles); a few basic scientists were included among the faculty as a token bow to Holy Mother Science, but research per se had no particular imperative.

The Hopkins example and the achievements of the new medical science did not go unnoticed.[13] The growing realization that what the doctor knew actually made a difference elevated the expectations of the public, which began to scrutinize medical practice with increasing connoisseurship. By the end of the nineteenth century, there was widespread discontent with the training and quality of many American physicians. It became clear that a substantial fraction of the nation's 170 or so medical schools were substandard.

A growing reform movement had already closed some of the weaker schools when Abraham Flexner, commissioned by the Carnegie Foundation to survey American medical education, published his now famous report in 1910. His analysis documented a medical education jungle. He lauded Hopkins, and found much to praise in a few other schools, but he considered many to have weaknesses so serious that closure was recommended. Georgetown's School of Medicine was among those considered by Flexner to have few redeeming virtues. His laconic objectivity serves as a useful antidote to the tendency of in-house histories toward discreet silences and a whiff or two of self-congratulation.

Flexner's specific section on Georgetown follows in its entirety:

> Georgetown University School of Medicine, organized 1851. A University department in name only.
> Entrance requirement: Less than a four-year high school course.
> Attendance: 89
> Teaching staff: 74, of whom 20 are professors; no one gives whole time to the medical school, except the dean, who has the chair of hygiene and is treasurer of both medical and dental schools.
> Resources available for maintenance: Fees only, amounting to $11,000 a year.
> Laboratory facilities: The equipment consists of a good dissecting-room, a single fairly well stocked laboratory for pathology, bacteriology, and histology, a fair equipment for experimental physiology, and an ordinary chemical laboratory. There is no library accessible to students, no museum, and no pharmacological laboratory.
> Clinical facilities: The school has recently built a hospital, in which there are 100 ward beds, not free, but available for clinical use. It is several miles distant. The usual supplementary clinics are held in other places also. A few rooms at the hospital are set aside for a dispensary; the attendance is small.
> Date of visit: March 1909.

He then went on to comment that "[Georgetown and George Washington] lack adequate resources as well as assured prospects. They are surrounded by medical schools . . . whose competition they cannot meet . . . Neither school is now equal to the task of training physicians of the modern type."[14]

The Flexner report markedly accelerated the housecleaning already under way, and by 1925 almost one hundred schools of medicine had disappeared. Georgetown was staggered by Flexner, but it refused to fall. After a thorough self-examination, a number of reforms were initiated. Under Kober's leadership, the faculty was organized into formal departments, an executive faculty was created, and efforts were initiated to increase the size of the faculty as well as the relative proportion of full-time salaried faculty (at that time almost all faculty were still supporting themselves by practice, which occupied most of their time). In 1912, it became policy to insist that all basic scientists be full-time. By 1915, the total faculty had grown to 101, and in 1923 Dr. Kober could announce that a new school building was needed because it had become necessary to turn down twenty or more applicants each year during the prior four years.[15]

Further, in a modest but precedent-establishing foray into fund-raising, he reminded those interested in Georgetown medicine that a school could not hope to remain in class "A" unless it had an annual endowment income of $25,000, a goal not reached for many years. Even today, the School's endowment is less than one-tenth the size of that of some of the more fortunate medical schools.

By 1929, class size had grown to eighty, and there were 141 faculty members. The future would see enormous growth in class size, faculty numbers, and physical plant, as well as almost continuous tinkering with the curriculum, but the essential elements of today's educational system were well in place by the time the present School of Medicine building was dedicated in 1930. (Not until 1938, however, did it become obligatory for all entering students to have a bachelor's degree.)[16]

Modern Times

The year 1929 was an important one for the School for several reasons. Dr. George Kober, a brilliant physician and administrator, whose remarkable achievements included the ability to survive for twenty-nine years as Dean of the School of Medicine, finally retired, having presided over the transmutation of the School from a local cottage industry into the formal, complex organization required by modern medical education. The year also saw a fundamental change in the relationship of the School to the University. At its inception, the School was administered by physicians, and it remained essentially under the control of the medical faculty throughout the nineteenth century and well into the twentieth, with little more than nominal linkage to the University. As the School grew in size and budget, and particularly as plans were being made for a move to a new building to be located on the campus, the University, understandably, began to pay closer attention.

For some time, the University president had been presiding over meetings of the executive faculty of the School of Medicine. In 1926, President W. Coleman Nevils, S.J., citing excessive demands on his time, instituted a fundamental change in governance by designating a surrogate to serve as liaison between School and University, and, in practice, to assume certain administrative responsibilities for the School. Walter G. Summers, S.J., was appointed as the first Regent of the School of Medicine. The School, which had heretofore enjoyed near-autonomy, would henceforth be governed to a greater or lesser extent on a day-to-day basis by someone (in most instances, not a health professional) sent from "the lower campus" to represent the president. The move clearly made the School part of the Union, and laid the foundation for the three-campus system of which the Medical Center with its three Schools and a University Hospital is a part. (The Medical Center was not officially so-called until 1946.)

The first Regent's important role in overseeing planning and construction of a new building to house the School established the precedent for the current system, which assigns responsibility for planning, physical development, and construction to the chief executive of the Medical Center. In 1961, the title of Regent was replaced by that of Vice-President, with corresponding escalation of authority over the deans and the hospital director.

Kober had proposed that a new School of Medicine and Dentistry be built on Thirty-seventh Street, but he was overruled by Nevils, who thought, wisely, that Kober's proposal would restrict growth. In his first official act as president of the University, Nevils insisted on the Reservoir Road location. The new building, dedicated in 1930, has been the School's home to the present day, and marked the first foothold of medical education on the University campus, a nidus for the development of the vast medical center now sprawled along the north campus. Some Georgetown residents of the time were less pleased than was Nevils, and viewed the Medical School building as a blight on the neighborhood, a view held by quite a few to this day.

In the 1960s, a perception that the United States had too few physicians gained increasing acceptance, and the government as well as private foundations urged that the system increase the number of physicians trained each year. The advice, perhaps because it was accompanied by the offer of large grants to the responsive, resulted in the first significant expansion in medical school numbers since the 1920s, when the post-Flexnerian weeding left approximately 75 schools standing. (By the mid-eighties there were 127 medical schools in the United States.) Concurrently, many existing schools increased class size significantly. Georgetown, whose class size had been 116 for many years, expanded to 145 in 1969. A further increase to 205 occurred in 1971 in response to the Physician's Augmentation Program initiated by the federal government two years earlier. Overnight, Georgetown became the second largest private medical school in the country (Jefferson is the largest).[17]

The carrots which induced such growth were of enormous value to the school in expanding faculty numbers, basic science, and clinical facilities, and in upgrading the library. In 1910, Flexner had sneered at Georgetown's annual budget of $11,000, but the current annual budget, which climbed to over $100,000,000 several years ago, is more likely to evoke pallor than scorn. Medical education has become big business. Fueled by class size expansion, marked increase in federal research funds, and the incorporation of practice fees into the School's fiscal structure, the medical education budget at Georgetown, as elsewhere, has grown to a size which raises some troublesome dog-versus-tail issues for the parent University.

Although bigger is not necessarily better, the School's growth was fruitful. Few would claim that a medical school with one full-time faculty member (Georgetown of 1909) is reaching for greatness. Excellence, however, does not come cheap. The first students enrolled paid $90 per year for the two-year course. Modest inflation brought the annual fee to $135 by 1868, but tuition *actually decreased* later to the $100 noted by Flexner. Subsequent increases brought the annual tuition to $500 in 1946, $1450 in 1963, and $2800 in 1972. The trend was clearly up, but Georgetown was still more or less on a par with comparable schools.

However, in the 1970s, the enormous increases in expenses generated by the expansion of class size, faculty, and physical plant, as well as the increasing costs of research (never entirely covered by extramural sources) necessitated major tuition jumps as the golden shower of federal incentive money ceased. The School was struggling to chew what it had bitten off. An unprecedented series of large increases brought tuition to $6800 in 1976, $12,500 in 1978,[18] and $17,500 by 1982. Georgetown became the most expensive medical school on the planet.

Exuberant growth in tuition subsided during the early 1980s, but even small annual increases to keep pace with inflation resulted by 1985 in a tuition of $22,500 each year for four years, a staggering sum. The School has scrupulously refused to introduce a means test into the admissions process, but now finds itself entangled continuously in the complex task of assisting students in obtaining huge loans. Troublesome questions have arisen about the extent to which such crippling tuition costs are influencing choices by those who are considering careers in medicine, or by medical students selecting a school or a specialty.

Up to now, careful observation has detected no effect on the quality of the students who choose to matriculate at Georgetown, a perennially popular school, which has consistently received applications each year during the eighties from almost twenty percent of all American medical school applicants. But it is inconceivable that the prospect of enormous debt burdens (frequently more than $100,000) at graduation escapes the notice of the applicants.

Georgetown is not intrinsically more expensive than comparable schools but, lacking state aid or a large endowment, the School, more than almost all other schools, must extract a significant fraction of the income needed to operate a modern medical school from the students. Increasing concern by faculty and dean over such crippling tuition costs resulted in deliberate belt-tightening, which permitted tuition to be frozen during 1988 and 1989, an admirable display of self-control which enabled Georgetown to relinquish with relief its title as most expensive, when three of Georgetown's private school sisters raised their annual charges to more than $22,500 in 1989. Nevertheless, the high cost of medical education is an ominous problem with which Georgetown, like all United States schools, will have to wrestle successfully if schools of medicine are to avoid, as they must, becoming an educational system for the well-to-do.

A Potpourri of Related Topics: Hospitals and Postgraduate Training

The hospital became the icon of Hygeia only in this century. Constructed in most instances to care for the poor, hospitals in the nineteenth century and earlier were frequently shoddy, arbitrary about admissions, autocratically run, and often did more harm than good to the hapless sick admitted to the spartan quarters. Those who could control their fate usually avoided hospitalization, believing with some justice that relatively few patients walked out. People of means had personal physicians who attended them at home.[19] Nevertheless, hospitals had been an important place for medical training for centuries because of a medical version of Sutton's Law, and physicians often fought for the privilege of attending hospitalized patients. Caring for the sick poor in a hospital setting simultaneously satisfied the ancient obligation of physicians to render charity care, provided an unparalleled opportunity to gain vast clinical experience, enhanced reputation, and sharpened skills which were useful in the private practice on which the physician depended for his living.

The role of hospitals in medical education at Georgetown and other schools was heavily influenced by the Hopkins model, and by changes in medicine which progressively improved the quality and effectiveness of hospitals to such an extent that the hospital, huge, frenetic, bristling with strange, expensive devices, is now the centerpiece of the medical care system. Georgetown's initial challenge in 1850 to that other school's National Hospital was to include six beds and a dispensary for the care of the sick poor in the original rented quarters.

In 1886, the facilities of Providence Hospital were made available for bedside instruction and outpatient service. Emergency, Garfield, and Children's Hospitals were subsequently affiliated, as emphasis on clinical experience grew. By 1896, however, just a few years after Hopkins showed the way, Georgetown's medical faculty began to call for a University Hospital, i.e., a hospital staffed by the faculty in which patient care, education, and, it was hoped, research could be integrated in a manner not possible as long as the School depended on facilities controlled by others. The University generously donated a plot at Thirty-fifth and N Streets, N.W., and by 1898, with funds solicited from the Washington community, Georgetown built a four-story University Hospital of thirty-three beds.

The new hospital quickly became so busy[20] that additional construction raised bed-capacity to 100 beds by 1903, and by a series of additions the Hospital attained a bed-capacity of 293 in 1927. So matters rested until 1947, when the core of the present University Hospital (initially 407 beds) was dedicated at the Reservoir Road site adjacent to the School of Medicine.[21] No longer needed for medical purposes, the old Hospital buildings were reclaimed by the University and are in use today. Extensive remodeling and new construction have been almost continuous in subsequent years, as Georgetown participated in the explosive expansion of health care facilities which has characterized recent decades. The official bird of Georgetown's Medical Center, it has been said, is the construction crane.

The University Hospital remains the central clinical teaching arena for Georgetown's medical students. However, the early pattern of using affiliated local hospitals has continued as a means of expanding the number of teaching beds, and to enrich the educational experience by exposing students to a variety of patient populations and health care delivery systems. (Plush suburban hospitals as well as such public inner city institutions as D.C. General Hospital and the Washington Veterans Administration Hospital are included in the empire.)

The almost exclusive focus on the hospital characteristic of American medical education today is facing increasing criticism as social forces are changing the patterns of hospital use. There is growing realization that a student whose training is restricted to the critical, high-technology problems which, increasingly, characterize the hospital patient population, never encounters the ten thousand ills for which patients consult their doctors in offices. Medical education, it appears, must learn how to recapture some of the outpatient experience which characterized clinical training for most of the nineteenth century.

Residency

The need for clinical experience has been evident to those who train physicians since the misty origins of the profession. In the late nineteenth century, it became more and more evident that the educational experience after graduation was sufficiently critical to warrant formal organization and supervision. Hopkins had stressed the need for supervised hospital experience for green physicians clutching fresh diplomas. During the twentieth century, the system grew, particularly in the years after World War II, into the present prolonged training period in which all American physicians spend long periods in postgraduate training as residents primarily involved in care of hospitalized patients.

At least one year is required for licensure, a year formerly called the internship, but now referred to as the first year of residency. After graduation, most Georgetown students serve three to five years as residents, sometimes more, to receive training in one or another of the specialties into which medicine has become divided by the almost overwhelming mass of the knowledge needed for expertise. It is an enriching feature of the educational process that the majority of students transfer to another medical center, often in another city, to obtain residency training. Gaining acceptance into the more prestigious residency programs is more difficult than getting into medical school, and the application process is a brief, intense period of stress for many senior medical students, almost all of whom participate in the national computerized "Match" which brings order to the varying preferences of students and hospitals.

The residency system with its associated Boards and specialty examinations has become a vital component of medical education at all American schools, and has gained international admiration. The white coats (or green scrub suits) of the resident physicians are a familiar sight at the University Hospital, which offers residency training in virtually all of the specialties. The residents play an essential role in providing medical care in hospitals. Because of their close contact with the third- and fourth-year medical students, the residents also do the lion's share of the teaching during this period of the training program. Georgetown, like all medical centers, is just beginning to grapple with the relatively recent public outcry against the long working hours traditionally expected of these trainees cum teachers cum employees (residents are often on duty from eighty to one hundred hours a week).

Through a series of historical accidents, the residency portion of medical education is generally more the responsibility of the university hospitals and the powerful national specialty organizations than of our schools of medicine. Residents are paid by the hospital, and are not working toward another university degree. However, the justifiable Georgetown practice (initiated in 1988) is to register the hospital's residents as graduate students in the School of Medicine. Such a custom is not universal, and at most university medical centers it is the hospital rather than the medical school which maintains records of the residents trained by the various specialty programs. Because the specialists who supervise the training of residents are, in fact, the faculty of the medical school, the issue of whether the School of Medicine or the University Hospital is responsible for this phase of medical education can become tangled, but the system works with only an occasional lurch.

Research

It is a post-Hopkins axiom of American medical schools that a first-rate medical education can be provided only in an atmosphere of intellectual inquiry in which, as a rarely attained ideal, all of the faculty are scholars and investigators as well as competent professionals and teachers. The enormous support for research provided by the National Institutes of Health during the past forty years has brought extraordinary advances in medical science, but the pursuit of such funds has changed the balance of effort at many schools significantly. At least a few thoughtful observers now argue that an overemphasis on biomedical investigation can pervert the educational mission. It must be acknowledged, however, that the prestige of a school of medicine today depends more on the research it produces than on any other single factor.

Although Georgetown has produced its fair share of notable medical scientists, the School, historically, has focused more on providing excellence in clinical training than on investigation. At present, Georgetown is closer to the median than to the leaders in the size of its research effort. An increased emphasis on biomedical research at Georgetown in the past few years has resulted in remarkable recent growth, and in 1988 the School introduced a joint M.D./Ph.D. program intended to facilitate the development of selected Georgetown medical students into the medical scientists of tomorrow. It remains to be seen whether or not an almost unbearably prolonged educational program or such rapid expansion of research can be sustained at a time when all such efforts have become increasingly costly, and the federal government is no longer in a giving vein.

The Students

What kind of person is the Georgetown medical student? All kinds, surely. Dr. Kober, a kindly man, characterized the students of the "sundown medicine" era as young men who "knew nothing of and cared less for alluring amusements, and many times the wee hours of the morning found them working together in the anatomical laboratory."[22] Maybe. In any event, such exemplars are seen rarely nowadays; perhaps the available amusements in Washington are more alluring than they used to be. Medical students today are very bright, and many are brilliant. The great majority are neither grade-hungry geeks nor budding Albert Schweitzers. Almost all are genuinely interested in using their knowledge to help the sick, and they are willing to work long hours for close to a decade of training to achieve competence. The educational gantlet converts a few into technicians of medicine *sans merci*, but none enter medical school hoping to be transformed into a robot.

Whether or not today's medical student is somehow less worthy than the saints of yore, not as nice a person, is a debatable matter. It was easier to attribute nobility to medical students during the nineteenth century and the early years of the twentieth when the income of most physicians in the United States was relatively modest except for a few superstars. The high income earned by most physicians today has not gone unnoticed by those considering their career options, but greed unconfined is not a commonly observed motivator, perhaps in part because any vision of sugar plums must contend with the reality of an extraordinarily difficult, long, and expensive period of education. (Which is not to say that medical students and physicians are impervious to the values of the "Me Decade" or to a sense of entitlement after such long labors.)

The flunk rate at Georgetown's School of Medicine was high during most of the School's history, perhaps *pour encourager les autres*. As noted by Flexner in his 1909 survey, some of Georgetown's matriculants had not finished high school, a rather low standard, which was, however, in accordance with the regulations of the AAMC, and no less demanding than that of most other American schools. Given such easy entrance requirements, a high failure rate was perhaps a form of mercy to the public, and was admired. In 1883, Georgetown received a letter from the Illinois Board of Health which praised the School's draconian policies: "The small percentage of your graduates to matriculates and the other marks of improvement are certainly to be commended."[23]

Why so many continued to fail even in later years as admission standards were progressively tightened is less clear. The class of 1939, which included a number of graduates who went on to distinguished careers, established an unenviable modern record, when thirty-nine percent of the matriculants failed to graduate. Despite the significant demand for physicians created by World War II, the faculty permitted only seventy percent of the class of 1946 to graduate. Attrition continued in the twelve to fifteen percent range during the 1950s and it was not until the 1960s that the failure rate dropped to about six percent.

In recent years, the failure rate at Georgetown, as at most American schools, runs at two to three percent, in large measure because of the extraordinary competition for places and correspondingly high aptitudes of accepted students. The remarkably strong qualifications of the applicants have continued despite a moderate drop since 1973 in numbers of college students interested in medical careers.[24] The patent ability of almost all who manage to get accepted has produced a marked change in the attitude of the faculty, which now makes every effort to bring all matriculants to graduation.[25] Indeed, behavioral or psychological flaws, rather than scholastic ineptitude, are responsible for almost all of the failures seen at Georgetown in the current decade.

Women and Blacks in the School of Medicine

For most of the School's history, women and blacks were welcome only as patients. Such institutionalized exclusivity was not peculiarly Georgetown's nor can it fairly be related to Catholicism. Georgetown is an American school, and it assumed the bigotry of the culture without calling attention to itself by display of either unusual virulence or outrage.

Although the University of Zurich had broken the ancient taboo by opening up its school of medicine to women in 1869, Georgetown was more cautious:

> In the Fall of 1898 one Louise Taylor applied for admission to the School. The medical faculty seems to have been somewhat upset by the request, but compromised by authorizing the professor of anatomy to give to the enterprising Miss Taylor a special course of instruction in that subject.[26]

In 1947, the School finally capitulated and began admitting women as regular students in the first-year class. (Sarah Stewart, a microbiologist, who subsequently had a distinguished career in cancer research, graduated with the Georgetown class of 1949, but had been admitted directly into the second year as a special case.) Since then, the proportion of women students has increased steadily, and is now over thirty percent. Perhaps more indicative of the admission committee's current enlightenment is the closely monitored statistic which indicates that the percentage of acceptances offered is about the same for male and female applicants.

The first black students were not admitted until the early 1970s. Since then, a genuine effort has been made to increase the enrollment of Blacks, but the attempt has been largely frustrated by the relatively high tuition, and scanty availability of scholarship funds at Georgetown. However, an affirmative action program (GEMS), initiated in 1977 for minority students with high intelligence and motivation but suboptimal aptitude scores, has been successful, and is the main source of the black students who now make up about ten percent of the student body.

The faculty, like the student body, was essentially white man's territory until recently. The proportion of women on the medical school's faculty has been rising in the past decade, but the rate of increase is slower than desirable, and at present none of the senior administrative posts (department chairman or above) is held by a woman. There are only a few black faculty members, and none in positions of authority.

Because integration of the student body has been successful in spirit, and increasingly so in actuality, the relatively glacial pace at which women and Blacks are being recruited into the faculty is puzzling. Some believe that the problem is not so much residual prejudice as unthinking networking, slow turnover in senior posts, and, for Blacks, a dearth of qualified applicants because the number of black physicians interested in academic careers is still relatively small. The result is troubling, whatever the cause. Some serious prodding may be in order.

What is Catholic about Georgetown's School of Medicine?

As a component of a Catholic, Jesuit University, Georgetown's School of Medicine is undeniably a Catholic medical school. But what, if anything, distinguishes it from plain vanilla medical schools? Is there something at Georgetown (to adapt the famous Turing Test) that would be noticed as different and somehow Catholic, if a professor or student from Secular Medical School were transported to Reservoir Road and not informed about the Jesuit heritage of the University? A simple answer will not do, in part because customs have come and gone over the life of the School. At least four areas in which Catholicity in one form or another could be expressed in a school of medicine deserve some attention.

1. To what extent are the clergy involved in the quotidian activities of the School?

Jesuits served as senior administrative officers of the Medical Center with one or another title for a relatively brief period beginning in 1929 with the first Regent and ending in 1969 when a layman was appointed as Vice-President of the Medical Center. At present, the relatively few priests in evidence are either chaplains or medical professionals serving as faculty members.

The original University Hospital was run by the Sisters of Saint Francis from Philadelphia, and the present Hospital was administered by the Sisters of Charity of Nazareth until 1963. However, in recent decades both administration and nursing in the University Hospital are carried out by laity.

Whether or not the period of Jesuit administration of the Medical Center in itself imparted a distinct Catholic flavor to one or another aspect of medical education is not obvious, but the visibility of clergy, like the presence of nursing sisters, would certainly have been a reminder of something to faculty, students, and patients alike. Some of the Jesuits who served as Regent gave lectures in morality and ethics to the students, and can be presumed to have stressed Catholic views.

2. To what extent were administrative, faculty, and student positions reserved for Roman Catholics?

The early School was ecumenical in faculty, and probably so in acceptance of students. Such is the case today. Although the Roman Catholic faith is heavily represented in the present faculty, student body, and among those with administrative responsibilities, significant numbers of Protestants and Jews can be found in each of these categories. However, it is believed by some seasoned observers that there have been periods in the past when the student body was almost exclusively Catholic by deliberate policy, and certain administrative posts, particularly the chairmanship of clinical departments, were reserved for Catholic physicians.

Restrictive policies with bias toward one or another group were flagrant among American universities as late as the 1950s, and if Georgetown did, indeed, favor Catholics from time to time, it was playing a popular game, however deplorable. In any event, few who are contemplating the idea of a university would hold that exclusion of non-Catholics makes an educational system Catholic in any important sense.

3. Is the medical education offered by the School compatible with specific church policies which govern certain aspects of medical care?

Although modern medicine does not, in the main, conflict with Catholic doctrine, a few components of medical practice which are both legal and acceptable to many non-Catholics are not acceptable to the church. Human reproduction has been the principal arena of dispute, with such topics as birth control, abortion, and some mother-versus-fetus issues receiving most of the attention. The Catholic position about such matters is not new, but it is only in the past few decades that advancing technology and changing mores in the general population have provided medical options (for contraception and for abortion, for example) which the church cannot condone. The position of the church on a number of health issues, including, among others, euthanasia, patient rights, birth control, and abortion, was codified and approved as the national code at the annual meeting of the National Conference of Catholic Bishops and the United States Catholic Conference in 1971.[27]

The clinical experience provided to students and the medical practice conducted at Georgetown University Hospital are in conformity with the bishops' directives. The matter is not a simple one. Georgetown's students have diverse backgrounds, religions, and beliefs, and they will be practicing medicine in a pluralistic society. They are informed about the position of the church and about the policies of Georgetown's Medical Center. However, they must be familiar with the advice, drugs, and procedures in use in the medical culture of this country, whatever decisions they make about what they themselves will advise or do as they practice medicine. Further, Georgetown students and residents receive part of their training in nondenominational hospitals within whose walls abortion, for example, is legally performed. A complex series of working rules has evolved to insulate the student from violation of the directives without leaving potentially harmful lacunae in the education provided.

Since the bishops met in 1971, technical advances (in vitro fertilization, prolonged life support, for example), and issues which revolve around homosexuality and AIDS have produced a host of difficult new questions which are under discussion, but about which no definitive Catholic position has been published. Should some new version of the directives appear, the Medical Center will surely pay attention. At present, it is in the rather circumscribed area of "pelvic theology," therefore, that medical education at Georgetown is clearly Catholic and distinguishable from that of secular medical centers.

4. Is there in the air at Georgetown some heightened sense of mission, of dedication to healing, of the moral responsibility of physicians, which can be attributed to the School's Catholic heritage?

No one could seriously claim that Georgetown's physicians and medical students are more noble than the physicians and students at other medical schools, nor is the medicine practiced at the Medical Center demonstrably more compassionate, diligent, ethical than that of the great secular institutions. And yet, there are those who say there is an intangible difference, that expectations of moral behavior are somehow higher at Georgetown for people of all faiths because of the connection with the church. Moral ambiance is not easily measured, and the matter will have to remain an interesting question for the thoughtful.

The Future

After 150 years, then, Georgetown's School of Medicine is healthy and respected. Indeed, if the School continues to increase its already significant commitment to biomedical research, Georgetown could eventually join the dozen or so medical schools which by common consent are acknowledged as our best. There are current problems which must be addressed: in curriculum (fact-cramming, ambulatory care, and the role of computers deserve particular attention), tuition costs, declining interest in medical careers, ethical issues spawned by the new technology, and a host of budget matters, including shrinkage of federal support for education and research. And, of course, medical education, which is necessarily intertwined with patient care, cannot escape involvement in the issue of escalating health care costs, which has alarmed the nation.[28] But these challenges must be faced by all schools, not Georgetown alone, and Georgetown has a 150-year track record of tough adaptability which inspires confidence in its future.

Such specific current itches must be scratched by those who administer medical schools, but what is arguably the darkest shadow to have fallen over modern medical education has yet to receive the urgent attention it deserves: entranced by test results (the "numbers") and marvelous machines, doctors are in danger of forgetting that the *raison d'être* of the physician is still the patient.[29]

In any age, the medical school curriculum reflects the medical *Zeitgeist*, and is designed to produce the model physician of the era. Society's view of its physicians has changed dramatically through the millennia as medicine shifted paradigms. Castiglioni summarized the role changes:

> The period then that begins at the end of the Eighteenth Century with revolutions was dominated by a positivist and biological current which brought a new aspect to the career of the physician. He is no longer the sorcerer of remote ages, the priest of ancient times, the clerk of the middle ages, the astrologer or alchemist of the fifteenth century, the bloodletter of the seventeenth, or the philosophizing academician of the eighteenth. He no longer depends on the church or on the state. The physician of the nineteenth century [and forever after] is simply the scientist.[30]

Thus, the seven ages of the doctor according to Castiglioni, but the last persona is wrong-headed. Olympian disinterest is not the stuff of a good physician: chilly technical precision addresses diseases, not sick human beings. Medicine which does not add values to its science has lost its way. It is the task of medical education to ensure that the physician is a concerned humanist informed by science, and not "simply a scientist." Our schools of medicine have just begun to realize that the spiral helix may be overshadowing something precious.

Whether medical schools can move beyond lip service and address this issue meaningfully remains to be seen. Those who point the finger need reminding that teaching values is not the same thing as instilling values, a problem no educational system has yet solved in any field. The commonly heard suggestion that all will be well if admission committees select more humanities majors (in itself, a good idea), while more or less ignoring measures of ability, is mindless. Even if it were demonstrated that literature majors, say, are inherently more compassionate than chemists, white-coated blockheads reciting Beowulf will make nothing useful happen in the intensive care unit. Georgetown, with its religious heritage and justly admired resources in biomedical ethics, could seize the day.

Notes

The citations of the papers of Hess, Nealon, and, especially Durkin, do not adequately describe my great debt to their publications, from which I obtained the majority of the specific facts and anecdotes about the School's history included in this paper. Dr. John Rose, whose knowledge of School lore is unrivaled, was helpful in a thousand ways, but particularly in providing information about the past three decades.

The assistance of Ms. Helen Bagdoyan, librarian of the History Room of Dahlgren Library, is gratefully acknowledged.

I, of course, am responsible for errors, interpretations, opinions, and tone.

1. E. H. Clarke et al., *A Century of American Medicine, 1776-1876* (Philadelphia: Henry C. Lea, 1876), 3.

2. J. Duffin, "Vitalism and Organicism in the Philosophy of R. T. H. Laennec," *Bulletin of the History of Medicine* 62(1988):525-45.

3. K. Klaus, *Rudolph Virchow. Medizin und Naturwissenschaft: Zwei Reden, 1845* (East Berlin: Akademie-Verlag, 1986), 60.

4. Minutes of the Directors of the Georgetown University Medical School, Vol. 1, transcript, Georgetown University Archives.

5. Joseph T. Durkin, S.J, *Georgetown University: First in the Nation's Capital* (New York: Doubleday and Company, 1964), 36.

6. S. W. Nealon, Jr., M.D., "The Georgetown University Medical Center," *Bulletin of Georgetown University Medical Center* 3(1950):222-231.

7. Joseph T. Durkin, S.J., "The History of Georgetown University School of Medicine to 1900," *Georgetown Medical Bulletin* 17(1963):113.

8. John Llewellin Eliot, M.D., "The History of the Foundation of the Medical Department of Georgetown University," typescript, 3 (1907), Georgetown University Archives.

9. Quoted by J. Blake, *Epilogue: Essays at the Bicentennial of Medicine in the United States*, Department of Health, Education, and Welfare publication no. NIH 77-1176, 4.

10. Cited in Durkin, "School of Medicine to 1900," 116-17.

11. In recent decades, desperate deans reacted to the explosion in knowledge

by piling lecture upon lecture at the expense of laboratory experience, wearing out both seats and brains of students. Reform is just beginning. *Plus ça change,* etc.

12. Cited in Durkin, "School of Medicine to 1900," 120.

13. Not all approved: Mark Twain, noting the progressive decrease in the death rate, regretted that the world could no longer rely on the incompetence of doctors to control overpopulation. Mark Twain, *Letters from the Earth,* ed. B. DeVoto (New York: Harper and Row, 1962), 91.

14. A. Flexner, *Medical Education in the United States and Canada.* A Report to the Carnegie Foundation, bulletin no. 4 (Boston: Merrymount Press, 1910), 201-202, 203.

15. W. C. Hess, Ph.D., "The History of the Georgetown University School of Medicine, 1900-1930," *Georgetown Medical Bulletin* 17(1964):240-45.

16. W. C. Hess, Ph.D., "The History of the Georgetown University School of Medicine, 1930-1964," *Georgetown Medical Bulletin* 18(1964):48-59.

17. Government opinion, which makes no fetish of consistency, now holds that there is a physician surplus, which, if true, was largely produced by federal *sjamboks* in the previous decade.

18. The D.C. government, in reluctant compliance with federal regulations, had been providing Georgetown with per capita support of approximately $5,000 per student for several years. The School compensated for the discontinuation of this program in 1977 with a startling escalation in tuition, which assuredly captured the attention of its students, and opened up new revenue possibilities to medical deans everywhere.

19. M. J. Vogel, "The Transformation of the American Hospital, 1850-1920," in *Health Care in America,* ed. S. Revner and D. Rosner (Philadelphia: Temple University Press, 1979), 105-16.

20. Heavy traffic and adjoining industry in northwest Washington of that period were a prolific source of injured patients. It is an ill wind . . .

21. $50,000 had sufficed to build the original University Hospital in 1898. The new one cost $3,600,000.

22. Cited in Durkin, "School of Medicine to 1900," 116.

23. Cited in Durkin, "School of Medicine to 1900," 118.

24. Applications to medical schools nationally increased dramatically throughout the 1960s and peaked in 1973 when there were about four applicants for each place. A subsequent drop caused concern to educators, but the applicant pool has now been stable for the past two years at slightly under two applicants for each place.

25. Any faculty tendency to harshness is probably also blunted a bit by guilty sensitivity to the large investment of time, effort, and money expended by medical students by the time they reach the last two years.

26. Durkin, "School of Medicine to 1900," 122.

27. *Ethical and Religious Directives for Catholic Health Facilities,* rev. ed. (St. Louis: Catholic Health Association of the United States, 1975).

28. Physicians and hospital administrators can justify spiraling costs persuasively, but even health professionals have been known to blanch when presented with a medical bill personally.

29. One can acknowledge that there is a problem without concluding that the profession as a whole has made a Faustian bargain. In recent polls, a large majority of those who believe that doctors do not care about people anymore consider their personal physician to be a prince.

30. A. Castiglioni, M.D., *A History of Medicine,* trans. E. B. Krumbhaar, M.D., Ph.D. (New York: Jason Aronson, 1969), 760.

MARK TUSHNET
Professor of Law

Catholic Legal Education at a National Law School: Reflections on the Georgetown Experience

In the early years of Georgetown University's law school, it purported to have a particular focus on legal ethics, legal philosophy, and legal history, because of its affiliation with the Catholic Church.[1] Yet, as Robert Stevens mordantly remarked, within a few years the law school had become an enormous factory for producing lawyers, where it is inconceivable that any specifically Catholic attitudes or values were imparted to students.[2] Stevens's observation is merely an instance of a more general point: Catholic legal education in the United States has been, and is, legal education first; it is Catholic no better, and often worse, than second. Thus, to understand the contributions that Catholic legal education and the church can make to each other, we must begin by understanding legal education.[3] The perspective I adopt here is intended to be analytical and descriptive, in the manner of a sociologist,[4] rather than prescriptive.

The primary distinction among law schools in the United States is that some are local and others are national. The local/national distinction refers in part to the geographical "draw" of the student body, but it refers in larger part to the activities in which the schools' graduates engage.[5] Local law schools train lawyers who will litigate in municipal and state courts, who will participate actively in local politics, who will serve as lawyers for municipal and sometimes state governments, and who will give legal advice to individuals and small proprietorships. National law schools train lawyers who will litigate infrequently and then mostly in the federal courts, who will not participate actively in politics, and who will give legal advice to large corporations. As a shorthand, we can say that graduates of local law schools deal mostly with people while graduates of national law schools deal mostly with organizations.[6] I will suggest in what follows a conclusion consistent with the more general one stated earlier. Not only is Catholic legal education primarily legal education; in addition, if a law school associated with a Catholic university seeks to become or becomes a national law school, it will find it extremely difficult to sustain activities in a strong way that either signal or embody its Catholic affiliation.

Law schools substantially expanded their enrollments in the 1960s and 1970s, and as a result expanded their faculties. The effect was to reinforce a dynamic that had already begun to affect most local law schools—the urge to become a national law school. Prior to the expansion of law school faculties, local law schools hired graduates of local law schools, usually their own graduates, and members of the local bar. As faculties expanded, local law schools were able to hire graduates of national law schools. These new teachers aspired to make their new institutions more like the ones from which they had graduated. This created a number of stresses. Older members of the faculty saw themselves being implicitly and sometimes explicitly criticized for being second-rate, that is, for having a local rather than a national orientation. Even as the numerical and other indicators of student aptitude rose at local law schools, students began to feel that they must be second-rate too, because their schools refrained from hiring their own graduates.

By the mid-1980s, some local law schools, including Georgetown's, had successfully navigated, or almost so, the transition to a national orientation. This alleviated some of the stresses just mentioned, though of course some of them persist, but it created new ones. In particular, many local law schools had developed an ideology of service to validate what they did as compared to national law schools. This ideology took a variety of forms. In Catholic law schools it was grounded in a humanistic philosophy inspired by the Bible. At other law schools, such as Tulane and the University of Wisconsin, the ideology of service stressed the contributions the law school and its graduates made to state governments. Once a school made the transition to national status, though, the ideology of service in its older form became quite unrealistic. Graduates of national law schools simply do not provide things like the attention to the legal problems individuals have arising from the stresses of modern urban life; they help corporations maneuver through the legal shoals.[7] The point may be symbolized by the drastic decline in the number of graduates of the Georgetown University Law Center whose first jobs were in public interest law. According to former Dean Robert Pitofsky, in 1979 "more than 25% of the class started their careers in federal, state and city government, prosecutors' offices, public interest law firms, and the like," while the comparable figure for 1988 was "about 7%."[8] Of course, this drop is the product of many factors, including the contraction of the public interest market and the widening gap between public interest and other salaries.[9] Its mere existence, though, makes the ideology of service seem the irrelevant product of an abandoned past.

The lack of realism of established ideologies of local service is compounded by another facet of the transition to national status, an ethnic/class element. Local law schools through most of their existence had been vehicles for class mobility and, in urban centers, for ethnic mobility as well. They provided opportunities for the children of working-class parents to enter the lower rungs of the professional classes, as low-status attorneys and low-level employees of municipal and state governments. In those capacities their class and ethnic affiliations were sometimes an advantage because of neighborhood, church, and other "old boy network" connections, but at least were not a disadvantage. Again, a symbolic point is that local law schools but not national ones had evening divisions, which allowed people with full-time jobs to obtain a professional degree. For most local law schools, though not Georgetown's, abandoning the evening division was part of the transition to national status.[10]

National law schools appear to draw their students from a substantially narrower class base than do local ones.[11] In the United States, class origin carries with it a manner of presenting oneself and of dealing with other people. Graduates of national law schools work with people in the middle and upper reaches of corporate hierarchies, and therefore must have the proper personal characteristics and the like. These can be acquired in the course of college education, but they are much more likely to be acquired before that, in the course of growing up in professional or upper-managerial families. The narrowing class base of the student body in national law schools obviously makes it more difficult to sustain the credibility of ideologies of local service.

Such ideologies could, of course, be transformed. Robert Gordon has shown, for example, how leaders of the corporate bar at the end of the nineteenth century continued to invoke the traditional images of republican virtue in defense of their work; they simply gave new content to that imagery, so that the sturdy independent yeoman whose republican virtue was the strength of a restrained democratic government was replaced by the capitalist whose independence from government supplied the basis for restraints on it.[12] Similarly, leaders of law schools making the transition from local to national status could transform their ideology into one of national service. There are several obstacles to such a transformation, entirely apart from the delicate politics within the law school that would arise were it attempted. First, service to the nation is likely to be most easily taken to mean service to the upper reaches of the national political system. Yet, the already established national law schools have quite a strong grip on that sort of service, because of the same kinds of "old boy" networks that had aided local law schools in placing their graduates. Further, the opportunities for such service are relatively restricted. Claims that a law school's graduates are providing that sort of service are therefore likely to ring hollow. Second, it is not easy to develop an ideology in which service to organizations carries as much value as service to people did in the ideologies of local service, at least in the United States, where general corporatist ideologies have been overwhelmed by individualist ones. Finally, with respect to Catholic law schools specifically, there may be particular theologically rooted difficulties associated with developing an ideology of service in which organizations have priority over people.[13]

Before considering in more detail what Catholic law schools and the Church might contribute to each other, there is one important additional qualification. Because Catholic legal education is legal education first, the distribution of activities in the community of Catholic law schools as a whole is quite likely to be the same as the distribution of activities in the law school community as a whole. Consider two examples drawn from the Georgetown experience. The *Georgetown Journal of Legal Ethics* began publishing in 1986 under the leadership of Robert F. Drinan, S.J. The first student-run law journal devoted to legal ethics, the *Journal* might be seen as the product of a Catholic institution's concern for ethics generally. Yet, almost simultaneously Harvard University, with a large contribution from its law school, began a program in professional ethics. The Georgetown University Law Center also has an extensive program of clinical education, whose justification lies in part in its provision of service to the community. Again that might be seen as the product of the institution's Catholic affiliation. Yet, the Stanford Law School, a national institution, has a more fully developed program of clinical education as community service, and the City University of New York at Queens College, a local law school, has a more extensive one.[14]

These examples suggest the more general point that a law school's leaders—deans and university presidents—feel the influence of general trends in legal education (such as the concern for legal ethics that surged with the involvement of so many lawyers in Watergate, or student pressure for a more "relevant" education), interpret those trends in the terms with which they are familiar, whether religious or secular, and develop programs responding to those trends that are roughly similar in content though sometimes different in stated justification. This point gains support when we examine Catholic legal education in the United States across the board and note that while certain Catholic institutions stand out with respect to particular activities, so do some secular institutions, thus undercutting the argument that specifically Catholic commitments generate such programs. Perhaps the most that can be said is that as institutions transform themselves, and in particular as local law schools seek to become national ones, Catholic law schools may focus in the initial stages on activities that seem to fit more easily with the Catholic tradition. The leading edge of the transformation, that is, may be chosen because of religious commitments, but the appearance that the institution is or is becoming distinctively Catholic may be misleading because it is drawn from an era of transition.[15]

These general observations about Catholic legal education as legal education form the background for the more detailed examination of models of church-law school interaction that follows. They do, of course, introduce a strongly cautionary note, that in the main we are unlikely to find much more than small effects on the margin.[16]

One model might be that of a national Catholic undergraduate college or, more to the point, a local Catholic law school. The former can make its mission the creation of a leadership group for the national Catholic community; the latter can similarly make its mission the creation of such a group for the local Catholic community. The very reasons that such institutions can have such missions, though, make it difficult for a national law school to adopt their analogue, that is, providing leadership for the national Catholic community. Undergraduate colleges deal with young people whose characters are still in the formative stages, and they can recruit a student body whose predisposition lies in the direction of Catholic leadership. Local law schools can recruit students whose ties to the community often will include participation in Catholic activities.

The graduates will use their community ties, again often with religious connections, to build practices that will serve, for example, the local Catholic small business community.

National law schools are in a different position. Their students, unlike those of undergraduate colleges, come to them with more fully formed characters. These law schools will inevitably have to recruit their students from a pool of applicants that is less heavily Catholic than the pool for colleges, if only because the graduates of Catholic colleges will be interested in a wide range of postgraduate activities, not just law school. The faculties at national law schools will be drawn predominantly from other, primarily secular, national law schools, and are unlikely to be comfortable if their institution defines its mission as providing Catholic leadership. At most, the students at a national Catholic law school will be disproportionately Catholic, though probably not enough so to give the organized life of the student body a distinctively Catholic tone. Thus, as they pass through law school, students at such an institution are unlikely to receive messages strong enough to have much influence on their already formed characters, to the effect that they should think of themselves as future leaders of the national Catholic community.

Finally, and perhaps most importantly, the careers of graduates of a national Catholic law school are unlikely to provide many opportunities for leadership *qua* Catholic lawyer. Local small business communities are often enough segmented by ethnicity and consequently by religion to allow a local lawyer to develop a practice among Catholics, thereby being in a position to provide local leadership. In countries other than the United States, the national economy may be similarly segmented. In the United States, though, graduates of national law schools are diffused throughout the economy, providing service and advice to large corporations that have no particular religious character. Neither in law school nor afterwards, then, are students at and graduates of a national Catholic law school likely to encounter conditions conducive to defining their roles as leaders of the Catholic community. Under these circumstances a law school with a Catholic orientation that defined itself as a national law school would be ill advised to take its Catholic mission to be providing such leaders.

A second model of church-law school interaction focuses primarily on the organized activities of the law school itself, and only secondarily on the long-term effects of those activities on law students. This is the model of the Catholic law school as the provider of service to the needy.

Of course, a law school might provide such service to demonstrate to its students in a concrete way that the law school values the activity, thereby assisting them to value it in the same way. The aim in this second model, though, is not to produce many graduates who will devote their careers to the direct provision of service to the needy; that would be unrealistic even for local law schools. Instead the aim is to produce lawyers who, as members of the bar, will support such organizations as the national Legal Services Corporation and local legal aid services even though they do not work for them.

Law schools provide services to the needy primarily through their programs of clinical legal education.[17] For present purposes it is sufficient to note that clinical legal education is a form of education in which students learn by providing services to individuals—impoverished consumers or tenants, prisoners or criminal defendants—and, sometimes, to governments. Clinical legal education has by now achieved an established but marginal position in law schools. It is likely to remain marginal for reasons that would make it difficult for a national Catholic law school to define its mission in terms of service to the needy.

First, faculties at national law schools tend to believe that clinicians are not as academically acute as members of the classroom faculty. They will admit one or two clinicians to the tenure track, but rarely will everyone whose full-time job is clinical education be on the tenure track, even though everyone whose full-time job is classroom education will be. This disparity alone would relegate clinical education to the margins.[18] Classroom faculty are probably wrong in their judgment of the intellectual quality of clinicians. Because law faculties have developed strong norms of conflict avoidance,[19] in their hiring they tend to defer to members of the faculty who assert special qualifications to assess the candidates for appointment in a particular area. The effect is that faculties tend to replicate themselves so that everyone will be satisfied that his or her own style of being a legal educator is valid. This pattern appears to characterize the hiring of clinical faculty as well, which means that the distribution of intellectual ability will be roughly the same in the classroom and clinical faculties. Nonetheless, law faculties, particularly those making the transition to national status, find it hard to acknowledge that fact. Hiring, retention, and promotion decisions are made one at a time, which means that it will be only the rare faculty member, or the one or two on the relevant committee(s), who will see the pattern. In addition, most faculty members regard the transition to national status as a process of upgrading. The argument that this particular clinician is at least as good as some of the lesser lights already in the classroom faculty will therefore carry little weight. Finally, the physical isolation of the clinical faculty means that members of the classroom faculty will not be as willing to give the benefit of the doubt to the clinicians; such willingness as to other members of the classroom faculty arises out of the regular social interactions that occur among people who share the same building. The perception of lower intellectual quality is thus likely to persist, and along with it the marginal status of clinical education.

The intellectual quality of clinical education, whatever it is, is related to a second problem faced by clinicians. Simply put, clinical education is more expensive than classroom education. It involves more teachers dealing intensively with fewer students. The fundamental question about the cost of clinical education is comparative: How cost-effective is clinical education compared to classroom education? Proselytizers for and dedicated opponents of clinical education have offered their judgments on that question, but we have essentially no answers of any substance. If, however, the previous point about the similarity in distribution of intellectual ability is correct, there is reason to believe that clinical education is not as cost-effective as classroom education.[20] Clinical educators have responded to cost concerns by characterizing their activities as "skills training," and by substituting less expensive educational methods such as simulations via videotape for client-contact methods. Although that substitution may allay cost concerns, it obviously undercuts the contributions clinical education makes to the service mission of the law school.

A third problem contributes to the difficulty a national Catholic law school would have in making service via clinical education central to its mission. Precisely because clinical education involves providing services to needy individuals—that is, to people—it is more consistent with the orientation of local than of national law schools. The corporate employers of graduates of national law schools tend to see clinical education as a frill, perhaps desirable when added to education in subjects thought to be important to serving organizational clients but certainly no substitute for that education. Further, to some extent a law school is national because of its reputation, and national reputations tend to rest on the contributions the law faculty makes to the fields of interest to organizational clients.[21] Concentrating on clinical education is, once again, unlikely to contribute to that reputation. Here too the national status of a law school and its Catholic mission conceived in terms of service are in tension.

A third model of church-law school interaction stresses the contribution the law school's intellectual work can make to the church. Timothy S. Healy, S.J., President of Georgetown University, 1976-89, has argued that the United States legal system has a rich body of law and insight dealing with an individual's relation to organizations that affect him or her. In particular, the due process concerns for fair procedures embodied in constitutional law could, Healy argues, inform the development of canon law. This model has several advantages. It flatters the faculty of the law school, and it allows the law school to see itself, or be seen, as Catholic without doing more than having some sort of specialization in constitutional law. Because constitutional law is one of the prestige specialties in national law schools,[22] this should be easy enough.

However, this model faces what might be called analytical and institutional difficulties. The analytical difficulties arise from the increased knowledge we have about the relation between due process and specific institutions. At the outset of the due process revolution, it seemed to the Warren Court that the core procedures of criminal trials—advance notice of charges specified in some detail, the opportunity to confront adverse witnesses, counsel, and the like—could be used without substantial modification in other contexts.[23] As due process ideas took hold in new contexts, though, it became clear that different institutions had characteristics that made the full-fledged due process model inapposite. The opportunity to confront adverse witnesses, for example, was problematic in the context of prisons.[24] It also became clear that institutions, like universities, which do not stand in as strongly an adversarial posture to their various clienteles are likely to develop procedures for dealing with situations in which adversarial positions are taken—student and faculty discipline, academic retention, faculty promotion—that are suitable to the institution and are fundamentally fair even if they do not fit the full-fledged due process model.[25]

We have learned that procedures are often institution-specific, and properly so.[26] It is therefore not analytically obvious that due process models developed to deal with the institutions that have been the subjects of constitutional litigation would be appropriate when applied to the church. Further analysis of the church might show, of course, that some analogies are appropriate. At this point, though, the institutional difficulties with this model of church-law school interaction arise. The faculty at a national law school is unlikely to be sensitive to the particular characteristics of the church insofar as those characteristics might affect fair procedures, for the reasons regarding faculty recruitment mentioned earlier. Under those circumstances it is not clear why the academic product of law schools should be appropriated by the church.

This difficulty could be reduced were the faculty to become educated in the problems of the church that intersect their secular specialties. It is not difficult to imagine an institutional form for that endeavor. A Catholic university following this model could locate an "Institute" at its law school. The Institute could be headed by an academically qualified Catholic who had specialized in constitutional law. It could sponsor faculty colloquia on relevant issues, use university and other resources to provide released time for faculty research on church-related issues, and the like. These activities would simultaneously educate the law school's faculty and validate their church-related research. Unfortunately, the institutional form of an institute, while probably essential to the success of the enterprise, may well conflict with the aspiration to national status. As mentioned earlier, reputation is one component of status. Law schools can sponsor specialized programs, but these will add to the school's reputation as a national law school only if the programs seem to have general significance, as with the Harvard program on professional ethics. Even worse, programs that lack this general appeal are likely to confirm the narrowness of the law school's aspirations, thus confining it to the same status as local law schools, which are thought to have similarly narrow aspirations. An institute devoted to church-related issues would be too obviously sectarian, and would therefore be likely to impair the law school's effort to gain national status.

Once a Catholic law school had secured national status, it might be free to pursue such initiatives without loss of reputation, secure in its national status and therefore able to retain a Catholic identity without fear of being regarded as a marginal institution. This suggests a final model, in which the national Catholic law school is Catholic because it orients itself to a distinctive Catholic tradition. One version of this model might be that a national law school is an essential component of a great Catholic university, whether or not the law school itself is distinctively Catholic, because the secular society values the national law school whose presence thereby validates the university's Catholic mission. The law school becomes, in this model, part of the university's, and the church's, "teaching dialogue with the world."

Here the Catholic law school provides legal education first, and perhaps, in some sense, exclusively, but it does so not to provide access for the children of immigrants to a form of professional power but to enhance the university's religious mission. The primary difficulty with this model is that such orientations are most often derived from the desires and characteristics of a law school's faculty. In this connection it seems significant that the Georgetown University Law Center, a Jesuit institution, has only one Jesuit on its faculty of over seventy members, and that no Catholic law school, local or national, has any significant numbers of faculty members from the teaching orders. This difficulty might be alleviated, though probably not entirely overcome, by a leadership that was sensitive to the law school's Catholic tradition. For example, a dean could include in his or her descriptions of programs the specifically Catholic reasons for the law school's choice of programs, along with the secular reasons common to all national law schools.

If we consider an alternative to an institute, we can see how each of the models discussed above might have some impact on the margins of a national law school's activities. Most law schools have some endowed lectureships to bring scholars of national reputation to deliver addresses to the law school community. Most law schools also have funds for faculty workshops and colloquia, in which work in progress is discussed less formally. A law school could devote a substantial portion of these resources to programs that would emphasize the school's Catholic affiliations. For example, a number of prominent religious thinkers, not all of them theologians, have devoted substantial attention to topics of interest to legal scholars.[27] These people could be invited to give endowed lectures. Precisely because such lectures are not well integrated in the law school's ongoing activities, giving them a religious focus would not impair the law school's status as a national law school. For the same reason, of course, they would not become an important part of the law school's self-defined mission.

In the end, something along those lines is the likely outcome of any effort to incorporate a specifically Catholic focus into a national law school. Some of the law school's activities might be somewhat intensified, as with clinical education and affirmative action, or directed in slightly different ways, as with the use of discretionary funds to support lectures, under a leadership that interpreted general trends in legal education by placing them within a Catholic framework. Such a law school would take its primary identification from its national status. Its identification as Catholic would be at best subsidiary. In this, of course, we see once again the pattern that Stevens identified at the outset of legal education at Georgetown.

Notes

I would like to thank Thomas Shaffer and David McCarthy, and the participants in the Bicentennial Faculty Seminar on American Catholic Higher Education, for their comments on a draft of this essay.

1. Joseph T. Durkin, S.J., *Georgetown University: The Middle Years, 1840-1900* (Washington, D.C.: Georgetown University Press, 1963), 95.

2. Robert Stevens, *Law School: Legal Education in America from the 1850s to the 1980s* (Chapel Hill, N.C., and London: University of North Carolina Press, 1983), 40, 74-75.

3. In this essay I use examples from Georgetown because it is the Catholic school with which I am most familiar, but I believe that the examples are indeed typical.

4. Though I have no specialized training as a participant-observer, the Bicentennial of Georgetown University is an appropriate occasion to examine this process. The University's Law Center successfully went through most of the transition from a local to a national school, and yet it did so recently enough for particular aspects of the process to be readily identified. More specifically, many of the faculty who were hired in the early years of the transition remember the institution as it was when they arrived, and often react to current proposals by invoking the imagery of backsliding and a return to the past. A participant-observer in the debates that occur at present thus can gain a rather good feel for how the transition reshaped—albeit incompletely—the institution's self-image.

5. The source of the following analysis is John P. Heinz and Edward O. Laumann, *Chicago Lawyers: The Social Structure of the Bar* (New York: Russell Sage Foundation; Chicago: American Bar Foundation, 1982), who studied the Chicago bar but whose conclusions are generally agreed to apply to the practice of law throughout the country. It should be noted, however, that there are some special cases for which the generalizations may hold true and yet for which the course of development I discuss was somewhat different.

6. The shorthand is inaccurate to the extent that it does not treat local governments, served by graduates of local law schools, as organizations. For additional discussion, see note 7 below.

7. Even when graduates of local law schools work for organizations, particularly for local governments, they tend to work as low-level line attorneys who implement rather than make public policy.

8. Robert Pitofsky, Letter to Law Center Alumni and Alumnae et al., 15 June 1989.

9. Like other law schools, Georgetown has responded to this gap by developing a relatively modest program of loan forgiveness for graduates who engage in public interest careers.

10. I should report that I do hear occasional comments at professional meetings on the fact that Georgetown still has an evening division. Usually, these comments come from teachers at local law schools who appear to take some comfort in the fact that Georgetown retains its evening division.

11. This statement is simply impressionistic on my part; I know of no statistics on the class origins of students at local and national law schools. Affirmative action programs, which seem to be somewhat more extensive at national law schools, do something to broaden the class base, though national law schools are in a better position to use affirmative action programs to "skim the cream" and draw from the upper reaches of the class hierarchy in minority communities.

12. Robert W. Gordon, "'The Ideal and the Actual in the Law': Fantasies and Practices of New York City Lawyers, 1870-1910," in *The New High Priests: Lawyers in Post-Civil War America*, ed. Gerald W. Gawalt (Westport, Conn., and London: Greenwood Press, 1984), 51.

13. Along the lines of the transformation of ideology described by Gordon, for example, Catholic legal educators can say, in accordance with certain aspects of Catholic social thought, that their students will work through organized bodies to provide the most effective service to people, as in the case of lawyers who provide "responsible" corporate counselling.

14. A similar point could be made about the commitment at Georgetown to affirmative action, a commitment that does not seem to differ substantially from that at a number of other law schools.

15. An example may be provided by the role that courses in jurisprudence play in Catholic law schools. In the past these courses undoubtedly focused on the natural law tradition in its Catholic incarnations, and that tradition provided the inspiration for Notre Dame's *American Journal of Jurisprudence*, but at present courses in jurisprudence in Catholic law schools almost certainly resemble jurisprudence courses in secular law schools. (My sense, drawn only from a quite informal exposure to law school catalogues, is that in the past jurisprudence courses at Catholic law schools were taught disproportionately by members of the teaching orders; I suspect that today an advanced degree in philosophy is disproportionately required. [I should add that of course there is no incompatibility between having such a degree and being a member of a teaching order.])

16. It may be worth noting that the arguments that follow suggest that it might be easier to preserve the Catholic character of local law schools than of national ones. However, an informal survey of deans of Catholic law schools, reported by Rex Lee, suggests that virtually all of them, most of whom were deans at local law schools, saw their institutions in the same way. *The Role of the Religious Law School*, 30 VILL. L.REV. 1175, 1176-77 (1985).

17. We could conceptualize affirmative action programs in similar terms. If so, problems parallel to those discussed in the text about clinical education would arise. In particular, there is necessarily a tension between efforts to "upgrade" a school using traditional criteria of quality, and affirmative action programs. Yet

those traditional criteria are precisely what must be utilized if a local law school is to become a national one. One hopes that the long-term effects of affirmative action programs will include a transformation of those criteria, but that seems not to have happened yet.

18. An indication of the marginality of clinical legal education is the fact that at a large majority of law schools the offices of the clinic are not in the same location as the law school. The articulated reasons tend to include that the clients of the clinic are elsewhere, that the clients are not entirely trustworthy and cannot be allowed to roam through the law school's premises, and that clinical programs expanded after law school buildings were completed. Some of the reasons are often valid, but the cumulative effect is to remove the clinic from the law school in a quite physical sense.

19. The reasons for the existence of those norms are not entirely clear to me. I suspect that they include the questionable intellectual status of much legal research. In departments of sciences and the humanities, there are strong conflicts over methods and the like. If such conflicts were allowed to arise in law schools, virtually everyone would discover that the emperor had no clothes. The resistance law faculties displayed to the scientific pretensions of advocates of "law and economics" analysis, and that they continue to display to the interdisciplinary scavenging of critical legal studies, suggests the difficulty.

20. And, of course, the point carries a fortiori if the classroom teachers' perception of the clinicians is correct.

21. For example, Georgetown and New York University Law School both have strong programs in corporate and tax law, which have materially helped them in making the transition. An exception to the generalization about reputation resting on contributions to areas of concern to organizational clients is the role that scholarship in torts and contracts has in generating a national reputation. For some discussion, see note 22 below.

22. Oddly enough, so are contracts and torts, quintessentially private law subjects. In part, prestige rests on having a combination of scholars who collectively cover the core of both private and public law. In part, the private law topics are prestigious because they are the domain in which hostility to government can be expressed.

23. Goldberg v. Kelly, 397 U.S. 254 (1970); In re Gault, 387 U.S. 1 (1967).

24. Baxter v. Palmigiano, 425 U.S. 308 (1976); Wolff v. McDonnell, 418 U.S. 539 (1974).

25. Board of Curators v. Horowitz, 435 U.S. 78 (1978).

26. I should emphasize that the process was not simply the abandonment by a conservative Supreme Court of liberal precedents. The Burger Court continued to endorse the due process model in contexts where it believed the model to fit. See, e.g., Wolff v. McDonnell, 418 U.S. 539 (1974); Vitek v. Jones, 445 U.S. 480 (1980).

27. I think of Bryan Hehir, Michael Novak, Stanley Hauerwas, and John Howard Yoder.

ELIZABETH PRELINGER
Department of Fine Arts

"From her Spires and Steeples Beaming": Mission and Image in Bricks and Stone

The occasion of Georgetown's Bicentennial provides an excellent opportunity to reflect upon the architecture of our hilltop campus. The subject has become of ever-increasing interest to all of us, not only as the University moves into its third century, but as our building programs become more and more ambitious. The Leavey Center was just completed last year and, strolling around the campus today, one can see such sights as Maguire undergoing thorough renovation, Harbin Hall receiving a new brick surface, and a newly landscaped plaza surrounding Dahlgren Chapel.

On the one hand, this campus has generated a great deal of affection; Healy Hall, in particular, is undoubtedly our symbol. On the other hand, people express confusion and frustration with what they view as a mish-mash of styles and an abundance of eyesores, with candidates for least favorite building ranging from New South to Lauinger Library. Even back in 1932, a student wrote: "When we Seniors first came to Georgetown, we had little answer to the joking remarks passed by our visitors from other colleges on the appearance of the school. The best answer we could supply was that the real worth of Georgetown was under the surface."[1] "Fortunately," observed another, "we have never tolerated the fallacy that buildings make the university; our history proves them the least important element in its economy."[2] This apologetic view has persisted throughout the history of the school.

Those days, one hopes, are over. Rather than making excuses, now is the time to try to understand our campus. This enterprise naturally rests on what for Georgetown is a belated, but nonetheless crucial, realization that, simply, architecture is important. Like the other arts, but even more visibly, architecture tells who we were, are, and what we want to be. In the interest of exploring how our buildings express the history of the school, several key questions need to be posed: Why does Georgetown look the way it does, both in terms of the layout of the buildings and their styles? How did we get where we are? Is there anything particularly Catholic about our architecture? How does the architecture of the Hilltop reflect our mission, or ideals? And where do we want to go in our third century? This essay will address these issues and suggest directions in which we might be headed.

Three principal factors seem to have affected the development of the campus and continue to dominate our notions of building and campus planning. The first is site. The college has a strong sense of place; sited up on the banks of the Potomac River, it overlooks the capital city of the United States, and is itself urban. Our location within the heavily regulated historic district of Georgetown has frequently determined planning and architectural styles. Because of stringent zoning, the University has been effectively confined to the one hundred and four acres it occupies and discouraged, when not outright prevented, from expanding further into the neighborhood. Consequently, the University has had to exploit the available land to its greatest potential. Buildings cluster together in intimate, even dense, configurations and multiple-use buildings dominate the campus in order to squeeze in as many functions as possible.

The second factor affecting campus growth has surely been finances. Lack of funds has been a severe problem and has probably made the most decisive impact on campus development. Frequently, Georgetown has had to settle for whatever was cheapest and most expedient, valuing function over appearance, with too little consideration for the fact that, in principle, it was building for posterity.

Third, perhaps partly due to funding, architecture has simply never been a priority here, as it has at other big eastern institutions. The officials of Georgetown did not seem to have the interest and possibly even the connections required to commission work from the most important practitioners of the eighteenth through the twentieth centuries, whose structures adorn other older East Coast campuses. There is no reason for this embedded in Jesuit tradition. Indeed, the baroque marvels of the European Jesuit tradition, such as the Society's main church in Rome, Il

Gesù, the mother church of the baroque style, suggest otherwise. Rather, our struggling institution in the New World sought to establish its Americanness, reflected in the simple styles it chose, while expressing its Catholic identity in other ways. The result of these three factors has been only a few great buildings and a lack of consistent, rational planning for our small, strictly circumscribed campus.

1. From the Founding to 1877

The development of the Hilltop may be roughly divided into four periods. The first represents the period from the founding through the antebellum era, from about 1788 to 1877, in which the early campus was laid out with its Federal style red-brick facilities.

Georgetown's first student, William Gaston, was so impressed on his first visit to the school that he wrote to his mother:

> A more beautiful situation than this in which the College is, could not be imagined; on a high hill with a view on one side of the river, on the other of the town, quite surrounded with trees, and everything that could make it either beautiful or useful, it stands as if it were made on purpose for the erecting of some such building.[4]

But unlike the University of Virginia, for example, where Thomas Jefferson's cultivated architectural vision created a unified grove of academe in the countryside of Charlottesville, Georgetown evolved in piecemeal fashion, filling needs in the best way possible as they arose.

Initially, there were few students and the campus subsisted on relatively minimal facilities until the building boom of the early twentieth century. It built according to need and finances, depending upon the initiative of the presidents, electing the most basic and most American style, the contemporary Federal, red-brick constructions of simple and classic proportions. The new college initially organized its facilities on the east-west axis, facing the Potomac River, and maintained that orientation until the construction of Healy, when it had quite a different statement to make.

The first building on the Hilltop was Old South, erected in 1788, and kept in service until 1904. It was used as an all-purpose building to house students and classrooms. McSherry, the oldest standing building on campus, was constructed in 1792; a former bakery, it now houses the most advanced telecommunications technology.

The first structure of major importance was Old North, whose plan was approved in 1792. The rather grand Georgian design may have been based on Princeton's Nassau Hall, 1753-55, with its tripartite organization and center pediment. Like Nassau Hall, it contained almost all of the college's functions, one of the first of Georgetown's many "mixed-use" facilities. This idea originated because the college had a small enrollment with little land or money, and it has continued to the recent construction of the Leavey Center.

When Old North was built, it was surely one of the grandest works in Washington, after the Capitol Building. School and college buildings were the biggest existing structures of this era, reflecting the country's commitment to education.[4] The towers were not added until 1808-10, as buttresses to keep the structure from sliding into the ravine. There are many legends connected with this red-brick building but George Washington did, in fact, visit Old North, as did General Lafayette and Marshal Foch. It also housed Union troops during the Civil War. The School of Business is currently located in its newly refurbished interior.

The school began to take shape as enrollment climbed in the first decades of the nineteenth century. By the beginning of 1814, we hear that there are one hundred and two residents of Georgetown college, permitting improvements in living arrangements, a new recreation room and guest room in Old North and a new parlor in Old South. Also, Father McElroy records that there is "a permanent gravel road from the new college door to the gate."[5]

For the next several decades, new facilities for the Jesuit community were built: what is now known as Gervase was built in two sections in 1830 and in 1848, Mulledy in 1833, and Maguire in 1854, extending the south axis and making the enclosure more pronounced. All conformed to the simple red-brick style existing on campus. In 1904, Old South was razed, with the elegant Ryan Hall added in its place, though it lives on in its porch, now attached to Gervase and commemorated by a plaque.

The college was also expanding in terms of research facilities. In the first of a number of instances in which Georgetown would follow fashionable trends in campus planning, an observatory was built in 1843-44 at a cost of $7,910.59. It was part of a fashion sweeping the country to "allow an even grander and more sublime view of nature," and was intended to counteract materialism by elevating "students' thought toward that fathomless fountain and author of being."[6] The site for many years of the pioneering work of astronomer John Hagan, S.J., who arrived in 1870, it is now listed in the National Register of Historic Places.

The Civil War followed and for a number of years all further progress on the campus was halted. But after the war, Georgetown began to build edifices appropriate to the major university it had become. This was largely due to the vision of Patrick Healy, who became president in 1873.

2. From Healy Hall to White-Gravenor

Among Patrick Healy's achievements, the one that most concerns us here is the construction of Healy Hall, the greatest landmark of the campus. Unlike his predecessors, Healy believed that an excellent physical plant, in addition to students and ideas, would create a great institution. Healy Hall in many ways physically embodies the soul of the school. Its grandeur signalled a new era in both the architectural and the general history of Georgetown, and it has become a visual symbol of the campus and a material embodiment of the ideals of the college. As is so frequently true with massive architectural projects, the building was as much a statement about the power and stature of Georgetown as the American Louvain as it was about the very real and crucial functions it fulfilled. Designated a National Historic Landmark in 1987, it was chosen to grace the postcard issued by the Post Office on the occasion of the Bicentennial.

Several interesting factors form the background of Healy Hall. Built some ninety years after Georgetown was founded, with the exterior completed in 1879, the timing of construction was also significant, following, as it did, the victory of the Northern states in the Civil War. The stability and permanence of the United States had been restored and there was a sense that a safe investment could be made in the future of the country as well as the school. Further, it was becoming clear to Patrick Healy that it was necessary to establish the legitimacy of Georgetown as the preeminent Catholic university in the country. Emmett Curran has suggested that Healy deliberately reoriented his building to face the city and not the river, effectively signalling Georgetown's wish to view itself as an educational institution of national importance and altering the direction of expansion on the campus for years to come. Healy Hall also served to enclose the quadrangle begun by Old South and its neighbors and Old North on the opposite side, though its principal façade did not face them.

To promote this ideal of permanence and power, Healy chose the firm of J.L. Smithmeyer & Co. Smithmeyer (1832-1903), an Austrian by birth, and his associate, the Prussian Paul Pelz (1841-1918), later went on to other distinguished commissions, such as the Library of Congress. Of the many eclectic styles prevailing in Victorian America, Smithmeyer and Pelz based their design on what has been called everything from "neo-Gothic, Medieval Revival, Victorian Gothic with an American sea-change, American Second Empire and Flemish or Rhineland Romanesque."[7] Certainly eclectic, like many major works of the period, it emphasizes heavy stone masonry, rounded arches, and picturesque turrets with decorative finials and imposing towers—in particular, the looming clock tower. Through this style, Smithmeyer and Pelz conjured up a stately European past, a milieu of culture and learning, while simultaneously being up-to-date. It was influenced by the Antwerp Town Hall and may even have had a modern precedent in the Parliament House in Ottawa, built in 1861-67 by Thomas Fuller, Chilion Jones, and others. The style was also related to, if less original than, the Romanesque Revival work of the preeminent architect of the time, Henry Hobson Richardson, whose designs set the current standard of quality and were widely copied. At this very time, Richardson was designing campus buildings for Harvard.

Massive in scale, Healy is 312 feet long and 95 feet wide, with the clock tower rising 200 feet. At its highest point, the spire soars to 334.40 feet above the Potomac, an impressive sight.[8] There are 3,000 cubic feet of stone, more than two million bricks and 350,000 feet of yellow Georgia pine. The heavy stones for Healy were transported from nearby Virginia and selected for their gray variations to produce a subtly colored façade. The richly pictorial quality effectively balances the massivity of its proportions, enhancing its aura of fortress-like strength, authority, and Victorian elegance. Visitors, as well as students, could only be awed by a building whose presence suggested the transition from the quiet, rather countrified campus to an imposing urban institution. This transition is literally built into Healy; the imposing ceremonial frontal façade is faced in expensive stone while the rear is faced in red brick to harmonize with the existing Federal style structures. Its appearance evokes church architecture and, on the rear façade, signs of the cross have been molded into the brick design.

The building was dogged from the first by financial problems, sadly not an untypical situation for the college. Durkin relates that, although

Healy Hall finally cost $300,000, the initial loan was inadequate, and it eventually all but wiped out Patrick Healy and the coffers of the college.[9]

Much like the Leavey Center today, slightly over a century later, Healy was designed as a comprehensive student complex. Students occupied living quarters on the top floors; they would then descend the stone stairways to the classrooms on the lower floors. Again, it is noteworthy that Georgetown chose not to separate living quarters from learning facilities. Rather than being guided by the notion of the residential college system, for example, based on the English university system, the college chose as its model an all-inclusive facility, perhaps comparable to an academy or monastery.

Currently, the more public functions of the building predominate. These include the offices of the president and the university chaplains, classrooms, and the bioethics library. Further, Healy Hall houses the historic Philodemic Society Room, the Hall of Cardinals, and the principal assembly room of the campus, Gaston Hall.

Due to the ever-present funding difficulties, in part because of the lack of alumni support, parts of Healy remained unfinished until as much as twenty years after completion of the façade. Gaston Hall, in particular, was left a large, open, "barn-like" space. This much needed auditorium remained draped in great cloths, largely because no permanent design satisfied the wishes of the architect, Paul Pelz. Finally, in 1900, the University hired Brother Francis Schroen, S.J., to decorate the room.

The talented young Schroen had lost his family to illness, in his grief experimented with the occult, and finally embraced the religious life, entering the Jesuit novitiate in 1898. Early on, he showed a talent for decorating churches. Gaston Hall was his first great commission as a Jesuit lay brother. Working entirely freehand, Brother Schroen painted a whole program of decorative and symbolic ornament and allegorical murals, emphasizing the great Jesuit ideals and educators. His work exemplifies the contemporary classical revival styles which were at that precise moment transforming the face of Washington, D.C., into the ideal of the City Beautiful. Schroen's goal of "nationalism, idealism and cosmopolitanism" was entirely consonant with the times and with the image that Georgetown wanted to promote.[10]

Among the most beautiful places on campus is the historic Riggs Library in the Healy building, which remained the college library until Lauinger opened in 1970. Completed about 1901, the beautifully decorated library comprised a reading room on the first floor and study space with four levels of open stacks spanning the second and third floors in the south pavilion of the building. In 1982 a renovation was completed, winning a first-place award from the American Institute of Architects.

The all-important construction of the Healy building represented a watershed in the history of the campus, significantly augmenting the prestige of the school. Linking Old North and Maguire, the new grouping of buildings formed a quadrangle, an integral feature of American campus planning, around which college activity centered. Until the 1930s, with the construction of Copley and White-Gravenor, this was the heart of the campus.

Dahlgren Chapel was an important addition to the Hilltop. The first building to be named after a non-Jesuit and the first to be completely financed by outside gifts, it anchored the historic quadrangle, surrounded by Healy, Old North, Maguire, Mulledy, Gervase, and later Ryan, and completed what became a consoling and protective enclave. The brick and stone structure was consecrated on June 9, 1893. The donors specified a roughly Gothic style, not to be too fancy and to cost ten thousand dollars. It maintains the red-brick motif of the campus.

The year 1926 saw the building of an addition to one of the college's earliest structures, Old North. Besides the brick façade, which we have come to expect and even to require, New North was conceived as another of the multi-functional facilities that the University has found so useful throughout its history.

Several years later, the orientation of the college would change once again with the construction of two works of central importance to the campus. Copley Hall[11] and White-Gravenor[12] were completed in 1932 and 1933, respectively, on the site of the former playing fields. These were crucial to the configuration of the Hilltop because now the main quadrangle was oriented away from the Healy-Old and New North-Maguire enclosure, to the lawns facing 37th Street and the historic district of Georgetown. The acceptance of this setting was confirmed some forty years later with the final spatial anchor set into place in the form of Lauinger Library.

Although the two buildings looked out onto the quaint Georgetown façades, they did not in fact conform architecturally with the use of brick. They diverged from existing styles by adopting the "Collegiate Gothic" mode, pioneered earlier in the century by Ralph Adams Cram, architect and designer of Princeton University. This look had become fashionable in the mid-nineteenth century and again in the 1920s, notably in many of the new residential colleges of Yale University.

Both Georgetown buildings were designed by the same architect, Emile G. Perrot, who was working from an accepted, even fashionable, trend of college planning when he chose this style. They look ecclesiastical but that was a factor of the style, and not a particularly Catholic outlook. What was Catholic and specifically Jesuit were the programs of decoration, which include the sign of the cross, the Latin motto of the Society of Jesus, and seals related to famous Jesuit educators and learned societies within the college. The materials, grayish-brown Port Deposit granite with lighter limestone trimmings, and the massing of the two buildings were intended to harmonize with the Healy building, so there was a sensitivity to context. The White-Gravenor building, companion piece to Copley, firmly and eloquently finishes off the north end of the front lawn.

With these new constructions, the campus and its growing activities were able to shift yet again as space permitted, and the ecclesiastical resonance of the buildings promoted the ideals of the college. At a recent senior dinner a student described his amazement upon his first visit to campus: "There were three churches in the quad!"

3. From World War II through the 1960s

The third period, from the late forties on, was characterized by functional, expedient building as Georgetown rapidly expanded the hospital facilities and increased student housing to provide for veterans in search of a college education and the rising number of women on campus. In 1946, the University even converted a barn near McSherry Hall into a dormitory, named in honor of Martin J. O'Gara, S.J., a military chaplain who died in a plane crash at the end of World War II.

The 1950s brought new commitment on the part of the University to athletics. Completed in 1951, McDonough Gymnasium served this purpose well for many years, but it has been superseded by the construction in 1979 of the Yates Field House.

As the Main Campus schools continued to grow, several functional but undistinguished dormitories were constructed or remodeled. New South was completed in September 1959; Harbin Hall and Darnall Hall were completed in November 1965. These buildings tended simply to respect the historical use of brick. In the late 1970s and 1980s as well, the college has made a concerted effort to build living quarters for as many students as possible. This harks back to the early years of the college and reflects the Jesuit ideal of living and learning as well as a time-honored notion of American college planning, namely, that "higher education is fully effective only when students eat, sleep, study, worship, and play together in a tight community."[13]

New South, built by Walton and Madden, is, in appearance, possibly the least favorite of all the buildings on campus; it is startlingly uncollegiate and unrelievedly utilitarian. According to some, it was based on prison design or on welfare housing projects.[14] Others claim that President Lyndon B. Johnson found it to be the most serious blight existing on the D.C. skyline.

A study of the archival materials reveals some interesting facts. Originally, the new dormitory was planned to fill in Healy lawn, to rise in the place now occupied by Lauinger Library. In that case, it would have been designed in the Collegiate Gothic style! As it stands, New South obviously represents the cheapest kind of construction available. It was completed under a deadline; new housing was needed by fall. The cafeteria opened to fanfare in February 1960, at the time the "biggest non-military food services in the Washington area."[15]

Harbin Hall was Georgetown's first high-rise dormitory, reflecting the contemporary hegemony of the skyscraper in American culture. Built upon some sixty to eighty feet of landfill over what used to be the beautiful "Walks," the original green spaces on campus, the building was evidently thought to be sensible in terms of space-saving, a maximum of footage with the minimum of acreage. It is currently being resurfaced with red brick to blend more harmoniously with its surroundings.

This third building period also saw construction of the Edmund A. Walsh Building for the School of Foreign Service. Designed by the firm of Murphy and Locraft, the building was dedicated by President Eisenhower on October 13, 1958. Containing classrooms and the Hall of Nations, Walsh was one of the first academic, as opposed to residential, facilities to leave the campus and venture into the neighborhood. Assembled in the prevailing institutional style of brick and glass, it nevertheless has a jazzy paint combination of dark turquoise and orange.

During the late 1950s and early 1960s, there was a boom in scientific and technological research. At Georgetown, this interest, which had started early in the history of the institution with the Observatory, led to the construction in 1962 of the Raymond Reiss Science Building.

With its brick façades and concrete entrance overhang, it is functional above all.

4. From Lauinger Library to the Leavey Center

The final period begins with the construction of Lauinger Library, for which ground was broken on April 6, 1970; it opened two years later. After years of residing in historic Riggs Library in Healy Hall, Georgetown's books and students finally had adequate space, a comfortable study environment, typing rooms, discussion rooms, lounges, and study carrels.

A big, abstract form, Lauinger seems, like nonfigurative art, to be very difficult for many people to like; they find it ugly and jarring and are astonished that its construction was permitted at all. The architectural firm of John Carl Warnecke intended Lauinger to blend in with the adjacent buildings. However, they were not interested in the conventional strategy of imitating historical forms, but in reinterpreting the shapes of the campus from a modernist perspective. So, while on first glance Lauinger might appear anomalous, with further study it emerges as subtle and appropriate. The Fine Arts Commission at the time the design was presented included Gordon Bunschaft, partner at Skidmore, Owings and Merrill, and architect, among other distinguished works, of the Hirshhorn Museum on the Mall. Himself a maker of strongly imagistic modern forms, Bunschaft supported the plan, which departs from the traditional red-brick Georgetown look but relates to the stone façades of the buildings surrounding Healy and Copley Lawns.

This building needs further study since it is more difficult and abstract than its fellows. Neatly closing off the quadrangle formed on the front side of Healy Hall with the construction of Copley and White-Gravenor Halls, the library is entirely modern, relating to a style of the 1950s and 1960s called Brutalism. It has been carefully and sensitively conceived to blend in with the surrounding buildings. Its massing, for example, evokes the forms of Healy and in its material, an exposed granite chip concrete aggregate, sandblasted for a softer effect, it relates directly to Copley and White-Gravenor as well.

Further, the image that informed Warnecke's conception of the Hilltop was that of Mont-Saint-Michel, the rocky island off the coast of Normandy, on which there rises a Benedictine abbey, dating from the twelfth to the fourteenth centuries, surrounded by its supporting buildings and a town, all perched on a steep hill. Warnecke saw Georgetown's situation as similar, the lower structures balancing but not competing with the picturesque projections of the taller buildings. Finally, the irregular massing of Lauinger, with its emphasis on verticality and the play of solids and voids across the façades, was intended to reflect the wavy wall surfaces of the other buildings surrounding the front lawn. Lauinger is surely one of the most challenging and interesting works on campus and deserves to be looked at again.

The same year the University broke ground for Lauinger, it also took a step that was long overdue. A University architect, Dean Price, AIA, was hired in 1970 to oversee the planning of Georgetown's campus. This was crucial for the future direction of the campus and was the first indication that the University recognized a need for continuous and unified professional attention to its physical plant. Under Price's direction, a campus Master Plan was drawn up for the first time in Georgetown's history, suggesting guidelines for future additions, based on an overall scheme. The plans conceived since 1970 have included consideration of long-range projections for use of our space as well as general guidelines for the maintenance of a Georgetown stylistic idiom, human scale, green space, and so forth. The Plan viewed Georgetown as a residential campus and many of its guidelines were incorporated into the new dormitories constructed in this fourth period.

Henle Village was finished in September 1976, Village A in 1980, Alumni Square in 1983 and, most recently, Village C in 1986. More responsive to its surroundings than earlier dormitories, Henle Village was designed as a small, brick, student village based upon the notion of a little medieval or "Victorian Italianate" town. The planners saw it as an "academic village," a term used by Thomas Jefferson, which had also been recently expounded by Eero Saarinen. Saarinen's experience of small Italian villages influenced his design for Morse and Stiles, two of Yale's residential colleges, designs which probably informed Henle's configuration.[16] This kind of "human scale village with Georgetown characteristics in architecture and landscaping," conforms to the Georgetown "idiom," as it has been called, in its brick facing, but is rather disconcertingly stark.[17]

Commitment to human scale as well as lodging for physically challenged students were important factors in the construction of Village A, designed by John Carl Warnecke, Architects, in 1980, next to their Lauinger Library. The facility was intended to resemble a series of brick townhouses and relate in that way to the adjacent neighborhoods.

Graded downwards toward the Potomac in the rear, layers of decks promote community within the Village as well as provide panoramic views of the river and the Virginia shore.

The University has also slowly been moving into the neighborhood of Georgetown to develop its residential properties. Among these are the Nevils Complex (the old hospital now converted into apartments), and the townhouses on 37th Street, christened by the students "Party Row."

The University hired the Georgetown architect, Hugh Newell Jacobsen, FAIA, to design Alumni Square, which echoes the rhythms of Party Row. The primary objective was to blend in with the neighborhood, to create "a more residential versus institutional design."[18] Brick, bay and circular windows, courtyards, and wrought iron railings give the appearance of townhouses within a large complex and it is the best of the new designs in its sensitivity to scale and detail.

Most recently, Village C has been constructed along similar lines within the campus area. It, too, has utilized features that seem more and more to be becoming the vocabulary of our architecture, or its "Georgetown characteristics." This means brick masonry with ornamentation and windows which refer to historical buildings on campus, in particular, the Federal style structures and, of course, Healy Hall. Rather than being particularly modern, our recent buildings may be loosely described as contextual, that is, they utilize architectural elements which have historical references and allude to traditional styles and contexts. This is the architectural strategy that currently prevails at Georgetown and that in this case was legislated by the building code of the Georgetown neighborhood. Village C is visually agreeable and suitable, if not as sensitive as Alumni Square, and it apparently successfully counteracts the monotonic profile of New South when viewed from the Virginia shore.

During the fourth period, another abstract, modernist work, the Edward B. Bunn, S.J., Intercultural Center (ICC) was erected. Although the ICC is situated well north of what has been considered the "center" of the campus, that is, Healy Hall, its construction has redefined the hub. Built to house the School of Foreign Service, the School of Languages and Linguistics, the Graduate School, and the School for Summer and Continuing Education, it also contains faculty offices, classrooms, language and computer labs, all grouped around a central atrium space that reflects contemporary corporate and hotel design rather than university architecture. Meant to symbolize intercultural education, it provides a space where one can literally see across a great open area where the flags of many nations have been ceremonially suspended. A sense of communication is certainly conveyed here and provides an interior quite unlike anything else on campus.

In its use of materials the ICC conforms to the Georgetown ideal. The massing, however, does not relate to its environment and the empty plaza in front of the ICC, popularly called "Red Square," has proved rather inhospitable. Part of the ICC's brutal, heroic, high-tech form, however, relates to its genuinely high-tech features, specifically, the roof. The top of the ICC is layered with more than 36,680 photovoltaic cells, intended to convert the sun's energy into electricity that would service both this building and the rest of the university. In fact, the design was largely determined by what Dean Price has called the "severe physics" of photovoltaics; for example, the roof had to face due south at a certain angle. Also, it was a marvel of funding—the University received generous grants for pioneering this technology and credibility for further support from Congress. So, all these practical factors played a role and must be considered when evaluating the design.

Another of Georgetown's innovative and experimental engineering projects was the construction in 1979 of the Yates Field House. Yates was specially designed to be underground, mainly to conserve energy. The idea was that, since it would remain at the temperature of the surrounding earth, 62 degrees Fahrenheit, it would not need air conditioning. It has worked fairly well, though problems have arisen with dehumidification, air circulation, concrete shell construction, and the Astroturf on the roof, which serves as an outdoor playing field.[19]

The style chosen for Georgetown's newest building, the Thomas and Dorothy Leavey Center, suggests that contextual designs are felt to be the most congenial to our campus, that is, the echoing of our traditional architecture rather than modernist, abstract reinterpretations, as in Lauinger or the ICC. Faced in red-brick masonry with light stone trimming, the façade of the Leavey Center is intended to reflect the rear face of the Healy Building, which itself is covered in brick, rather than the more expensive stone. In its use of towers, it also echoes the massing of Healy. Yet again, the center of campus has shifted. It seems likely that, for the near future, especially since the new Academic Facility is planned to go up near the Reiss Science Building, University activities will be concentrated in this northern area of the campus.

A facility of colossal proportions, the Leavey Center houses Student

Affairs, the Georgetown University Student Association, clubs, activities, the University Book Store, student-run food shops, two restaurants, a student cafe, the faculty club, and a giant parking garage. The Marriott Corporation runs a guest house and conference facilities, a large part of the marketing of the facility. The densely packed room assignments are surrounded by long hallways around the perimeter of the building, for the most part containing seats in front of tall windows. On the top of the main building, a landscaped roof actually adds to the acreage of open green space on the campus.

Leavey suffers from a number of problems, of which scale is the greatest. Its proportions, described by one member of the Georgetown community as those of an international airport, make intimacy difficult. Further, the detailing and interior color scheme are rather weak and lacking in character. Nonetheless, Benjamin Forgey, architecture critic for the *Washington Post*, has aptly noted:

> In more recent projects the university has become more sensitive to its own architectural traditions and to the delicate balances between buildings and sections of the campus. The step—a leap, really—in the right direction and in the right place, too: The Leavey Center is strategically located to mediate between the institutional modern architecture of the medical complex and the finer textures of the historic campus.[20]

In fact, barring the recreation of the campus as a showcase of diverse architectural masterpieces, the historical style represented by Leavey is very probably the direction that makes the most sense for us on our small and densely settled Hilltop.

5. Looking to the Future

What about the future? What are our goals for the Hilltop campus?

There are different strategies. For example, A. Whitney Griswold, president of Yale in the 1950s, saw his campus as a laboratory. He commissioned the greatest architects of the twentieth century to design works for the much more spread-out New Haven campus, creating a diverse selection of masterpieces. At Princeton, the firm of Venturi, Rauch and Scott-Brown, which many consider to be the most significant and innovative firm working today, has designed exciting contextual works like

Gordon Wu Hall and the Lewis Thomas Biological Laboratories. These pick up on the historical textures of the existing campus while simultaneously making witty and completely original statements.

This more traditional contextualism is probably the ideal scenario for our own campus too, given our circumscribed space, dense organization and limited funds. One can convincingly argue for the wisdom of carefully organized configurations of buildings, adhering to architectural styles and materials that reflect and reinterpret our most valued existing buildings, in particular, our Federal style structures and Healy Hall. The Leavey Center has surely pointed us in that direction even if it has not been entirely successful. Further, it is part of a master plan that intends to maximize our usable acreage while maintaining green space and gradually becoming fuel efficient.

Leavey Center is the first of a planned series of "socioenergy podia" which will descend toward the Potomac, a visionary concept developed by the University architect. Like Leavey, these podia are layered configurations with green space on the top, and, immediately below, levels of multipurpose academic and educational support space. Below that are parking levels and various kinds of circulation systems. On the lowest level are energy conservation and cogeneration systems. Healy Circle has already been closed to routine vehicular traffic in preparation for the new south entrance, which would be marked with an elegant building whose design has been refined even further from the 1983 Campus Plan. It would welcome the visitor to this rationalized City Beautiful scheme, based on clear strong axes, which evokes the pavilions of the University of Virginia. The new rendering in the Bicentennial Master Plan shows even more green space and a pedestrian footway around the western border, along with increased footage for faculty, graduate, and staff housing. An energy-efficient and nonpolluting bus system would circulate around the campus and fuel-cell batteries placed in various areas would eventually make us largely energy-independent. It is a remarkable idea that presents an option for our future.

Nonetheless, for Dean Price and the other contributing members of campus planning committees, the Master Plan, as it unfolds, is not written in stone, or brick for that matter, but is rather a "living, daily effort."[21] This living plan would build upon judicious use of limited space, respect for context in architectural styles, both within the campus and within the community, and creation of a sense of place.

A fixed plan would, in fact, be neither desirable nor workable; a more fruitful way of addressing the problem might be to emphasize the establishment of "principles for future growth."[22] As Joseph Hudnut, dean of Harvard's Graduate School of Design, observed some forty years ago:

> Every attempt to bind [universities] to a pattern laid out in advance has failed and ought to have failed. . . . We must set them free to develop their environment in whatever way may best suit their existing needs. . . . The task to be performed in university buildings and the methods by which they are built constantly change. Their nature tomorrow cannot be predicted. No program is possible which extends beyond a dozen years. . . . Let's imagine the university, as city planners imagine the city, as a growing organism whose form lies partly in the past, partly in the future. Our university will never be completed. . . . If we make a master plan then, it must be in such general terms as will admit of new interpretations and unexpected development. We can take nothing for granted.[23]

To conclude, I think we can say that at its two hundredth birthday Georgetown University has shown remarkable growth since Gaston first admired the location of Old South, making great progress in fulfilling the Jesuit ideal of living and learning, accommodating a significant percentage of students on campus, providing extensive facilities and constantly looking to the future. It is to be hoped that our rapid growth will persist, but no longer at the expense of aesthetics and quality.

There are several areas where we must remain constantly vigilant. First, as we refine and expand our facilities, we need to be conscious of historic preservation, rather than simple renovation that can destroy our heritage. Our sense of our history, renewed through these Bicentennial reflections, should make us especially sensitive to this issue. Second, the University architect will be retiring before long, and there is apparently a danger of losing the position. Responsibility for our architecture should be placed in the hands of architects and professional campus planners; it should not be merely an administrative matter. Third, the University should be encouraged to pursue actively the most original and exciting solutions that vision can conceive and funding can tolerate. Inviting innovative architectural firms that specialize in our kinds of problems, such as Venturi, Rauch and Scott Brown, for example, to participate in open discussions and competitions could lead to brilliant solutions.

Though at present we remain constrained by space and finances, the experience of the Bicentennial will, one hopes, reinforce the understanding that architecture is important for our sense of self as well as for the proper and satisfying functioning of our physical surroundings. While a university may be "first and foremost a community of people," as Royden B. Davis, S.J. has affirmed, the environment the community elects not only expresses who we are but also affects how we live.

Notes

1. Arch J. Collins, "Progress at Georgetown," editorial, *Georgetown College Journal* 61:1 (November 1932), 50.

2. "New North Building," n.s., *Georgetown College Journal* 54:8 (June 1926), 598.

3. November 5, 1791. Gaston MS quoted by J. Herman Schauinger, *William Gaston, Carolinian* (Milwaukee: Bruce, 1949), 10; cited in John M. Daley, S.J., *Georgetown University: Origin and Early Years* (Washington, D.C.: Georgetown University Press, 1957), 63.

4. Paul Venable Turner, *Campus. An American Planning Tradition* (New York: Architectural History Foundation; Cambridge, Mass., and London: MIT Press, 1984), 17-18.

5. Diary of John McElroy, 1814, MS GUA, 256; cited in Daley, *Origin and Early Years*, 182.

6. Turner, *Campus*, 106. The first permanent installation was constructed at Williams College in 1837.

7. Joseph T. Durkin, S.J., "Healy Hall: Harbinger of Change," *Annual Report*, Georgetown University, Washington, D.C., 1979, n.p.

8. Extensive technical details are contained in the booklet "Georgetown Architecture, Northwest Washington, District of Columbia. Historic American Buildings Survey Selections, Number 10," issued jointly by the Commission of Fine Arts and the Historic American Buildings Survey, United States Department of the Interior, National Park Service, Office of Archeology and Historic Preservation, 1970; see also Hardy George, "Georgetown University's Healy Building," *Journal of the Society of Architectural Historians* 31:3 (October 1972), 208-16.

9. Durkin, "Healy Hall," n.p.

10. Cited in *American Renaissance 1876-1917*, ex.cat. The Brooklyn Museum, 1979, 28.

11. See John G. Bowen, "Copley Hall," *Georgetown College Journal* 61:6 (April 1933), 418-26.

12. See John G. Bowen, "The White-Gravenor Building," *Georgetown College Journal* 61:5 (March 1933), 319-24.

13. Turner, *Campus*, 23.

14. This would not be unprecedented. It appears that the great early

nineteenth-century architect, Andrew Jackson Davis, "who did much collegiate work during this period, thought of college buildings as belonging to an architectural category that also included prisons and asylums." Turner, *Campus*, 89-90.

15. "GU Inaugurates Large Dining Hall," n.s., *Standard* (February 1960), n.p., clipping in File: New South, 388-6,7, GUA.

16. See Turner, *Campus*, 294-95.

17. "Summary," Long Range Development Plan (Master Plan), Master Plan Revisions, 8/20/71, Henle 41, File 1288, File 40:02, 52.

18. Leslie Thomas, "Village B Coming Soon," *The Hoya* 63:17 (24 September 1982), 3.

19. Caption, *The Hoya* 63:10 (16 April 1982), 7.

20. Benjamin Forgey, "The Inside Story. A Look at Georgetown's New Leavey Center," *Washington Post*, 19 November 1988, C, 1, 5.

21. Conversation with Dean Price, 25 August 1988.

22. Turner, *Campus*, 260.

23. Joseph Hudnut, "On Form in Universities," *Architectural Forum* (December 1947), 90-92; cited in Turner, *Campus*, 260.